LEARNING

from

THE GERMANS

LEARNING

from

THE GERMANS

❧

*Race
and the
Memory of Evil*

SUSAN NEIMAN

Farrar, Straus and Giroux
New York

Farrar, Straus and Giroux
120 Broadway, New York 10271

Library of Congress Cataloging-in-Publication Data
Names: Neiman, Susan, author.
Title: Learning from the Germans : race and the memory of evil / Susan Neiman.
Other titles: Race and the memory of evil
Description: First edition. | New York : Farrar, Straus and Giroux, 2019. | Includes
    bibliographical references and index.
Identifiers: LCCN 2018060804 | ISBN 9780374184469 (hardcover)
Subjects: LCSH: Collective memory—Germany. | World War, 1939–1945—Atrocities—
    Germany—Public opinion. | National socialism—Public opinion. | Denazification—
    Germany. | African Americans—Crimes against—Public opinion. | Racism—United
    States—Public opinion. | Civil rights movements—United States—History. | Collective
    memory—United States. | Public opinion—United States. | Public opinion—Germany.
Classification: LCC DD256.48 .N45 2019 | DDC 305.800973—dc23
LC record available at https://lccn.loc.gov/2018060804

Designed by Abby Kagan

Our books may be purchased in bulk for promotional, educational, or business use.
Please contact your local bookseller or the Macmillan Corporate and
Premium Sales Department at 1-800-221-7945, extension 5442,
or by e-mail at MacmillanSpecialMarkets@macmillan.com.

www.fsgbooks.com
www.twitter.com/fsgbooks • www.facebook.com/fsgbooks

1 3 5 7 9 10 8 6 4 2

What happened, happened. This sentence is just as true as it is hostile to morals and intellect. The moral power to resist contains the protest, the revolt against reality, which is rational only as long as it is moral.

—**JEAN AMÉRY**, *At the Mind's Limits*

Not everything that is faced can be changed, but nothing can be changed until it is faced.

—**JAMES BALDWIN**, "As Much Truth as One Can Bear"

History will not go away, except through our perfect acknowledgment of it.

—**STANLEY CAVELL**, *Must We Mean What We Say?*

Contents

LEARNING

from

THE GERMANS

Prologue

I began life as a white girl in the segregated South, and I'm likely to end it as a Jewish woman in Berlin. Lest you suppose I'm tracing an arc that strides the space from perpetrator to victim, let me complicate the story. The question of whether Jews should count as white people was not quite settled in the South where I was born. "There's an old saying," Reverend Wheeler Parker, who was Emmett Till's cousin, told me. "If I was Catholic and I lived in the South, I'd be worried. If I was Jewish, I'd be packing up. If I was black, I'd be gone."

When I was eight years old, my best friend solemnly declared she could no longer play with me. We had a lot in common: a preference for building tree houses over playing with Barbie dolls, a love of books whose games in the woods often revolved around searching for a door to Narnia. Still, she ended our friendship after hearing that the Jews had killed Jesus. The temple where my family worshipped had been firebombed, and most of the Jewish community kept their heads down. I am proud that my mother did not. My parents had moved from Chicago to Atlanta shortly before my birth in 1955. My mother's involvement in the campaign to desegregate Atlanta's public schools was sufficient to earn her a photo in *Look* magazine and a number of late-night calls from the Klan.

If we could not be reckoned to the perpetrators, neither did we consider ourselves victims. Jews *had been* slaves in the land of Egypt and, as such, were obliged to liberal solidarity with other oppressed peoples. That was the major tenet of my mother's homespun theology. Much later, it must have played a role in my decision to study philosophy, and to find my way within philosophy to the work of Immanuel Kant, that dry Prussian professor who wrote the metaphysics of universal justice. It was Kant who insisted that all rational beings should obey the same moral law, and not even God is exempt.

None of my family was a victim of a concentration camp or, as far as I know, a pogrom. Safely landed in Chicago by the early twentieth century, my grandparents never spoke of the eastern Europe they'd left behind. On the contrary, the only grandfather I knew was fiercely American. The first in his family born outside of Odessa, he had a touch of Yiddish accent, but he adored Teddy Roosevelt, visited all the national parks, and served in both world wars. His love of Lincoln was so strong that when he came to visit his Atlanta grandchildren, he taught us all the words to "Marching Through Georgia," which we blithely sang in an open convertible, oblivious to any impact it may have had on those Atlantans disinclined to celebrate the march that burned their city to the ground. Today it's easy to smile: no wonder I never felt at home in the place. At the time, it only enforced my sense that we were fighters for justice and right. Like any American child, I learned something about the Holocaust, but it was too far away to dent, or even shadow, my own life.

What were present were moments like the sticky summer day in Georgia when my mother invited an African American friend to bring her children across town to play in our yard. Five years after *Brown v. Board of Education*, native white Atlantans were threatening to close down the school system rather than integrate it, a threat some counties carried out. Using skills she'd learned in an early stint in advertising, my mother and her friends from the newly organized HOPE—Help Our Public Education—were working to forestall the violence the Supreme Court decision ignited elsewhere. Meanwhile, she wanted to prepare her children for desegregation by arranging what was not yet called a playdate. The black folks we knew were all someone's servants, and she wanted us to have equal and normal relations with African Americans who were not. That's why her friend from the movement was there.

Our backyard was large and surrounded by woods where we could hide, hunt for arrowheads, play Capture the Flag. But it was too hot for any of that, and no amount of lemonade could change it.

"Let's go to the pool," I said.

"We can't," said my mother shortly.

"Why *not*?" I began to whine. "We *always* go to the pool when it gets this hot."

"We just can't," said my mother. I was too young to notice whether she and her friend exchanged glances.

"Then can we go to the lake?" The park at Red Top Mountain was usually muddy, not as nice as the pool, but the air was getting stickier by the minute.

"We can't go to the lake today either," said my mother.

"Why *not*?" I demanded, encouraging my little brother to chime in.

In the end we had to settle for playing under the sprinkler that watered the grass. I didn't settle graciously. How could I guess that it was against the law for black and white children to swim together, not only in the big concrete pools to which white Southerners flocked on such days but in the lakes that studded the county by the grace of God? As far as I could tell, my mother was just being unreasonable. Perhaps it was unreasonable to imagine she could construct normal relations, even for an afternoon, in a system as unreasonable and violent as the segregated South. I'm still glad she tried. By the time I knew enough to apologize for the embarrassment my fuss surely caused her, she had trouble remembering the day.

Southern plants still pull me deep, as though I had roots there. Dogwood, honeysuckle, azalea, even a magnolia tree in the backyard of my childhood. The newness of green: chlorophyll sounds like medicine, but that green is the color of life itself. It's the promise that grips us, the world that begins again with each new leaf and each new life, unmarred by sticky fingers or sandbox scuffles. My mother always wanted to follow the springtime, starting in the Deep South and driving steadily north to catch that moment of color ever again. She never did. Every budding tree reminds me of her longing.

Apart from the plants, what sticks in memory are the places I made my own: the smell of hot rain as it hit the marble steps of the local library I visited every week, the kudzu-draped ruins in the woods that must have been a mansion burned by Sherman's troops. We lived in one of the prettier not-quite-suburbs on the edge of northwest Atlanta, but everything made it apparent: we were never of them. My insufficiently Southern accent was suspicious. One day I turned in a homework assignment that the teacher had requested: we'd been told to ask our parents about their hobbies, the organizations to which they belonged. I still remember the look on my teacher's face upon reading that my mother belonged to the ACLU. "Isn't that a subversive organization?" ("Mommy, what's subversive?" I had to ask when I got home.)

My mother's friends were the few liberals, mostly white and Episcopalian or Unitarian, who shared her political views. After the dismal failure of my own first friendship, I didn't try very hard to make more. And there wasn't another girl in the area who got lost in long discussions of the books she loved or preferred the woods to Barbies. To be honest, I was pudgy, nearsighted, and terrible at sports, any one of which could have left me feeling lonely even in Brooklyn. But I'd never been to Brooklyn, and I spent my childhood dreaming of leaving the South—either for Europe, which I knew entirely from Ludwig Bemelmans's *Madeline* books, or for Greenwich Village, which I imagined as a leafy but talkative town.

At the age of twelve, I got lucky. I joined the first integrated youth group in the city, the Actors and Writers Workshop, an after-school program that offered a handful of budding liberal bohemians a house where they felt at home. We were taught that theater and writing required hard work, not just goodwill. We all shared convictions about the issues at the forefront of Atlanta politics, but we didn't meet three times a week just to feel good about ourselves, though it did feel good to be somewhere we could share what were, at that time and place, minority values. We were making art, and the director we called Rob took his job as seriously as if he'd been on Broadway, not directing a bunch of lonely, lost kids who, in the years we got a grant from the city, performed on a flatbed truck parked in one ghetto parking lot or another. Our parents soon learned that the best way to get us to do anything, like homework, was to threaten to prevent us from going to the workshop. Even on the rare Saturday when there were no rehearsals or classes, we'd gladly come to Juniper Street just to sweep the floors or diaper the baby. None of us suspected she would become Julia Roberts, and it wouldn't have mattered anyway.

The workshop was an outpost, itself not altogether at home in Atlanta. We came to offer helpless condolences at Martin Luther King's house the day after he was shot, for the three eldest King children were part of our classes. Not much of the white South was in mourning when Dr. King died. "Alabamans didn't cheer the way we did when Kennedy was shot," says the Alabama historian Diane McWhorter, whose finger on the Southern pulse is surer than mine. "But at the time we did think our troubles were over and the South would go back to normal without King stirring it up."

If the South never felt quite like home, five years in Tel Aviv, decades later, failed to make me Israeli. Perhaps that's why I feel so easy in today's Berlin, which has become a haven for many who feel at home nowhere else. I'd hardly felt easy on first arriving at Bahnhof Zoo station to a gaggle of punks panhandling on the stairway, German shepherds at their feet. In my imagination, German shepherds called up ghosts screaming *Halt!* or *Juden raus!* A couple of months at a Goethe-Institut in Freiburg had extended my vocabulary but barely dented my fears.

Berlin in 1982 was so far off the beaten track that it wasn't hard to convince more than one foundation to support me for the year I'd said would be spent studying German philosophy, though it was hardly the whole truth. Berlin had an aura that radiated, however faintly, all the way to Cambridge, Massachusetts, where I'd studied for eight years. When I was asked, rather often, "How can a nice Jewish American set foot in Germany, and for a whole year at that?" I countered with a question: Forty years after the war, wasn't it as racist to condemn the whole German nation as it had been for Germans to condemn the Jews? My answer suggested that *I* had worked through the Nazi past sufficiently to forget all about it and focus on Kant and Goethe. I may even have believed it at the time. Now I know better: I came to Berlin not because I'd gotten over the Nazis; I came because I wanted to know more about them. I was writing about the nature of reason, and they provided a world-historical question mark.

I soon felt exalted by the heady sense of abandon, the feeling of being forgotten in a city in limbo. Neither East nor West, but a state-subsidized playground between them, Berlin was studded with reminders of the war that no one had the inclination or the money to remove. We lived in splendid old apartments whose ceilings often sported cracked plaster angels, whose facades often sported mortar holes. We carried buckets of coal from the cellars to heat the tall ovens that kept us warm. And there was, of course, the Wall, which was often the subject of dark irony, at least in the West. What else could you do with an object that, two decades after its construction, felt like a piece of the natural world? With ruins of one kind or another in your face at any moment—one popular bar called In the Ruins punkily fetishized its crumbling walls—it would take a great deal of effort, or a great deal of intoxication, *not* to think about history.

And that was the most thrilling of all. *Vergangenheitsaufarbeitung—*

working-off-the-past—was one of the first words I added to my German vocabulary, which was slowly freeing itself from images of tight-lipped men in
uniform barking *Jawohl!* Working off Germany's criminal past was not an
academic exercise; it was too intimate for that. It meant confronting parents
and teachers and calling their authority rotten. The 1960s in Germany were
more turbulent than the '60s in Paris or Prague—not to mention Berkeley—
because they were not focused on crimes committed by someone or other in
far-off Vietnam, but those considerably closer to home, committed by the
people from whom life's earliest lessons were learned.

That autumn of 1982, those who came of age in the '60s were adults in
their thirties, working-off-the-past with special intensity, for the fiftieth anniversary of Hitler's election was approaching. There seemed no end of books
and speeches, as well as exhibits like *The Architecture of Destroyed Synagogues, Gays and Fascism, Women in the Third Reich, Resistance in Neukölln.* The arts academy offered workshops on making films about the Third
Reich. There were performances of music the Nazis banned and performances of music they promoted, with lectures accompanying each. Neighborhoods competed with each other to explore their own dark history. This
and much more could be found in Berlin, where a play called *It Wasn't Me,
Hitler Did It* that opened in 1977 would run for thirty-five years. My new
friends warned me that Berlin was unique: it had always leaned left, while
the rest of Germany was less inclined to face the skeletons in its closets. But
I wasn't in West Germany, I was in the former capital of the Reich, whose
eastern and western halves vied with each other to produce the best form
of working-off-the-past. As I took it all in, the half-buried fears I'd brought
with me began to recede, leaving sympathy and admiration in their place.

In 1982, most Americans in the city were members of the occupying
army, and I was often the first Jew many Germans had met. Raised with images of Jews that were confined to gaunt prisoners in concentration camps
or Orthodox men in prayer shawls, it didn't occur to them to apply the word
to me. Conversation involved a perpetual balance between announcing it
and avoiding it. I hadn't been raised in a particularly Jewish community; I
hadn't yet been to Israel; if any book about Jewish identity seemed written
for me, it was Isaac Deutscher's *The Non-Jewish Jew.* I had no inclination to
deny it, if only they would ask. They never did. What happened instead was
the sort of conversation I had with a pleasant man at a party of left-leaning
activists and diplomats. "You know," he said after a second glass of wine had
loosened our tongues, "I bet you come from the southern part of the United
States." "How did you guess?" I replied. "I can't say exactly," he replied. "It's

something about the way you move—your voice, your hands—I imagine it's like the difference between northern Europeans and Mediterranean peoples." I began to laugh. "As it happens, I was born in Atlanta," I told him. "But I'm an atypical Southerner. What you're noticing is that I'm Jewish." The gentleman was mortified. "Oh *no!*" he cried. "That isn't something I would *notice!* That plays no role for me at all."

Given minimal familiarity with American culture, and about a minute in my company, most people assume I grew up on the Upper West Side. It's not just the dark curly hair or the fact that I tend to talk fast and wave my hands at the same time. I can't explain it either, but the mixture seems to signal *New York Jew.* Such people find this story hilarious. Germans do not get what's funny. They were raised with the notion that Jewishness is something unpleasant, and probably smelly, so that noticing it would be a sign of bad manners. Like white Americans proudly asserting that they do not notice color, they fail to notice the history of assumptions behind *that* claim. (Don't notice color? Is the sky blue or gray today? The leaves red or green?)

In 1982 I could not have known that the year I'd planned to spend there would mark me for life, turning a vague fascination with a city into a deep, complex love. Staying in Berlin made thinking about ethics a grounded, constant presence; any concrete slab or bullet hole could remind you of moral questions. We are historical beings, unable to describe ourselves without describing ourselves in space and time. And unlike other animals, we cannot grow up without considerable input from our parents, with whom we need to come to terms if we are ever to truly separate from them.

❧

Two decades after I unwittingly embarrassed the man at the party, I was part of the national German committee to plan celebrations for the 2005 Einstein Year. One hundred years after Einstein made his most famous discoveries, the left-leaning government had decided to spend 20 million euros to show its support of science in general and of left-wing cosmopolitan (ahem!) intellectuals in particular. As the only Jew on the committee, my main function would be as what Orthodox Jews call a *mashgiach*—someone who guarantees that the premises are kosher. There were exhibits, there were banners, there were lectures, and more. What if they made a mistake?

I spotted one in an early brochure, where Einstein was described as a "fellow-citizen-of-Jewish-background." Did the committee know, I asked, that Einstein had expressly ridiculed that weird circumlocution? "He just called himself a Jew," I said. "Jews don't consider the word insulting." "Is that so, Frau Neiman?" replied the minister of science. She was flustered. "That's very helpful, just the sort of thing we need to know." *Jew* in German has two syllables, not one, and I suppose that buried deep in some dreams are memories of sinister mobs shouting *Ju-dah! Ju-dah!* Perhaps even for atheists, echoes of Judas Iscariot play a role. Germans use phrases with nine syllables, like *fellow-citizen-of-Jewish-extraction* or *fellow-citizen-of-Jewish-heritage*, in order to avoid using the obvious two. The habit is so engrained that despite my objection, the second draft of the brochure used the same phrase. "I know we all have many duties here," I said at the next meeting. "But perhaps it has been forgotten that I mentioned that Einstein didn't like this designation. He made fun of it several times." I was learning to use certain forms of polite circumlocution myself. "Of course," said the minister's deputy. "We'll see it gets changed." They never did; too many nightmares worked against them.

Between the encounter at the party and the committee meeting, my life took several turns. I'd seen nascent working-off-the-past in the 1980s, and I left Berlin because stories like the first bothered me more than the occasional right-wing rhetoric or traces of Nazi jargon. I had married a Berlin poet, and after our son was born, I began to long for a place where a Jewish child could be someone ordinary. That wish, I confess, was compounded by the widespread Berlin opinion that nothing very interesting would ever happen there again. My first book, *Slow Fire*, described Berlin life in the '80s, which were drawing to a close around the consensus that the action had moved elsewhere. A year before the Wall fell in 1989, I accepted an offer to teach philosophy at Yale.

Even without a premonition of what might be in store for the city I'd left behind, I spent my second night in Connecticut drinking an entire bottle of wine, in tears. The difference between Berlin's intensity and New Haven's dismal mixture of suburb and ghetto was screaming. But a contract had been signed, an apartment abandoned, and I settled in to enjoy what there was to enjoy: wonderful students, interesting new friends. After my twin daughters were born, there was no time for regret, or much of anything else. I did apply for a professorship in Potsdam, but my marriage had ended by the time I received it. Instead I took my children to Israel for a sabbatical, hoping to find a home. We stayed five years and became Israeli citizens while I taught philosophy at Tel Aviv University. They were young enough to assimilate easily, while I chewed on Ben-Gurion's claim that the first generation of immigrants to Israel would always be lost; all that mattered were the children. My misgivings were not political: the peace process had yet to collapse, the second intifada was still to come. But when approached by the Einstein Forum, which was looking for a new director, I wasn't entirely closed to alternatives, even though I said no at the start.

"Do you actually know what the Einstein Forum is?"

The more I learned, the more I was tempted. The Einstein Forum was founded just after German reunification with two concerns in mind. The first was the wish to build intellectual and cultural institutions in the former East Germany, whose own institutions had been gutted through the removal of anyone considered close to the fallen communist regime. There were already complaints that the wave of removals served as an excuse to find jobs for West intellectuals who'd been unable to get them on their own turf. Hiring an American, therefore, was one way to sidestep East-West strife. The second concern was less local. Disturbing signs of right-wing nationalism had emerged in the wake of reunification, and every single one attracted international press. At the same time, Brandenburg—the largest of the new states, which surrounds Berlin as Virginia and Maryland surround Washington—discovered that it had symbolic treasure in the form of a dilapidated wooden cottage Albert Einstein built in 1929. What better way to send a signal for internationalism and progress than to throw a little money in its direction and hope something interesting might emerge?

I knew none of this when invited to apply for the job. "Is there an intellectual agenda I'd have to follow?" I asked at one of several interviews. "Because if you're hiring me to be a Jew coming to Germany from Israel, I have to say I don't intend to spend the rest of my life talking about *Vergangenheitsaufarbeitung*." (Somewhat hilariously, I thought I was done with the subject at the time.)

"You'd be free to do whatever you want," I was told.

"Like talk about the Enlightenment?"

"This is Potsdam. We'd love it."

Most of my philosophical work has been devoted to defending the much-maligned Enlightenment, that eighteenth-century movement which created the foundations for universal human rights. Potsdam is the home of the summer palace where Frederick the Great entertained Voltaire and other Enlightenment thinkers. The emperor later had the philosopher arrested, but for two years they had a good run discussing the best and the worst of all worlds. My teenage heroes were de Beauvoir and Sartre, so I'd never felt entirely at home in the Ivy League. The chance to open philosophical questions to a broad general audience was unique, and Potsdam was close enough to Berlin to allow me to live in the city that still touched my heart like an unresolved love: *it couldn't be all over between us!*

There remained the question of what it meant to raise three children who considered themselves Israeli in the former capital of the Third Reich. Today, nothing in Tel Aviv is trendier, but in 2000 I was called a traitor for merely considering leaving Israel for Germany. A decade earlier, I'd decided against it; there seemed no way that foreigners, much less Jews, could feel truly at ease in Berlin. But watching an African man in dreadlocks talk back to a careless driver on one of several trips I made to discuss the job convinced me: the new Berlin wasn't just a matter of hype. The thought of a foreign—any kind of foreign—comeback at a German on a street corner was unimaginable in the '80s. We were all too frightened. Was it the change from a long conservative tradition to a Social Democratic–Green government? The fact that the capital, and with it more foreigners, had moved to Berlin? Whatever the causes, you could feel it on the street: the changes were dramatic, certainly enough to suppose that three Israeli-American-German children could grow up there without feeling they had to cower.

Twenty years later, I still wake most mornings feeling grateful for my good fortune. The Einstein Forum is thriving, and I was lucky to find a lovely apartment in a neighborhood still dicey enough to be affordable. On sunny summer days you'd be forgiven for thinking you've landed in multicultural heaven. On my block alone there's a Kurdish, a Finnish, and a Brazilian café where live music spills out onto the sidewalk on warm evenings; a Danish bakery; a Moroccan restaurant; and a Greek delicatessen. Walk ten minutes in any direction, and you'll find one of nine small bookstores. One specializes in Polish literature, with poetry readings and music some evenings; another in English fiction. On Tuesdays and Fridays you can buy bread and fish, fruit and cheese, and most anything else you need at the outdoor market next to the canal that used to be called Oriental. Though about half the vendors and a third of the buyers are Turkish, some functionary in the new Berlin clearly worried about orientalism and changed the name to something innocuous. (I cannot swear that the functionary read Edward Said, but I know that the police chief of my district saw the movie about Hannah Arendt.) There are many women who cover their heads, the older ones rather grimly, the younger ones with style and sass. In this part of town, the jostling, bargaining, and banter between Muslims and non-Muslims at the market is unfailingly friendly.

Yes of course I read the news, and even if I didn't, I have plenty of friends who do. In the wake of the heavy press coverage of the Israeli-Arab attacked in 2018 for wearing a kippah, one worried old friend wrote from Los Angeles: Were my children and I safe? Anti-Semitic incidents in Germany get more international press than such incidents elsewhere. What receives far less attention is the way that Germany reacts. Even before the kippah attack was recorded on video, Chancellor Merkel had created a new, high-ranking office to combat anti-Semitism. After the attack, twenty-five hundred Berliners, including the foreign minister, demonstratively wore kippot at a rally in front of the Jewish Community Center, and the demonstration was front-page news for days: BERLIN WEARS A KIPPAH was the headline in my local daily paper. A few days later, the parliament voted unanimously to officially declare the existence of the State of Israel a part of German *Staatsräson*—reason of state, or national interest. Anti-Semitism, says the new official in charge of combating it, has remained fairly constant in 20 percent of the population, now intensified by two complicating factors I'll discuss in the final chapter of this book: the rise of the far-right AfD (Alternative for Deutschland) party and the influx of Muslim refugees raised on anti-Jewish propaganda. It's not far from the percentage of anti-Semitism in the United States as soon as you leave the large cities, and it's certainly no worse than the levels of anti-Semitism in Great Britain. The difference lies in the response to it. In Germany, condemnation of anti-Semitism was swift, sharp, and serious. It came from the top of the government and was echoed by most voices outside it. In the United States, after Charlottesville, Nazis were excused. In Britain, the Labour Party's response to charges of anti-Semitism was self-destructively slow.

No one in Germany denies there's more work to be done. This became especially clear in 2017 when Merkel's conservative party lost votes and the new far-right party gained them in the wake of her 2015 decision to admit a million refugees. Good Germans are ever on the watch for signs of resurgent racism. They view those developments with gloom and expect that worse will follow. What will develop in a world where the number of refugees is growing is anyone's guess; what's clear is that Germany's past no longer provides complete immunization against the wave of nationalism now sweeping the world. None of those developments cut against the fact that Germany was the only country in the world that showed any leadership on the refugee crisis. The German historian Jan Plamper showed that despite the AfD, active engagement to support refugee integration grew from 10 percent of the German population in 2015 to 19 percent in 2018. The last figure was determined by Germany's renowned Allensbach Institute, and it showed that far more Germans supported the refugees than voted for right-wing parties.

What's been termed "the welcome culture" is the largest and broadest social movement in Germany since the war.[1] Had Americans wished to compete with German generosity, they would have had to absorb five million refugees within a year on a fraction of the landmass. Instead, anti-immigrant campaigns succeeded in persuading Britons to leave the EU, and electing an unhinged swindler in America.

What about the Jewish question? Thirty years ago I wished that Germans were aware I was Jewish, or at least weren't shocked when they found it out. Although they often knew quite a lot about concentration camps, they knew next to nothing about living, breathing Jews. This year, several German friends sent emails wishing me happy new year, in Hebrew. A Swiss Jewish historian is the president of the German Historical Museum. Berlin now hosts an annual Jewish film festival, a Jewish Culture week, an Israeli-German arts festival, several Jewish magazines, and no end of hummus joints. Should you wish to become a rabbi, you can choose between a Reform, a Conservative, and an Orthodox seminary. Thanks to Chabbad immigrants from Russia, and the Lauder Foundation, the Orthodox Jewish community is growing, as is the community of Israelis who leave their country to escape its Orthodox-dominated government. Being Jewish is so fashionable that a number of German rabbis are actually converts. Buying matzo in the '80s was not quite secret, but it carried an aura of stealth. There was only one store that sold it, along with kosher wine, gefilte fish, mezzuzot, and falafel. After the store was bombed in 1977, the owners exchanged the sign reading SHALOM for one that read ORIENTAL SPECIALTIES. You had to know where you were going in order to get there. Now the only problem in shopping for Pesach is the fact of competition, as I discovered on a last-minute search for matzo meal last year. Everyone was sold out. "We underestimated," said one owner. "Don't bother going across town. There's no matzo meal left in Berlin." As I was wondering how long it would take to grind matzo piece by piece, I remembered that the parents of Israeli friends who were coming for Pesach might bring an extra box. You read that correctly. Israelis left home to enjoy the Seder with their children and grandson in Berlin. Next year in Jerusalem?

Nothing reflects the change in spirit more than the commemoration of May 8. In 1985, President Richard von Weizsäcker made headlines as the first major West German politician to call the day the war ended a day of liberation. Until then the German defeat was viewed with ambivalence, and whoever was not ambivalent kept quiet. I failed to appreciate the speech at the time, for I could not grasp that the taste of defeat was still so bitter forty years after the war that Weizsäcker's use of the word *liberation* was revolutionary. (Imagine Virginians celebrating the Confederate surrender at Appomattox, and you'll have a rough idea of the effect.) Today, one of the directors of the Maxim Gorki Theater is Israeli, and the theater produced a three-day festival to commemorate the war's end. There were edgy theater and video productions, sassy dialogue about Jewish and Muslim gay men, a comedy about circumcision, and a discotheque playing a mishmash of hip-hop and Russian folk. "We have something to celebrate!" shouted one of the organizers as we danced to an accordion in the foyer. Outside the theater, over Berlin's largest boulevard, a flag fluttered. WE WON, it read in German, English, and Russian. After Weizsäcker's speech, antifascist Germans, for-eigners, and the few Jews in town breathed a sigh of caustic relief: finally, a West German politician admitted that May 8 was not a day to mourn. But celebrate it with a flag that declared WE WON? I cannot imagine who would have dared.

⌘

Years ago I promised myself to answer every stranger who took the trouble to write to me, at least once. That probably reflects the letter I received from C. S. Lewis when I was seven, after I wrote to say that I too wanted to be a writer and enclosed a poem about Narnia. He was kind enough to overlook the quality of the poem and send an encouraging answer. I was elated.

Stewart's letter contained some praise for a short article of mine that be-came the kernel of this book. The article had landed on the internet, and Stewart's letter was immensely serious. I reproduce it here in part:

> I have lived in Mississippi my entire life (Oxford now) and I am a white con-servative. Hilariously (at this point) that must mean I am a racist, I sup-pose. But in fact I—and many like me—genuinely do wonder what the right thing to do is with regard to the history of the southern states in America and the history of the United States in general. Your article provided sub-stantial guidance for me.

But Stewart wanted more, and his letter continued with a list of questions.

> What do you think? Should we tear down all Confederate statues? Should we rename all buildings and streets? Should we take this cleansing past things relating to the Civil War and take Washington off the dollar bill? For

your reference, I have asked numerous alleged civil rights leaders in Mississippi, and I even had the opportunity to eat dinner with James Meredith and hear his take on the issue. The sides are split, but man oh man, those who think we need to eliminate all vestiges of the slavery era are the angriest. But are they right?

I wrote back to offer a few concrete suggestions and concluded by noting that if all self-described white conservatives were as thoughtful as he, the country was in better shape than I thought.

I didn't need the election of Donald Trump, as terrifying as it was ludicrous, to prove that it's not. Had it started in Ferguson? With the acquittal of the man who shot Trayvon Martin? By the time a smirking, dead-eyed kid named Dylann Storm Roof killed nine African Americans at a Bible study group in Charleston, the crisis seemed as clear to the white people who'd been able to ignore it as it was to the black people who'd never forgotten it. The heartache that gripped America was not just about the fact that the massacre took place in a sanctuary. There were also the voices of many victims' families declaring hate would not win.

Roof's computer was full of white supremacist propaganda and pictures of himself holding a Confederate flag. There seemed to be a moment of consensus, even in the South. The video that showed massive goodness responding to purest evil lowered the flag and moved President Obama to Charleston to deliver one of his most powerful speeches. The president looked ashen as he began, presumably sickened by the thought that those bullets were meant for him. The recent rise in racist terror is not in spite, but because of the fact that we finally elected a black president, and the huge security detail surrounding him led white supremacists to seek softer targets. Looking shaken in the beginning, Obama talked himself into the cadence of the mighty black church, mixing politics and religion into a binding, spellbinding whole. Taking down that flag, he said, is not an insult to the valor of Confederate soldiers, but simply an acknowledgment that the cause for which they fought was wrong. Nor did he stop there. "By taking down that flag, we express God's grace." And after a long riff on grace just as deft as any jazzman's, Obama began to sing "Amazing Grace" in a voice so good it made you wonder why he hadn't chosen an easier line of work. The delighted audience sprang to its feet and sang with him.

It was working, wasn't it? Obama's eulogy called on the nation to use history as a manual for avoiding the mistakes of the past, a road map toward a better world, and with Southern states voluntarily shedding Confederate symbols, something new was clearly happening in America. Like that of every other Deep Southern state, South Carolina's governor was Republican, and still she presided over the ceremony that lowered the flag from the state capitol and readied it for a museum. Alabama's governor followed suit. Some stores announced they would no longer stock Confederate memorabilia. In that bitterly hopeful moment, I resolved to write a book expanding on the essay that prompted Stewart's letter. It seemed a time when Americans and others could use an example from someone else's violent history to learn how to come to terms with our own. A couple of weeks after the president's speech I got another email from Stewart. In the wake of all the post-Charleston discussions, he wanted me to speak at his alma mater, Ole Miss. I wanted to look into what was being done by those who work on race and history in the Deep South. That's how I wound up as a guest of the William Winter Institute for Racial Reconciliation in Oxford, Mississippi.

◦❧◦

By tracing the differences between *Vergangenheitsaufarbeitung* in Germany and the United States, this book will encourage Americans and other peoples to learn from the Germans. It's significant that while there are many variations on the concept in German—*Vergangenheitsverarbeitung, Vergangenheitsbewältigung, Erinnerungskultur*—no similar concept exists in English, or in other languages, as far as I could find. In the three years during which I wrote this book, most every German I know rejected the comparison between the crimes of the Nazis and those of American racists—even after the 2017 demonstrations in Charlottesville showed they now use the same symbols and are equally ready to kill. That rejection, I'll argue, is itself a sign of how far Germany has come in taking responsibility for its criminal history. For entirely different reasons, many Americans reject the comparison too. Thus the book begins with an attempt to answer their arguments, while acknowledging the obvious: no two histories are ever entirely alike.

The first two parts of the book are, broadly speaking, empirical. Part One sketches the history of Germany's attempts to come to terms with the Nazi period, both before and after reunification. In rejecting the common view that the GDR did not confront the Nazi period, I do not claim its confrontation was flawless. By examining the attempts of the pre-1989 BRD and GDR with equal seriousness, I compare the different flaws that riddled the ways each half of Germany faced, and avoided, its Nazi past. Nothing fueled Cold War hostilities in Germany like the charge that the other side lived in unbroken continuity with its Nazi legacy. If contemporary East and West Germany could recognize that each side made (different) progress in breaking that continuity, while each managed (differently) to maintain it, a deeper reunification would be possible.

Part Two is devoted to the legacy of racism in the American Deep South. Concentrating research there by no means implies that racism is absent in the rest of the United States, but the consciousness of history to be found in Mississippi, for example, puts all the questions out in the open. Adam Nossiter argued that Mississippi is as culturally distinct from the South as the South is from the rest of the country, comparing it to a laboratory—"a continuous experiment in which people are forced to learn how to live with their past."[2] C. Vann Woodward wrote that "the experience of evil and the experience of tragedy are parts of the Southern heritage that are as difficult to reconcile with the American legend of innocence and social felicity as the experience of poverty and defeat are to reconcile with the legends of abundance and success."[3] I spent half a year there learning from people working in the South to change American culture at its broken heart. While systematic racism infects processes and affects lives all over America, Southern awareness of history makes it impossible to ignore. Moreover, the influence of the South on American political culture is disproportionate to the size of the region. Focusing on the Deep South is not a matter of ignoring the rest of the country, but of holding a magnifying glass to it.

The surveys of these two very different histories of confronting—and avoiding—national legacies should give the reader an overview of how things are today. In Part Three I wrestle with questions of how things ought to be. What is our responsibility to our national pasts? How should children be educated, monuments built or removed, reparations for injustice organized, political cultures constructed? This book does not pretend to offer answers to all the questions it raises; if it provokes others to think further, its purpose will be served.

I was trained by the great theorist of justice John Rawls, but Rawls, as he regularly and diffidently insisted, wrote in the abstract. In writing this book, I sought as much particularity as possible. I spent much of 2016 and 2017 recording hundreds of hours of interviews, in Germany and the American South, with people who have played major roles in contesting and reframing their nations' public memory, as well as people who have been affected by them.

There are good books in English, and whole libraries full of them in German, examining Germany's confrontation with its past, as there is an increasing body of work detailing American responses to Reconstruction or the age of racial terror rendered harmless by the silly expression "Jim Crow." I make no effort to add to historical records, however often I have drawn on them. To quote the Bulgarian-French critic Tzvetan Todorov, "The historical facts are well known and easy to look up. But facts don't come with their meanings attached, and it is the meaning that interests me."[4] Although philosophy, like history, is always a search for understanding, it's a discipline whose bones are normative through and through. How should we live in a world riven with evil? is the question that has driven philosophy since its beginnings. (If the world were as it should be, thought Schopenhauer, philosophy would have no reason to raise any questions at all.[5]) Since I believe that abstract ideas become most compelling when refracted through particular experience, I have alternated between analysis and anecdote, in the conviction that concrete historical examples will not obscure general moral questions but illuminate them. The goal is to wrestle with questions about how working-off-the-past can prepare the ground for freer futures, and how it can become a process that blocks access to them instead. My aim is to explore how the past should, and should not, be used in thinking about our moral and political futures. This kind of moral training helps us recognize complex forms of evil as well as simple ones and prepares us to begin to prevent them. It's training that should not be confined to historians but must become a matter of shared public memory—history no thinking man or woman can honorably ignore.

Some historical claims made in these pages will be controversial. While I've worked to support them, particularly through my choice of interviews, I'm well aware that other subjects would tell stories differently. I am not a neutral observer; this story is also my own. The decision to use a first-person voice was not, however, born from conviction that history is irrevocably subjective. It's a way of locating and taking responsibility for my claims. Where I have models for philosophical reflection on urgent moral questions, they are Jean Améry and Hannah Arendt. Each provides standards for that critical thinking which, in an age that values science and technology over every other intellectual enterprise, is needed more than ever.

These pages will show how excruciatingly hard it was for Germany to accept the burdens of its shameful history—and that acceptance was nonetheless possible. The rise of the AfD has led many to doubt the progress Germany has made in the past several decades, and even to lament that we're living through a Nietzschean eternal return. Yet it's absurd to give up on the process of *Vergangenheitsaufarbeitung* just at the moment when it's under attack. *Vergangenheitsaufarbeitung* isn't a foolproof inoculation against racism and reaction; the world is unlikely to suffer a shortage of fools. Progressive democratic values show their merit in the ways they respond to those who seek to undermine them. When the AfD attacks decades of efforts to work off the Nazi past as shameful, it is imperative that the rest of us insist that shame can be the first step toward responsibility, and with that, toward genuine national pride. By examining German attempts at redemption through the lens of the failures of others, we can learn to cherish the work that has been done—and to safeguard it from those who seek to undo it.

PART ONE

German Lessons

1

On the Use and Abuse of Historical Comparison

Evil is what others do. Our people are always *very fine people.* In the ancient world, an evil action could pollute the community without being intentional, as the story of Oedipus reminds us. Even those who subscribe to the doctrine of original sin in the abstract tend to ignore it when things get particular. We have a natural impulse to believe that we, and our tribe, may make mistakes, but nothing that merits a word like *evil.* The impulse is just as strong toward evils past as evils present. We want our ancestors to be honorable, and honored. *My grandfather died for the homeland he loved; what's criminal about that? My great-uncle wasn't a racist, he was simply defending his home.* If you followed the debates over the removal of Confederate flags and monuments that began to swell after nine churchgoers were massacred in Charleston in 2015, you will recognize such remarks. Some were made by white supremacists who, enraged by the presence of a black man in the White House, knew exactly why they wanted to keep Confederate flags flying. Those who were less malicious, if also less honest, clung vaguely to family tradition. As those debates continue, you will hear variations on that theme from Richmond to New Orleans.

Unless you've lived a long time in Germany, you'll be surprised to learn that descendants of the Wehrmacht made the same claims as the descendants of the Confederate Army. Not only in the dark, shell-shocked days that followed the unconditional surrender outside Berlin in 1945; such remarks continued to be made in public through the end of the twentieth century, when the Wehrmacht Exhibit broke West Germany's final taboo. Created by the Hamburg Institute for Social Research, the exhibit used soldiers' letters and photographs to reveal that Nazi military crimes were not limited to elite SS units, nor confined to a few bad apples. The institute, which organized the exhibit to commemorate the fiftieth anniversary of the war's end, never expected the reactions it provoked. After all, the claim that the Wehrmacht systematically committed war crimes seemed—to foreign observers and even most German historians—about as controversial as the claim that the earth is round. But the gap between historical scholarship and ordinary public memory proved tremendous. With eighteen million members, the Wehrmacht included a broader scope of German society than any other Nazi organization. Every German had a father, a son, or a brother who served in it, if they didn't serve themselves, and reactions to the exhibit showed how many still believed the myth that the Wehrmacht was clean, even gallant. *Those brave men who defended their homeland against the Bolshevik menace were no better or worse than millions of soldiers before or after them.*

Originally planned as a limited project, the exhibit was seen in thirty-three cities by nearly a million viewers. It ignited media discussions, filled talk shows, and eventually provoked a debate in parliament. Protesters balked at what they saw as an attempt to drag their forebears through the mud. In Munich, five thousand neo-Nazis carried signs bearing slogans like GERMAN SOLDIERS—HEROIC DEEDS. In German it rhymes. The good news was that even in Munich, the Nazis' original stronghold, ten thousand counter-demonstrators turned out to protest them.

The furor revealed how hard it is for scholarship to penetrate personal memory. For decades, German historians had worked to provide a detailed reckoning with the Nazi period, but there were layers of popular consciousness that work had not reached. The impact of the Wehrmacht Exhibit was profound; as its initiator, Jan Philipp Reemtsma, told me, the claim that the Wehrmacht was a criminal organization, so controversial at the time, now is self-evident. The exhibit became part of the history of postwar Germany; no German listening to the media at the time, or studying postwar Germany since, can fail to know something about it. When people point to

Germany's attempts to come to terms with its criminal past, the Wehrmacht Exhibit is Exhibit A.

"But surely . . ." said a sweet-tempered sixtyish man in Mississippi after I'd explained that the first generation of postwar Germans sounded like nothing so much as the defenders of the Lost Cause version of Confederate history, "Surely they knew—at the latest when they opened the camps—that what they'd done was pure evil?"

They did not.

This book shows how the German people worked, slowly and fitfully, to acknowledge the evils their nation committed. Many books have been written urging us to draw lessons from the Holocaust, some of them dubious. My interest is in what we can learn from Germany after the catastrophe was over. The story should give hope, particularly to Americans currently struggling to come to terms with our own divided history. Here's a key to understanding contemporary Germany: nearly every German I know, from public intellectual to pop star, laughed out loud when they heard I was writing a book with this title. The exception was a former culture minister who didn't find it the least bit funny, raising his voice in a Berlin restaurant to tell me that I should under no circumstances publish a book suggesting there was something to be learned from the Germans. Just as it's become axiomatic for decent Germans to insist that the Holocaust was the worst crime in human history, which should never be relativized by comparison with anything, it's become axiomatic that this insight itself was far too slow in coming. German *Vergangenheitsaufarbeitung* was too little, too late, and above all incomplete, as the defensive reactions to the Wehrmacht Exhibit revealed. *Don't I know how long it took for Germans to make the switch from viewing themselves as Worst Victims to viewing themselves as Worst Perpetrators? Don't I know that many of them never made the switch at all? Don't I know there's still racism in Germany, currently represented by the AfD, the first radically right party since the war that won enough votes to be seated in parliament?*

Having spent most of the last four decades in Berlin, I do know these things. I'm a philosopher, not a historian or a sociologist, but for reasons that were deep and urgent I've been straining to gauge the temperature of this once-fevered nation since 1982—most crucially, to determine whether it was a place fit for raising Jewish children. In 1988, I decided it was not. By 2000, I had changed my mind, for the changes that tentatively began in the '80s had taken root.

In fact, it's the failures of *Vergangenheitsaufarbeitung* that should give hope to other nations facing similar problems, but that's only an apparent paradox. Social justice activists in the South, for example, who are struggling to force their neighbors to face the ways their racist history informs the racist present, are above all aware of how hard it all is. The acknowledgments are too defensive, the racism too tenacious, the impulse to insist on one's own victimization too strong. Learning that it took decades of hard work before those who committed what are arguably the greatest crimes in history could acknowledge those crimes, and begin to atone for them, brings enormous relief to those working toward similar acknowledgment in the United States. If even those raised in the heart of darkness needed time and trouble to see the light, why shouldn't it take time and trouble to bring Americans—nurtured for years on messages of their own exceptional goodness—to come to terms with homegrown crimes? The mechanisms and mistakes of the postwar German experience show a slow and faulty process that reflects the tentative steps America is taking toward justice and reconciliation.

Failures foster hope where it's clear that they lead not to final solutions, but to progress that can be gauged by real differences in people's lives. For a few, the differences were lives made worse: in Frankfurt am Main and Philadelphia, Mississippi, men were finally sent to jail for murders committed in times and places where the murders were not considered crimes. For many more, lives were made better. A million refugees were welcomed by cheering Germans eager to reverse the racism of their forebears, and the later backlash does not change that fact. And two terms in a row, my president was black. The achievements of Obama's presidency, especially impressive in the face of massive opposition to every move he made, undermined the last rationalizations for white supremacy—which is just what provoked the massive backlash that led to the election of the least qualified man ever to approach the White House. Obama's term in office could not overcome the wave of hatred he and his family endured with such grace. But the fact that it was possible is a fact to be cherished, for if the hopes it raised were possible, they are possible again. I will argue that the 2016 election resulted, in large part, from America's failure to confront its own history.

∽

In American and British life, the symbolic importance of the Nazis stands in inverse relation to common knowledge about them. *Nazi* just means: the black hole at the heart of history, the apex of evil, the sin for which no expiation is possible, no condemnation sufficient. There is, of course, a wealth of scholarship about the Nazi period produced by American and British historians, upon which I have often drawn in addition to German sources. But my interest is public memory: what every half-educated member of a culture knows in her sinews, for it seeped into them in ways she can hardly remember. Things like your country's geography: few Americans need pause to consider whether Colorado is west of Connecticut, as few Britons have to wonder whether Leeds is north of London. If you've forgotten everything else from your school days, you're likely to remember that.

Britons and Americans know that six million Jews were murdered by the Nazis, as they know that Henry VIII had six wives or George Washington chopped down a cherry tree, but the absence of detail makes the Holocaust more of a mystery than anything else. There's detail aplenty about the mechanisms of murder; the appetite for yet another description of life within or on the way to the death camps seems insatiable. But with little knowledge of what led to fascism in Germany, and next to none of what happened after it, it's unsurprising that *Nazi* is simply a term of abuse that has been applied to everything from Obamacare (by Ben Carson) to Saddam Hussein (by George Bush). Bill O'Reilly even used it to describe Black Lives Matter. No wonder a comparison between the violence inflicted on Jews by the Nazis and the violence inflicted on African Americans by Caucasians raises hackles, even indignation. "Tendentious" is the mildest objection white people raise. *Slavery was wrong, but it was an economic issue. How can you compare it to the deliberate murder of millions?*

Who has the right to make comparisons? This is not a trivial question. The first people to compare Nazi racial policies with American ones were the Nazis themselves. It's noxious enough to learn how frequently those comparisons were made after the war in wretched attempts at exoneration. Even in playground brawls, *He did it first!* is a miserable excuse. It's considerably worse when the genocide of Native Americans is invoked to justify the murder of millions of Slavic peoples. Alas, historians have shown that Nazi interest in American racial practices was present not only after the fact but considerably before it. In the 1920s, Nazis looked to the American eugenics movement to support their own bumbling race science. Hitler took American westward expansion, with its destruction of Native peoples, as the template for the eastward expansion he said was needed to provide Germans with *Lebensraum*—room to live. Nazi jurists studied American race laws extensively, particularly concerning citizenship rights, immigration, and miscegenation, before drafting the notorious Nuremberg Laws. Chillingly, those jurists found American racial policies too harsh to apply in Germany, and replaced the infamous "one drop of blood" model by which American law determined race with more lenient criteria, allowing Germans possessing but one Jewish grandparent to count, shakily, as citizens. On the other hand, they appreciated the ways in which American legal realism "demonstrated that it was perfectly possible to have racist legislation even if it was technically infeasible to come up with a scientific definition of race."[1] The best of those jurists dug up the worst quotes of Lincoln and Jefferson in support of racist policy. None of this suggests that American racism was the cause of German racism. Racism is a universal phenomenon that takes many forms. The fact that the United States had the world's best developed racist legislation, which the Nazis eagerly studied in the 1930s while formulating their own, is disturbing enough without causal connections.

After the war had leveled their cities, Germans were no less inclined to compare. *Wasn't the massive Allied bombing of civilians a war crime as severe as anything the SS had committed?* While the focus was usually on the firebombings of Hamburg and Dresden, which were seared into postwar memory, references to the "atomic holocaust of the Japanese" can still be heard in Germany and Austria, but only from those whose political allegiances tilt far right. Those comparisons were always central for Germans who tried to exonerate Germany by arguing that Wehrmacht war crimes were no worse than those of the Allies, Nazi genocide no worse than the European genocide of Native Americans.

I do my best to follow Tzvetan Todorov's wise injunction: Germans should talk about the singularity of the Holocaust, Jews should talk about its universality. You can derive the principle from Kant, but it's also a variation on an idea we should have learned in kindergarten: if everyone cleans up her own mess, we won't have to worry about anyone else's. Todorov's claim will only be problematic for those who think statements are exhausted by their truth value. In fact, as ordinary language philosophy has taught us, statements are often forms of action. A German who talks about the singularity of the Holocaust is taking responsibility; a German who talks of its universality is denying it. Germans insisting on universality are seeking exoneration; if everyone commits mass murder one way or another, how could they help doing it too?

Germans were not the only ones to compare their own racist crimes with those of others. In the early '60s, before the Holocaust became sacrosanct, many African Americans did so too. When W.E.B. Du Bois visited the Warsaw ghetto in 1949, he was shaken by the parallels he drew with what he'd called the century's greatest problem, the color line. After the 1963 Birmingham church bombing, James Baldwin said that white Americans share collective guilt for the persecution of black Americans as Germans did for their silence during the Nazi persecution of Jews.[2] Our history isn't bloodier than others, he continued, but it is bloody.[3] In conversation with Baldwin shortly after the Eichmann trial, Malcolm X remarked, "What was done to the Jews twenty years ago keeps us on the edge of our seat wanting to kill Eichmann. No one tells them to forget the past."[4] The comparisons were made by the civil rights hero Medgar Evers, who risked his life in the fight against fascism at Normandy, and even by the NAACP president Roy Wilkins, who was hardly known for radical views. Tellingly, no African American I met while researching this book found the comparison problematic. But after white nationalist demonstrators screamed "Blood and Soil" in Charlottesville, does the comparison require further argument? *"Blut und Boden"* is a Nazi slogan. Nor is there anything *neo* about them: What's new about torchlight parades, Heil Hitler salutes, and swastikas—except their increasing appearance on American soil?

A Jew who insists on what Todorov called the universality of the Holocaust need not argue for exact equivalence between the Holocaust and the crimes of other nations; it's a matter of taking responsibility for the latter. Though I have spent almost as many years of my life outside the United States as in it, I remain at heart an American Jew. (Readers who belong to neither tribe should note that there are as many ways to be American as there are to be a Jew.) As such, I write appalled by my country's procrastination in confronting our own national crimes. A mixture of secondary school education and a steady stream of popular movies, television, and radio programs insure that you needn't be a historian to know basic facts about Auschwitz. Indeed, to avoid information about Auschwitz, you must have spent the last thirty years in a hermitage. Unless you're a historian specializing in contemporary Germany, you are unlikely to have learned much about what Germans have done over the past seventy years to contend with the shadow Auschwitz cast.

Germany's relationship to its history is complex enough to have spawned several long compound words. Though they've been called Germany's most distinctive export, there is no real translation of any of them, but *working-off-the-past* is a reasonable approximation. The German word for *debt* is the same as the word for *guilt*; both, it seems, can be worked off with sufficient effort. More recently, all those words are being replaced by the much vaguer term *Erinnerungskultur*—memory culture—to suggest that the debt can never be paid. In this book I will use the older term, working-off-the-past, since there is no other point to the exercises in memory. *Vergangenheitsauf-arbeitung* came into use in the '60s, an abstract polysyllabic way of saying *We have to do something about the Nazis*. Outside Germany, many still think the Nazis' strength depended on illiterate mobs, a view unfortunately reinforced by the dreadful book and subsequent movie *The Reader*. In fact, the highest proportion of Nazi Party members came from the educated classes. Their children demanded that their institutions be overhauled from top to bottom.

For several decades, that overhaul has included not only legal examinations and school curricula; it has dominated public debate; created countless works of art, film, literature, and television; and changed the landscape of many German cities. In addition to the famous Holocaust Memorial, built on the most prominent piece of empty space in reunited Berlin, there are more than sixty-one thousand much smaller but more unsettling stumbling stones, which the German artist Gunter Demnig has hammered into sidewalks in front of buildings where Jews lived before the war. Each small brass plaque lists a name, and dates of birth and deportation.

For comparison: Imagine a monument to the Middle Passage or the genocide of Native Americans at the center of the Washington Mall. Suppose you could walk down a New York street and step on a reminder that this building was constructed with slave labor, or that this site was the home of a Native American tribe before it was ethnically cleansed? In the past few years, some universities have begun to mark the relationship between some of their spaces and the labor of slaves. What about the rest of the country?

Both Washington's Mall and London's Hyde Park devote space to commemorating one instance of evil: the Holocaust. It's puzzling that an event that happened in Europe should assume such a prominent place in American or British national symbolism—particularly when the United States did so little to save Jewish refugees before the Holocaust and so much to insure that former Nazis emigrated to the U.S. after it. And though a majority of British citizens favored changing visa restrictions in order to admit Jewish refugees, Foreign Office memoranda reveal that policy makers feared that the Germans might "abandon extermination and aim instead at embarrassing other countries with floods of alien immigrants" if they did so.[5] Can the resources devoted to commemorating an evil that neither country did much to prevent be simply motivated by guilt?

The question is seldom raised openly, for the only intelligible answer seems to be an anti-Semitic reference to the Jewish lobby. But as often in history,

Jews can be used on the front line of many agendas. The prominence of the Holocaust in American culture—and to a lesser but significant extent in Britain—serves a crucial function: we know what evil is, and we know who was responsible for it. Though it's no secret that genocidal slaughter didn't begin or end with the Nazis, the claim that rounding people up and sending them to gas chambers is evil is the only claim that commands nearly universal moral consensus today. In a world where every moral claim is viewed with increasing skepticism, any agreement at all may be welcome. The problem is that a symbol of absolute evil gives us a gold standard by which other evil actions can look like common coin. The focus on Auschwitz distorts our moral vision: like extremely nearsighted people, we can only recognize large, bold objects, while everything else remains vague and dim. Or, to put the matter in psychoanalytic terms, the focus on Auschwitz is a form of displacement for what we don't want to know about our own national crimes.

Until very recently, the amount of material about the darker sides of American history has been far easier to overlook. The information was there, but it took work to seek it out. Once confined to university libraries and departments of African American or postcolonial studies, the history of slavery and the Jim Crow reign of terror are now part of general history curricula and popular culture. (Though its critics overlooked the references, at least one turning point, Quentin Tarantino's film *Django Unchained*, was influenced by German memory culture that the director witnessed while in Berlin to make his previous movie.) British public discussion is more hesitant. As the former British Museum director Neil MacGregor put it, "What is very remarkable about German history as a whole is that the Germans use their history to think about the future, where the British tend to use their history to comfort themselves."[6] British schoolchildren learn that Britain abolished slavery before America did, but rarely about British responsibility for the slave trade. Most college students there are vaguely aware of a problem called Ireland, but lack the most basic knowledge of which part of the country belongs to the Crown. And the history of British imperialism—*we built them roads and weren't half as bad as the Belgians!*—is so small a part of public consciousness that even educated Britons can be surprised to learn that their country is generally considered to be part of the history of European colonialism.

Is an American's attempt to examine her country's crimes by the light, or the dark, of German history an exercise in self-hatred? Before you conclude this, you should consider that self-hatred is a running theme of the German right, which routinely refers to efforts like the Wehrmacht Exhibit as "dirtying one's nest." In fact, they're better described as Herculean acts of nest-scrubbing, which make cleaning stables look simple. What readmitted Germany to the family of civilized nations only decades after the Holocaust and allowed it to become the leading power in Europe was the recognition of its crimes. Having the will to face your shameful history can become a show of strength.

᠔

Evil isn't a matter for competition, though it is often treated as one.

The deliberate high-tech murder of millions is worse than the economically driven exploitation of slave labor!

But more people died in the Middle Passage that brought captured Africans to the New World than were murdered at Auschwitz!

If you want to focus on form, you could add that the Nazis went to great lengths to murder Jews even after it was clear that trains and troops were desperately needed for the war effort; Nazi devotion to genocide was so great that it outrode even instrumental interests of reason. (You should, however, remember that the gas chambers accounted for less than half the murders of European Jews, and none of the twenty million Slavic peoples. The rest were killed by low-tech means: more or less organized shooting, burning, and bludgeoning were the preferred ways of killing on the Eastern Front.) If you want to focus on number, you could argue that the number of hours captured Africans spent crammed into the holds of slave ships was higher than the number of hours spent by Jews pushed into cattle cars. Examples like these show the folly of entering into an Olympics of suffering. Quite apart from the fact that competitive suffering is bad for the soul, we have no means to measure evil's scale. Trying to determine which evil is worse than another is a political project, not a moral one, and weighing evils against each other for political purposes is morally unacceptable. Today there's at least this much consensus: both the Holocaust and slavery and its aftermath were evil. Now what?

This book is about comparative redemption, not comparative evil. Suppose you accept the view that the racism that led to the gas chambers and the racism that led to slavery and terror can be compared. Still, you may wonder: Can we compare the processes that are meant to heal the wounds of such different historical events? Postwar Germany was ravaged and occupied by four victorious armies. Contemporary America is not. Even those who acknowledge that both have been infected with murderous racism may wonder about the cure. With such very different circumstances in the present, how can one attempt to overcome the past provide lessons for another?[7]

Let's begin by counting the differences.

1. *Germany was an occupied country for forty-five years; not until 1990 did a peace treaty declare the war to be over. As a thoroughly defeated nation, Germany had no choice but to acknowledge its crimes. The United States, by contrast, emerged from World War II not only victorious but as a victor whom even pacifists acknowledged had been on the side of truth and right. Who could force them to admit they had sins to repair?*

The dates are incontestable. What's also never contested is the fact that the denazification imposed by the Allies in West Germany was a consummate failure. (As I'll show, the situation in East Germany was more complicated.) Like defeated Southerners under Reconstruction, postwar West Germans initially chafed under what they called victors' justice, and they mocked Allied attempts to impose a change of consciousness. From the Nuremberg Trials to the forced visits to Bergen-Belsen accompanied by posters screaming YOU ARE GUILTY OF THESE CRIMES!, official efforts to insist on acknowledgment were almost uniformly despised. The best-selling West German novel of the '50s was *The Questionnaire*, one right-wing author's use of a denazification questionnaire to frame his own life story in a way that sneers *the Allies are too stupid to get it* on every page. Admitting the failure of reeducation programs and eager to put aside past enmities in the service of the Cold War, Western Allies discontinued those programs in 1951. Working-off-the-past is not something that can be imposed from without. Only the internal confrontation, begun in the late '60s by the children of those who opposed any confrontation with the past at all, would have a chance.

The history of racism in America is longer than the history of racism in Germany. The first slave was brought to Jamestown in 1619; in 1951, a delegation of clergymen visiting the White House with a letter of support from the ailing Albert Einstein failed to convince Harry Truman to make lynching a federal crime. This would have left it subject to federal rather than local prosecution at a time when local justice officials were often part of lynch mobs, and certainly disinclined to prosecute them. Politically dependent on the support of white Southern Democrats, Truman said the moment was inopportune. With murderous racism so deep and long-standing, how can Americans hope to work off a past that the Germans have already begun to master?

Once again the dates will stand, but they need to be complicated by others. German racism has a long history too. As in other European nations, Jews were forced to live in ghettos, and rarely free from fear of pogroms, through the late Middle Ages. They gained citizenship status only when Napoleon carried the principles of the French Revolution eastward on swordpoint, and the vaunted German-Jewish symbiosis was as late as it was wobbly. Though hailed in his day as the German Socrates, the philosopher Moses Mendelssohn was denied membership in the Prussian Academy. One hundred and fifty years later, Einstein's membership was secured only after a recommendation assured that august institute that he was "free of all unpleasant Jewish characteristics." The year was 1914; he had already discovered relativity theory. The question is not which racism was longer, stronger, and more devastating. But rather: Did the forms it took in America preclude the sort of atonement that has taken place in Germany?

2. *The Civil War was over in 1865; World War II concluded eighty years later. If Germany has already proceeded quite a way down the path to redemption, what's taking the United States so long?*

Dates, once again. Diane McWhorter, author of a Pulitzer prizewinning history of the Birmingham civil rights movement, suggests that we should start counting from the passage of the Civil Rights Act in 1964. For however many forms of racism still continue, that was the moment racist policy was banned by law. *De facto* racist policies continue to this day, but their *de jure* abolition marked a dividing line. If you accept that reckoning, we are only fifty years from zero hour, about the place where Germany was when the Wehrmacht Exhibit provoked the kind of backlash that the removal of Confederate monuments provoked in New Orleans.

There are several reasons for American slowness in facing our history, and one is fairly simple: there's a hundred-year hole in it, and few white Americans are even aware of that. For most of us, the period between the 1863 Emancipation Proclamation and the 1955 Montgomery bus boycott is a vague and cloudy blur. My own ignorance was enormous before I began work on this book. Even as knowledgeable a politician as Hillary Clinton managed to confuse Jim Crow and Reconstruction on the 2016 campaign trail. With all due allowance for campaign exhaustion, you should not have to think in order to be clear about the difference between them, any more than you'd have to think about whether Memphis is the same thing as Montana. Excellent work by Michelle Alexander, Edward Baptist, Douglas Blackmon, Eric Foner, Bryan Stevenson, and others has made us conscious of the ways that chattel slavery turned into slavery by other means. I will sketch that work in chapter 8. Until this becomes the kind of knowledge that is mandatory in our classrooms and visible in our public spaces, we'll continue to hear the refrain: *Slavery ended in the nineteenth century, why are we still talking about it in the twenty-first?*

There are sinister explanations for the presence of this hole in American memory, beginning with the concerted efforts of the defenders of the Lost Cause narrative of Confederate history, but one explanation is perfectly innocent: Americans prefer narratives of progress. Call them happy endings. Our stories are more aspirational than actual. We may acknowledge that wrongs were committed in the past, but we want to believe they were righted in a roughly straight line. Shortly after Trump's election, President Obama tried to cheer us with the remark that American history zigs and zags, but while the metaphor may have been soothing in a moment of national anxiety, it's too abstract to describe the turns America has taken. Frederick Douglass, the former slave turned abolitionist, said it early on: racist violence occurs most often when black people advance.[8] The Klan was founded in the wake of Reconstruction, the brief period following the Civil War when African Americans began to enjoy the rights that the Union victory had assured them. Decades later, black men proud to serve in the U.S. Army came home from world wars to face lynch mobs. Some scholars argue that fury over *Brown v. Board of Education* played a role in the murder of Emmett Till. The Confederate flag was raised in South Carolina and the Stone Mountain Confederate Memorial completed in Georgia in response to early successes of the civil rights movement in the '60s. And there's no doubt that the presence of a black family in the White House enraged a sufficient number of Americans to insure the election of a swindling, violent successor whose policies, such as they are, are at odds with the interests of all but a handful of billionaires. This is not an elegy for the possibility of progress. Barack Obama's election fulfilled dreams we didn't dare to dream in that most hopeful of decades, 1960s America, and it stirred hopes and hearts around the world. Until we realize, however, that the zigs and zags are not accidental, but have a clear and particular structure, we will be unable to make systematic progress again.

3. *The Jewish community of Germany may be the fastest-growing one in Europe, but it's still far below what it was at the time of the Nazi takeover—when it was less than 1 percent of the population. However you count them, the Jewish population of Germany will never be close to the 14 percent of the U.S. population African Americans make up.*

Jews in Germany are very hard to count because the only way to be counted is to join the official Jewish Community. Doing so automatically tithes 1 percent of your income, but even those undaunted by the tax often feel alienated by the Community, which is both strife-ridden and conservative. None of the thousands of Israelis currently living in Berlin take that step, and hence remain uncounted. As do I. It's undeniable that African Americans are far more present in American life than Jews are in Germany, but that cuts both ways. The fact that so many Americans of African descent refuse to be anything but a vital part of American culture is also an advantage. Germans have been mourning the holes in their own culture since they drove out the Jews, and those of us who came, or came back, after the war cannot make up for those losses. Since Frederick Douglass, at the latest, the great majority of African Americans have rejected proposals to return to Africa. Instead, they have insisted on remaining to claim their full rights as American citizens. The American economy was built on the backs of enslaved men and women who cleared the land and tended the crops that created the wealth that was the foundation of U.S. prosperity. Equally important, American culture is unimaginable without the contributions of generations of black artists who forged forms of expression the world has come to know as quintessentially American. African Americans are inextricably part of American life, past and present, and that is a reason for hope. Forty million voices with four hundred years of history cannot be swept aside.

4. Perhaps not. But that *argument cuts two ways as well. For white racism continues, and continues to be deadly, throughout America: it's not just a matter of an unexamined past but of a pounding, brutal present. In Germany, by contrast, there are no longer enough targets left for racism.*

In Germany, to some extent, Turks and other people of color became the target of the venom once directed toward Jews. Nine of them were randomly murdered by young neo-Nazis between 2000 and 2007. The trial of the one accomplice who remained alive after a self-made bomb blew up the others shocked Germany, and the National Socialist Underground murders were not the only attacks of violence against brown people committed in Germany in recent years. It was disgust at an attack on a refugee asylum in 2015 that drove thousands of Germans to protest by streaming onto railway platforms to welcome trainload after trainload of incoming refugees from Syria, Iraq, and Afghanistan; it was fear over that welcome that gave seats in parliament to the first far-right party in Germany since the war. There is no doubt that vigilance will be needed for the foreseeable future. The past continues to seep into and infect the present. Working-off is never finished or final.

And for all the work that's been done to face anti-Semitism, even *that* hasn't entirely disappeared from Germany. My friends say I don't hear the worst of it; few Germans would tell a public intellectual who's known to be Jewish the things they say behind her back. I'm sure my friends are right, since I do hear the softer sorts of insult: the suspicion that my professional success in Germany is a result of affirmative action will haunt whatever I do, as it haunts many an African American in the United States. But what matters most is change over time. I left Berlin in 1988, largely because I wanted my son to grow up with a sense of normality that seemed impossible in a land with so many ghosts. One day-care worker had told me, "If I'd known he was Jewish, I wouldn't have taken him. Not because I have anything against Jews, they can't help what they're born as, but I couldn't have treated him like any other toddler." At least she was honest. Twelve years, two children, and a change of government later, I returned to Berlin convinced that past and prejudice had been sufficiently worked off to allow Jewish children to grow up without feeling they had to remain in hiding. Two of them, now adults, still live in the city that welcomes more foreigners every day. This is significant change. I would not have taken them to a place where they, or I, would be forced to live in fear. Put slightly differently: I would not have taken them to a place where they'd be forced to walk past Hans Wehrmacht statues or flags flying swastikas.

In sum, the circumstances surrounding racism in Germany and America, past and present, are not the same. How could they be? History is just as particular as the individuals who make and are made by it; what worked in one place can't be straightforwardly transferred to another. Seen in one light, the differences between German and American racist histories are glaring. Seen in another, what's clear is what the similarities can teach us about guilt and atonement, memory and oblivion, and the presence of past in preparing for the future. Many of the similarities are cross-cultural, as relevant for thinking about British as about Dutch colonization, though every attempt to work off past debts must attend to each nation's particular history. *Forget the past and move on* isn't even helpful in the realms of individual psychology; as political advice, it is worthless. When pasts fester, they become open wounds.

What's common to both starts with language: in Germany, as in the southern United States, "the War" is a singular reference. Everybody knows that one was decisive, and its repercussions are with us today. This knowledge is more conscious in a Deep South that was occupied, and almost as devastated as Germany, than in the rest of the United States. Still, many authors have argued for the continuing influence of the Civil War in American life, and some even claim that mainstream American political culture is a reflection of Southern attempts to win the war by other means.[9]

The centrality of the Civil War for all the American history that came after it is less clear to most Americans than the centrality of World War II for Europe. The great historian Tony Judt rightly called his examination of late-twentieth-century European history *Postwar.* The title could do for post-1865 America, were anyone to undertake as magisterial a survey of it, for the Civil War has cast an even longer shadow. Rather than focusing on the details of difference, we should use whatever lessons we can gather as we seek to come out of the shade.

~Q~

Germany was once proud to call itself the land of poets and thinkers. In the first angry attempts to confront the Nazi period, more than one wag suggested calling it the land of judges and hangmen. (*Dichter* and *Denker* rhymes with *Richter* and *Henker.*) Initially, German thinkers absconded from what should have been a moral obligation to reflect on the Nazis' assault on reason and right; Heidegger was merely the most prominent example. As most philosophers, like most other professors, supported the regime while it lasted, they avoided the subject once it was gone. But Karl Jaspers and his student Hannah Arendt, Theodor Adorno and his student Jürgen Habermas, as well as thinkers like the brilliant autodidact Jean Améry, all wrote many essays devoted to the question: What does it mean to live in the wake of past crime? German intellectual traditions prepared the way for this work in a way that American and British traditions, with few exceptions, do not. (One distinguished English philosopher told me he was no more interested in the question of why some Germans became Nazis than he'd be interested in thinking about someone who declared he was a teapot. "Both are simply mad," he said.) Having learned much from German philosophy, my goal is to encourage a discussion of guilt and responsibility as serious as the German one—not in order to provide a set of directions, but rather a sense of orientation won through reflection that is no less passionate for being nuanced.

Rules are rarely useful in matters of moment. There, judgment, which can only be based on serious reflection about particulars, is necessary. Understanding how the Germans have confronted their past will not provide recipes for confronting a different one—even were the German confrontation without flaw. Even in a single culture there are seldom clear directions.

Over lunch one afternoon the president of Berlin's Academy of Sciences asked me if I'd come to take a look at the mosaic in the academy's vestibule floor. He wanted a Jewish opinion, though he wouldn't tell me about what. As I stared at the floor, I saw that it was one of those duck-rabbit designs: if you looked at it one way, you saw an innocuous pattern; blink, and you saw a series of interlocking swastikas. No one had noticed them until the president of Israel paid the academy a ceremonial visit. Pacing in the vestibule, his bodyguard saw swastikas. Since displaying a swastika is illegal in Germany, the president of the academy received a summons from the district attorney. Had the floor been laid by the Nazis, there would have been few doubts about what to do. The trouble was that the floor was laid in 1903, nearly twenty years before the Nazi Party existed. It's an old Indian design, after all. Should they tear up the floor they had just spent part of 10 million euros to renovate? Put a rug on top of it? Put a plaque explaining the history? This is the usual solution for such questions in Berlin, and it is the one that president chose. His successor thought it better to take down the plaque and solve the problem with a rug.

Examples like these show how endlessly complicated every confrontation with the past must be. Which streets should be renamed, which statues dismantled, how those who committed crimes should be remembered and how their wrongs should be requited—none of these questions can be decided abstractly, once and for all. However similar national crimes may be, they are also relentlessly particular, and any attempt at reparation must be particular too. Only direct analyses of particular cases and contexts can help us to get the balance right.

Critical thought about history and memory is evident in recent American debates that give reason for hope, as Americans begin to see how the unexamined past forces its way into the present. It's too soon to tell, but the process that began in Frankfurt and Berlin in the '60s and changed the German nation may foreshadow the movement that began in Charleston and Charlottesville. However many the differences, all are animated by the conviction that our past will continue to haunt us if we do not face it down. An open reckoning with that past is a crucial step toward maturity that will allow us to envision a full-bodied future, for a grown-up relationship to one's culture is like a grown-up relationship to your parents. We all benefit from inheritances we did not choose and cannot change. Growing up involves sifting through all the things you couldn't help inheriting and figuring out what you want to claim as your own—and what you have to do to dispose of the rest of it.

2

Sins of the Fathers

Nothing I ever learned in Berlin surprised me more than the recognition that most Germans once put their own misery front and center. For decades after the war ended, Germans were obsessed with the suffering they'd endured, not the suffering they'd caused. Hadn't they lost sons and husbands, fathers and brothers on the field? Hadn't most of the men who survived been taken prisoner, as often as not to Siberia? Hadn't the women and children spent night after night shivering in cellars from cold and from fear of the bombs that burned or blew their cities to bits? Hadn't they lost a quarter of the territory that belonged to Germany for centuries? Wasn't the winter after the war so bitter that the great trees that lined city streets were sacrificed to keep civilians from freezing to death? Hadn't they survived on dandelion greens and potato peels? Nor was all they endured during the war enough: now they were being beaten with what would later be called a moral club. Did they really have to hear that the cause for which they'd fought and suffered was not only senseless but positively criminal?

Younger Germans couldn't entirely overlook the discrepancy between their parents' view of the matter and the views of the rest of the world. It's what led thousands born after the war to pass themselves off as Danish or Dutch when they traveled abroad. They knew what reactions the truth would provoke. There were cold shoulders, glasses slammed on a counter, even occasional spit. This was as true for young West Germans visiting Paris as it was for young East Germans visiting Poland, and they sought repair in different forms. But their parents had told them that the world's reaction was a case of victor's justice, if their parents told them anything at all. Most often they did not.

What the U.S. Declaration of Independence called "a decent respect to the opinions of mankind" may be absent in many a nation, but postwar Germany felt particularly entitled to do without it. Hadn't the rest of the world been wrong before? Only twenty years separated the end of one war from the beginning of another, and the memory of the Versailles Treaty was still fresh. Germans did no more at the beginning of that war than participate in the imperial power struggles few Europeans found problematic at the time. At the end of World War I, the carnage was so shocking that the victors looked for someone to blame and someone to punish: not only did Germany lose quite a bit of territory, it was saddled with a bill for war reparations that left its economy dysfunctional.

West German children of the war generation told me often enough that their parents opposed their own nascent attempts at atoning for the Nazi period, but they never conveyed the collective whine that was the emotional power behind their parents' opposition: *Haven't we paid enough already?* I needed decades to learn how deep those emotions had been.

The German war generation paid quite a lot. First and foremost, seven million lives. This was significantly less than the twenty-seven million killed by the Wehrmacht in the Soviet Union alone, but seven million was more than a tenth of the total German population, and hardly a family was spared. At least a million of the dead were civilians, though no one knows the exact number killed in the Allied air raids begun in retaliation for London and Coventry. If you lived in one of the cities they targeted, you were likely to lose your home and everything in it as well. When it was all over, like thousands of others, you combed through the rubble, grateful for an old photo, a child's doll, or a locket, anything that might anchor a memory of your past. There was very little to eat, and the winter of '46 was the coldest in living memory.

Another number: one-quarter of German territory was permanently surrendered. This meant that one-quarter of the population lost whatever they couldn't carry when they fled west, fearing the Red Army might do to them what the Wehrmacht had done to Russian civilians. For the most part it did not, but that couldn't be predicted, so millions of refugees swept westward, overwhelming compatriots who were likely as not to be bombed out themselves. This was hardest, of course, on the refugees, but not easy on their new neighbors, for the refugees were a daily reminder of Germany's total defeat. For comparison, imagine that China conquered the West Coast of the United States and everyone west of Wyoming went east to seek shelter.

I've sometimes wondered whose resentment was greater—the men's or the women's. The men had lived through misery, especially if they were on the Eastern Front. Their aspirations had been honed in the language of glory, and they returned as louse-infested losers. Talk of master race and machismo had conditioned their youth; now they'd been fucked in the ass, as many who had served on the Western Front put it. It was humiliating enough to be emasculated on the Western Front by the Americans, but unthinkable to acknowledge that they were subjugated in the east by the Slavs they'd always heard were scum. As men, they were so devastated that it's not hard to understand how sorry they felt for themselves.

It was the women, however, who kept the home fires burning. During the war, when front leave was just long enough to produce another baby for the Führer, they were the ones who managed the rations and dragged the mattress to the cellar when the air-raid sirens sounded night after night. After the war, if they were lucky, their men were merely missing, but often they waited years to find out. Meanwhile, the work of carting off the ruins of their homes remained when they weren't scrambling for firewood or food. Their children remember a tight-lipped grimness that filled every room. Even memories that ought to be pleasant were rimmed with shadow. "The whole city was our sandbox," recalls the writer Daniela Dahn. Sometimes they even found an old helmet to dig with, there in the ruins. "Being loser and perpetrator was a doubly hard burden," says the author Alexandra Senfft. Therapists in postwar Germany were exceedingly rare; the Nazis had branded psychoanalysis as a Jewish science, and analysts who were lucky emigrated to America or Britain. Meanwhile, the sins of the fathers continue to traumatize: many Germans of the first postwar generation refused to have children because of their own childhoods. The men said the very concept of paternal authority was contaminated. The women simply experienced family life as depression. For the first generation born after 1940, procreation could be a heroic act.

Men and women captured by their own traumas were blind to any others. Returning from exile in London, the Viennese writer Hilde Spiel was greeted with envy: *Lucky you got to spend the war abroad!* Though her father had converted from Judaism to Catholicism and cherished his Iron Cross, Spiel would have shared the fate of her grandmother, who perished in Theresienstadt, had she not left her native land. For their former neighbors, however, one thing mattered most: the returning émigrés had spent the war away from the terror that reigned in places like Vienna and Frankfurt— terror created both by the Nazi regime and the Allied attacks on it. After the bombings came hunger and cold. Surely the émigrés should feel grateful— or anyway lucky?

Spiel's experience was not unique. Non-Jewish returning refugees, who could have stayed in Nazi Germany had they not chosen to leave for political reasons, were branded as traitors. Marlene Dietrich's love songs to her native Berlin are legion, but she preferred to sing for Allied troops rather than accept Goebbels's sumptuous offer to leave Hollywood in 1936. When she returned to Berlin in 1960, she was greeted with picket signs denouncing her betrayal of the Fatherland; rotten eggs were thrown during a concert in Düsseldorf. Dietrich retired to Paris, never to return. The most famous non-Jewish returning refugee was Willy Brandt, and nothing illustrates the chasm that separates early postwar German views of the war from the views of other nations than the way Brandt was treated in his homeland. Willy Brandt's kneeling before the memorial to the Warsaw ghetto moved the world. We were thrilled to see the man who had belonged to the resistance atone for crimes of his nation, cracking open a door to the thought that the sins of the fathers need not contaminate the sons forever. But when he knelt in 1970, most of the West German public were as distressed by it as the rest of the world was delighted. The gesture suggested not just humility but humiliation. Kneeling was read as capitulation, and, even worse, capitulation to the Poles, whom years of remorseless propaganda had taught them to consider as *Untermenschen.* And why did Brandt feel the need for an apology tour at all? Less than a decade earlier, West Germany's first chancellor, Konrad Adenauer, had campaigned against Brandt with the slogan "What was Herr Brandt doing for twelve years abroad? We know what we were doing in Germany." Foreigners can barely grasp that the very thing that made him a Good German in the eyes of the world—Brandt's 1933 flight to Norway—could have been a political liability in the eyes of his compatriots. Times have changed. Germans today are ashamed of the slogan, which now appears on the glass front of the little Willy Brandt museum on the great boulevard Unter den Linden. To find out the slogan's source, however, you have to dig quite a lot. The Christian Democratic Union has yet to work off the past of Adenauer, who remains revered as the founding chancellor of the Federal Republic.

The postwar West German sense of victimhood ran so deep that it is almost invisible today. Berlin was thrilled to welcome Neil MacGregor as the founding director of the museum created in a replica of the former imperial palace, not least for his work on German history. Yet when MacGregor's 2015 BBC radio series on Germany turns to examine the women who cleared away the rubble left by Allied bombers, he concludes, "Unlike Londoners, they could hardly think of themselves as victims." In fact, that's exactly what they did. The rubble women—*Trümmerfrauen*—saw themselves as significantly worse victims than their London counterparts. Not only was there more rubble to clear in Berlin and Hamburg than in London and Bristol, but however backbreaking the work might have been in England, the task of clearing rubble was lightened by the knowledge that they'd won a righteous war. No such consolation brightened the work of the German women, who stood in long lines passing buckets of brick that had once been their homes. It took me years of reading, listening, and open eyes to get it: the majority of Germans put their own misery *über alles*.

If the pain of defeat and the absence of remorse went so deep that foreigners have trouble grasping it, Germans find it hard to grasp that foreigners don't. Growing up with family photos of fallen heroes in jackboots, they find it self-evident. The sting of defeat penetrated childhood so thoroughly that they found it hard to separate from childhood itself; now that they're grown, shame prevents them from mentioning it much. The shame is all the greater with the realization that their parents, in the best case, were not only party to war crimes, but considered themselves to be victims of them. Even the cultural historian Wolfgang Schivelbusch's brilliant study *The Culture of Defeat* only takes on the aftermath of World War I, which he compares with the Confederate defeat of 1865.[1] For a German writer born in 1941, comparing the experience of defeat in 1945 with anyone else's would cross moral red lines. Todorov's rule urging Germans to focus on the singularity of the Holocaust prevents decent Germans from comparing those who created it to anyone else.

～

Yet the evidence is there, though you won't find it in histories like Schivelbusch's or MacGregor's. One surprising place to look is early postwar German philosophy. The most famous is the case of Martin Heidegger. The man who some find the most important philosopher of the twentieth century not only joined the Nazi Party but also agreed to take the top post at the University of Freiburg. Philosophers and historians still argue about the importance of those facts. In his inaugural lecture he gave a rousing defense of the new spirit created by the Nazi revolution that drove his own assistants into unemployment or exile. (His comments about that are confined to complaints about the extra work created for him by the edict banning Jews from universities.) It's true that his tenure as rector was too short and his work too abstract to provide concrete ideological support for Nazi ideology. Heidegger's students, and their students, have argued that Heidegger's concern was not the petty details of politics, but the deeper questions about the nature of Being that took him back to the pre-Socratics. In fact, the recently published letters to his brother, who did not share the philosopher's enthusiasm for the new regime, reveal that Martin followed the day-to-day turn of political events very closely. His private notebooks were even more damning, particularly since Heidegger, always obsessed with his legacy, left exact instructions in his testament about the order in which they were to be published. It's stunning to imagine the man in his Black Forest cabin decades after the war's end, preparing for the 2014 publication of passages about "World Jewry" that are more ponderous than Goebbels's tirades, but hardly different in substance.

At least as chilling as the anti-Semitic passages are the antimodern ones. Infamously, Heidegger wrote that there was no fundamental difference between the killing machines of the death camps and the growth of mechanized agriculture. The notebooks go even further: modernity, which he sometimes thought began with Socrates, is the source of all our woes. Anti-Semitism and antimodernism often go together, as the image of the wandering, rootless cosmopolitan Jew shows. The difference is that straightforward anti-Semitism is (mostly) condemned in the United States and Germany, while antimodernism runs stronger than ever. Will progressive intellectuals continue to talk of reading Heidegger against Heidegger when they read the *Black Notebooks* passage declaring that the Allies' refusal to allow him to return to teaching was "a greater brutality than any of Hitler's"?[2] The monstrous narcissism thus unveiled was too much even for Günter Figal, the longtime head of the Heidegger Society, who gave up his chairmanship when the ninety-eighth notebook was published in 2014.

Unlike Heidegger, the influential legal philosopher Carl Schmitt didn't even apply to the Allies for permission to teach. Probably suspecting he wouldn't receive it anyway, Schmitt refused to undergo the denazification process he and his friends called "terror." He spent the rest of his long life holding forth in small circles against "preachers of repentance like Jaspers." Schmitt's rants against the "criminalizers in Nuremberg" and the "constructors of crimes against humanity and genocide" were founded on his critique of the concept of universal value as liberal hype. "The crimes against humanity are committed by the Germans. The crimes for humanity are committed against the Germans. That is the entire difference." "Anyone who uses the word 'humanity,'" he famously wrote, "wants to deceive." The deceit, thought Schmitt, is a matter of cloaking partisan preferences in terms that disguise the truth: moral concepts are irrelevant in politics, where the only categories that matter are friend and foe. Liberal democrats who seek neutral frameworks to settle competing claims by way of justice rather than power are hypocrites or fools, for any framework claiming neutrality represents nothing but the triumph of a stronger over a weaker faction. It's an old claim that goes back to pre-Socratic sophists, though someone feels the need to revive it every generation or so. Progressive thinkers who think they can take up Schmitt's critique of the more hypocritical aspects of liberal democracy without swallowing the rest are due for a shock.

Jürgen Habermas called Schmitt pathological: his inability to recognize the gap between his own grievances and the suffering his party inflicted on millions is breathtaking, and it can hardly be called a failure of understanding.[3] Likewise, Heidegger's conviction that nothing Hitler did was as brutal as the Allies' refusal to allow him to infect German youth with his murky antimodernism almost beggars belief. By the time he wrote that sentence, the dead had been counted. What kind of a mind weighs withholding permission to teach at a university against the murder of millions? For the sake of argument, however, let's suppose that the only two wartime German philosophers still read widely today were anomalies whose failures of judgment were as colossal as their fame. What about the rest of their compatriots?

Like many other conservative Germans who saw the Nazis as the bulwark that would save Europe from bolshevizing Russians on one side and soulless Anglo-Americans on the other, the philosopher Karl Jaspers was not initially opposed to the Nazis. Forced to retire from the university in 1937, forbidden to publish in 1938, and enduring considerable hardship after resisting Nazi pressure to divorce his Jewish wife, Jaspers later broke with earlier colleagues like Heidegger and insisted on German guilt. With the possible exception of those whose political opposition led to imprisonment, Jaspers held every German, including himself, morally responsible for doing too little to stop the Nazis' rise. His famous essay *The Question of German*

Guilt makes for curious reading today. Its arguments seem so obvious, you will wonder why anyone bothered to make them, until you reflect on his audience. The essay was originally part of a series of lectures delivered in 1946 to young men whose minds had been so thoroughly deformed by Nazi ideology they were unable to recognize truths that seem trivial today. As philosophy, Jaspers's arguments seem directed at straw men. As history, they remind us that those men were as real as flesh and blood can be. Through Jaspers's painstaking efforts to prove what now seems banal, we can see just how much postwar Germans had to learn. He explained to his students that not all suffering is created equal:

> Most everyone suffered, but it's completely different whether one suffered and lost in battle at the front, at home, or in a concentration camp; whether one suffered as a victim of the Gestapo or was one of those who used the regime, albeit in fear. Almost everyone lost close friends and family, but whether he lost them through battle, bombs or mass murder has very different consequences.[4]

Contemporary readers will hold these truths to be so evident they will wonder how anyone could fail to see them. How could an entire nation so reverse fortune and failure, cause and effect?

Jaspers's essay tried to answer that question by anticipating his audience's reaction. Defeat was the basic experience, resentment the most common emotion, leaving little room for guilt, shame, or even regret—except for the lands and lives Germany lost in the war. The memory of Versailles hung heavy over Nuremberg. Was it victors' justice—the winner's attempt to disguise base revenge against the loser by cloaking that revenge in moral rhetoric? Jaspers attacked this widespread view by distinguishing between the two world wars: while Germans were unfairly blamed for the first, *we* must accept guilt for the second. Jaspers used the first-person plural throughout. He believed the first clumsy attempts to force acknowledgment of guilt were no help. Shortly after the war's end, posters went up all over the British and American zones. Under a photograph of corpses at Bergen-Belsen was printed the sentence: THIS IS YOUR FAULT. The German word for *fault* is the same as the word for *guilt*, something notoriously hard to impose from outside. Jaspers described the reaction most Germans had upon seeing the posters: "There something rebelled: Who is accusing me? No signature, no name of an authority—the poster came from empty space. It is only human that someone accused, whether fairly or not, will seek to defend himself."[5]

Tactics were somewhat savvier in the Russian zone, though Jaspers didn't discuss them. Berlin was still largely a collection of rubble when the Soviet authorities organized the first theater production in 1945. *Nathan the Wise*, Gotthold Lessing's classic Enlightenment drama urging equal rights for Jews, Christians, and Muslims was meant to remind the audience of better voices from their own tradition. As the returning émigré philosopher Theodor Adorno later argued, the most important part of *Vergangenheitsaufarbeitung* affects the unconscious. The Frankfurt School emphasized the importance of psychoanalysis, and if raking through the past was going to heal anything, individually or nationally, it had to come from within. Reproaches from others are only likely to create resistance. "Whatever happens as propaganda remains ambivalent," Adorno insisted. That's just how we're built: attack us from the outside, we'll be quick to defend our ground.

What were the defenses? How was responsibility deflected? Jaspers ran through all the excuses and demolished them one by one. *State terror made resistance impossible, unless you were ready to die.* Inside German borders, Jaspers countered, concentration camps were full of political prisoners who resisted. In 1944, more than four thousand were arrested every month. The fact that concentration camps inside Germany operated until the war's end showed there was internal opposition to the Nazis, and though it wasn't very effective, it wasn't often fatal. *Germany's geographical cards were worse than those of other nations. It's easy to develop open and liberal political cultures when you live on an island that hasn't been invaded since 1066.* Geography isn't destiny; just look at the Romans. *Every state in the world recognized Hitler's government. They streamed into Berlin for the 1936 Olympics, and many expressed admiration for the new regime.* Indeed they did. Winston Churchill, for example, wrote in 1937, "One may dislike Hitler's system and yet admire his patriotic achievement. If our country were defeated, I hope we should find a champion as indomitable to restore our courage and lead us back to our place among the nations."[6] As a general truth, Jaspers acknowledged that others were no better. The particular historical truth, however, was that the others actually were better those past twelve years.

Jaspers went on to make a less obvious and more interesting point: it would be a relief if the others *were* fundamentally better than his compatriots. Were the victors nothing but selfless world rulers, there would be no moral confusion, and the reeducation of Germany would be certain and assured. Moreover, if the Germans were uniquely awash in original sin, who could blame them for acting it out? As Jaspers's student Hannah Arendt put it: where everyone is guilty, no one is. Decades later, German sales figures for Daniel Goldhagen's *Hitler's Willing Executioners*, which emphasized the continuity of anti-Semitism in German history, provoked suspicion that the book was experienced as exoneration. If everyone in the nation was anti-Semitic to the marrow, how could anyone be blamed for failing to act against the Nazis? But even though Jaspers and his wife, fearful she would be deported, lived through the end of the war with cyanide pills in their pockets, he wrote, "At no time was German anti-Semitism a popular response (*Volksaktion*). The population did not join the German pogroms, there was no spontaneous cruelty. The masses were simply silent, and withdrew."[7]

Yet even those who may be willing to acknowledge responsibility for their silence worry that too much atonement can sap a nation's strength. Without commitment to shared national traditions, what holds a people together? What allows them to keep their heads high enough to raise their children with a measure of pride? Jaspers's answer was struggling and tentative; he began a dialogue that continues to this day. For some, German tradition is poisoned, if not absolutely fatally, by those twelve unfathomable years. They work to fathom, or at least to expose them. Year after year, sons and daughters of that history publish painstaking studies on the complicities of the wartime foreign service, or the ways that leading lights of literary theory were influenced by an SS past they quietly concealed. Others clamor: *Enough is enough.*

Jaspers was unhappy with his compatriots' response to what he called his "little book"; few, he wrote, had read it, and even fewer were open to it. He was countered with the claim that Bolshevik terror was worse than Nazi terror, and criticized for undertaking a "campaign" against Germany. One visitor to the original lectures reported that students laughed and scraped the floor with their feet when Jaspers spoke of democracy in connection with the spiritual renewal of Germany.[8] Few were prepared to follow even his insistence that the victims of war should be distinguished. In 1952, what was planned as a memorial day commemorating the victims of fascism was turned into a National Day of Mourning—*Volkstrauertag*—that drew no distinctions between all those who had suffered in the war. Even in Germany, philosophers have limited influence.

Real data about what broad swaths of the country were thinking, and not thinking, was provided five years later by another philosopher, who constructed an extraordinary experiment. In 1933, ten years after the Frankfurt Institute for Social Research was founded, its members were forced to flee, not only because most of them came from (secular) Jewish families but because their work was informed by both Marx and Freud, either one of whom was enough to make them anathema to the Nazis. One member of the institute, Walter Benjamin, later took his own life when escape over the Pyrenees looked hopeless. The rest reached America and survived there until the University of Frankfurt, unlike most West German universities, called Max Horkheimer and Theodor Adorno back. In a 1948 trip to explore whether to return to the land of the murderers, Horkheimer wrote that the mass of Germans seemed even more evil than during the Third Reich.[9] That fact, he continued, did not discourage him from taking up a job from which he'd been fired when the Nazis dismissed Jewish professors from the universities. On the contrary, he felt compelled to support those Germans who had genuinely resisted the Nazis, however few they had been. And the chance to play a role in reeducating a new generation was hard to turn down. Besides, Horkheimer and Adorno were curious. Whatever were their former compatriots thinking? Thus arose the Group Experiment, in which eighteen hundred people—farmers and doctors, housewives and high school students, officers and secretaries—were encouraged to speak about German guilt. Forming small groups in which people talked to each other was meant to create an atmosphere like that of strangers on a train, who might speak more naturally and openly than they would with a single interviewer.

Though the participants represented a large variety of occupations and education, their language and historical references suggest fairly high capacities for reflection. They just didn't use them. None expressed a desire to return to the good old days of the Third Reich. Perhaps they were wary of doing so in front of the experimenters facilitating the discussions, but whatever memories they had of peace, prosperity, and pride in the '30s were battered by what followed. Stalingrad at the front and bombed-out cities at home produced shock and shame that were amply clear in 1950. The shame, however, had no moral component. Nearly every participant in the Group Experiment denied any suggestion of guilt.

One former soldier went so far as to deny that Germany had started the war. It was America, he said, that sent Germany to Russia so that Germany would bear the brunt of fighting communism at its source.[10] Even those who didn't go that far insisted that the world should be grateful for the German attack on Bolshevism, which would have overtaken not just Europe but America too had the Wehrmacht not exhausted the Red Army.[11] Germany's fight against Bolshevism was the reason for the war, and had the West only allied with Germany, there'd be no problems in Korea today and no worries about a third world war tomorrow.[12] Others suggested that the causes of war began earlier: as a cultured nation, we too wanted more land in the nineteenth century, but the other colonial powers did not want another rival.[13]

Pointing to other nations' sins, with a special focus on America, was a favored defense against recognizing their own. Why didn't America take in more Jewish refugees?[14] Several brought up lynching, arguing that American treatment of black people was worse than German treatment of Jews. After all, blacks were always treated as second-class citizens, whereas Jews had not been until the Nuremberg Laws. And lynching, which is driven by hate, is worse than mass murder taking place in an orderly fashion. Besides, lynching is mob violence that takes place in public, whereas Nazi mass murder was hidden away in secret camps in Poland.[15] Moreover, if the Nazis were so bad, why did all the foreign diplomats—who surely had more information about what went on behind the scenes than we ordinary folk—act as if they were normal? Before the war, the French ambassador went hunting with Himmler. If they knew they were dealing with murderers, why did they sit down at their tables?[16] It was the bombing of German civilians, which most participants had experienced directly, that came up most often: anyone guilty of that has no right to accuse others of war crimes.[17]

Adorno and his researchers often comment on the contradictions in their subjects' responses. How many knots can the psyche tie itself into to defend itself against moral truth? Quite a number of subjects declared themselves free of anti-Semitism, though many of them followed their declarations with anti-Semitic remarks. Along with memories of kind Jewish doctors or favorite Jewish schoolmates, the participants expressed other positions. Kosher butchers torture animals.[18] Jews prefer cheating to honest labor; just look at how many are working on the black market.[19] German Jews were all right, since they weren't really Jewish anymore; it was those weird-looking *Ostjuden* who couldn't speak proper German that caused all the trouble.[20] Alternatively, Hitler was wrong to *kill* the Jews, but it's a good thing he got them out of prominent positions, because they were running the country, and they weren't real Germans at all.

The most extraordinary instances of moral myopia were expressed in the subjects' descriptions of postwar German-Jewish relations. After 1945, said one participant, we wanted good relations with the Jews, and we reached out our hand—but they didn't take it, so now we owe them nothing.[21] Others said the problem with the Allied Occupation was that it was infected with bitter émigrés who wanted revenge.[22] One subject raged about his time in an American POW camp, which he said was run by Jews who were "horrible people." His example of the horror? "They cut our rations to a minimum and made us look at photographs from Buchenwald, where the dead, who allegedly came from concentration camps, were exhumed. No one wanted to look, but if they saw you close your eyes they'd shove you in the back to make sure you were awake. That was definitely not democratic."[23]

Only a single participant in the Group Experiment expressed the kind of moral reflection you might expect. She was an older Catholic woman, one of the few subjects to use religious language. "I take my being bombed out as atonement for the great guilt we incurred toward the innocent. The Americans are right that we murdered more Jews than they murder Negroes in a year. That is the truth. I was bombed out three times. I haven't done enough wrong in my life to justify that, but I would not ask God 'What have you done to me?' There was so much guilt to atone for that a part of the nation must atone for it on earth. Even if our children must atone for it again."[24]

Adorno and his team of researchers commented on most of the interviews. They were trying to understand how a whole people managed to defend itself against feelings of guilt, and they often used psychoanalytic concepts: this subject displayed clinical paranoia; that one revealed the infantile assumption that the occupying Americans were obliged to feed the German population *and* to work to gain its sympathies.[25] They do not seek to analyze why one woman responded to moral catastrophe in the right way, with a knowledge of sin and a sense of guilt that demanded expiation, cost what it may for herself and her children. No guile, no defense, no twisted logic.

Are we better at analyzing evil than goodness? Or is goodness, finally, impossible to analyze: it's just something simple?

∽

Bettina Stangneth is one philosopher who is not impressed with German efforts to work off the past. Born in 1966, Stangneth would be a phenomenon anywhere. She was raised in a home without books in a village in northern West Germany. No one there could imagine why she wanted to earn a Ph.D. There wasn't much political conversation in her family, but she does remember the phrase *you don't say that in school* repeated rather often.

"One didn't dare say what one's father had been doing during the Nazi period. Almost everyone lied during their denazification hearings, but there was a lot of drinking in those days, and people would say things when drunk. And then tell the children *don't repeat that.* There was no consciousness of wrongdoing, just the sense that we are the losers and the victors are in charge now."

Stangneth can't quite explain how her childhood longing to understand sparked the voracious reading that began at sixteen by "falling hopelessly in love" with Goethe and continued with a dissertation on Kant's concept of radical evil. Somehow it led her to become one of the most erudite, eloquent, and original philosophers writing today. I suspect it is not only a sparse academic job market but her fierce and self-assured independence that made a university position unlikely. The international success of her masterly *Eichmann Before Jerusalem* made a professorship unnecessary, and she now lives in Hamburg without one. Occasionally she accepts invitations to lecture, wearing flowing swaths of Thai silk. But she spends most of her time thinking about the questions that do not let her go.

Eichmann Before Jerusalem, published in 2011, is a brilliant and impassioned dialogue with Hannah Arendt's classic *Eichmann in Jerusalem*. No work of twentieth-century philosophy continues to arouse so much passionate ire.[26] Yet unlike other critiques, Stangneth's had no interest in speculating about Arendt's alleged Jewish self-hatred or blaming of victims. Through a breathtaking analysis of sources Arendt could not access, Stangneth simply showed that Eichmann's attempt to play a dull-witted bureaucrat at his trial was a calculated effort to save his skin. This claim is not entirely new. Stangneth proved it, in part, by focusing not on Eichmann himself, but on the people who surrounded and aided him. For his act in Jerusalem should have worked, as it did for many of his comrades. No Nazi since Nuremberg had received more than a few years' prison term, and even those light sentences were often commuted. Thus, wrote Stangneth, Eichmann's calculations were entirely rational. How he really felt about the crimes for which he was eventually executed was revealed in a series of documents, created in the 1950s in Argentina, which Stangneth painstakingly studied.

The bulk of these are transcriptions of tapes made in the home of Willem Sassen, a Dutch SS officer who organized meetings with Eichmann every weekend for most of 1957. Eichmann annotated and edited every transcript by hand. The meetings were attended by Nazis who had fled to Perón's Argentina to escape prosecution and remained committed to most every aspect of Nazi ideology. Chafing in Buenos Aires, they followed German politics closely, and everything they saw raised their hopes of ending exile and returning to power. They knew how many of their former colleagues held high positions in the chancellor's office, the foreign service, the army, and the courts of the Federal Republic. They also knew how the early Allied efforts at denazification were scorned by the general West German public and quietly abandoned altogether by the Western Allies as the Cold War unfolded. The climate for a rebirth of Nazism, give or take a revision or two, was auspicious. All that stood in the way, they thought, was what they called the Holocaust Lie. Nazis to the core, they considered Jews eternal enemies, and since most of them fought at the front, they knew Jews were killed there. But that was war, after all. Hadn't countless civilians been killed by Allied bombers from Hamburg to Dresden? The claim that six million Jews were the victims of calculated mass murder was another order entirely, and these men were sure that the claim was a piece of enemy propaganda designed to extort money from the Germans. Who could better counteract that propaganda than the man now living as the manager of a rabbit farm in an unimpressive house in the suburbs who was once the adviser for Jewish affairs? Surely Ricardo Klement, Eichmann's alias in Argentina, could further their cause by providing a detailed reckoning of just how many Jews had been murdered.

Eichmann's testimony in Buenos Aires sorely disappointed his listeners, for in addition to confirming the early estimate of six million, the only regret he expressed was about his failure to murder all eleven million Jews of Europe, as had been originally planned. The most fervent hope he expressed was that "millions of Muslims, to whom I have a strong inner connection since I met the grand mufti of Jerusalem" would finish the task.[27] His confessions were too much for many of his fellow Nazis. The logic of their beliefs should have led them to Eichmann's conclusions: the virulent anti-Semitism, unbearable attempts at humor, sentimental nationalism, and paranoid conviction that an all-powerful world Jewry was out to destroy them might have made the total elimination of the Jewish people seem a rational course of action. But even fanatical SS officers like Sassen found Eichmann's description of the mechanical murder of children hard to stomach. There is no evidence that Eichmann's testimony caused the group's members any deep changes of mind or heart, but they had to abandon their hopes of returning to power by refuting the Holocaust Lie after Eichmann exposed it as truth.

The most striking feature of *Eichmann Before Jerusalem* is not the revelation of Eichmann's efforts to set out and defend, with disturbingly acute classical references, the philosophical worldview whose conclusion was genocide. That worldview was shared by most of his comrades. As Walter Gruss, head of the Nazis' Racial and Political Office, put it in 1939: "There can be no possible agreement with international intellectual systems because they are not true and not honest, but simply based on an incredible lie, namely the lie of the equality of human beings."[28] The drive to world domination, they believed, is simply a law of nature. Having neither a state nor an army, the Jews sought domination with intellectual weapons, most prominently the doctrine of internationalism, beginning with the prophetic texts of the Hebrew Bible, continuing through Freemasonry and the French Revolution, and culminating most dangerously in Marxism. The information that Eichmann brandished such views will be of interest to those still concerned with his biography, or his exact place in the hierarchy of the machine whose levers he moved to set gas chambers in motion—though it does not undermine Arendt's general claim that most of the genocide was enabled by thoughtlessness.

Stangneth's research revealed an atmosphere in which views like Eichmann's seemed entirely plausible. Well into the '60s, West German commitments to democratic order were precarious, and the possibility of a return to a sanitized Nazism could not be ruled out. Courts and universities were staffed with former Nazis, and not simply, as was claimed, because there was no one left with sufficient skill to replace them. "All they had to do was to invite the emigrants to return, instead of systemically making that difficult," said Stangneth. "Adenauer's willingness to hire former Nazis sent a message to the millions waiting uncertainly in the new Federal Republic: there's room for you here too. All you need to do is behave in an orderly fashion and we won't look closely at your past." The Adenauer government knew of Eichmann's whereabouts as early as 1952, but a trial was not in the German government's interest; his defense could reveal how many of his comrades were filling powerful positions in the new era. Nor was that government alone in its desire to avoid unpleasant revelations. The Vatican put it most clearly: "The leading Nazis of World War II should no longer be prosecuted; now they belong to the active side of the defense of Western civilization against communism, and today it is more necessary than ever to gather together all anticommunist forces."[29] The statement was written in 1960, as Vatican diplomats demanded Eichmann's return to Argentina. And as Stangneth told me, "Anticommunism is the only aspect of Nazi heritage you can still practice without anyone objecting."

A decade spent studying those for whom the Nazi cause was not yet lost has made Stangneth particularly vigilant for the traces they left in contemporary Germany. "Perhaps it's because I have an exceptionally good sense of hearing," she said. "In a literal sense. Even as a child I was always overhearing things I wasn't meant to hear." She's not convinced that Germans have faced the worst fact about the Nazi period: not the ignorant masses, but the educated elites were the driving forces behind the regime. Of the fifteen officials present at the Wannsee Conference, where the Final Solution was settled, eight had Ph.D.s. "After the war the Nazis were pictured as bloodthirsty aliens, preferably with knives between their teeth. None of the professors wanted to acknowledge that they'd accommodated themselves to the system, and done very nicely thereby." Because of this, Stangneth believes we have yet to acknowledge the connections between Nazi thinking and contemporary thought. She has researched the continuity between the books taught at Nazi universities and those that are currently assigned.[30] Nor does she think this continuity is confined to Germany. "People voted for Hitler as they voted for Putin and Trump, because they didn't want to give up their own privileges. This isn't a matter of ignorance. They understand exactly the price of enlightenment: that the equality of humankind means the equality of humankind, and not only after I've secured my own comfort. I too must obey moral laws." Like me, she is appalled at the ways in which progressive-minded German philosophers continued the attack on the Enlightenment that Nazi thinkers began—"the fact that victims of the regime like Adorno and Horkheimer barely escaped Germany in order to spread Nazi anti-Enlightenment thought through the world is too awful to put into words." There is, she continued, only one single weapon against racism and chauvinism, and that is the critique of reason that shows us our own capacities for understanding along with the recognition of reason's limits. "People abandoned this most powerful weapon because they let themselves be told that it was the problem. The Nazis knew exactly that the best way to disarm someone is to persuade them to lay down their own weapons by convincing them they are useless."

While I share her philosophical convictions, I cannot share all her conclusions about continuities between Nazi and contemporary German practices, much as I admire her relentless commitment to watchfulness. Among my German friends, watchfulness is a matter of good taste. Even when reflecting on a single crime, would we trust a man who took pride in the depth of his remorse, the extent of his good behavior in prison, the exemplary nature of his rehabilitation? Good taste prevents good Germans from anything that could possibly be construed as boasting about repentance.

"I don't understand why Germans were accepted into the world community," she continued, "except for the fact that the judgment at Nuremberg was also a lesson for the future: we will punish the criminals, but not the people as a whole. We don't do race war; that's a German form of craziness. They should have hanged the whole lot at Nuremberg, but the Allies wanted to show that they could make distinctions between degrees of guilt. It was a peace offering to the German people. We weren't exactly offered an outstretched hand, but it was an open door. Whether the German people have earned that gift is not yet clear. At Nuremberg, Goering said that people would be building monuments to him fifty or sixty years after the trial. We turned Robin Hood into a hero, a man who smashed in travelers' skulls in order to rob them. Who knows how we'll see Hitler a hundred years from now? Germans have a great talent for interpretation, and we know how to throw sand in people's eyes."

Relativism, she insisted, is not a post-structuralist invention. If you believe there is no truth but the truth of the victor, you can build frameworks to interpret things in just the terms that will appeal to the victors. "That's how it was done, East and West. We've always understood how to give foreigners the feeling that they can explain us to ourselves in a way that leads to the conclusion: man, you're terrific."

"That's my biggest fear in writing this book," I told her.

"You should be afraid. You don't want to be embraced to death. And the Germans who will embrace you are people you don't want at all. The sort who secretly want all this atonement to stop. They're not even particularly secret about it—"

"Bettina," I interjected. "May I remind you how things are in other countries?"

"You're asking about my country. If the soup is too salty, it's too salty. Doesn't matter if you can't get better soup anywhere else."

I reminded her of the days after the Charleston massacre, which moved many Southern states to take down the Confederate flags the murderer had brandished. "Steve Bannon, who was Trump's chief strategist, wrote articles urging people to keep the flag flying, and fly it proud. That would be impossible to do with a swastika in this country."

"Of course it would be impossible," she answered. "It would be awful if *nothing* had changed. We catapulted ourselves out of the world community, and we were rightly put on probation for years."

"I think you've passed probation."

"I don't."

If Stangneth's conclusion is common enough among non-Jewish Germans who have studied postwar German history, many Jewish Germans see it differently. Like Cilly Kugelmann, recently retired as program director of the Jewish Museum in Berlin, who lives in a neighborhood that once was a center for educated German Jews; Albert Einstein lived around the corner. Nowadays in Schöneberg, there's a memorial to Jewish absence: two artists created an installation listing laws passed against Jews, statute by statute, hanging from the high lampposts that line the streets.

Kugelmann was born in 1947 in Frankfurt to parents who were newly liberated from Auschwitz, where their first child was murdered. Though her father testified at the Auschwitz trial, he never spoke about Auschwitz to her. "Parents have a right *not* to tell their children how degraded they were," she said. "Parents want to protect their children—not to show themselves as broken people who weren't able to do so." She grew up in what she describes as the ghettoized world of Frankfurt's survivors, who were too broken, or exhausted, to face the prospect of moving elsewhere. Like most of their children, she moved to Israel on finishing high school; like most of them, she returned to Frankfurt after a few years. There she cofounded the journal *Babylon*, the first postwar Jewish intellectual journal in Germany, which sparked many to imagine a revival of Jewish culture in a place once committed to rooting it out. "There were four of us," she said ruefully when I told her how the journal had created excitement in mid-'80s Berlin. Now, she pointed out, there are so many Israelis in Berlin that it may be the place where a young generation of sophisticated secular Israelis can create a new type of Hebrew society. ("Maybe they'll even become Jewish," said her lifelong friend Micha Brumlik.) Kugelmann became program director of the new Jewish Museum, which was built with federal funding, Daniel Libeskind's architectural design, and a great deal of fanfare meant to herald a new era in German-Jewish history. "People who visit rarely have a particular interest in the history of Jews in Germany," she told me. "They want to see *Vergangenheitsaufarbeitung.*"

Kugelmann's background might have predestined her to become the sort of mournful soul that often peoples institutions designed to remember a culture, unable to see any sorrow but their own. Instead she filled her role with grace, nerve, and wit. The celebration she prepared for the museum's tenth anniversary centered around a three-day symposium entitled "Visions of Belonging: Jews, Turks, and other Germans" in which Muslim intellectuals outnumbered Jewish ones, and both groups discussed how to deal with the dramatic changes occurring as Germany reconceives itself as a nation where 20 percent of the population has immigrant roots.

The anticipation surrounding the museum's opening a decade earlier had been enormous. The capital had only recently moved from Bonn to Berlin, and the fact that the Jewish Museum's grand opening was the most sought-after invitation in the new Republic was heralded as a sign that Germany had turned a corner. In the weeks leading up to it, I was asked about the dress code by several German women who thought I, as a Jew, must know. *It says "fancy dress" on the invitation, but how fancy can I get? How much décolleté? Is glitter appropriate?* Accustomed to associate *Jewish* with *tragedy*, the ladies were unsure. In the end we all dressed with style and sparkle, Chancellor Schröder opened the ceremonies, and nobody remembered what food was served, for the private opening with the coveted invitations took place on the evening of September 10, 2001. The public opening that had been scheduled for the next day was quickly canceled. "We knew immediately that the world had changed," said Kugelmann.

Still, her focus is on the change in Germany, which she believes is deep and vital. The 2000 law that separated the right to German citizenship from the possession of German blood was fundamental. The renaissance of Jewish culture in Germany is fundamental. "Germany is one of the safest countries for Jews in the world," she said. "And that's thanks to decades of public working-off-the-past. A politician who said something anti-Semitic in public would lose his job. That doesn't mean there's no anti-Semitism or racism left; we still have to be vigilant." But that, she insisted, is an international problem. What matters is the arc that Germany has traced.

More typical of the next generation is Polina Aronson, a sociologist who was born in St. Petersburg in 1980. The majority of Jews now living in Germany come from the former Soviet Union. Both the size of that majority and the nature of its Jewishness are still debated. According to Jewish law, which recognizes only those born to Jewish mothers, about half would be counted. According to Jewish custom, which assumes some knowledge of tradition, even fewer would qualify. But they were Jewish enough to have their Soviet passports stamped on the line where ethnic identity was listed, which was enough to assure them an exit permit before the Soviet Union collapsed, or a visa to Germany thereafter.

"People often ascribed Jewish identities to me," she said, "both positive and negative. From being smart to being canny. We all know how that goes; you don't have to name it."

"No. But you look Jewish," I said. "If I saw a photo of you, I'd bet you were a young professional in a suburban Ohio synagogue."

"Of course. But this is something you will never hear in German."

"Of course not."

Polina describes herself as a child of the glasnost era. Her grandfather left the shtetl early to become a communist; he worked as a printer. Until she read his diaries, she could not understand her own love for Berlin: "its bleak architecture, its sour humor, its dialect, flat and broad like the Prussian landscape." For her grandfather, as for her parents, the distinction between Germans and Nazis was clear. Two grandparents survived the siege of Leningrad, which took the lives of some 750,000 others, and survived the battlefields as well: her grandfather as a soldier in the Red Army, her grand-mother as a doctor in the field. But they were raised in the tradition of the Communist International, in which Germans had played such a role that it never occurred to them to lump Karl Liebknecht with Heinrich Himmler.

Before she came to Berlin, Polina told me, she had "zero knowledge of Jewish culture." Changing diapers in the baby corner of her local gym, she was addressed by another mother, who'd heard her speaking Russian to her daughter. As it turned out, their babies were not only born weeks apart, they were also named Adam and Eva. The two mothers became fast friends, and Marianna, a television anchorwoman who was raised in a Russian community in Brooklyn, introduced Polina to basic elements of Jewish tradition.

One Friday evening I was invited to celebrate Shabbat with their fami-lies. The door opened to the sweet smell of fresh challah. Polina was bak-ing with the older children, while their fathers, both non-Jewish Germans, tried to keep the younger boys and their Lego pieces in some sort of order. Initially, the two families considered sending the children to a local Jewish kindergarten.

"We thought it would be a Brooklyn-style kindergarten where they make bagels," said Polina. "Instead, there were Russian women wearing wigs, and little boys with kippot and tzitzit. I had no idea what tzitzit were." She laughed. Marianna had to explain the tassled undergarments worn by Orthodox men.

Polina enjoyed "the beautiful messiness of their lives" but decided to send her daughter to a secular kindergarten instead. Since kindergarten spots are rare goods in Berlin, Marianna and her husband, Mark, gave the Orthodox kindergarten a try, but they quit because of the dinosaurs.

"Dinosaurs?"

There was a parents' meeting at which one mother complained that the children were subjected to a book with pictures of dinosaurs. The Torah says nothing about dinosaurs, and the Jewish calendar reckons the world was created in 3761 before the Common Era, whereas dinosaurs, allegedly, are . . . Mariana and Mark took their son out of kindergarten when they realized they were the only parents who didn't object to dinosaurs.

"Who are these people?" I asked.

"Mostly young families from the former Soviet Union, but some of them come from England as well. Word has spread that Berlin is a good place to be Orthodox."

Polina likes the ritual of Friday night dinners, though her Saturdays are full; she brings her children to the other side of town, where they attend

Russian classes, "an even more important part of their identity." She hasn't learned all the prayers, so sometimes she just bakes challah, lights the candles, and says "Shabbat Shalom." "For me, it's a big middle finger in the face of Adolf Hitler and company. They tried to kill us, they failed, let's eat. I can't say more."

"Have you ever run into anti-Semitism here?"

"Never," Polina said. She has lived in Berlin since 2004. "I ran into other things. I couldn't tell a Jewish joke for a long time, and there are so many fantastic Jewish jokes." She told me one I didn't know, and I had to agree: there's a certain kind of self-abnegating Jewish humor that frightens good Germans, who find it offensive. And it *could* be offensive, if told by a German. For Polina, it's part of the free-flowing Jewish identity she remembers from her grandparents' home in St. Petersburg.

If she misses dark Jewish humor in Germany, she is warmed by the kindness expressed in the offers of help toward the refugees, which she feels is particularly German. "It's just something very genuine: the readiness to distinguish between good and bad and act on it." She believes this is a result of German historical reflection.

When the refugees came, Polina too volunteered her help. She began by cooking at a festival organized to raise support for the new arrivals, which is how she came to offer her spare room to Mustapha, a twenty-five-year-old computer engineer from Aleppo. He'd found a job washing industrial refrigerators, but he was sleeping in a park; his sleeping bag had been lost in the Mediterranean, along with his other possessions. When her husband was traveling on business, she acknowledged a moment of fear: she had, after all, opened her home to a total stranger. "What if he's shopping in a drugstore for cactus fertilizer to make a bomb?" But she thought of the ways her family had been helped by strangers before and after the war, how they had given help in turn. She thought of the Russian Jewish writer Vasily Grossman, who wrote that the instinctive thirst to help our fellow humans—often contrary to all reason—can overcome the wildest hatred.[31] So Mustapha lived in her spare room until he found a place of his own.

"How did he react to your being Jewish?"

"He was happy to wear a kippah one Shabbat, but we didn't really talk about it. He has other things to worry about; his family is still in Aleppo. We did get into an argument about hummus recipes. He wanted to make it with yogurt."

I asked Polina what other countries can learn from the Germans.

"Relentless self-questioning," she answered immediately. "Even when we may not be satisfied with the answers." Self-reflection, she continued, shows respect both for history itself and for the people who lived through it.

Bettina Stangneth remains skeptical. "I'm outraged that since we've become aware of the Muslims, we've suddenly discovered Christian-Judeo tradition as the foundation of German culture. We use a group that wouldn't exist today, had it been up to us, to undermine a new enemy that can't defend itself. That's part of our great talent for reinterpretation." She warns against the tones she sometimes hears on television—*that guilt business has to end sometime*—for she fears that a silent majority is just waiting for the right moment to take off the cloak of repentance. "Instead of being grateful for the second chance the Allies gave us, many Germans still feel they're the victim of a great injustice. That's why they love historians like Timothy Snyder, who come from abroad to exonerate them."

Stangneth's views are supported by the message of her work on Eichmann. Arendt's mistake, she argued, didn't result from her failure to attend the whole trial; no observer did. Nor is it surprising that she was hoodwinked by the demeanor of "a nobody"—in the words of Avner Less, Eichmann's chief investigator. Stangneth came to know him well, and wrote a book about him too, for everyone who saw Eichmann was hoodwinked by what Arendt would later call his banality. Arendt, Stangneth argued, simply could not grasp the idea that thinking people could consciously do evil, or fail to repent when confronted with the extent of their crimes. Philosophers come by this attitude honestly. The idea that no one willingly and knowingly does evil goes all the way back to Socrates. "We've understood that people who grew up in psychologically deforming circumstances will do damage," Stangneth said. "But all that we've understood doesn't explain what happened: the conscious anti-Enlightenment sentiment from people who were not psychologically damaged, who were in a position to reflect, and nevertheless decided for the worst." Thinking people too may keep turning on the wheel of their own suffering—even when that suffering can only be seen, by outsiders, as just punishment for abominable crimes.

Stangneth reminded me that many of Heidegger's notebooks are still unpublished. "Anyone who still could write in '47 that the Allies were more brutal than the Nazis will hardly say something better in '61. If you're that pig-headed, you're bound to get worse over time. The notebooks that have been published were written before he saw Arendt again. Do we want to know what he wrote about her in his black notebook after the war? Of course we want to know, but can we bear it?"

❧

The inclination to set one's own suffering *über alles* isn't particularly German, nor is it particularly new. Voltaire's *Candide* includes a marvelous old woman, missing an eye and half a buttock, who accompanies Cunégonde on her travels. Setting sail for the New World, she proposes a little entertainment: "Just for fun, why not get each passenger to tell you the story of his life, and if there is one single one of them who hasn't often cursed the day he was born and hasn't often said to himself that he was the most unfortunate man alive, you can throw me into the sea head first."[32] Competitive victimhood may be as close to a universal law of human nature as we're ever going to get; it is surely an old and universal sport. Postwar Germany was no less inclined to participate in it than the defeated American South. Though the South's defeat is older, you can hear the same litany: the loss of their bravest sons, the destruction of their homes, the poverty and hunger that followed—combined with resentment at occupying forces they regarded as generally loutish, who had the gall to insist their suffering was deserved. If Germany could come to shift its focus from the suffering it experienced to the suffering it created, what's to prevent any other nation from doing the same?

Out of that suffering some will weave a theodicy. All that pain cannot be without meaning. The weavers need not be those who remember the suffering directly. Often it's the suffering of their ancestors, more imagined than experienced, that drives the search for a framework with which to understand it. The myth of the Lost Cause was created by Southerners idealizing a childhood most could barely remember. And counted from start to finish, the Third Reich lasted only twelve years. Since the good times were over after Stalingrad, there was barely a decade in which memories of new roads and Volkswagens, free vacations on the Baltic, and torches in twilight parades could be mythologized. Germans and Southerners both viewed themselves as guardians of old codes of honor against the mercantile materialism of their enemies, but the number of Germans who truly long for the old days is very small. There's a group of people who call themselves *Reichsbürger*— citizens of the empire—and refuse to acknowledge the legitimacy of the Federal Republic, which they view as a construction of the Allies. (As it was, in fact, for almost fifty years. Good thing, too.) Their numbers are small enough—about thirteen thousand—to be kept on the watch list of the German equivalent of the FBI. Anti-immigrant sentiment has made a new right-wing party stronger, but even a conservative German president recently acknowledged that "Islam belongs to Germany."

I am under no illusion: much of Germany is unhappy about the refugees. The so-called welcome culture that took in a million of them is often the subject of sarcasm and fear, both from those who are educated and privileged and those who are not. The citizens who gave the AfD party 12 percent of the national vote in 2017 were not all poor people from the East, though those are the ones who got the media's attention. Had I not met them in a street or a salon, I would have encountered them in print. An article about the refugee question was to be published by the leading newsweekly *Der Spiegel*, and as so often in Germany, they wanted to know what philosophers thought. Asked for a comment, I replied that at a time when people drown every day in the Mediterranean, I was less interested in philosophical discussion about the definition of helpfulness than in practical questions. There are empty villages from Poland to Portugal. Why not give refugees a chance to rebuild them? The viciousness of readers' reactions was chilling. *Didn't I know the majority of migrants are African, who have no experience overcoming difficulties through hard work? How could I expect them to develop abandoned villages? And speaking of abandoned: the young people have abandoned those villages, but older people remain. How can I propose to let their world be overrun by dominating African hordes?*

The author of this email went on to suggest that it was scandalous that the director of an institute named after Einstein should think so poorly. He was clearly unaware that Einstein was a refugee himself, who spent considerable amounts of energy and money helping less privileged refugees escape the Third Reich.

So I know how many sides there are to this story. Racism has hardly disappeared in Germany, as comments like that only begin to show. The only thing of which I am certain is that Germany's treatment of the refugees has been far better than that of most of its neighbors—ask anyone in Poland or France or Great Britain—and that the German response to the refugees was born as a response to its own history. Even more important is that the initial response came from the ground up. Angela Merkel received both credit and blame for the decision to absorb a million refugees. I won't make light of what became, for a time, a brave political stand, but the chancellor waited twelve long days before taking it. In those last days of August 2015 something extraordinary took place. Disgusted by a right-wing attack on a refugee shelter, thousands of Germans came out to welcome refugees by the trainload. Sometimes this meant literally standing on station platforms, waving signs of greeting; more often it was a matter of collecting food, clothes, and bedding for the shelters. Thousands more signed up to offer German lessons or play soccer or music with the refugees. The wave of support was truly popular, engulfing hip young artists and staid, settled shopkeepers alike; nearly everyone I met in Berlin wanted to do something. When asked why, some said they just couldn't stand the thought of the Mediterranean becoming a graveyard. For most, historical references were front and center. Their grandparents had been refugees when East Prussia became Poland after the war; their grandparents had created refugees when they supported the Nazi Party that forced the luckier victims to flee from their homes. Even those who didn't mention their own grandparents felt bound by a bequest from the past. The attack on a refugee shelter in Heidenau was a pogrom against the Other, the consequences of which every German has been taught to remember. And despite the backlash that gave political power to the AfD, quieter efforts to help refugees integrate continue three years after the official wave of welcome. Among my neighbors, an upper-crust journalist and a young woman financing her studies with cleaning jobs both donate time every week to teach their language to Syrians. Among my acquaintances, a young family and an aging scientist have refugees living in their spare rooms. In his 2019 history of refugees in Germany, Jan Plamper could conclude, "While there is still too much racism in Germany, at the end of the day this is a story of success and progress."[33]

◦◦◦

Do the sins of the fathers contaminate the children? And if so, for how long?

It's a question that quietly underlies German discourse, from sociological tomes to tabloids, since the late 1960s. The fear has overshadowed so many German lives that it's hard to find anyone who's entirely free of it. This is psychology, not piety. It's not easy to feel touched by what your great-grandfather did; chances are, you never knew him. It's another story if his sins continue down another generation or so, and that is indeed the problem. None of us can entirely escape the residues of attitude transmitted from mother to daughter, father to son, unless we are bitterly scrupulous. Even then, those who make an effort to reject those attitudes are likely to retain their traces.

Alexandra Senfft was born in 1961 to a liberal family in Hamburg. Her father was a left-leaning lawyer; her mother suffered from deep depression that often left her unable to care for her children. Trying to understand her mother's misery long after her early death, Alexandra wrote a poignant book called *Silence Hurts*. Her thesis: her mother's mental illness stemmed from her own father's execution when she was fourteen and the fact that the family never acknowledged his participation in the Holocaust. Hanns Ludin was the Third Reich's envoy to Slovakia who signed the deportation orders for the Slovak Jews. "He must have had a feeling of guilt," said a friend of Ludin's years later—"the guilt that torments every honest Nazi, since he realized what had gone on behind his back as well as in his name . . . now that he realizes how often he closed his own eyes in order not to look too closely."[34] Alexandra's mother, Erika, had been Hanns Ludin's oldest and favorite child, and her memories of early life in occupied Bratislava were warm and happy—playing accordion and theater in the garden of the villa that was stolen from its Jewish owners in order to house the Nazi envoy, his family and servants; good, fresh food; horses to ride on; ski trips in the mountains. The family was evacuated back to Germany as the war drew to a close, but the head of the family handed himself over to the Americans. He was tried in Bratislava and sentenced to death for war crimes. One day in 1947 Erika learned that her father had been executed. It was shortly before Christmas; the packet she'd sent to the prison arrived too late for him to open. Alexandra's grandmother raised their six children alone. She kept a house full of music and warmth, and though Alexandra never heard her say a good word about the Nazis, she also never said a bad word about her late husband. Alexandra's search to understand began after her grandmother's death. The book she produced made her the black sheep of the family. Feeling she had besmirched the glorious image of their mother, none of her aunts in the once close-knit family accept her position.

"But your book is so gentle, and generous," I told her. "You are trying to understand your grandparents."

"I have no sympathy for people who cling to Nazism. Anyone who is not in denial, who is not covering up their crimes, who is trying to understand how their family members got into that—we have a basis for a dialogue."

Her books express that. The success of *Silence Hurts* may have led to ostracism from her extended family, but it led to something else as well. Letters from readers with similar stories made clear that not only the children of Nazis were struggling with their parents' crimes; the grandchildren were deeply affected as well. She wrote another book, *The Long Shadow of the Perpetrators*, that moved through her own experience to include the stories of others.

Alexandra believes that many in her parents' generation, whose own parents were Nazis, did a good job confronting the Nazi past intellectually and politically. But that was pure reason. What they couldn't face was emotion. Nobody likes admitting mistakes. What does it take to admit that your parents were *world-historically* wrong?

Trapped in that circle, children of Nazis took many routes. Some, like Alexandra's mother, self-destructed. Others cut themselves off from their families entirely and refused to start families of their own. And some, like Richard von Weizsäcker, went on to become president and make seminal speeches acknowledging Germany's guilt—but always maintained that his own father was innocent. *He only took the job as chief assistant to Foreign Minister Joachim von Ribbentrop to prevent other people from doing things that were worse.* Weizsäcker was a young law student when he defended his father at Nuremberg. His defense was unsuccessful: his father received a sentence of five years in prison, though, like most Nazis, he was freed after less than a year. The president always regarded the judgment as "unfair and inhuman."

"Weizsäcker's speech really was a paradigm shift," said Alexandra. "But he failed to face up to his own father's guilt. He turned a perpetrator into a victim—making it easy for Germans to do the same."

"How do you explain his defense of his father?"

"That's just the classic ambivalence about confronting the victimizer in a person you love. It's easy to talk about other people who were Nazis and not so easy to talk about your own people. To be sure, most Nazis refused to talk about the war within their families, but there are alternatives: you can read letters, look at the archives, go into groups or therapy."

There are a number of groups in Germany in which children, and now grandchildren, of Nazis engage in dialogue with the children or grandchildren of those the Nazis tried to wipe out. They're not unlike the groups led by the William Winter Institute in Mississippi, or those in which descendants of slave owners work to communicate with descendants of slaves. Alexandra has worked with several such German groups, beginning with one led by the late Israeli psychiatrist Dan Bar-On, who published several books documenting the work. "Dan's approach was based on the idea that when people tell their stories, you can always find something that is yours too, and then they're not strangers anymore. I've seen it happen with people who initially refused to look at each other."

I had seen it happen in Mississippi too, but had never been to one of the German groups, and I asked Alexandra to get me invited. In Köln, Peter Pogany-Wendt greeted me warmly. He was born in 1954 in Budapest to parents who survived concentration camps and drew the lesson: better to hide. Wherever they wandered, they were reluctant to identify as Jewish, and for half his life Peter did not do so either. Now he is a psychiatrist who treats many people, particularly those who have lived with one or another trauma of exile. He has also been instrumental in organizing a group called the Working Group for Intergenerational Consequences of the Holocaust, in which Jews and Germans meet to talk about the pasts they are still working off. "Phenomenologically," said Peter, "children of perpetrators and children of victims are very similar." Björn Krondorfer, a German professor of religious studies at Northern Arizona University, is also director of the Martin-Springer Institute, which seeks "global engagement through Holocaust awareness." Together Peter and Björn prepared a series of exercises for the weekend. They didn't mind having an outsider in the group of twenty people—as long as I agreed to be a participant, not just an observer.

During one exercise Björn laid out a long strip of paper on the floor; on it were marked a series of dates in German and Jewish history. We were asked to walk through the line, placing ourselves at those points in history with which we identify most. Does 1939 feel more like the beginning of World War II or the date of the first ghettos in Poland? If 1953 is the date of the first treaty between Germany and Israel, do we feel closer to Adenauer or Ben-Gurion? And how are we going to talk about it?

I had agreed to participate, not simply observe, so I was bound to go along with the exercise, but I also felt compelled to speak honestly. I cannot really identify with either side. I am American, not German, and no one in my family was a Holocaust victim. "No one?" say several people, surprised. "Most American Jews had some family members who were affected by the Holocaust." I do not. Hence I believe that identifying with them would trivialize victims' experiences. I wasn't even particularly interested in the Holocaust till I came to Germany at the age of twenty-eight. The rest of the group felt squarely identified with one side or the other, but they accepted my hesitation.

For Alexandra, such groups are important. "You need people around you who are also seeking the truth, because you face a lot of opposition from your own family and your environment for breaching loyalty. You need support from people who have had the same experience." She views her own work as a bridge between emotional and cognitive wrestling with the past. "That's the work you have to do if you have Nazi parents or grandparents. People who don't do the work—who go into denial—pass their unprocessed feelings on to their children, leaving them disoriented. If you're uneasy about foreigners, your children will feel that too. I discuss these questions clearly with my children, knowing there is still so much xenophobia in this society."

"Don't you think that has changed?"

"Yes and no. A lot of people have learned their lessons and have changed fundamentally, but I would say the majority of people have not. Values can change, and sometimes it's a creeping process. Democracies are young, and you need to work at them."

Like many others, Alexandra is very worried about the anti-EU, anti-immigrant party that has grown in the past two years. There is still a taboo against openly anti-Semitic statements, but anti-Muslim sentiment is deeply racist, and growing. "It's okay to be against those Semites," I said, and we both laughed. Darkly. Weakly. Alexandra predicts that anti-Muslim attitudes will open the gates to more anti-Semitism and racism. She and her husband occasionally speak of leaving the country if the AfD wins an election.

"But for now we've decided to stay, to fight for democracy and remind people about our history."

↶↷

"Being German in my generation," says the prizewinning author Carolin Emcke, "means distrusting yourself." She was born in 1967.

Exact birth dates are important in Germany. If you were born before 1910, your education was not soaked through with Nazi propaganda, and you probably knew enough Jews to inoculate you against the worst of it. If you were born after 1928, your education was in Nazi hands, but you were too young to be drafted into the Wehrmacht, though you might have been a *Flakhelfer* in the war's last desperate days. In between, you were likely out of luck. Postwar dates matter just as much. If you were born after 1960, it's unlikely that your father was in the army, though his school days would have been informed by it, as well as the memory of the bombs that fell in the course of what Goebbels called Total War. Born a little earlier, you are probably torn and frayed. I know no honest man or woman of that generation who wasn't in some unreachable place broken. If you've ever had the misfortune to learn an awful truth about your parents, you can put yourself in German shoes. Whatever else they did or failed to do, your parents remain the people who gave you milk and wiped your ass and made sure you didn't perish before the age of two, as you probably would have without them. Even finding out they were Nazis cannot change that.

They are called the '68ers, the generation born in the '40s that watched the Eichmann and the Auschwitz trials on television and had epiphanies: suddenly the grim-lipped brutal silence of their parents and teachers had a cause. "It mirrored the silence of the victims," said Cilly Kugelmann. "But it had another ground. The victims were silent from shame; the perpetrators from guilt." Alexander and Margarete Mitscherlich, German psychoanalysts whose book *The Inability to Mourn* was part of the awakening, put the nation on the couch. Germans of the war generation had to radically shift identity within twenty years. The heroes of the Wehrmacht had become the victims and losers of bombs and POW camps, a difficult enough transition; now they had to get used to being perpetrators. From *hero* to *victim* to *perpetrator*: How to wrap one's head around that? The Mitscherlichs argued that one couldn't, and the nation was consequently stuck. Unable to mourn the loss of their beloved Führer and the self-image he had given them, they could not mourn the deaths his regime had caused.

Because their parents could not mourn, acknowledge responsibility, or even speak about the war, the next generation was damned to express it. Some say the Federal Republic could not have been rebuilt without that silence; cleaning up the ruins was hard enough without having to reflect on how they got there. No wonder the expressions came out off-key, and often worse. Unable to identify with their parents, they rushed to identify with the victims, who could be, alternately, Jews, Palestinians, or the Vietcong. The Mitscherlichs called it an envy of innocence, and many spoke that envy out loud: how they wished their own parents had been on the other side of the barbed wire. Those who had children themselves often gave them Hebrew names. In the 1980s, you could shout "Jakob!" on most any Berlin playground and watch three little blond heads turn.

They sometimes lurched into righteous self-pity. Even those who weren't much inclined to theory read Adorno, Horkheimer, and Benjamin, but their reaction to living Jews was awkward at best. "Every time I see you, I think of Dachau," said one to me as we sat in a rainy *Biergarten* in 1983. Sometimes they replaced the anti-Semitism of their parents with a philo-Semitism that felt no better, at least to this Jew. Sometimes they simply tweaked the anti-Semitism, whether or not they knew it; many were relieved and some even rejoiced when they learned that Israelis too could be cruel during an occupation.

Looking back on the German '60s, some now say that the Nazis provided an excuse, and a violent twist, to a rebellion against the parents that would have happened anyway. "Suddenly they had arguments instead of hormones," said Bettina Stangneth. And yet it was the generation that broke the silence, even if their slogans were, well, not unproblematic. *Better to occupy empty houses than foreign countries* was a particular favorite of the squatters who rushed to take over Berlin apartments that owners had abandoned after the war.

One result of the tumult the late '60s unleashed was a flurry of official nods to the need to say *something*. When the noise died down, some of the noisemakers began the long march through the institutions, creating a spate of institutionalized atonement ceremonies. Often it feels like an inverse Jewish calendar, each year peppered with dates to be marked. Many of the ceremonies were so formulaic that there were days when I thought silence might be preferable, but as time went by, the efforts to break the silence became more reflective and sound.

∽

No one in Germany has devoted more serious thought and time to working-off-the-past than Jan Philipp Reemtsma. He has also spent a considerable amount of his fortune in the process. "I grew up with war and death," he once wrote. Born in 1952, Jan Philipp falls through many a standard crack. His father was badly wounded in the First World War, so he didn't have to fight in the second. Nor was he a Nazi, just an opportunist who privately upheld his own code of honor. As soon as the war was over, he located his Jewish partner in New York and paid him the fair share of the business that had been officially Aryanized. "Some of my parents' best friends really *were* Jews," Jan Philipp told me. "We visited each other. Not to say there were no problems." As a child, he'd asked his mother, "What exactly did Hitler have against the Jews?" His mother made no reply, but asked her Jewish friend what she should tell him. Her Jewish friend gave no advice, but answered that she was glad they were being forced to listen to such questions. Jan Philipp's mother was indignant: What kind of a friend says that? Except for that occasion, Jan Philipp remembers no anti-Semitic comments in his home, aside from the time his mother told him not to marry a Jew. It would make life difficult for the children to know where they belong.

"I'm not sure that counts as anti-Semitic," I answered. "My mother said the same thing about marrying a goy: it's hard on the children."

Jan Philipp and I had known each other for fifteen years when he surprised me by saying that many people think he is Jewish. They assume that's the reason he does much of what he does. Once, he was accosted by an old classmate who had read an early essay he wrote. Among other things, the essay discussed the fate of the Marranos, Jews whom the Spanish Inquisition forcibly converted and then observed to see if they were secretly practicing

Judaism. Was smoke coming out of the chimney on Shabbat? Jan Philipp wrote that he hoped the Marranos kept their traditions—while hating the Christian community that surrounded them. "Not to be able to do that would be succumbing to victim pathology," he said. His erstwhile schoolmate saw things differently. Moving close, almost threatening, he asked, "Are you Jewish? If you weren't Jewish, you wouldn't write something like that."

Jan Philipp has a fine, complex mind and a brilliant capacity for irony, but everything else about him says *northern Europe*, from his pale blond frame to his dignified efforts to unstiffen in the company of people he likes. He is the only German of my generation with whom I feel completely at ease joking about matters Jewish. With him I never have to fear any reaction that might come out philo- or anti-Semitic.

"And besides"—I laughed—"it's not exactly a secret . . ."

"I know. My father had a virtual monopoly on cigarette production during the Third Reich. How exactly could I be Jewish?"

At a time when a smoke was the only comfort eighteen million men on the front had at hand, a cigarette manufacturer could make a fortune. Though he never joined the Nazi Party, the elder Reemtsma had good connections to Goering. Both had been pilots in the last war and could speak comrade-to-comrade in the next one. Goering exacted a price for his preferential treatment of the firm. "The Herr Reichsmarschall would like to have a Rembrandt. The Herr Reichsmarschall would be very pleased if Herr Reemtsma would donate five million for a new theater." It was more blackmail on Goering's part than bribery on Reemtsma's, and with former Jewish colleagues returning from emigration to testify in his favor, the elder Reemtsma was acquitted of the corruption charges filed against him after the war.

Jan Philipp was only seven when his father died, too young to ask about the war years, but he opened his archives to independent historians who researched the family. He grew up in a home filled with the spirit of Calvinism; his father's middle name was Fürchtegott, "Fear God." Photos of his dead half brothers lined the hallway. Since all three died young—two of them on the front—Jan Philipp inherited the bulk of the war-profiteering fortune. He studied literature, philosophy, and sociology, and when he came of age, he sold his share in the cigarette firm. He has spent much of his life figuring out the honorable thing to do with the proceeds.

Some things are relatively easy to figure. He hired an art historian to examine whether any of his paintings had been stolen or bought at cut-rate prices from Jews seeking to flee. "I don't want stolen art on my walls," he said. "If I'd been particularly attached to something, I would have offered the heirs a fair price for it, but stolen art?" He frowned with disgust. Starting in the '50s, the Federal Republic paid reparations to Jewish concentration camp survivors, but the question of compensating non-Jewish slave laborers was not settled until the twenty-first century. "There was a legend in the family that the firm didn't use slave labor, but I hired a historian to find out. The research went all the way to the Crimea. Had the Nazis won the war, I would have grown up on a tobacco plantation in the Ukraine, surrounded by men in striped uniforms." He showed the research to a cousin and suggested that they contribute more than the commission for compensation required. "We carry this name. And it's not as if a contribution would leave anyone *poor.*" The cousins wanted no part of it. Jan Philipp gave to this cause as he's given to many others: forgotten authors whose work he wants to preserve, or their widows, Jewish institutions in Israel and Germany. He founded and funded the Hamburg Institute for Social Research, which studies violence and how to prevent it. He has written more than twenty books on subjects ranging from Nazi crimes to Muhammad Ali. Still, in Germany he is most famous for two things that took place in the '90s. He was kidnapped, terrorized, and held until his wife was able to deliver the largest ransom ever paid in the nation, and he was set free, a changed man. The media circus surrounding the kidnapping was second only to that which surrounded the other event: the Wehrmacht Exhibit.

Envy may forgive either wealth or intelligence, but rarely both together. As one of the smartest as well as the richest men in Germany, Jan Philipp attracts a mixture of sycophancy and resentment. Good taste preserves him from complaining, but his is not an easy life. Since the kidnapping, private bodyguards accompany him when he makes a public appearance, sweeping the rooms before he enters. Until he retired from the institute he founded, every package sent there was scanned for explosives. The Wehrmacht Exhibit had been firebombed in Saarbrücken, after all.

Neither Jan Philipp nor his staff were prepared for the reaction the exhibit provoked. The Wehrmacht had been deliberately exempted from indictment at Nuremberg. This was partly meant, we saw, as a lesson for the future; the Allies wanted to suggest that racial war was a German problem, and unlike the Germans, they were not going to punish entire peoples. The German army was as heterogeneous as any other army; the only way to get out of service was to do something even worse than serving in it, such as working in a concentration camp. The judgment at Nuremberg indicted the SS, which could be joined only voluntarily, but not the Wehrmacht, for which millions were drafted. (Although it was well aware that the army committed war

crimes, the tribunal maintained that this was a legal but not a moral declaration of innocence.) There was also a less enlightened motive for leaving
the Wehrmacht out of the list of criminal organizations: most crimes of the
Wehrmacht took place on the Eastern Front, and years of propaganda had
contributed to the idea that Slavs were *Untermenschen*. At the least, a dead
Pole was not as appalling as a dead Frenchman.

Although the Wehrmacht was not on trial at Nuremberg, in the intervening decades historians formed a consensus. The murders committed by
the Wehrmacht were not the fault of a few bad apples; they were widespread,
systematic, and crucial to the war effort. Nor did the murder of massive
numbers of civilians take place in a normative void. There were laws of war,
particularly concerning treatment of civilians and prisoners, and every officer knew it. Deliberate destruction of those norms was part of the ava-
lanche of destruction that took place on the Eastern Front. Moreover, there
was room for individual action. There were all kinds of ways to respond to
orders, from outright resistance to refusal to obey to voluntarily causing
more violence than commanded. Soldiers are not simply cogs in machines,
even in the heat of war.

The exhibit sought to do no more than display those widely accepted
truths by focusing on three cases of war crimes in Serbia, Poland, and
Belorussia. The public reaction, however, revealed the depth of the gulf
between professional historians and public memory. Many visitors came
carrying small photos of their fathers or grandfathers to compare with the
photographs in the exhibit. They were actively looking for truth about
matters long avoided in their families—in some cases because the soldiers in
question never returned from the war. Those whose relatives did not appear
in the photos of ordinary men tormenting civilians expressed relief. Those
who found the evidence they'd feared often expressed gratitude for the
clarity that evidence brought: now they understood why Papa or Uncle Franz
returned from the war a different man. Others protested vehemently against
the dishonoring of their dead. Children and grandchildren of Wehrmacht
veterans were not the only ones to attend the exhibit. Many veterans came
themselves, and their reactions were equally divided. Some bitterly complained that the exhibit slandered their actions and those of their fallen
comrades; others said quietly, "That's just how it was." As it became clear
that the exhibit unleashed a torrent of private emotion, the organizers sought
ways for visitors to express it, and the responses to the exhibit became themselves an object of study.

They revealed the variety of ways human beings deflect guilt. There's the reference to *force majeure*—the Bolshevik menace, as well as the fear of punishment if orders were not followed. There's the insistence on one's own victimhood—the soldiers' suffering on the Eastern Front, the bombing of their cities at home—as well as other nations' war crimes. One critic argued that "the execution of hostages was also horrible for many soldiers commanded to do it. Allied bombers were spared such scenes; they caused a thousandfold miserable deaths in cellars they never had to see." There was the appeal to the private decency of the soldiers now reviled as murderers, as well as the invocation of patriotism: the wish that Germany, like other normal nations, would honor those who defended their country.

The popular protests were mirrored by the media, which eventually found a Polish historian researching crimes committed by the Soviet Union during the partition of Poland. Though the claims that the exhibit had falsified photos were laid to rest, the historian found several that were improperly identified. In particular, one photo showed Polish citizens who were murdered by the Soviet Army; the incoming Nazis had blamed the Jews for the murder in order to incite a local pogrom. The historian alleged that the corpses were represented as if they were murdered Jews rather than Poles. Shortly before the exhibit was set to travel to New York, Jan Philipp decided to close it until an independent commission of international historians could review the entire exhibit to ensure that every claim stood up to scrutiny.

After confirming that no historical exhibit has ever been so thoroughly scrutinized, the commission's report bemoaned the fact that historians pay too little attention to the difficulties of reliably identifying photographs. Nevertheless, in the sort of painful detail that once made Germany the birthplace of those who sought to make history an exact science, the commission argued that

> Photo 69/1 shows how a man in a light coat threatens a Red Army soldier cowering on the ground. The photo also shows coffins marked with crosses, and corpses covered with cloth. The objection that several of the soldiers in the picture were holding handkerchiefs over their noses and mouths to protect against the stench of the decaying corpses at their feet is not proof. The gesture need not mean that the smell of putrefaction comes from the corpses that are visible in the photo. It could just as well come from the corpses that have been exhumed on another side of the courtyard which is not visible in the photo.[35]

And so on. In painful detail.

After a year's worth of research, the commission concluded that fewer than twenty of 1,433 photos shown in the exhibit should be removed because the crimes they depicted were likely committed by Finns, Hungarians, or the Soviet secret police. The commission also proposed a few changes that would make the exhibit clearer. Above all, however, they concluded that the major claims of the exhibit were true: with three million dead Soviet prisoners of war, countless reprisals against the civilian population—one hundred hostages shot for every Wehrmacht soldier killed, fifty for every one wounded, and the murder of Belorussian peasants shot searching for food—the war on the Eastern Front was a war against the entire population. The revised exhibit was twice as large, and it opened in 2001 to unmistakable acclaim. A few hundred neo-Nazis demonstrated against it, but this time the judgment of the media was clear. The second exhibit proved beyond doubt that the Wehrmacht as a whole was a criminal organization, whatever individual soldiers may have decided or done. "The Wehrmacht exhibit was the first time that memories of the war and memories of the Holocaust were fused," said Aleida Assmann, the author of seminal works on German memory culture.

Jan Philipp himself continued to be attacked—though rarely to his face—as a nest fouler, someone who washes dirty laundry in public. *Race traitor* is not an acceptable term of abuse in Germany, but that's what they mean. His own infinitely complicated relationship to the Wehrmacht may be revealed by something he barely mentioned in public. During the thirty-three days he spent chained in a cellar, not knowing if he'd survive the kidnapping, he realized that he did not want his dead body to be left in a wood. He would rather it be placed somewhere where visitors could come, if they chose. Perhaps lay a flower. Or simply pause and think. The realization led him to find out more about a half brother he'd never known, Uwe Reemtsma, an officer who took part in the occupation of Denmark and the invasion of the Ukraine. He was shot on a street in Dubno while attacking the Soviet army barracks, and he died the same night, just twenty years old. The Organization for the Care of German War Graves recently found his grave in Ukraine. On hearing this, Jan Philipp had his bones brought back to Hamburg to lie with the rest of the family.

I asked him about the remnants of Lost Cause ideology in Germany.

"There were no veterans' clubs, as there were in Austria. Vienna was the first place where the Wehrmacht exhibit was really attacked. In Germany, veterans might talk at their local pubs, but they were never organized. Perhaps they feared the Allies would not have accepted it, but after Nuremberg it was clear what sort of gang was sitting in the dock. Brecht's *Arturo Ui* described it pretty well."

At the time, however, people who were later reckoned to the progressive forces in Germany saw Nuremberg as a case of victors' justice. In 1947, Gustav Heinemann, who would later be president of Germany, argued that the trials had the opposite effect of what was intended: "Instead of isolating those who had been responsible for the Third Reich, a new German solidarity was created against the Allies which can only be adequately termed as 'renazification.'" Even Marion Countess Dönhoff, the much-admired founder of *Die Zeit*, was, Jan Philipp told me, "an unbelievably dishonest person. She always flirted with the claim that she'd been close to Stauffenberg's resistance, and at the same time said she'd never heard of Auschwitz. How does someone maintain both?" Still, he argued, the Nuremberg Trials had a subcutaneous effect on the population. "At the very least, nobody ever came close to fulfilling Goering's prophecy: in fifty years you'll be building monuments to us."

There were plenty of other subcutaneous influences, though few reached the surface. Group 47 was a group of young writers who came together in 1947 with the goal of renewing German literature after the war. It included such well-known figures as Heinrich Böll, Günter Grass, Hans Magnus Enzensberger, Peter Handke, Paul Celan, and many others. "A very difficult story," said Jan Philipp, whose doctoral degree is in literature. "Celan had terrible experiences there. Plenty of them were hostile to the émigrés and proud of having been Wehrmacht soldiers. Not all of them, but the majority."

Then there was *Das Diktat der Menschenverachtung*, a book Alexander Mitscherlich wrote about the crimes of Nazi doctors after he observed their trials in 1946. The German Medical Association bought all twenty-five thousand copies of the book and destroyed them in the hopes of preventing information about the medical experiments on concentration camp prisoners from reaching a wide audience. "Mitscherlich said: there were too many," Jan Philipp told me. "There are not as many perverse sadists in the population as there were doctors without scruples." Though the book was revised and republished years later, Mitscherlich never again held a position at a medical school, though he later became a professor of psychology and philosophy at Frankfurt.

One by one, however, most every facet of the Nazi regime was investigated, usually by the professional heirs of those who concealed their own or their colleagues' transgressions. After the doctors, the judges. The banks, the Foreign Office, the Max Planck Institute. Now that it has become ordinary, or anyway expected, I've heard young historians complain about the opportunism of some of their colleagues. In a tight academic job market, the offer of a three-year contract to investigate *anything*, be it old Nazis or butterflies, is hard to refuse. Nor are the motives behind opening up a new facet for investigation always admirable. "The question of stolen art was on the table in '45," Jan Philipp explained. "There were certainly enough lawyers who tried to get stolen art restored to the emigrants, but there was no legal basis for doing so. It was only after the Soviet Union collapsed and Germany wanted to retrieve its stolen art in Russia that anyone began to address the problem of art stolen from the emigrants."

I asked him what mistakes were made in the working-off process that took so many decades. He paused for a long moment. "I don't think it could have happened earlier," he said. "Look at Adorno's Group Experiment. He concluded that they were psychologically overwhelmed. Between the bombs and the losses in the families, they were so focused on the horror as a whole, they could no longer distinguish between guilt and misery. Fortunately, the occupation was long." He also believes that postwar prosperity played a role. "Not because I believe that unemployment led to Hitler. We all know how many wealthy people supported him. But the relatively quick prosperity after the war meant that no one could complain that the Allies left us beggars. Without that cushion, the working off would have come even later. It came late enough."

Still, it came, and it stayed, and the results seem to be solid. According to all the indices of all the pollsters, Germans are less open to radical-right views than citizens of England or France. "I cannot say it happened because of one single factor," Jan Philipp added. "I can only say that several things came together, as they usually do in life. There is rarely one cause for anything."

This is true. He declined to name one experience that led him to devote so much of his life to working off the German past. He was too young to watch the Eichmann trial or be part of the '68 rebellions. "Something is missing if you haven't seen Auschwitz," he allowed. "There are things you cannot prepare for, no matter how much you've read about them. The enormous cabinets full of packed suitcases; people brought soap and shoe polish, thinking they would have a use for them. You can't prepare yourself for the moment you see that. The other thing that shocked me was the barbed wire, which is not particularly massive. When you're inside, you can't get out, but from the outside you could push it over with a tractor. It never occurred to them that anyone would try. That's the first impression: the self-assuredness of those people. As I stood before the ARBEIT MACHT FREI sign, I had a moment of realization—as if a part of me had never entirely believed it at all."

Yet he has spent most of his life working to understand it—without being crushed by it. His masterpiece, *Trust and Violence*, begins with the question he thinks is specious: How could perfectly ordinary people become so violent as the Nazis? The question is wrong, he wrote, because it happens all the time. Ordinary people create violence because there aren't enough sadists to go around. The better question is this one: How can we trust modernity when it led to Auschwitz?

Jan Philipp believes that our ability to ask that question is itself a sign of progress, for only in modernity is violence regarded as something abnormal. Through the Thirty Years' War the culture was drunk with violence, often understood as entertainment. The Romans created the Coliseum, their largest standing monument, as a place to watch murder the way we watch football. Christianity created Hell, where violence was eternal. Our assumption that violence should be contained, our hope that it should be eliminated are entirely new. That assumption and that hope have been the basis for reducing violent practices, from human sacrifice to torture. And our capacity for self-criticism in light of our failures to reduce them further is itself a sign of the very progress in modernity that is called into question. We still have violence, and abuses of power, but the fact that we can call the perpetrators to reckoning is a great achievement of world history.

In fact, *Trust and Violence* argued, it is trust, not violence, that is the basis of society. This is true even in dictatorial regimes. No tyrant can depend on violence entirely, for he'll have to sleep after thirty-six hours, at the latest—and he'll have to trust someone in order to do so. We cannot *not* trust. And with that trust we can, as a society, refuse to accept violence. "When the first refugee asylum was attacked, everyone worried that the violence would continue. But there were large demonstrations of people who said we do not accept this. That made a difference."

The attack on that asylum was not the last one, but there have not been as many as was feared. You may say even one is too many, but Jan Philipp takes a wider perspective: "Most of the soldiers went along with the My Lai massacre. They'd all heard the same propaganda: *the village is riddled with Vietcong, women and children included.* Some of them went crazy shooting them down—but one threatened to shoot his comrades if they did not stop. It took a long time, but later he was decorated for it."

Jan Philipp Reemtsma walks a very fine line. He knows how often postwar

Germans have pointed to other nations' violence in order to excuse their own. Nothing could be further from his intention. Intentions aside, the years he has spent confronting German crimes allows him to explore the international history of violence without violating Todorov's principle. He could not possibly say *We made moral decisions where others did not.* Yet *Trust and Violence* ends with a question about self-assurance: *Who are you to tell us anything about morals?* Jan Philipp believes there's just one answer: *I am not one of the murderers.*[36] It's an answer that resonates with the most important passage of *Eichmann in Jerusalem*:

> During the few minutes it took Kovner to tell of the help that had come from a German sergeant, a hush settled over the courtroom; it was as though the crowd had spontaneously decided to observe the usual two minutes of silence in honor of the man named Anton Schmidt. And in those two minutes, which were like a sudden burst of light in the midst of impenetrable, unfathomable darkness, a single thought stood out clearly, irrefutably, beyond question—how utterly different everything would be today in this courtroom, in Israel, in Germany, in all of Europe, and perhaps in all the countries of the world, if only more such stories could have been told. . . . For the lesson of such stories is simple and within everybody's grasp. Politically speaking, it is that under conditions of terror most people will comply but *some people will not*, just as the lesson of the countries to which the Final Solution was proposed is that "it could happen" in most places but *it did not happen everywhere.* Humanly speaking, no more is required, and no more can reasonably be asked, for this planet to remain a place fit for human habitation.[37]

3

Cold War Memory

Though the other chapters of this book deliberately leave many questions open, this one has a clear and simple thesis: East Germany did a better job of working off the Nazi past than West Germany. Like any attempt to make normative judgments about history, this one can, and will, be complicated. Still, the judgment will be a surprise to most Anglo-American readers. For most Germans, the claim is the philosophical equivalent of throwing down a glove in an old-fashioned duel.

The reunification of Germany is now celebrated as one of the few happy moments in twentieth-century history, but in the 1990 negotiations leading up to it, everyone outside Germany was scared. The original Allies, who still occupied the country, were particularly anxious: Would a reunited Germany return to its disastrous past? They sought to work some guarantees into the peace treaty that had waited forty-five years to be signed. Margaret Thatcher invited historians to investigate whether the Germans posed a threat to Europe, and she went herself to Moscow to enlist Gorbachev against reunification she feared would threaten world security. Hoping to support the continued existence of the GDR, François Mitterrand did the same.

When that began to look impossible, he demanded that Germany give up the mark and accept the euro as the price of reunification. Gorbachev insisted that the reunited nation maintain, in perpetuity, the memorials to the Red Army soldiers who had died to liberate the country from fascism. The head of the U.S. Justice Department's department for Nazi crimes, Neal Sher, knew his East German counterparts well enough to issue one request on his last visit to East Germany's attorney general in June 1990: that a reunited Germany would assume East Germany's standards, not the West's, when examining Nazi crimes.[1]

It did not happen, and East Germany's ways of working-off-the-past have been largely forgotten. The very nicest thing a West German will say about them is that East Germany had *verordneter* antifascism—antifascism by decree. Such remarks bring East Germans to laughter on good days and angry incomprehension on others. "Antifascism was state policy, *and rightly so*," said the writer Ingo Schulze. For British and American readers, even this much has been forgotten; not many remember how the war was won. The Red Army had been fighting, and dying, for three long years before Stalin persuaded the other Allies to open up that Western Front. Thirty-seven thousand Allied ground troops and seventeen thousand Allied air force members lost their lives in the Battle of Normandy. Twenty-seven million Soviet citizens—twelve million of them members of the army—lost their lives in the course of the war.

My trust in *The New York Times*'s foreign reporting was undermined when the paper ran an article explaining the context of the terrorist bombing that shook Berlin in December 2016. Pointing out that a ruined church towered over the market where the murders took place, the author opined, "After the war, East Germany rebuilt historic landmarks, hoping to erase the memory of Nazism. But West Berliners preserved the Gedächtniskirche as a ruin—a testament to the destruction and terror Germans brought upon themselves, a daily reminder never to forget."[2]

Almost nothing in this claim is true. East Berlin tore down many historic landmarks, most notably the central palace now being rebuilt from scratch, for they wanted to excise every symbol of bombastic imperialism. Not far from the palace, they installed two memorials to guard against forgetfulness. One is a grand monument to the victims of fascism and militarism, complete with honor guard, eternal flame, and Käthe Kollwitz's peasant take on the *Pietà*. (The honor guard, a troop of stiff soldiers, disappeared when the GDR did.) The smaller memorial is dedicated to the Red Orchestra, the name the Gestapo gave to a bundle of resistance groups, most of whom the Nazis executed. West Berlin had nothing comparable. The plaque before the ruined church tower read A REMINDER OF THE JUDGMENT OF GOD. Judgments of God are notoriously unpolitical, though politicians the world over read every stroke of lightning as a sign that God is on their side. Throughout the 1980s, progressive West Berliners vigorously argued for a worthier monument to the main victims of the war. For the ruined church tower with its vapid plaque suggests, without actually asserting, that the worst victims were those Germans whose churches and homes were bombed. The *Times* got the story exactly backward, despite the fact that the author of the piece lived in Berlin for two years. It's impossible to walk down the city's main boulevard without seeing both East German monuments. When he strolled down Unter den Linden, what did the journalist fail to see?

German readers cannot be so uninformed, but their perception is beset by a different kind of problem. Three decades after reunification, many tensions between East and West remain. Some have roots in old rivalries, and some of the tensions are new. It's now common to say that the events of 1989 brought not a reunion of East and West, but a colonization of the East by the West. Three decades later, all but 1.7 percent of the leading positions in politics, industry, media, and academia in the East are still filled by West Germans. Most East Germans find the colonization narrative self-evident.

I have no intention to argue that the GDR was a model state, nor do I intend to excuse its most famous institution, the Stasi. It's worth remembering, however, that even Edward Snowden's most enthusiastic supporters refrained from reducing the entire United States of America to its surveillance programs. The GDR deserves the same courtesy.

Nothing raises East-West hackles more than the question: Whose *Vergangenheitsaufarbeitung* was better? Did the East bring more Nazis to trial? Did the West support the State of Israel? German working-off-the-past must be understood through this most interesting of Cold War rivalries. When I first came to Berlin, in 1982, I worked on my language skills by listening to the news from opposing channels. From West German television I learned about the Soviet invasion of Afghanistan; East German television offered news about U.S. support for right-wing militias in Central America. Listening to both, I was pretty well informed.

It was a crucial moment in my own education. In divided Berlin I learned how much background noise shapes our perception of the world. Even those who'd been taught to think critically, as I had, could not help seeing the world through the philosophical frameworks that surround us. Those frameworks are all the more powerful for looking like banalities that are altogether free of philosophical assumptions. This doesn't mean I'd suddenly switched frameworks to decide that the Eastern version of history was the right one, still less that I'd decided that nothing is true. I just became aware that you need to see events from many different angles before you can get as close as possible to the truth about them.

My American passport and a generous fellowship during my first two years in the city allowed me to experience both sides directly. All I had to do was take a subway to a border crossing, answer a question or two from a guard, exchange twenty-five West marks for twenty-five East marks, and I was behind the Iron Curtain. The rivalry between the city's two halves was often expressed in physical terms: if West Berlin had one opera house, East Berlin had two; and to make up for the larger area of square kilometers allotted to the French, British, and American zones that combined to form West Berlin, East Berlin went for height. The tallest building in the city, which couldn't be missed for miles around, towered over Alexanderplatz. It was the kind of sparring that made for subsidized easy living on both sides of town. Both halves of the city were showcases that devoted considerable resources to putting their best feet forward. On one point, however, the sparks flew so fiercely that no one could see straight: each side accused the other of failing to come to terms with fascism, and each insisted it had done so itself.

How did each half of the country work, however fitfully, to turn German self-perception from victim to perpetrator? Looking at *Vergangenheitsaufarbeitung* through the prism of East-West rivalry is a way to look at the elements that must be part of any nation's attempt to face its national crimes. The Cold War makes the German case unique, but no less an example to other nations for all that. Every case is unique, and each one requires a great deal of contextual understanding. Still, some aspects of *Vergangenheitsaufarbeitung* seem common to any culture.

～∾～

These are crucial facets of any successful attempt to work off a nation's criminal past.

1. The nation must achieve a coherent and widely accepted national narrative. Here language is front and center. Was the Civil War about

slavery or states' rights? The U.S. Department of Citizenship and Immigration Services isn't certain. Was May 8, 1945, a Day of Liberation or a Day of Unconditional Capitulation to Foreign Powers? Since the GDR called it a "Day of Liberation" from its inception, Chancellor Konrad Adenauer thought the use of the word *liberation* was communist. Although the East German narrative, like most any narrative, was incomplete, its tenor was very clear: NAZIS WERE BAD, DEFEATING THEM GOOD was never in doubt in one side of the country. For a good thirty years in the West, by contrast, that simple claim was drenched in ambivalence.

2. Narratives start with words and are reinforced by symbols, and many symbols involve remembering the dead. Which heroes do we valorize, which victims do we mourn? The United States has hundreds of monuments depicting a noble-looking Robert E. Lee, commander of the Confederate Army. In 2018, Bryan Stevenson dedicated a national monument to honor the victims of lynching, but where are the national monuments to the freedom fighter John Brown—or at least to Harriet Tubman? There are no monuments to the Nazis in Germany, East or West, but only after reunification did West Germany build significant monuments to the victims.

3. Narratives are transported through education. What are children taught to remember, and what are they meant to forget? American textbooks have been improved since I was a child, when the heroic story of western expansion left out the genocide of Native Americans entirely, glossed over the horrors of slavery, and never mentioned Jim Crow. East German history textbooks were resolutely antifascist from the beginning. In the first decades after the war, West German children were left with the impression that history stopped after 1933; neither their teachers nor their textbooks discussed the Nazi period. Today Nazism is not merely covered in history classes; it has a central place in subjects like literature and art.

4. Words are even more powerful when set to music. So can we sing "Dixie"? What about the German national anthem? It gives most foreigners a chill, for they cannot help thinking of "Deutschland über alles." The anthem's defenders are keen to point out that the tune was written by Joseph Haydn long ago. That notwithstanding, the GDR wrote new music as well as lyrics for its own national anthem. A national anthem, done properly, expresses its people's best hopes. Done properly. It may be time for the United States to rewrite our national

anthem, with its unsingable tune and its reference to a war no one remembers. If it weren't hopelessly old-fashioned, I'd vote for Paul Robeson's version of "Ballad for Americans," the only song ever played at the Democratic, Republican, and Communist party national conventions. The year was 1940.

5. What about things that are less symbolic: hard, cold things like prison cells and cash? Are perpetrators brought to justice and placed behind bars? Is restitution made to victims of injustice? It took decades to bring the murderers in the most famous civil rights cases—Medgar Evers, Chaney, Goodman, and Schwerner—to justice, and most criminals never faced justice at all. The Emmett Till case was reopened in 2018—sixty-three years after the murder. But what about the men who have killed unarmed black children in recent years? The man who shot Trayvon Martin is free; Tamir Rice's killer was never indicted, though he was fired from the Cleveland police force, but he was hired by the police in another Ohio town. The list could be easily continued. West German justice prosecuted only a tiny number of Nazis and usually commuted the sentences of those who were convicted. East Germany tried and convicted a far greater proportion of war criminals. Both countries paid reparations, in different ways, for crimes committed in the Nazi era. As of this writing, the United States has refused to consider a congressional resolution to discuss the possibility of reparations for slavery.

This list is not exhaustive. Depending on time and place, other elements may come into play in a country's attempt to work off its debts to the past. Any attempt that does not include these elements, however, is likely to be partial and thin. Without remembering Martin Luther King's calls for economic justice, making his birthday a national holiday is hollow.

◆

Before comparing eastern and western narratives of the war, it's important to understand the changes in the narrative through which the West remembered the East. Both came together in the Historians' Debate (*Historikerstreit*), which rocked West Germany in 1986. It began with a metaphorical bombshell thrown by the conservative historian and Heidegger student Ernst Nolte. He charged that all of Hitler's crimes, and the misdemeanors as well, were a reaction to Stalin, whom Hitler had imitated. The ensuing debate took up more than a year of media time, involving not just historians and philosophers but nearly every journalist in the country. From its beginnings in the question of who started what, the debate unfolded into a discussion of whether fascism and communism can ever be compared. The left-leaning philosopher Jürgen Habermas was not the only one to argue they cannot. The centrist Rudolf Augstein used the magazine he published, *Der Spiegel*, to reinforce the point in no uncertain terms: Comparing communism to fascism, he wrote, was not only a way of avoiding responsibility for the latter, but a way of trivializing the nature of Nazi crimes. Nothing is worse than the deliberate murder of millions for being a member of the wrong tribe.

It's important to note that the debate concerned the legitimacy of comparing Hitler's Germany to Stalin's Soviet Union. Stalin's crimes in the '30s and the extent of the gulag system were known well enough in 1986. Still, Habermas, Augstein, and many others insisted that any comparison between those crimes and the crimes of the Nazis was morally illegitimate. The crimes of neighboring East Germany played no part at all in the debate. Despite a Stalinist period in the '50s, the GDR's offenses were trivial when compared with its Soviet big brother. As the East German playwright Heiner Müller would later say, the GDR left behind mountains of Stasi files, not mountains of corpses. Or as the historian Mary Fulbrook later put it laconically, there is a difference between having been a party secretary and having been a mass murderer. In his book of open letters to Adolf Eichmann's son Klaus, *We, Sons of Eichmann*, the philosopher Günther Anders wrote:

> It's true—and that's awful enough—that Stalin was willing to accept millions of victims year after year. Nevertheless, and we must not obscure the difference—*the thought of industrial liquidation of masses of human beings, a systematic production of corpses like Hitler and Eichmann produced, never crossed his mind.* Not even the partisan German historians in the *Historikerstreit* dared to accuse Stalin of that.[3]

After a fitful start, late '80s West Germany seemed to have achieved a consensus: Nazi crimes are incomparable to any others, and any attempt to compare them is an attempt to get the Germans off the hook. One-half of Todorov's principle—Germans should focus on the singularity of the Holocaust—was accepted.

Few but historians remember the Historians' Debate today, and the consensus it produced has been forgotten. Under cover of vague claims about totalitarianism, comparisons between communism and fascism support a small intellectual industry. Well-meaning West Germans often preface remarks on the subject with the formula "I don't want to equate them, but . . ." before going on to equate them by implication. The phrase "the two German dictatorships," a not very subtle way of denying the differences between them, now trips off many a tongue. There are monuments where the words TO THE VICTIMS OF THE TWO GERMAN DICTATORSHIPS are literally chiseled in the stone. Before 1990, the word *Vergangenheitsaufarbeitung* itself referred only to the need to work off Nazi history. After reunification there were demands for a second wave of working-off-the-past that would work off communist crimes in a way, its advocates admitted, that West Germany had failed to work off Nazi ones. The complexities of the second wave are beyond the scope of this work, but the very insistence on it was another way of saying that Nazism and communism were equally destructive.

To be sure, the German Democratic Republic was democratic only in name. The media was heavily censored, the borders were closed, and elections were a national joke. But once you equate the GDR with Nazi Germany, everything about the GDR is poisoned. Much like the 1950s tendency to describe communism as a malevolent disease, it moves the discourse from politics to pathology.[4] This leaves no room for any reasoned discussion of political principles and practices. All you can do with Nazis and diseases is get rid of them.

The international drive to equate fascism and communism is not just a problem for understanding twentieth-century history. How we remember the past constrains the possibilities we consider for the future. If communism is painted black, neoliberalism has won. Any appeal to solidarity— or human motives other than the endless competition neoliberals view as natural—will be read as a call for bloodshed. For the moment I'm concerned with the ways the equation falsified historical memory, leading to nearly complete amnesia about East Germany's antifascist past. Some historians have examined the subject, but most popular memory now assumes that Germany's working off the Nazi past began with reunification.

The fact that the division of Germany was viewed as punishment for its war crimes lends a little credence to that claim. The Nobel laureate Günter Grass, for example, opposed reunification in 1990 on the grounds that the penance for Auschwitz had not yet been paid. And the joy with which the fall of the Wall was celebrated in Berlin hadn't much to do with seeing long-lost cousins or compatriots; after a few days of hugging strangers, tensions between East and West remained fraught. The rejoicing was grounded in another feeling, which many expressed the moment they teetered joyfully on that Wall: the war, they shouted, is finally over. But although the Wall's end symbolized the war's end, designating 1989 as the beginning of German working-off-the-past is a slick but sloppy way of ignoring all that the GDR had done before.

∾

The difference between grand monuments in Berlin is staggering. The Holocaust Memorial is the size of two football fields, and it occupies one of the most central and expensive pieces of real estate in Germany's capital. Rather than selling it off to a major insurance or automobile company, the government decided it should be used for a memorial to the victims of the Holocaust. Five acres right next to the country's national symbol, Brandenburg Gate, was a dramatic statement from the reunited republic, and it's been controversial. As late as 2017 a candidate for the right-wing AfD party complained about the "symbol of national shame" at the heart of the capital. Nor was it easy to get the monument built, for such attitudes were very common in the 1990s.

The first demands for a significant Holocaust memorial in place of the bombed-out church came from a small group of West Berliners, including the philosopher Margherita von Brentano, the historian Eberhard Jäckel, and the journalist Lea Rosh, who took over the initiative entirely after von Brentano's death. After considerable lobbying, parliament agreed to build something, and sent out a call for designs. The ensuing debate, along with the fifty proposals that made the short list, fills a volume the size of a Manhattan phone book. The winning proposal was drafted by the American architect Peter Eisenman, whose 2,711 concrete stelae now fill the space, looking like a postmodern take on an old Jewish cemetery. After critics complained that the monument is abstract enough to represent almost anything, a center documenting the murder of Europe's Jews, with texts and photos, was placed underground. You can find all the information you want there, but few of the thousands of visitors taking selfies before the slabs decide to enter it. To increasing irritation that public behavior at the monument is inappropriate for such somber space, Eisenman had few words: he'd built the monument the way he built it; now it was up to the visitors to decide how it was used.

I attended the dedication of the Memorial to the Murdered Jews of Europe, as the memorial is officially called. It was a cool morning in May 2005, and speakers included, among others, the president of parliament and the head of the official Jewish Community. They were accompanied by somber Jewish music and a rabbi who said Kaddish at the end. The memorial was not yet dotted with scantily clad tourists eating ice cream. Descriptions of it had filled the press long before the opening, so I knew that the differing heights and angles of the stelae were not really meant to evoke an old graveyard, but were placed to create the sense of fear and alienation that concentration camp prisoners sensed every day. I wandered in search of that sense. I tried to think about Auschwitz, or the million murdered children in whose names, among others, the stelae had been raised. I failed. After weaving my body through the slabs a little longer, I walked out into the day, discontent.

In the center of the city, the Holocaust Memorial is very hard to miss. To see the Soviet Memorial of Honor, the largest war monument in what once was East Berlin, you must go out to the park in Treptow. One day a year, the place is very full. By the time the unconditional surrender took place in a small villa on Berlin's outskirts on May 8, 1945, it was May 9 in Moscow, which thus became the most important holiday in the Soviet calendar, and today in the Russian. That's the date when the Liberation is celebrated in Treptow, where children in dress clothes and occasional copies of Red Army uniforms play catch or Frisbee as their parents pose for pictures. Many are earnest, laying single red carnations at one or another station of the memorial. Some wear tags with the name of a fallen relative; some explain the events to their children. Others are mainly there to picnic with friends from Kirghiz or Kazakhstan, celebrating a holiday that, like American Memorial Day, has less to do with the battle that occasioned it than a chance to relive a celebration of their youth, and that on a fine spring day. Presumably their children will continue the ritual. In insisting on the preservation of this and other Soviet monuments, Gorbachev was right to fear that the West would prefer to forget the Red Army's contribution to the fascist defeat. Even many who were alive at the time already have.

On any other day of the year the giant memorial is almost empty, leaving the few visitors a chance to face its monumental solemnity. Seven thousand of the seventy-three thousand Red Army soldiers who lost their lives in the battle for Berlin are buried there. The first thing you see on entering the memorial is a mourning mother, her bowed head and body cut into large stone, surrounded by poplars. Turn left onto the walkway bordered by weeping willows and you'll see a half arch, each side decorated by a soldier, helmet in hand, kneeling to honor his fallen comrades. Like the mother's, the soldiers' statues are larger than life, and they seem even larger until you look up and see the centerpiece of the memorial, far away on a hilltop: a thirty-meter-high statue of a Red Army soldier. His left arm holds a child he has saved from destruction; his right holds a sword, with which he has smashed the swastika at his feet. Unveiled in 1949, it was intended by the Soviet command to be the largest war memorial in the world.

All the texts at the memorial were written by Stalin. You must walk a long way from the weeping willows to the soldier on the mound, past unmarked graves covered with ivy and flanked by two lines of marble sarcophagi, each decorated with a bas-relief telling part of the story of the Great Patriotic War. On one side in German, the other in Russian, the sarcophagi-like structures use Stalin's words to tell the war's history. Most are simple references to the brutality of the Wehrmacht, the bravery of the Red Army, the steadfastness of the population behind the lines. Sometimes criminals can tell the truth too. Only the first quote, which says that everything in the Soviet Union was fine until the Germans invaded, is false.

∾

Mischa Gabowitsch was born in 1977 in Moscow, but grew up in the German-French borderlands. He was the longtime editor of two major social science journals in Russia and is currently writing a history of Soviet war memorials. He has also written critically about Russian liberals' admiration of German atonement. On a raw December day, just after he'd published a book about practices surrounding Soviet war memorials in five European countries, I asked him to walk me through Treptow.

"Treptow and the Holocaust Memorial stand for different sides of history, but they aren't complementary," Mischa told me. "Each one is missing a major part of history the other one contains. The Holocaust Memorial doesn't stand for the Holocaust in the East, but only for what happened in the extermination camps. The fact that millions of others were shot, burned, and buried alive is mentioned in the underground museum, but it isn't present symbolically." The Holocaust Memorial leaves out millions of victims to focus on the Jews; the Soviet monument has little room for victims at all. It commemorates heroes, and even they are anonymized. "Even if you leave out Stalin's own victims, there's nothing about the Siege of Leningrad, nothing about the prisoners of war," Mischa charged. What Treptow tells, and tells quite literally, is a triumphal narrative. Evil, in the shape of a smashed-up swastika, was overcome by the courage and kindness—remember the rescued child on the soldier's arm—of the Red Army. That is indeed part of the story, along with the Red Army's less savory actions, but narratives of good smashing evil make many uneasy. Some say we live in a post-heroic moment; it's easier to acknowledge victims than to lift up heroes. "It would be nice to be able to say that putting both monuments together would give us the whole story," says Mischa, "but that wouldn't be enough. Each is missing too much. Still, it would be good if we could at least begin to look at them together."

I asked him about a common complaint about Soviet-era monuments: even when they commemorate victims rather than heroes, they seldom use the word *Jew.* "First of all," he said, "this is only partly true." In fact, hundreds of monuments were built at the initiative of Jewish survivors that featured Jewish symbolism or inscriptions in Hebrew or Yiddish. Most of them are near extermination sites in small towns or villages and so they have been less visible than the giant memorials in big cities—this has been called the Babi Yar syndrome.[5] "But," he continued, "to the extent that ethnicity was indeed suppressed, there was a deliberate decision to describe the victims as Soviet citizens." More than 120 recognized ethnic groups lived in the Soviet Union. "Why single out one group of people based on ethnicity when there was a village of non-Jews next door that was burned down for other reasons, whose people died just as horribly?" Non-Jewish urban dwellers and peasants were massacred in retaliation for partisan activities, and three million prisoners of war died of mistreatment. Slavic lives hardly mattered, even though Slavs were slated for slavery rather than death. "Not every Slav was designated for extermination, but should we discriminate against the people who happened to be in a category that was less systematically exterminated than another? I don't know," he said. One reason Jews were hardly mentioned in the official Soviet narrative was the same reason they were hardly mentioned by Roosevelt. Both the Russian and the American government were aware of native anti-Semitism.

"You have to categorize people one way or another," Mischa continued. "You can categorize them in the ethnic-based language of the perpetrators, or you can call them Soviet citizens. The last is very problematic when you think about residents of Western Ukraine, who'd been forcibly made into Soviet citizens two years before the Nazis arrived. It's certainly not the way they viewed themselves. Still, there's an argument for rejecting the categories of the perpetrator, though I think people should commemorate their dead in whatever terms they choose."

Lately, people from the former Soviet Union have turned from anonymous heroic collective commemorations to seeking the graves where their loved ones were buried. Mischa pointed out the paper signs, often written by children, that decorate some of the mass graves with the names of individual soldiers. Their birth dates are different, but their death days are close: they all fell within a few days fighting the brutal and desperate attempt the Nazis made to defend Berlin to the end.

Mischa spoke of the tension within Berlin's Jewish community, a majority of whose members now come from the former Soviet Union. The Russian Jews want less talk of the Holocaust, more about their parents and grandparents who were soldiers in the Red Army. They are tired of the focus on victims; they want to remember the heroes—or if we are to remember the victims, it should be all of them: Jews along with millions of others in the Soviet Union. Riffing on Todorov's principle, Mischa agreed that the focus must change from country to country. "Russia *should* talk more about what the Holocaust against the Jews meant, since it failed to do so before. In Germany the main challenge now is to make people understand that there are other perspectives on the war, and if you're not exclusively focused on the Holocaust, you're not denying it or engaging in anti-Semitism." He thought the long parliamentary debate about the Holocaust Memorial was framed as a generational legacy. "We have enshrined one narrative: the national crime was that Germans killed Jews. By solidifying the narrative in stones, they made it impossible for future generations to think about it in any other way."

❧

The official GDR narrative was simple: we are the other Germany, antifascists from the start. For the political and cultural leadership, the narrative was actually true. Some were communists who fled Germany just after the Nazis took power; those who didn't landed as political prisoners in Nazi concentration camps. Hitler's first victims were communists. Many who would form the Communist Party's elite were what the United States called "prematurely antifascist," who fought for the Republic in Spain. They returned to Germany a decade later in the wake of the Red Army. On June 11, 1945, the Central Committee of the newly constituted German Communist Party issued a founding statement:

> In every German the conscience and shame must burn. The German
> people carry a significant part of guilt and responsibility for the war and

its consequences. Hitler is not the only one who is guilty of crimes against humanity! Part of the guilt must be borne by the ten million Germans who voted for Hitler in 1932, although we communists warned: whoever votes for Hitler votes for war . . . It was our misfortune that broad sections of the population lost the elementary feeling for decency and justice and followed Hitler when he promised them a well-filled table at the cost of war and plunder.[6]

No such claim was made by any German authority in the Western Zones. Their narrative was not quite the Lost Cause saga. The good times under the Nazis had been too short, and the war too devastating, to develop the kind of nostalgia for dirndls that Southerners feel for hoopskirts. As incapable of real nostalgia for the Nazi past as they were incapable of celebrating its ending, most West Germans floundered in the muck of victimhood for two or three decades. The proud and decisive call to atonement that rang out in the East just a month after Berlin was surrendered was absent in the West.

But that was official, antifascism by decree. Did East German citizens identify with the antifascist politics that were prescribed, or did they swallow it because of a need to toe party lines? I decided to interview friends and acquaintances who'd grown up in the GDR. Three of them were Jewish, all of them were critical of much GDR policy, and several had been active dissidents. As any historian can tell you, memories often distort. Yet by choosing those who, with one exception, had been openly critical of the GDR while it lasted, I knew I was speaking with people who had not been bound by party lines.

I began, however, with a West German who headed the West German diplomatic mission to East Germany. He couldn't be called the ambassador, because it couldn't be called an embassy. That would have meant that the West acknowledged East Germany as a country, which would have meant accepting the division of Germany as final. Hence Hans Otto Bräutigam was called the permanent representative during most of the ten years he lived in East Berlin.

The words *old-school gentleman* don't do the man justice. Hans Otto Bräutigam was born into a Catholic family in a small Westphalian town. His father was a naval officer in World War I who later directed the chemical division of a steel factory. Bräutigam's father had no respect for Hitler, whom he contemptuously referred to as "the corporal," but he joined the Nazi Party early on because he agreed with its foreign policy: revising the Versailles Treaty, defending Germany against Bolshevism.

"Anti-Bolshevism was far more important than anti-Semitism," Bräutigam explained. "Most Germans believed that our national destiny was to protect Europe from communism. As a former officer who felt loyal to his comrades, my father tried to enlist in the Wehrmacht. Since his job at the steel factory was important for the arms industry, the Wehrmacht turned him down."

"That was fortunate." I know too many Germans who, to this day, remain torn by images of what their fathers did, or did not do, on one front or another. Unless Papa was one of the few Nazis who were actually tried for war crimes, what he did in the war was left to his children's imaginations.

"Yes," said Bräutigam, but his voice still quavered all these decades later. "But why did he even *think* about enlisting? He was a nationalist patriot, or a patriotic nationalist. Like so many others, he distinguished between Hitler and the German nation, and he felt loyal to the latter. The priority was fighting communism. His brother felt the same. None of them were anti-Semites."

"Then it's interesting that most of your professional life was focused on the East."

"True enough. But there my family didn't really influence me; they never experienced the GDR. My interest was another: I always believed that the German question could only be resolved if both East and West viewed each other with respect. I wasn't inclined to the left in those days, and certainly not to the GDR's version of socialism. Like Willy Brandt, I sought a certain closeness to the GDR for diplomatic and political reasons. Then I met so many people I admired there. Writers like Christa Wolf and Christoph Hein, church people like Manfred Stolpe and Friedrich Schorlemmer. Ordinary people, too, who wanted nothing to do with politics."

All that was much later. Hans Otto Bräutigam, who was born in 1931, was lucky. He remembers bombs falling on neighbors' houses, but his own was not hit. Like every other ten-year-old, he joined the junior wing of Hitler Youth, but he was spared much further entanglement in Nazi organizations. The family's conservative Catholic roots, and his father's contempt for the corporal, provided an alternative to Nazi ideology. After the war, the Americans dismantled the steel factory where his father oversaw the labor that provided parts for the Nazi war machine. His father found a job with a small family firm that produced industrial polish. Hans Otto left the provinces to become a lawyer, eventually attaining a Ph.D. in international law. In 1956 he received a fellowship to spend a year at Harvard Law School.

Bräutigam returned from Harvard to the silence and repression that characterized the time. He joined the foreign service and soon found himself specializing in West Germany's relations with the East. In his long professional career he came to know it like no other West German I've met. In 1974, even mutual acknowledgment was a diplomatic achievement. Long negotiations on every detail were required to establish the Permanent Mission—down to the question of whether *Permanent* and *Mission* should be capitalized or not. Bräutigam saw his task as building diplomatic relations that would lead to concrete improvements in human lives: allowing families divided by the border more access to each other, organizing better energy and transit policies for encircled West Berlin. Though carefully refraining from supporting any dissident activities, the Permanent Mission, settled in the heart of East Berlin, became a place where GDR citizens could come for information as well as for informal jazz concerts and poetry readings. In the Cold War era, it was often the only contact between citizens of two countries who'd been taught to regard each other as the worst of enemies. Reunification was an unimaginable goal; the highest hope was that small, slow steps might lead the two countries to the sort of loose confederation of states that had made up Germany through the late nineteenth century. Such small steps were crucial in those moments in the '80s when the Cold War threatened to boil over. After American nuclear missiles were stationed on West German territory, the decade of increasingly close cooperation on minor issues played a role in averting major disasters.

Bräutigam headed the mission, where he did his "duty with pleasure" until he became the West German ambassador to the UN. After nearly two decades of preoccupation with German-German relations, he looked forward to experiencing the wider world he'd hoped to encounter when he joined the foreign services in his youth. By the time he was appointed to the UN, it was early 1989, and he wondered if it was the right time to go. Opposition in the GDR was growing. Despite his intimate knowledge of the country, Bräutigam no more predicted the peaceful revolution than anyone else that winter. His feeling that something was about to change was only a feeling, after all, and the bureaucratic wheels had already rolled. He couldn't find a serious reason to prevent him from doing his duty, though he left for New York with a heavy heart. That's where he was when the reunification he'd spent so many years working to prepare took place. He never thought he'd live to see it. "I really suffered, being away from Berlin at that moment."

Bräutigam shook his head with a disbelieving smile when I told him the name of the book for which I wanted an interview. "I don't believe we can be a model for others," he said, turning serious. "In the years after the war we had a very hard time taking responsibility. It took twenty years before we began to develop the consciousness for it—through the Auschwitz trial, which was more important within Germany than the Eichmann trial. The Nuremberg Trials were quietly and bitterly rejected as victors' justice. I don't see Germany as a model," he repeated. "It took us too long, and too many people rejected responsibility."

That's a claim most thoughtful Germans repeat. Ralph Giordano, a half-Jewish German journalist, devoted a thick book called *The Second Guilt* to the deep repression of what had happened in the war and who was to blame for it. West Germans, who made up much of what once had been the German nation, confined their memories to the end of the war: the bombings, the losses, the hunger. The idea that any of this might be considered deserved punishment for starting and supporting the deadliest war in human history crossed hardly a mind. The nation stewed in its own pain, and devoted itself to cleaning up the cracked brick and broken concrete strewn through its cities. It took decades before there was much interest in tackling the moral ruins.

"But that's important for other countries to know," I assured Bräutigam. "*Vergangenheitsaufarbeitung* is a process. It takes time."

I turned to the main question that concerned me, for I hoped to find in him one of the few people who can talk about German-German relations without resentment or bias. His perspective is probably unique, now that his predecessor as permanent representative, Günter Gaus, has died. Did Bräutigam think East German antifascism was for real?

"Antifascism was GDR ideology from the beginning," he replied. "You could call it their *Staatsräson*. I thought one of East Germany's greatest strengths was the way they condemned fascism, far earlier than the Federal Republic."

"Western critics call it 'antifascism by decree.'"

"That's not how I experienced it. It was the deepest part of their belief system."

The West's position is meant to convey that antifascism in the East was prescribed from above, as part of a policy that was sometimes used to justify acts of state that were ultimately unjustifiable. But wasn't it right to decree that the seventeen million Germans left in the Soviet zone should reject fascism rather than see themselves as the war's primary victims?

Initially, East Germans were no more naturally inclined to do so than their Western compatriots. The best sources on the subject are the diaries of Victor Klemperer, a German-Jewish scholar of the French Enlightenment whose deportation was prevented by his loyal Aryan wife, who refused state pressure to divorce him. After he was forced to resign his professorship, Klemperer took to writing excruciatingly detailed journals that provide a unique picture of daily life in Nazi Dresden. When published in 1988, after his death, the meticulous, monumental volumes became bestsellers. Public curiosity about life under the Nazis did not extend to the journals he wrote in the first years after the war, for although they were published, they did not receive the attention of the earlier journals. (Instead of an English version of *Ich sitze zwischen allen Stuhlen—I am sitting between all the camps*—the English translation was published under the title *The Lesser Evil*, embodying a political judgment completely at odds with the book itself.) This is unfortunate, since the later journals are at least as informative as the earlier bestsellers.

In them Klemperer described scenes that are both harrowing and funny: former Nazis who came to him seeking testimony of their good character to ease the path to employment, or at least better rations. A music teacher wanted credit for the fact that she never stopped playing Mendelssohn-Bartholdy; a former student wanted him to attest to the antifascist tenor of his doctoral dissertation. The few people who had continued to greet him on the street during the Nazi era wanted him to corroborate that; some even offered to pay him. Knowing how craven most characters had been led the very bourgeois Klemperer to join the Communist Party, a move he had once found unthinkable. Because he had the opportunity to observe Dresdeners all through the war, he confided to his diary in May '46, "Who do I still trust in Germany? No one." In February '46 he had already written, "I am tending even more to support a state of East Germany that would be a part of Soviet Russia. That's how much I've changed!" Klemperer wasn't blaming the petty bourgeoisie or the illiterate mob. On a trip to Berlin in January 1946 he recorded, "Reactionaries were supported by three pillars: the Junkers, the army, and the universities. Only the first two have fallen (with the Liberation)." The universities remained elite bastions of Nazi supporters. Klemperer was only one of many who believed that a long and thoroughgoing "antifascism by decree" was needed to root out the racist and reactionary sentiments still present throughout German society.

"I was so impressed by Klemperer's diaries that I bought copies for each of my children," said Bräutigam. "I told them they were required reading."

Bräutigam confirmed other facts that have quietly dropped out of so many accounts of postwar history: East Germany put far more old Nazis on trial, and out of office, than the West. The occupying forces in the American and British zones initially planned a large denazification program that would divide Germans into five categories according to their degree of guilt, and would absolve, punish, or reeducate accordingly, but the task was overwhelming. There were nowhere near enough Allied soldiers with the linguistic competence to read and evaluate the questionnaires distributed to Germans who held positions of power in the Nazi regime. And when the Cold War began, the United States and Britain were far more interested in securing allies against the Soviet Union than in digging up their sordid pasts. The denazification program was turned over to the West German government, which had no inclination to pursue it. Soon thereafter the efforts were discontinued. Instead of examining and punishing perpetrators, Adenauer's government turned to recompensing victims.

Konrad Adenauer, a conservative Catholic who became the first chancellor of the Federal Republic, made a deal that few in Germany mentioned but everyone understood. His decision to pay significant amounts of money to the State of Israel, and to individual Holocaust survivors, was controversial in his native country. That was one reason the payments were called compensation rather than reparations, a word that reminded too many of the detested Versailles Treaty.

"The Federal Republic managed to avoid the question of reparations for decades by arguing they should be determined by a peace treaty that hadn't been signed yet," said Bräutigam. "But paying compensation, however we called it, and establishing diplomatic relations with Israel were necessary conditions for our acceptance into the community of nations. After all the terrible things Germans had done, it was not at all obvious that we should be accepted."

"But wasn't the unspoken bargain for the payments the understanding that West Germany would not engage in *Vergangenheitsaufarbeitung*? That Adenauer's government could continue to employ high-ranking Nazis in prominent places, that there would be no political or cultural confrontation with the Third Reich—"

"You're right," he said. "Adenauer spoke of silent forgetting, but he was hardly the only West German who hoped that if we never spoke of the Nazi period, it would all be forgotten. That's changed in the last few decades. No one complains anymore that we lost the eastern territories to Poland. Perhaps it wasn't possible to do more, those first years after the war. People were exhausted. The country had to be rebuilt. It made sense in the '50s to look to the future rather than the past."

West Germany's economic miracle has been described as a colossal act of collective repression, the way shoveling shit from dawn to dusk might take your mind off a love story that went wrong. The philosopher Hermann Lübbe, who had been what he called a harmless Nazi, put the matter more ponderously: the country could not have been rebuilt, he argued, without "communicative silence." While the Marshall Plan was crucial in rebuilding the West German economy, another spur to all that silent, stolid hard work was the desire for distraction. It's a process that functioned well on both sides of divided Germany.

Bräutigam's work has been focused on things one can measure: compensation, reparations, hard facts of foreign policy, but they are prepared through the forms of soft diplomacy he practiced. I am equally interested in the symbolic; above all, making sure things are called by their proper names. When President Richard von Weizsäcker made German history in 1985 by calling May 8 the Day of Liberation, I couldn't understand the fanfare that followed. The tone of his speech reflected the arid, measured coolness most German politicians project, and its content seemed banal. *We shouldn't remember the end of the war without remembering its beginning. No nation is free from war and violence, but the genocide of the Jews is without example in history. Other peoples were victims of a war that Germany initiated before we fell victim to it ourselves.* The dry, droning prose went on for nearly an hour. Who needed to hear this, forty years after the war?

Millions of West Germans, as it turned out, who had hitherto called it the Day of Defeat—or of Unconditional Surrender, if they were aiming for neutrality. Most avoided the reference altogether. Chancellor Gerhard Schröder would later praise the speech for having created a collective norm, a new historical identity. Reading the speech today, I understand its importance, for I now understand what had seemed incomprehensible. Up to that moment the majority of West Germans considered themselves to be the war's worst victims. Von Weizsäcker knew his audience far better than I did, for his famous speech began by acknowledging all that. Only by taking their sense of suffering seriously could he lead them to acknowledge that they owed the Allies a debt for bringing them the liberation they were too weak and too blinded to bring on themselves.

In a particularly elegant piece of rhetoric, the president's speech ended by identifying the German people with the children of Israel. On the fortieth anniversary of the end of the war, why not take a leaf from the book that sustained the people his army tried to destroy? *Israel stayed in the desert for forty years before a new historical epoch could begin. Forty years were necessary for a complete change of the generation of fathers who were responsible at the time.* Was he comparing slavish longing for the fleshpots of Egypt with the bootlicking service in a murderous regime? Probably not. Nor is there evidence that Weizsäcker identified with Moses. But his hair was all white and his father long gone, enabling him to say what the rest of the world took for granted: there were many who suffered more than the Germans, and their suffering was Germany's fault.

"But wasn't it always called the Day of Liberation in the East?" I asked Bräutigam.

"It was, and it was celebrated, along with the victory of the Soviet Union. This wasn't just an obligation; many East Germans truly felt grateful."

When the East German writer Daniela Dahn met Richard von Weizsäcker years after the famous speech, she pointed out to him that the GDR had always referred to May 8 as the Day of Liberation, and had made it a national holiday. "Weizsäcker laughed, he was friendly, but I could see that the penny had dropped. He'd never thought about it. Everyone in the West behaved as if no one had ever thought to call May 8 the Day of Liberation."

"Were the East German commemorations of the liberation genuine?" I asked Bräutigam. "I know schoolchildren were taught to sing songs like 'Thank You, Soviet Soldiers.' Did they mean it?"

"Many really did, and many had strong emotional ties to the Soviet Union. Christa Wolf, for example, or Jens Reich. They were much like the feelings my generation had for America, in the West: gratitude for the liberation. Gratitude for the peace. It's no longer so emotional, but it's an important part of German history."

"There aren't many West Germans who share your perspective on German history."

"That is true."

"I take it you don't share the current inclination to talk of two German dictatorships, as if fascism and communism were equivalent."

"Absolutely not," he answered, speaking louder and more vehemently than before. "*Ganz und gar nicht.* They weren't similar at all. I thought the comparison was absurd from the start."

"So why do you think the comparison has become so common?"

Bräutigam sighed. "Perhaps it's a normal process. The GDR is nearer in time, so the history is more present. There aren't many left who actually experienced the Nazi years."

"If it were former East Germans making the comparison, it might make sense, but—"

"People from the East never make the comparison."

"That's what I thought."

"Most of them think Nazism and communism aren't comparable at all. They know the GDR was much more complex than it's pictured in the West, something that's obscured by this eternal Stasi discussion—which is of very little value if you really want to understand the country." He sighed once again. "Look, there's always been a tendency in West Germany to try to forget the Nazi period entirely. It's not as bad as it was in the '50s, but the tendency is still there."

I suspect that the equivalence now drawn between fascism and communism serves an even darker purpose than repression. I don't think it's conscious, but that makes it even stronger. Few Wehrmacht soldiers were moved to take up arms in order to mow down Jewish civilians, though few disobeyed orders to do so once behind the front lines. After 1935 there was a draft on, which could usually be avoided only if, like Bräutigam's father, you worked in a vital war industry or in a concentration camp. But no dictatorship gets far by merely commanding its troops; it has to inspire them. The heroic ethos the Nazis cultivated would not have been furthered by exhorting recruits to shoot long-bearded old men or to bayonet babies; those acts took place, but they were not advertised.[7] The call to defend Europe from the communist menace was loud, clear, and far more effective. Sometimes communists were depicted with the same hooked noses that graced caricatures of fat bankers, as every student of Nazi propaganda has noted. But especially after the war began in earnest, the emphasis was less on the Jewish and more on the Bolshevik menaces. After the tide turned at Stalingrad, the call to defend home and family from the Soviets wasn't even propaganda, for it was clear that the Red Army would not end its answer to the German invasion until it entered the gates of Berlin.

As Hitler wrote after the defeat of France, "I could have thrown myself heart and soul into the destruction of bolshevism, which is Germany's essential task, the ambition of my life, and the *raison d'être* of National Socialism." That drive to destroy bolshevism "would have been coupled with the conquest of vast spaces in the east . . . to ensure the future well-being of the German people."[8] The Wehrmacht did not invade Poland and Russia in order to maximize the number of Jews it could murder; its mission was wider in scope. To say this is not, of course, to engage in Holocaust denial, or to overlook the ways in which anti-Semitism was essential to Nazi ideology. Arno Mayer, one of the few historians writing in English who has emphasized the centrality of anticommunism to the Nazi program, wrote that "there is no question but that in Germany the assault on Jews was grafted onto a violent backlash against democratic liberalism, advanced capitalism and cultural modernism. All three had been critical pillars and vehicles of Jewish emancipation."[9] But he also insisted that "although antisemitism was an essential tenet of the Nazi worldview, it was neither its foundation nor its principal or sole intention."[10] During the war, similar views were echoed by official American sources. In 1944, for example, the philosopher Arthur O. Lovejoy wrote a pamphlet for American soldiers explaining the causes of the war. Territorial expansion, and the interests of arms manufacturers, take first place; anti-Semitism is mentioned in passing.[11]

No one in Germany doubts that anti-Semitism polluted most of the air left to breathe in those twelve poisoned years. But everyone in Germany knows that the heroic aura that still surrounds the Wehrmacht's survivors, and its fallen, derives from the lost battle with the communist foe. Only right-wing forces actually assert it. Still, the lingering guilt few Germans can entirely shake off could be assuaged by revamping Nazi anticommunism. Papa, or Grandpa, probably did *not* pick up his gun to kill helpless Jews. It was Bolsheviks he was after; Jews were just in the way. The worse the Bolsheviks now appear, the better the Nazis look in retrospect. If fascism and communism are equal, weren't Papa and Grandpa fighting evil too?

"There we're in agreement," said Bräutigam. "I think that's the decisive reason for the equivalence: there's still a deep, unspoken need for exoneration for the Nazis. That's why people prefer to focus on the GDR."

෴

In 2003 the historian Tony Judt asked me to co-organize an international conference comparing fascism and communism. He thought it would be good for philosophers and historians to discuss the question together, and he wanted to do so at the Einstein Forum. The Remarque Institute at NYU, which he headed, could put up half the funds if I could find the other. Sitting in a basement restaurant in New York City, we began to plot the program.

"One difference is this," said Tony, who'd been one of the first Western thinkers to criticize East European socialism from the left. "I'd sit down at a table with an ex-Stalinist. I wouldn't sit down with an ex-Nazi."

Only much later did I reflect that for most West Germans, the opposite was true. As children, they'd been likely to sit at the breakfast table every morning with an ex-Nazi or two; they were unlikely to have ever met an ex-Stalinist. At the time, I could only agree, and suggest an ex-Stalinist to invite.

"Markus Wolf is a stroke of genius," said Tony. "Do you think you can get him?"

During most of the many years that Markus Wolf headed the East German equivalent of the CIA, he was known as the man without a face, for he'd never been photographed. He was also said to run the best intelligence agency in the world, with the possible exception of the Mossad. In 1986 he retired and began to criticize the GDR government. He spent the first years of his retirement writing a moving and thoughtful memoir of his extraordinary life.

Born in 1923 in Germany, Mischa Wolf, as he was known, fled to Moscow with his parents and brother Konrad when the Nazis took power. His father, Friedrich, wasn't religious, but like many others, he would have fallen foul of the Nazis on racial grounds. Friedrich didn't wait for the Nuremberg Laws but left Germany in 1934, as he was not only a Jew but a communist who had dedicated his life as a doctor to improving health conditions among the poor, and writing antifascist plays on the side.

The family grew up in Moscow, under the shadow of Stalin's terror but not directly affected by it, unlike many of their friends in the émigré community. (Possibly because Friedrich volunteered to serve as a doctor in Spain, believing, like many, that the Spanish Civil War was a less dangerous place than Moscow at the height of the Terror.) Unlike his younger brother, Konrad, who fought with the Red Army all the way to Berlin, Mischa worked behind the lines building airplanes. When the war was over, the family returned to Berlin, where their history and talents made them part of the GDR elite. Friedrich became the country's first ambassador to Poland, Konrad became East Germany's best filmmaker and later president of its Academy of Arts, and Mischa rose to become head of the Foreign Intelligence Service. When the Wall finally fell, Mischa was indicted for treason. After briefly fleeing to Moscow, he returned to stand trial in Berlin, where he was acquitted of all charges. The court agreed with the defense: every nation is entitled to a foreign intelligence service, and he was guilty of nothing but running East Germany's very well.

Mischa Wolf said he'd be happy to accept our invitation, and asked what he should do for the conference. We'd agreed that informal dialogue would be better than a formal lecture. The question was, with whom? I asked Hans Otto Bräutigam if he would agree to a public discussion with Wolf. He asked for three days' time to think it over. Wolf was happy to speak with Bräutigam, but as he'd never been allowed inside an English-speaking country, he wasn't sure his English would be up to the task. I assured him that Tony and I would be happy to translate if the need arose, and that, I thought, was that.

It proved easier to interest historians in the conference topic than it was to engage philosophers; my field isn't known for much reflection on actual events. But Tony was the sort of person who could persuade the distinguished historian Eric Hobsbawm to attend, even after lambasting his autobiography in *The New York Review*, so with a superb list of historians and others, I wrote to several German organizations that fund this sort of thing. They all gave the same answer: the conference looks splendid, they'd be happy to fund it—as long as I disinvited Markus Wolf.

I understood why Bräutigam had asked for time to think it over; he knew how controversial it would be. In the end I got the funding from the Open Society Foundation in New York, and the conference, which took place in 2005, was excellent. The discussion between Bräutigam and Wolf produced no earthshaking insights. They agreed on most essential matters; both held that though Stalinism was a perversion of an ideal of equality that began in the Enlightenment, Nazism had no ideals, beyond rampant tribalism, to pervert at all. Under Stalin, at the latest, communism turned totalitarian. But unless you believe states of mind have no meaning, there's a world of difference between a person who began by fighting for equality and solidarity and one who began from a racist worldview. That's why Tony was willing to meet with one, but wouldn't share a table with the other.

Other speakers at the conference talked of differences between ideology and ethics, intention and circumstance, gray zones and accountability. Wolf's English turned out to be better than he'd feared, and Tony and I were so impressed by him that we wanted to keep the conversation going. At the closing dinner of the conference, Tony invited Wolf to be a guest at the Remarque Institute the following year. Wolf was glad to agree; he'd never been to New York, he had a half brother in the States whom he hadn't seen in half a century, and they were both getting on in years. Tony and I began to plan another joint event, this time in New York. I still have emails from him brimming with excitement over details.

But Mischa Wolf wasn't granted a visa to enter the United States of America. After a number of angry inquiries, Tony learned that the refusal came from close to the top. Condoleezza Rice had conferred with Angela Merkel, who was not yet chancellor but the head of the opposition Christian Democratic Union. Both of them decided: no way. Tony protested and went through back channels, but the State Department stayed firm and the party

Tony had planned so carefully never happened. Mischa Wolf died in his sleep a year later. He never got to see his half brother.

The story shows something about East-West relations and the difficulty of openly discussing the way the Nazi years continued to live on past the war and drive the deepest tensions between East and West. It became even more interesting a few years later, when *The New York Review* published a long article after Tony's tragically untimely death. The author of the tribute was Timothy Snyder, who later made some questionable equations between fascism and communism. He had been at the conference and thought it worthwhile to write that "once, at a conference in Berlin, the former East German spymaster Markus Wolf maliciously asked him to repeat a question in German. Tony did so, but with a kind of hesitation that was uncharacteristic of him . . . The Holocaust, on Tony's account, was everywhere and nowhere in his upbringing, like a vapor."[12]

Reading the piece, I was stunned. There had been nothing malicious in Wolf's use of German. He'd been promised help with simultaneous translation, if needed, and if Tony hesitated, it was only because his German wasn't perfect. In any case, the efforts he made to get Wolf to New York the following year proved he had taken no offense at the question; quite the contrary. How could Snyder interpret the exchange as malicious—except on the assumption that anything said by an ex-communist is said with evil intent?

◦◦◦

A conservative West German who spent ten years of his life as a diplomat in East Germany is one source of information that's as untainted as possible by ideological loyalty. Numbers could be another one. In the past twenty years Germany has devoted significant resources to careful historical examinations of its Nazi past. Major government organizations like the Foreign Office or the Justice Department have commissioned studies showing how many former Nazis continued to work in them after the war. Major industries followed suit. With so much meticulous research concerning so many details, surely someone must have tabulated an overview: How many old Nazis were left in power, East and West? How many were put on trial, and how many of those were convicted? How much money did the West spend on reparations to the State of Israel, and how much did East Germany pay to the Soviet Union? I've never believed that numbers reveal everything; I just thought they would be reliable.

Perhaps it is a case of such detailed research into trees that no one asked about the forest, but as I pored over hundreds of pages on the history of *Vergangenheitsaufarbeitung*, I grew increasingly discouraged. When two studies, conducted two years apart, gave different figures about the numbers of Nazis tried and convicted in both German states, what hope could I have of getting the numbers right? An American historian consoled me. "We don't even know how many Americans were killed in the Civil War," said Jennifer Stollman. "Not to mention how many Africans died in the Middle Passage. Estimates range from four million to twenty million. The first thing you learn in cliometrics is that numbers are written down by people."

That means that although numbers are available, some of them will be political. Sometimes the politics behind the counting are obvious. After reunification, the government commissioned a study of how many grave desecrations were taking place in the former GDR. The number of tombstones knocked over or smeared with swastikas were certainly disturbing. The trouble was that no one bothered to commission a study of the number of desecrations in the West during the same period. There turned out to be more, but since no one was interested in devoting resources to hiring someone to count them, the figures are inexact.[13] Political interests make the question of counting the number of old Nazis who were left in office— government, police, universities—almost maddening. Too many institutions did not want to know. Having cast itself as an antifascist state, the GDR did not want to acknowledge any at all, though everyone knew there were more than a few. The western side of the story is so complicated that it could be a subject for dark comedy, if you like that sort of thing. At the end of the war the American army captured a cache of 10.7 million Nazi Party membership cards, which it kept in American hands. Given how many SS officers tried to exchange their uniforms for jackets with yellow stars, Americans did not trust the Germans to preserve the definitive records of who was a Nazi or not. A little later, the Cold War made the question *who can we trust not to be a Nazi?* far less important than the question *who can we trust to be anticommunist?* Recognizing the names of many prominent politicians while looking through the party cards, the Americans put the evidence under lock and key at the Berlin Document Center. Access was severely restricted, as they didn't want to embarrass their most important allies in the Cold War. The German allies found it very convenient to leave the documents under American control. Hans-Dietrich Genscher, for example, the prominent foreign minister who knew that his own party card was in the file, asked the Americans to resist growing pressure to turn over the archives to West Germany. Finally tired of bearing the blame for not releasing information, the Americans insisted that the Germans take over the archives in 1994—two years after Genscher retired.

And that's just an introduction to the question of why all things Nazi are hard to count. Records are incomplete, whether lost in the fires of war or deliberately suppressed. Comparisons are hard to calculate: it's not easy to determine the value of the plants and train tracks that flowed from East Germany to the Soviet Union in relation to the value of the money transfers that flowed from West Germany to Israel. Quite a lot of research is still in progress, and ten years' time may yield more reliable figures. For now, these estimates are compiled from the least tendentious sources.

TRIALS

In East Germany, 12,890 Nazis were found guilty, 129 were sentenced to death, and the others were given prison terms of varying lengths. In West Germany, 6,488 were found guilty, no death sentences were carried out, and most prison sentences were quickly commuted. Most were tried not as murderers, but as accomplices to murder. As a result, for example, a certain Josef Oberhauser, tried as an accomplice to murder of more than three hundred thousand people in Belzec, was sentenced to four and a half years in prison; this amounts to 7.8 minutes for each murder.[14] Similar but not identical figures are recorded by Andreas Eichmüller and Malte Herwig.[15] As the (West) German professor of criminal justice Ingo Müller concludes from these numbers:

> In East Germany there were thus twice as many convictions as in West Germany; relative to population numbers six times as many. Thereby it must be considered that the majority of those former Nazis who were most heavily implicated preferred to go to the Western Zones when possible.[16]

The paucity of convictions in the West is no surprise, given how many former Nazis worked at the Ministry of Justice—66 percent of leading officials as late as 1966—and the Bundeskriminalamt, the equivalent of the FBI, three-quarters of whose executive employees had been Nazis, with more than half of those belonging to the SS.[17] The German Federal Intelligence Service was, with the help of the CIA, led by Reinhard Gehlen—not only a Nazi but the general in charge of military intelligence during the war against Russia, who afterward helped his comrades, like Adolf Eichmann's chief assistant, escape prosecution. Such facts explain why the West German government was hardly dogged about pursuing and prosecuting others.

NAZIS IN OFFICE

The progressive Left and Green parties have led the cry in parliament for thoroughgoing investigations of Nazi influences in West German ministries, particularly after the investigation of the terrorist group National Socialist Underground was suspiciously hampered by those federal agencies that should have investigated the murders of nine brown citizens from 2000 to 2007. Predictably, some Christian Democratic parliamentarians opposed approving funds for thoroughgoing historical investigations of West German ministries, on the grounds that "there were old Nazis in East Germany too." It's unlikely that the latter will ever be exactly counted, but in 2016 the government voted to devote 4 million euros to a comprehensive investigation of the West.

The troubles they will encounter are foreshadowed by the reception of *The Office and the Past* (*Das Amt und die Vergangenheit*), an 880-page book devoted to the Foreign Office during the Third Reich. Largely because of Deputy Foreign Minister Ernst von Weizsäcker's deceptive testimony during the Nuremberg Trials, the Foreign Office had an undeserved reputation as an office of quiet resistance during the Nazi era. A commission of five internationally renowned historians, including one from Israel and one from the United States, drew the opposite conclusion: the Foreign Office was crucially involved in making the Holocaust happen. This book, published in 2010, created so much debate that the debate is now itself a subject of historical investigation.[18] Historians not included in the commission complained that the commission's sources were inadequate; the commission complained of files destroyed and documents disappeared. The excluded historians complained that the commission should take an introductory course in historical method; the commission responded by suggesting that the colleagues were simply jealous that they hadn't been chosen to join in the work. These were only some of the arguments among the community of professional historians. Outside that community, some called the book a witch hunt reminiscent of East German propaganda; others responded by calling *them* old Nazis attempting to restore the honor of their fallen colleagues. Those debates took place between 2011 and 2015.

A preliminary study of the Ministries of the Interior found that, at its highest level in 1961, 66 percent of employees of the West German Interior Ministry had been Nazis; between 1962 and 1970 the percentage was 50 percent. The percentage of Nazis in the East German Interior Ministry was 14 percent. This was significantly higher than the GDR wished to admit, but significantly lower than what was the case in the West.[19]

In short, though all reliable sources agree that there were far more old Nazis in office in West than in East Germany, exact numbers are hard to get—even for a single ministry. The figures given above must be understood as preliminary. The 4-million-euro comprehensive study commissioned in 2016 is scheduled to be published in 2020. Given that the German desire for thoroughness often overrides the German desire for punctuality, I wouldn't hold my breath waiting.

MONUMENTS

The Federal Office of Political Education published a study of all the monuments erected to the victims of National Socialism before 1990. Since Berlin is the best place to make East/West comparisons, I will limit myself to those. Counting everything from a small plaque on a building to a large sculptured monument, the tally is 246 in the East, 177 in the West.[20] While we are counting, we should also remember that East Berlin in 1989 had a population of 1,297,212 and an area of 409 square kilometers, while West Berlin contained 1,854,552 people in an area of 480 square kilometers. On both sides, the monuments include memorials to places where synagogues once stood, as well as tributes to Jews and other opponents of the regime who were murdered by the Nazis. There are expected differences. East Berlin commemorated more resistance heroes, particularly if they were communists, as well as the five thousand Germans who were prematurely antifascist enough to join the International Brigades in the Spanish Civil War. West Berlin contains more monuments dedicated to Christian leaders who fell victim to the Nazis, and one that honors the many gay victims who often go uncounted. Scanning the careful compilation, one fact is striking: nearly half of the West Berlin monuments were constructed in the 1980s, when the popular pressure that eventually led to the construction of the Holocaust Memorial produced a wave of smaller monuments that engaged West Berliners felt should have been erected long before.

One particular sort of monument outside Berlin itself can be compared fairly easily. In the GDR, the concentration camps Buchenwald, Ravensbrück, and Sachsenhausen were restored and turned into museums. The funds for the restoration came from both the state and individual donations, and every schoolchild, at some point in their education, was taken to visit at least one. In the West, by contrast, there was no public funding for Dachau until 1965. Only then did the pressure of the Comité international de Dachau, an organization of former prisoners, compel the state of Bavaria to construct a memorial. The hundreds of smaller camps in the state remain unmarked. Until reunification, West Germany offered no federal funding for the preservation or support of any concentration camp memorial.

REPARATIONS

Calculating these numbers is particularly complicated because so many components are involved. Compensation to individual victims of the Nazis is one thing; reparation to entire nations for the damage the Wehrmacht inflicted on their people and property is another. Nor is it clear how to calculate the latter alone. Billions of marks in physical plant were transferred from East Germany to the Soviet Union. When calculating their value, does one calculate the worth of the factories in 1953 or the lost income the factories would have generated had they remained on German soil?

According to the most reliable studies, the Federal Republic (BRD) paid about 80 billion DM in compensation to individual victims, which include lump sum payments to the State of Israel and the Jewish Claims Conference.[21] Totals for the German Democratic Republic are harder to find; the best estimates range from 1 to 2 billion DM. The GDR paid compensation only to victims who were living in the GDR—one reason why this sum looks paltry in comparison with what was paid by the West. When one looks at reparations, however, the percentages are reversed. The most conservative estimate of GDR reparations is 90 billion DM, while the BRD payed 19.5 billion DM. (These figures are calculated according to the value of the deutschmark in 1953. In today's currency, the GDR would have paid 180 billion euros in reparations.) Because East Germany had only 40 percent of the population of West Germany, the difference in per capita amount of reparations paid is even more striking: the ratio is roughly 110 (East) to 3 (West).[22] The effect on the East German economy was devastating, a major reason it fell significantly behind the West. Although the Potsdam Agreement originally stipulated that both Germanys would compensate the Soviet Union for the devastation the Wehrmacht wreaked, East Germans paid the lion's share of the bill.

∽

If numbers are problematic, symbols are simply complicated.

When "Deutschland über alles" was written in 1841, it meant something different entirely. It wasn't a sinister expression of German superiority, but a plea to put petty differences behind and unite thirty-seven principalities into a national whole. But even the West German government, which banned the first two verses in 1952, knew that an appeal to originalism wouldn't fly. The references to German women, and territorial claims no longer possible, were contaminated, but all that was left after they were removed was the harmless but hackneyed third stanza, which is now sung alone as the national anthem.

> Unity, justice and liberty
> For the German fatherland
> Let us all strive for that
> In brotherhood with heart and hand!
> Unity, justice and liberty
> Are the foundation for happiness
> Flourish in the radiance of this happiness
> Bloom, oh German fatherland

There was an alternative. In 1949 the GDR commissioned a new national anthem, "Risen from the Ruins." The tune Hanns Eisler wrote for it combines sweet major with rousing minor strains in a stirring if schmaltzy way particularly suited to inspiring national sentiment. The words written by the official poet Johannes R. Becher expressed as much commitment to *Vergangenheitsaufarbeitung* as a national anthem can contain. These are the first verses:

> From the ruins risen newly
> To the future turned we stand
> May we serve your good weal truly
> Deutschland our fatherland

Triumph over bygone sorrow
Can in unity be won
For we must attain a morrow
When over Germany
Shines a radiant sun

May joy and peace inspire
Germany our fatherland
Peace is all the world's desire
To the peoples give your hand
In brotherhood united
We shall crush the people's foe
May our path by peace be lighted
That no mother shall ever again have to
Mourn her son in woe

When the East abandoned its demand for unification in exchange for hard cash and better relations with its western neighbor, the words were no longer sung in public. All that remained was Hanns Eisler's tune.

"Risen from the Ruins" could have been the ideal anthem for the newly united Germany, acknowledging the terror of the past, proclaiming the hopes for another future. Does it matter that Becher, who wrote the lyrics, later served the state in its most Stalinist phase? Do we know what later happened to Francis Scott Key, who wrote the words to "The Star-Spangled Banner"? Or the unknown author of "God Save the Queen"? That was roughly the argument of Lothar de Maizière, the first and last democratically elected chancellor of the GDR. In the feverishly hurried negotiations leading up to reunification, he pointed out that the words could be sung to the old Haydn tune the world knows as "Deutschland über alles" if the West insisted on retaining a piece of *its* past. Holding all the economic cards in their hands, the West answered: no. With the Christian Democrats in power, it was not surprising. They needed decades to acknowledge the need for any form of working off the German past, and they never explored what needs to be worked off in their own party history. Why would they want to be reminded of that past every time the national anthem was sung?

The only vestige of an East German symbol that survives in Berlin today is the jaunty little man who signals stop and go at traffic lights, decidedly more appealing than the robotic-looking figures that once regulated West Berlin pedestrians. If you want to take home a mug or a T-shirt with an emblem of the city, it's the easiest one to find. The souvenir shops will never tell you how contested it all was, and the younger sales clerks are unlikely to know it themselves.

But a national anthem is part of state propaganda, decreed from above. The GDR used its antifascism as a weapon to accuse its western neighbor.

East Germany was quick to use as propaganda for its own state the fact that West Germany neither investigated nor prosecuted former Nazis, but the fact is no less true. In both German states, everyone knew the Nazi years were still present, but that fact was either hardened into dogma or left entirely unspoken. The East German dogma: As the first antifascist state on German soil, we have broken every continuity with the fascist past. The West German dogma: As a totalitarian ideology that suppresses individual freedom, communism is no better than fascism; hence the GDR is no break with the past at all. Since neither dogma fit the facts, silence was often preferred.

There were old Nazis in the GDR too.

Of course there were. It had been the same nation, after all. The East had fewer Nazis to start with, since so many fled to the West as the Eastern Front crumbled. Between Nazi propaganda about barbaric Bolshevik hordes and their own fear of retaliation for what the Wehrmacht had done in the Soviet Union, most Nazis preferred to await defeat in the American zone. This meant that East Germany had fewer big fish on their hands from the start, but they tried far more of those Nazis who were left than West Germany did. Most important, although the majority of the population in both East and West had been equally entwined with the Nazi cause, this was not the case with the leadership. East German leaders—in politics, civil service, media, and the arts—were antifascists in their bones, and some of those who survived had paid for it with their blood. West German leaders had been, at the least, complicit; even those who were not openly anti-Semitic were openly and bitterly anticommunist. West Berlin refused to allow resistance heroes to speak of their wartime experiences in public schools because most of those who survived had been communists. In West Germany, serving communism was always worse than serving fascism. This became clear in monetary terms when a new pension law was passed after reunification. The years you may have spent as an SS officer or driving a cattle car to Auschwitz were counted toward your pension. The years you may have spent doing obligatory military service in the GDR or driving an ordinary train there were not.[23]

East German antifascism was displayed to win favor with the Soviet occupiers.

As West German reparations payments were made to win favor with the American occupiers. Both sides used different forms of working-off-the-past to curry favor with the overlords who occupied the country till the peace treaties were signed in 1990. *Vergangenheitsaufarbeitung* is never merely internal. Every country that undertakes it is always making a statement to the outside world. President Kennedy used civil rights legislation as a tool in the Cold War after the Soviet Union, in the wake of postcolonial revolutions in Africa, pointed out that American segregation was thoroughly at odds with American ideals. Whatever outside pressures helped to produce the civil rights legislation of the '60s, its passage was a good. Whatever outside pressures strengthened the GDR's public commitment to antifascism, that commitment was a good.

East Germany used antifascism as an excuse to conceal its own injustice and repression.

It did indeed. The most clear and stupid instance was building a 128-kilometer concrete barrier around West Berlin and calling it the Antifascist Protection Wall. Everyone knew that its purpose was not to keep invaders out, but to keep citizens in. The name the government used for the Wall probably created more contempt and cynicism than anything else it did. *Vergangenheitsaufarbeitung* is always political, and like anything else, including baby pictures and the Bible, it can be politically abused. Still, even those former dissidents who wish the GDR had spent more time working off its Stalinist crimes believe it did well in working off the Nazi ones.

By claiming its place in history as the antifascist state risen from the ruins on German soil and suggesting that the Nazis were a West German problem, the GDR did distort. And its claim that getting rid of capitalism would get rid of fascism was as one-sided as the BRD's claim that getting rid of open anti-Semitism was all it would take to get rid of fascism. By valorizing the Red Army, the GDR managed to suggest that they were part of its victory— so much so, it's occasionally claimed, that children were confused about which army their fathers had served in the war. The government's position left most East Germans convinced they were, by nature, on the right side of history. And this in turn is a dangerous suggestion, for being on the right side of history in one moment is no guarantee that you will remain there— as the career of Erich Mielke, who began by fighting fascists in the Spanish Civil War and ended as the head of the Stasi, surely shows. Nonetheless, in putting itself on the side of antifascism and inviting those forced to emigrate during the Nazi years to return to rebuild another Germany, the GDR put itself on the right side of history at least once.

East German working off was superficial. It may have been government policy, but it didn't extend to personal confrontation.

The philosopher Stanley Cavell divided thinkers into those whose main categories are political and those whose categories are primarily psychological.[24] For East Germans, political categories were front and center; West Germans focused on the psychological.[25] When the West German '68ers exploded in rage over the lack of working off in the first postwar decades, they insisted that working off meant reckoning—and often violent confrontation—with their parents. This kind of personal encounter rarely took place in the GDR. As the (West German) philosopher Bettina Stangneth put it, "Working through history there wasn't a matter of self-enlightenment. Marxism said that change is a matter of changing political and economic relations. Once you change those relations, and the political leadership, evil is overcome, and you need no further enlightenment. It's an overly optimistic ideology."

I believe a thoroughgoing working off of a nation's crimes requires both political and psychological changes. But if I had to set priorities, I'd prefer that political commitments—expressed in laws preventing expressions of racism, punishing racist crime, and roundly condemning it from the highest levels of government to the teachings in elementary schools—come first.

East Germany was anti-Semitic.

In 1991 the West German research institute EMNID published a study comparing anti-Semitic attitudes in East and West. It was so soon after reunification that the lines between the two former states were still clear. Their verdict: 16 percent of the population of West German states showed extreme anti-Semitic tendencies, while 4 percent of the East German population did.[26] Jews in the GDR who survived the Nazi years received a host of benefits, ranging from a large state pension to privileged housing to free public transportation. And though the Nazis' anticommunism was emphasized more than their anti-Semitism, East Germany also thoroughly documented the latter. The historian Renate Kirchner counted 1,086 books the GDR published about Jews and anti-Semitism. More than one thousand films and television programs regularly presented the Holocaust to a broad public long before West German television showed the American television series *Holocaust*.[27]

The anti-Semitism that coincided with Stalin's worst anti-Semitic policies cannot be ignored. It's also true that, like the Soviet Union, the GDR sided with the Arab states during the Six-Day War in 1967. Virtually everything else about West and East German forms of working-off-the-past remains a matter of argument. As the historian Mario Kessler summarized: "Reading all these works, which often refer to the same sources to support their claims, shows how historians can draw very different conclusions, or rather how much their ideological and political standpoints influence their judgment."[28]

If the GDR was so good at working off the crimes of Nazism, why didn't it tackle the crimes of Stalinism?

Excellent question. Many East Germans think the GDR might have survived if it had.

❧

Jens Reich is a molecular biologist who was a prominent dissident in the GDR—so prominent that he lost his job leading a biology institute when he refused to join the party and pledge loyalty to the system. He was given a less interesting job in the provinces, where he continued both his scientific research and his political work organizing others in critical discussion groups that were hoping to change East Germany.

We met in his house in a decidedly bourgeois corner of what was formerly West Berlin. "We didn't want to end the GDR, but to reform it." Everyone who was actually involved in the opposition says the same thing.

Jens Reich's father served as a doctor on the Eastern Front. I asked if they ever argued about the war.

"My father insisted that the Wehrmacht did not only consist of criminals."

"This was before the Wehrmacht Exhibit?"

"In the GDR we were talking about the criminality of the Wehrmacht in the 1950s. My father was on the front, and he also spoke of building clinics in the villages that served the local population as well as the soldiers." They also fought about the behavior of the American forces during the war. "Father was angry because they immediately withdrew from cities where they encountered resistance, and bombed from the air." This led to thousands of civilian deaths. "I thought it was understandable. Since they were suffering in the Pacific, they couldn't afford to lose soldiers here."

The arguments cannot have been bitter ones, for Jens speaks of his father with love and respect. Returning from the war, he joined the Communist Party, wanting to help build a new, socialist Germany. Since most doctors had gone to the West, where salaries were far higher, his services were welcome. He built up a hospital. "Father suffered under the stupidities of an authoritarian system, but he never said a word against the Soviet Union, nor against the GDR."

Jens Reich remembers how the history of the Nazi period was discussed in school. The main focus was on the heroes of the antifascist resistance, but stories of the victims were told as well. "I don't know anyone who thought the Day of Liberation was a Day of Foreign Domination, as was common in the West. It was a day of defeat, but many really experienced it as liberation." The celebration of resistance heroes helped avoid psychological burdens, so that children didn't have to grow up feeling they were part of a criminal nation. "We didn't learn everything, but we learned a lot. In the West the history lessons ended with Kaiser Wilhelm."

Like others, Reich insists on distinguishing between particular epochs in the GDR. The Stalinism of the '50s gave way to "a sad time; after the Wall was built, we couldn't leave, but it was no longer a brutal dictatorship." There was still a lot of censorship, but what Reich remembers today is how easy it was to get around it. In his own experience there was no anti-Semitism. Most educated citizens, he said, didn't approve of the government's position during the Six-Day War. "In the West the left was very anti-Israel, which was not the case with us." Nor did he detect any anti-Russian sentiment. "Anyone who was fanatically anti-Russian went to the West. The rest of us knew about the Wehrmacht and the SS and thought *What the hell did we do there?*" Reich was a member of the organization for German-Soviet friendship and had many colleagues—half of them Jewish—in the Soviet Union. Nor did he sense xenophobia toward other nationalities: "Look, we were cut off from much of the world. We were happy to see every foreigner."

The informed GDR citizen, he said, was always in an ambivalent position. Many of those who truly wanted to build a new Germany were given honorary posts where they couldn't influence anything. "Many were frustrated with the party as it held on to its foundational antifascist narrative when the party itself had become so stiff and hardened that the young could no longer believe in it. The older people should have faced up to it earlier and said *this is not my socialism*. Still, the reproach that our antifascism was empty is not one I can accept. In those matters I have no complaint."

∾

Friedrich Schorlemmer is a tall, fine-featured man whose sonorous voice must have served him during the years he spent as pastor of the church where Martin Luther did, or did not, nail the ninety-five theses. Historians still disagree about that, but Schorlemmer pointed out the door where the theses would have been fastened if the story is true. Though he's retired, Schorlemmer is clearly at home in the cathedral, where he showed me the renovations for the five-hundredth anniversary of the Reformation. He's also at home in Wittenberg itself, where nearly every passerby greets him on the cobblestone streets; if the passersby are tourists, Schorlemmer stops to help them find their way. Those who know him do not forget the movement he organized in 1983 called Swords into Plowshares. A fierce pacifist, he protested against GDR militarism. Even those who missed the demonstration itself remember the famous photo of the bare-armed blacksmith whom Schorlemmer invited in order to make the metaphor explicit by beating an actual weapon of war into an agricultural tool. A monument now marks the spot. He was also among the first to protest against the GDR's environmental policies, or lack thereof.

"Western journalists didn't know what to call us. We weren't the opposition, and 'dissident' wasn't quite right either, so they called us civil rights activists. The Stasi estimated there were fifty thousand of us, but I think that's rather high."

I told him that Hans Otto Bräutigam insisted I speak with him. "Bräutigam is a lovely, clear-sighted man. He asked questions, and he listened. His picture of the GDR was neither too dark nor too pretty." Schorlemmer recalled speaking in his usual resounding voice while traveling on a ferry with Bräutigam, who wanted to protect him by warning him to speak softly. He appreciated the concern, but "My attitude was always: they should know what I have to say."

"Didn't everyone know they were being overheard by the Stasi?"

"Some say that to justify the fact that they did nothing; others say it to make out that they were braver than they were. I knew they were listening, though I didn't know they'd gone so far as to wire the bathroom and the hallway. I had a major who accompanied my whole life, and I learned more from him after reunification than I did from my Stasi files." He shook his head. "The Stasi was there, but I wouldn't compare it with the surveillance in

South Africa, for example. It didn't determine our lives. We spent most of our time enjoying ordinary things: a wonderful Gouda, a drinkable red wine."

Born in a small village in 1944, Friedrich Schorlemmer cannot remember the war. But his father, who was also a pastor, served as a medical orderly on the Eastern Front, and he left his son a diary that, had anyone found it, would have sent him to prison—at best. As fifteen-year-old Friedrich began to read Holocaust literature, he attacked his parents: *How could you permit this to happen?* His mother cried; his father looked stonefaced, but later offered to talk to him about the war at length.

As a medical orderly, Friedrich's father never fired a shot, but he considered himself a perpetrator anyway, for he moved with the troops all the way to the outskirts of Moscow. Schorlemmer brought his father's diary from the study and read me an entry from February 13, 1942. "'We've just received sharp orders: the civilian population should be more afraid of German soldiers than of Russian partisans. Villages that shelter partisans should be extinguished: man, woman, and child. We're to take everything: the last cow, the last seeds. This is no heroic war, but a war of destruction in its bloodiest form.'" The diary also told how his father was saved by a Russian babushka who let him sleep on her oven. Without her he would have frozen to death. Though her own sons had been killed by the Wehrmacht, she didn't view him as a murderer, just a young man in need of help. "My father told me about the greatness of the Soviet human being—so it was called at the time—because he'd experienced it."

The consensus in the GDR, said Schorlemmer, was clear, even among families who talked less openly about the war than his did. "We didn't call it World War Two, we called it the German War of Theft and Extermination. Period. In contrast to West Germany, there was widespread acknowledgment of the suffering we caused. Everyone knew about the starvation in Leningrad and who was responsible for it. Or the incredible Battle of Stalingrad."

There's at least one East German who describes himself as a victim of the war: Joachim Gauck, a different East German pastor, who became president of Germany in 2012. His autobiography exudes outrage over the moment when Soviet soldiers took his father away to a POW camp. When I mentioned the book, Schorlemmer grew indignant. "That book is dishonest because it hides so much. Why was his father arrested? He was a fervent Nazi, one of the first to join the party, and he was an important man in the marines. On top of that, he came back after five years; many did not. What does Gauck have to whine about?"

"If few in the East echoed Gauck's reaction, how was the war commemorated?"

"In my father's generation there were still people who said privately *At least we managed to hold out against the world for six years.* People who suffered under the Nazis experienced May 8 as a day of liberation, and they wanted it to be honored. It wasn't really internalized by the masses, though Weizsäcker's speech had an impact on the East too. Today I think it was also a speech about German unity: we are united in guilt, whatever system we lived in. We're united in common responsibility."

Schorlemmer praised East German art, particularly film and literature, for working off the Nazi past as well as developing sympathy for Russia. He said he can still be shocked when he sees a film about the war—and wonders whether he can be certain he would not have joined in the killing himself. As for Russia: "We had to deal with the nation that made the most sacrifices in the war. They'd been despised as Slavic *Untermenschen*, and suddenly they were our conquerors." It was hard to swallow, but many East Germans wound up considering the conquerors as friends. "Some of them, like the officers Klemperer knew who admired German culture, were trying out progressive cultural ideas they couldn't have tried at home under Stalin." The West Germans identified with Americans, but "the American losses weren't comparable to the Russian ones—" He interrupted himself; he is a pastor after all. "Every single death is evil, it can't be a matter of numbers. But the scorched-earth policy we left behind in Russia was unique."

Schorlemmer still serves often as pastor, and he recently presided over the burial of someone who had gone to a Soviet prison in his father's stead. The prisoners had to clear minefields in the Oderbruch; only one in eight survived. "Can one blame the Russians for sending prisoners of war to do that? They were German mines that were meant for the Red Army. And the man's father wasn't sentenced by accident. He would have been a Nazi, though as pastor, I didn't want to ask at the funeral."

We talk about East German symbols. He finds the Treptow monument more moving than the Holocaust Memorial. "Those blocks are not accessible." He can still get teary when he hears the line from the former national anthem: "*Never again shall a mother have to mourn her son.*" "It's a little bombastic, but sometimes the soul needs that kind of thing to break the hard crust that forms around it. The GDR had a lot of peace songs, and people still sing along when I quote them at lectures. They're romantic songs in the best sense—the sense that people long for something and feel lifted up by that longing."

As different as working-off-the-past was in East and West, Schorlemmer thinks they had something in common: both were able to create the feeling that the Nazis were responsible—and that the Nazis were someone else. In the West, the Nazis were *those big bosses at the top*. In the East, the identification with the victims went so far that they were able to forget their own complicity and view the Nazis as a Western problem. Though there were more Nazis in the West and more identification with the victims in the East, "that's only half the story," he said. "As Germans in the East, we never fully worked through our own responsibility."

I reminded Schorlemmer that we'd first met years earlier, when he invited me to a symposium about racism he had organized for Martin Luther King's birthday. What does he think other countries can learn from Germany's unfinished, imperfect working off of its debts?

He answered without hesitating. "You can learn that no country, no culture, no religion is immune to falling into the abyss into which we fell. And once it begins, there will always be people who shut down their consciences and side with the strongman. Knowing that, we need to develop a kind of preventative uncertainty. If even the land of Beethoven and Bach and Thomas Mann and Kant and Hegel could do *that*—" He paused. "But it also means we are all capable of asking for forgiveness, and of giving it as well—without denying what happened. That takes time. I don't mean that time heals all wounds, but it takes time to realize that one was a perpetrator before one was a victim and that one became a victim *because* one began as a perpetrator. But if we don't believe that self-knowledge and conversion and building a society based on human rights is possible, then the damage starts all over again."

❧

Hermann Simon owes his life to the Red Army. His mother was a young middle-class Jew who spent the war hidden in Berlin. Before her death, he persuaded her to dictate a memoir of her wartime experience, now published as *Untergetaucht* (*In Hiding*). Her description of life underground— avoiding betrayal, seeking shelter and, when possible, food—is so exact and so gripping that after reading it, I was moved to trace some of her steps. The house where she stayed most often is not far from my own. It is one of the few in the neighborhood that retains the gray-brown plaster unrenovated since the war. Other than that, it looks perfectly ordinary. It had been a shelter from the fear, and often the sexual exploitation, she found elsewhere during the war. Impressed by the fact that simple working people helped her far more often than the better-situated bourgeoisie, she joined the Communist Party soon after liberation.

"Of course we called it liberation," said Simon.

His mother became a professor of philosophy at the Humboldt University, where his father, who fought with the British during the war, became a professor of Jewish studies. Unlike most communists, they were members of the Jewish Community. "I was lucky," said Simon. "My parents registered me at birth as a Jew. I had a bar mitzvah. Everyone knew we were Jewish; it was never a fact that had to be discovered."

Hermann Simon studied history and spent years researching old coins before he decided that researching old Jews was more interesting. He published a history of the Oranienburgerstrasse synagogue when it was still in ruins, and he was one of the people responsible for the GDR commemorations of the fiftieth anniversary of Kristallnacht. In November 1988 there were speeches aplenty on the other side of the Wall. East Germany took the occasion to begin renovating the synagogue, once the largest in Germany, and establishing a Jewish Center inside it. The center now hosts an exhibit, a large library, and a research center, and the only Berlin synagogue where men and women can sit together. Hermann Simon was its director for twenty-seven years, until he retired in 2014. His tenure was marred by reports that he had contact with the Stasi, but he was cleared of any damaging charges and honored by the present state.

He is skeptical about some of the ways in which East Germany worked off its Nazi past. "We were the new Germany, the victors. There were children who thought their West grandpa was in the Wehrmacht, their East grandpa in the Red Army. It took time for the young to realize that the Nazi terror wasn't confined to West Berlin neighborhoods like Schöneberg or Wedding; it happened right here in Berlin Mitte, the capital of the GDR." He always found the monument at Treptow kitschy. "Still, I've never forgotten that I have the Red Army to thank for my own existence."

Nor could he complain about anti-Semitism in the GDR. "Everyone has anti-Semitic experiences. My relatives in Canada can sing you songs about it. There was very little in East Germany, partly because the law came down hard on it and partly because the worst Nazis went to the West, where they were safer. There may have been anti-Semitism in corners of the country, but I never experienced it. In a sense, we lived on an island, like my American friends. None of them has ever met a Trump voter."

He recalled many discussions of anti-Semitism and the Holocaust in school, as well as the enormous amount of reparations that were paid to the Soviet Union, and he never heard a word of resentment about them. He was cautious, however, about predicting the future; he knew the country he grew up in, but reunification has produced a new one. After twenty-seven years living in it, he doesn't feel he's known it long enough to make a judgment.

"The current attitude is, we are the perpetrators, not the victims. I don't know how long that will last. Attitudes can change very suddenly."

It's a German sort of skepticism that has nothing to do with Simon's background. Everyone warns of the need for continued vigilance.

⌘

Jalda Rebling was born in 1951 in Amsterdam after her mother returned there from Auschwitz and Bergen-Belsen, where she was with Anne and Margot Frank when they died. Jalda's mother was both a Jew and a communist. Her father was neither; he emigrated from Germany to Holland just because he loathed the Nazis. He later was honored by Yad Vashem for risking his life trying to save Jews from deportation. Jalda's mother was among them when the Gestapo found them in 1944.

"They were betrayed by the Dutch, not the Germans. Nowhere did the deportations function so smoothly as in Holland. The Dutch are loyal servants of the state. If the state tells them to do something, they do it." More people were deported to Auschwitz from Amsterdam than anywhere else. Lin Jaldati—Jalda's mother—and her aunt were the only members of their family to survive. Jalda's older sister, who was two at the time, was hidden with a Dutch family hours before the Gestapo arrived. She always feared she might have babbled something that gave them away.

After the war, Lin Jaldati found her husband and daughter waiting, but the return to Amsterdam was hard to bear, particularly after 1948, when McCarthyite anticommunism made it impossible for people with their political views to earn a living. When her father was offered a job as music critic for a GDR newspaper in 1953, the family moved to Berlin. There her mother became famous as a singer of Yiddish songs. Her voice and her story were celebrated as heroic; only her daughter knew how often she succumbed to panic attacks and depression.

Having parents who were resistance heroes and the first to perform Yiddish music onstage gave Jalda a protected life. "I was a VIP child; I could get away with things." During the Six-Day War a functionary told her to take off the Star of David she always wore, saying it was a symbol of Zionist aggression. "It's a symbol of my grandparents who were murdered in Auschwitz," she replied. That shut him up.

"I don't miss the GDR for a moment, and I don't play along with anyone who tells me how wonderful it was. But I also don't play along with anyone who tells me it was awful."

"So you weren't a party member like your parents?"

"Sure I was a party member." She laughed ruefully. "I wanted to change the world and thought I could best do so from inside the party. Much later I understood that the world could only be changed from the outside."

Jalda didn't intend to follow in her mother's footsteps, but when her mother asked her to join her for a concert commemorating Anne Frank, she discovered that she too loved to sing Yiddish music. A concert tour in America brought Jalda together with the Jewish Renewal movement, where she found the joy she'd experienced in her mother's songs. "Before that, I only thought of synagogues as places of mourning." She went on to study in the United States and became a cantor. Jalda founded a small congregation just outside of Berlin, where she lives with her wife, Amy Adam, a Jewish artist whose own mother also survived Auschwitz. The two of them often work together on projects meant to spread the message that Judaism isn't all about tragedy.

"Yiddish is the language of the powerless," said Jalda. "It has everything the German language doesn't have. Humor, irony—which great German writer has those?"

"Well, there's Heine."

"Exactly. Heine and Tucholsky." We laughed, knowing that both were Jewish. I wonder why East Berlin has a street named after Heine and a statue of him in the city center. West Berlin's poets' quarter has none, though there are several streets named after Goethe and Schiller. This could be accidental. Or not.

"Yiddish songs were taken up by the civil rights movement in the GDR. It was a way of identifying with the power of the powerless."

Still, she told me there was anti-Semitism under the surface in the GDR. "A swastika was smeared on our mailbox. That could have been anticommunist or anti-Semitic. You never know."

Jalda has noticed subtle anti-Semitism in the klezmer scene. Before giving a concert at a large Berlin theater, she was introduced by someone who expressed his gratitude that Yiddish had been preserved in America so it could return to Germany. "So the Shoah was not that bad after all?" she shot back. The story reminded me of the way some Southern plantations market the blues along with hoopskirts and mint juleps. *Could slavery have been so awful if it produced that great music?* But is that rank racism, or a lack of sensitivity for nuance?

Jalda described another concert with a mixed group of musicians at the Jewish Community Center. She wore a concert dress, but the non-Jewish musicians were dressed in jeans. "The members of the Community—you know, the kind who wear too much gold and too much perfume, but they were survivors—found it disrespectful. They decided they'd never again invite goyim to play klezmer. So there was a discussion in the klezmer scene over who has the right to play Yiddish music. Only Jews? And does that mean Jews can't play Bach? Utter nonsense," she concluded. I decided that a conversation about cultural appropriation would take us into the morning hours.

She knows that serious discussions of the Nazi past are taking place now. "Too late, but at least they're taking place, unlike in Holland or France." Jalda doesn't think that average citizens want enlightenment. They care about being left in peace, staying healthy, having a decent apartment. "People who ask questions that don't have simple answers have always been rare."

I disagreed. Unexamined pasts eventually seep into the quiet lives people try to lead. "Human beings need more than bread and circuses."

"Of course they do. The question is whether they want it."

She doesn't believe the Enlightenment has failed us in regard to anti-Semitism; she thinks we need more of it. Books and lectures don't work alone; the only thing that's effective is personal interaction. She described the project her wife created, in which the two of them take a painted bus to small towns and talk to people about Judaism. "We put a question mark in the children's heads. We start with the Muslim children."

"But that's enlightenment too. I saw it happen in Mississippi."

She wasn't sure whether to agree. "Perhaps we need more books and lectures too. Before talking to you, I didn't realize that the Russian side of the war isn't present in the U.S. and Great Britain. Now it explains some of the conversations I've had there. We always knew what went on in the Western world. I didn't know how little they knew about the Eastern one."

Ingo Schulze's novels are bestsellers in German, and they've been translated into thirty other languages. That's why he's often described as the best writer to come out of the East. "It's meant as a compliment, but they're not conscious of the impact. Would anyone call someone the best writer to come out of the West?"

"It's like calling someone in America the best black philosopher."

"Exactly."

He was born in 1962, a child of the GDR. "Antifascism was everywhere, and with good reason too. It's nonsense to call it prescribed. The communists were the first group the Nazis persecuted. Then came the Social Democrats, then everyone else." There were school visits from resistance veterans, a class trip to Buchenwald. His connection to Russian culture is particularly strong because of his family's story. His grandfather built airplanes during World War II. The Russians took him, as the Americans took Wernher von Braun and others. They lived on the Volga, north of Moscow, for ten years. "Compared to living conditions in the GDR just after the war, things were comfortable. Afterwards my mother was often homesick for Russia." He never discussed the war with his family, "though it was rough to know your grandfather built planes for the Nazis."

Soviet literature and film played a big role in Ingo's life; he collected Soviet army medals as a child. "And then, crazily enough, the impulse to revolution came from Russia." One month before the Wall fell, Gorbachev had warned party leader Erich Honecker: Life punishes those who come too late. Support for the dissidents came from the Soviet Union. "It was German communists—not communists really, but party bosses—who opposed reform." And, Ingo repeated, it was the Red Army that liberated Auschwitz.

"Did you learn about the American contributions at Normandy?"

"Our relationship to America was ambivalent. We heard about how long they took to open a second front; we heard about the Anglo-American terror attack on Dresden. And everything was overshadowed by Hiroshima." From Berlin to Vladivostok, everyone in Eastern Europe was brought up with the knowledge that only one country in the world ever actually deployed nuclear weapons.

As a child, however, it felt strange to identify with the Russians, and no one wanted to identify with the Germans. "So we played cowboys and Indians. The only problem was that everyone wanted to be an Indian. Nobody wanted to play the greedy occupiers." Despite his childhood knowledge of what the palefaces did to Native Americans, Ingo grew up with a strong sense of another America. He saw Harry Belafonte cry over the great actor and activist Paul Robeson during a concert in East Berlin, which still has a street named after Robeson.

When I arrived in Berlin in 1982, the stationing of nuclear missiles in Germany and the wars in Central America were on many minds. In West Berlin cafés, exiled Chileans far outnumbered American expats. West Berliners' reactions when they heard I was American were very hard to take. If they didn't blame me for Ronald Reagan, they attacked me over McDonald's. East Berliners, who were even less likely to meet Americans, had other associations; they usually asked if I knew the radical philosopher Angela Davis.

"I spent my allowance for Angela Davis," says Ingo. "That was normal, like solidarity with Chile. Even we dissidents knew the putsch was a crime. Lots of things were named after Salvador Allende."

When he isn't writing novels or spending time with his daughters, Ingo is politically active. He writes pieces that are deep and clever, gives speeches and interviews about current affairs in Germany. His criticism of the neoliberal order is as fierce as his long-ago criticism of the East German one. Since he grew up in Dresden, I asked why he thinks the far right has gained such a stronghold there.

"Dresden was always conservative," he said. "And conservatives always move to the right when they're dissatisfied. So they call it a scandal that German pensioners have to collect bottles out of trash cans while all the refugees are given money. It is a scandal that people don't have decent pensions, but the one has nothing to do with the other." The living conditions of many citizens whose lifelong work left them with inadequate pensions is often appalling, and they do collect bottles to recycle for pennies. Ingo sees this as a growing problem; it just happened earlier in the East, where pensions are lower and savings were unnecessary. The state took care of its own.

"Conservatives think in national terms rather than social ones. You're not going to win votes by telling people the truth: that our comfortable lifestyle is dependent on exploiting developing countries. That's a major cause of the flood of refugees. Still, one has to say it: you can't really work for social justice in one country without working for it in the rest of the world."

There is something about Ingo that's as upright and good-hearted as the hero of his latest novel, *Peter Holtz*, which some critics dismissed as kitschy. Who still believes there could be someone who always tries to act in the name of the universal common good? Ingo was on his way to a reading of the new novel, and I hurried to ask him what he thinks was wrong with East Germany's antifascism.

"If the working off of the Nazi era had been better, the GDR would have been a different country. But that would have meant speaking about Stalinist crimes as well. Everybody knew about them, but they weren't discussed in public."

What can other countries learn from the German experience?

"To look at your own country as if it were a foreign one. It's crucial to have a broken relationship to your past, to be ready to see your own history with shame and horror. Germany didn't do it willingly. It's still not completed. Even today we have problems thinking about the cruelties of our colonial history."

◦ᢙ◦

One dreary day in November 2016 some forty historians, sociologists, and writers arrived at the Jewish Museum Berlin to exchange notes at a private conference about Jews in East Germany. None of them were young, and many of them were East German Jews. From the West came a few Germans, a Frenchwoman, and three Americans, including myself. We shared many points of agreement.

1. The West never invited Jewish émigrés to return; the East did. Not everyone in the East wanted them back, but enough leaders in culture and science did. It was the Aryans at the universities who insisted on hiring the Jewish professors that were needed, and the GDR government sent the invitation.

2. Those Jews and others who did return had a deep desire to build a better Germany. They didn't want to be victims, but to be active; they didn't want their suffering to have been in vain. They had a strong sense of social responsibility and a belief that social injustice leads to violence. As Germans, they refused to accept the Nazi view that they did not belong there. Whose Germany was it, anyway? And as left-leaning as they were, they were appalled by the American anti-communism of the McCarthy years. "My parents came back after they witnessed the Rosenberg trial," said one participant. The United States executed Ethel and Julius Rosenberg in 1953 for passing nuclear secrets to the Soviet Union. Bertolt Brecht didn't wait that long; he left America after being questioned by the HUAC.

3. There was anti-Semitism in both East and West populations. What was different was the leadership, and the leadership set very different

tones. Still, both sides were concerned to impress the rest of the world with signals against anti-Semitism.

4. Every state has its own myths. In the GDR it was the myth of the anti-fascist state. In the BRD the myth was another: from dogcatcher to diplomat, nobody but the handful of criminals in charge had any idea of what was happening in the East. Our men at the front there were gallant fighters, not criminals.

The East German faces looked tense. They acknowledged the truth of these claims, but they didn't like the tone. One remarked that after they've lost everything else, even East Germany's history has been appropriated. Since 1989 the sovereign interpretations of East German history, which claim it was hard to be Jewish there, all come from the West. "That's not how I remember it," said one East German Jew.

"They're talking about a country I never lived in," said Daniela Dahn, an East German writer best known for a series of sharp, fierce critiques of the reunification process. Nor does she understand those who say the Holocaust was not discussed in the GDR. "Where *were* they?" In the seventh and eighth grades, half of all the literature taught in German classes was devoted to it; in the final year of school, it was still a third. "It was rather too much than too little, especially since we all had to visit Buchenwald. Not to mention all the war films made by DEFA, the East German state film studio, at a time when West German film was waxing lyrical about country girls in Bavaria."

Since many at the conference were historians, there was a discussion of the differences between history and memory. "Why are written sources sacrosanct?" asked the French historian Sonia Combe. "Stasi files can lie. Records are incomplete. Even if testimonies don't provide the same information as the documents, I often find that witnesses provide answers where documents cannot."

Watching the other faces, I remembered a 1993 conference at the University of Minnesota. Shortly after reunification there were attacks on refugee asylums, East and West. Thousands of Germans formed lines, holding candles to protest, but everyone who watched Germany was worried: Had reunification opened the door to racist nationalism?

Having just published my first book, *Slow Fire: Jewish Notes from Berlin*, I'd been invited as the voice of Jews who'd lived in Germany. An Afro-German woman and a Turkish man rounded out the representatives of those who were expected to talk about xenophobia from the inside. The rest of the speakers were West Germans.

My talk had nothing to do with East-West comparisons, though one sentence mentioned that I'd felt more comfortable as a Jew and a foreigner in East than in West Berlin. The room erupted. Though the claim was incidental to my talk, it was all anyone wished to discuss. The West Germans were enraged. One after the other stood up to correct me.

"I'm talking about my own experience," I said.

"And mine," said the Afro-German.

"And mine," said the Turk.

If you invite representative voices, shouldn't you listen to them, even when their claims are at odds with what you want to believe? West German beliefs about East Germany are so tenacious that the subjects of concern went unheard. In America, when white people tell black people how to feel about their own history, it's called whitesplaining. There isn't a word for it in German.

I turned back to the present, watching faces grow tenser. The conference at the Jewish museum was composed of experts on the subject of East Germany and its Jews. It concluded with another claim on which all could agree: Isn't it amazing that we're still arguing about these matters a quarter century past reunification?

I left the conference more convinced than ever: German reunification will not be complete until both sides stop competing with each other and acknowledge that the other side's efforts, while partial and framed by Cold War ideologies, were genuine efforts too.

∾

The most thoughtful Germans, East and West, are reluctant to praise German *Vergangenheitsaufarbeitung*. They are too aware of its flaws, its incompleteness on both sides of the Wall. The greatest flaw was common to both, as Friedrich Schorlemmer pointed out: far too often, the real fascists were the Others. In both cases, responsibility was deflected. In neither case were many able to say *I was guilty*. In both cases, every form of working off was instrumentalized, indeed weaponized as potent ammunition against each other in the long Cold War.

Yet looking at the evidence, it's hard to disagree with Malte Herwig: "If *Vergangenheitsaufarbeitung* were an Olympic sport, the GDR justice system would be ahead of the BRD to the very end." Those who contest the reality of East German *Vergangenheitsaufarbeitung* should at least begin to doubt. First and most important, those who experienced life in East Germany experienced *Vergangenheitsaufarbeitung* as genuine, even when they were critical of most other aspects of that life. Second: Shouldn't some form of antifascism have been imposed by the government? All the Allies originally believed it was necessary; the Western Allies simply gave it up early. As a result, almost any West German who attended school in the '50s and '60s can tell a story about one teacher or another who was given to egregious Nazi expressions, each more militaristic or racist than the other. And since, with the exception of prominent figures like Heidegger or Schmitt, former Nazis remained in their professorships after the war, the steady drip of Nazi-like propaganda would continue until the students were well into their twenties.[29] East Germany removed such possibilities from its inception. On August 24, 1949, the Executive Committee of the Party decreed:

> The resolute continuation of democratic school reform is of essential importance in the further development of social conditions in Germany, especially the consolidation of the anti-Fascist democratic order . . . In view of the intensification and inevitability of this struggle, these tasks can be fulfilled only if every teacher and educator combats all reactionary and neo-Fascist, militaristic, war-mongering and especially anti-Soviet influences and theories, any religious, national and racial hatred.

The history textbooks were standardized throughout the country; new editions appeared every few years, and every school received them at the same time. As elsewhere, that history was put into the service of the Cold War. Every East German textbook written until 1990 contained the following quote from Harry Truman: "If we see that Germany is winning, we ought to help Russia, and if Russia is winning, we ought to help Germany, and that way let them kill as many as possible." It was used as propaganda, but the accuracy of the quote is undeniable. Truman gave it to *The New York Times* in 1941, when he was still a senator.

To repeat: being on the right side of history at one time is no guarantee that you'll be on the right side of history at another. The GDR had periods of that Stalinism which is the death of real socialism. Lies were numerous, and lives were destroyed. But there were moments when it was on the right side of history. To forget that is to falsify not only history but politics and morals as well. For that amnesia is a way of externalizing and demonizing evil—the surest way to perpetuate evils in the future.

PART TWO

Southern Discomfort

4

Everybody Knows About Mississippi

Goddam. There's more than one way to pronounce that word. Nina Simone did it with the wrath of a prophet, giving voice to the fury the term originally conveyed. When the God of mercy damns you, you are well and truly lost. Southern radio banned "Mississippi Goddam" in the '60s; they said it took the Lord's name in vain.

Yet *goddam* can also express something like revelation, or even wonder. For what everybody knows about Mississippi is largely mythic. *The heart of darkness, the middle of the iceberg*—at the very least, the place you don't want to be caught after sundown. The state gets first prize in every contest you don't want to win, from the highest number of lynchings (in the past) to the highest level of obesity (in the present). Despite occasional competition from neighboring Alabama and Louisiana, it is last on every list of goods we value: the worst health, the least wealth, the poorest quality of education.

All those things could be improved by legislation and taxes. Anything imposed by the government, however, raises half-buried memories of Reconstruction, the period between 1865 and 1877 when the federal government tried to cope with the consequences of the Civil War. The radical reconstructionist wing of Congress supported progressive legislation, including full civil rights for the nearly four million liberated African Americans, and they were prepared to keep federal troops occupying the South to ensure that legislation was enforced. The defeated Southern states found the occupation intolerable, and its memory fuels resistance to anything *those Yankees try to tell us to do.* Few will say it out loud, but the not-quite-conscious conviction that anything coming out of Washington is a Yankee military measure underlies opposition to every program that might benefit the South from outside, whether it's infrastructure or Obamacare. If we knew more about Reconstruction, we would know that this conviction has some history behind it: there was no mandatory public schooling until the Radical Republicans introduced it. Schools and roads and public institutions for the care of orphans, as well as the introduction of taxes to support them, were all products of the wide-ranging structural reforms that even, for a moment, succeeded in suppressing the Klan.[1] The line from Southern hatred of Reconstruction to Southern opposition to government programs is a straight one, though it's rarely explicitly drawn. So Mississippi prefers potholes that can ruin your wheels in its capital, and schools that leave their graduates illiterate in its countryside, to imposing taxes that might fix them.

Mississippi wasn't always the poorest state in America. When it was settled in the early nineteenth century, much of its land was wilderness, teeming with bears and panthers. By the time of the Civil War, the white gold in its fields made Mississippi the fifth-richest state in the nation, for cotton was the sort of international currency that oil is today. Of the seventy-eight thousand of its sons who took up arms for the Confederacy, only twenty-eight thousand returned. A third of these left at least one limb on the battlefield. Imagine Germany without the Marshall Plan and you can imagine the devastation the war left on the Deep South. The inability of Reconstruction to impose a thorough plan for physically or morally restructuring the land left it to fester. When the Radical Republicans lost the support of Congress, there was no force that could urge Mississippians to reconsider their past. On the contrary: Mississippi was the first state to introduce the Black Codes, which effectively revoked all the rights freedmen and -women had been promised with emancipation. Since the rest of the country preferred to think of racial problems as Southern problems, the better to ignore its own complicity in sustaining them, Mississippi was left to itself. Thousands of African Americans fleeing terror and poverty went up north as soon as they could buy a ticket. In fact, with the possible exception of William Faulkner, any Mississippian with any sense was inclined to start life over elsewhere.

I'd driven through the state many years earlier—twice, real fast, without even stopping for gas. Mississippi sends chills down many a spine. *Nonsense, I told myself, you are white. Then again,* I remembered, *so were Schwerner and Goodman,* the murdered Jewish volunteers who came to register voters during the Freedom Summer of 1964. Countless men and women were murdered in Mississippi in the '60s, and only two of them were white and Jewish. But their names were the ones that rang in my ears when I crossed the state line in 2016. I was struck by the straightness of highway, the flatness of terrain. All the names were familiar, sometimes eerily so. And no wonder: these days Mississippi markets itself as the birthplace of American music. Who indeed can imagine American culture without the blues? Without Elvis? Aretha? This is just as true as the fact that Mississippi was called the lynching capital of the world not too long ago.

Suddenly all the references made sense. Jackson, Leland, Tupelo, names I'd heard sung but never quite imagined in space. If it's set to music, you can start me off with a line and my usually mediocre memory clicks into overdrive. Crossing the bridge over a stream marked TALLAHATCHIE, I was hurled back decades to remember all the lyrics of Bobbie Gentry's "Ode to Billie Joe." The song was sinister enough even before I recalled the name of the river where they found the body of Emmett Till. The county where his mangled corpse was left is still debated in the Delta, but there's no doubt that the fourteen-year-old black youth was kidnapped, tortured, murdered, and thrown into that muddy rolling water.

All that was on my mind as I saw a sign advertising a Mississippi Welcome Center. The paunchy white man at the counter offered me a cup of coffee so affably and insistently that I gave in and took it. "Ah, Oxford," he said when I told him my destination. "You go in for literature?" He handed me a brochure for Faulkner's house, which I duly promised to visit. I smiled, took a brochure describing the Mississippi Blues Trail, and walked out the door. The coffee was as tasteless as expected, but I waited till I was out of sight to pour it out.

More than two dozen American towns are named for the city of dreaming spires in Oxfordshire, England. Most of that naming was done in the hope that a great university would follow, and Oxford, Mississippi, was no different. Inside the state, the town is known for its flagship university, still the first choice of the scions of business and politics who hold the Mississippi reins of power. They can be sure that Daddy will visit often, since many alumni come up every weekend during football season. Their wives lay out linen and china for the elegant pregame picnics that take place in the Grove, an ample space of tree-shaded ground in the center of campus. Not many of them remember how the Grove was once filled with fire when "two men died 'neath the Mississippi moon," as Bob Dylan sang in "Oxford Town."

Outside the state, Oxford is famous for two things. In 1962 it was the site of what's been called the last battle of the Civil War, when governor Ross Barnett tried to prevent a young veteran named James Meredith from becoming the first African American to study at the state's leading university. The governor was supported by thousands of rioting students, and the case was resolved only with the help of the thirty thousand troops President Kennedy sent to restore order. All over the South, brave young black men and women integrated universities under threat of violence; in Oxford the violence was so explosive it became a national turning point. If the name Ole Miss evokes football fields and magnolias for its alumni, it evokes tear gas and shotguns for others. Among those who remember the violence, Ole Miss is not an affectionate nickname, but a racially loaded reference harking back to the days when slaves spoke of "Ole Miss" and "Ole Massa." As James Meredith wrote:

> The 'Ole Miss' of the plantation was by far the most important person in Mississippi. She held the keys to every lock on the plantation. She was the monitor of culture, the developer of Christian virtue, the matchmaker and the director of education and training. Above all, she was the queen of white supremacy. The University of Mississippi played all these roles for the state. It is a fitting nickname, for Ole Miss was and is the dominant, most powerful institution in the state.[2]

So I learned to call the place by its official name, the University of Mississippi, though it has ten syllables instead of two.

Oxford's other distinction: it's the home of William Faulkner, the South's only Nobel laureate in literature. I use the present tense deliberately; he died in 1962, but Faulkner's ghost still hovers over the town today. Though he was loathed by most of his neighbors during his lifetime—"Count No Account" was the local nickname—Faulkner's language turned the proud, twisted history of the postwar South into world literature. Today's locals are mighty pleased to tell you that their home was the template for Faulkner's fictitious Yoknapatawpha County. Faulkner's house, Rowan Oak, is now a lovely museum full of memorabilia, where seminars on his work are sometimes held on the gracious lawn. His grave at the local cemetery is regularly adorned with fresh flowers and bottles of his preferred brand of bourbon. And just in case you might be inclined to forget him, there's a life-size bronze statue of the writer sitting on a bench in front of the town hall. Faulkner's ghost draws other writers, along with literary conferences and archives, and it's surely a reason why Square Books is one of the nation's best bookstores. Joining the citizens who retire to the City Grocery bar for a whiskey after a bookstore reading, I felt I'd arrived at a small, warm haven of literacy and gentility. Even though the bar's balcony looks right out onto a statue of Johnny Reb, the iconic Confederate soldier invented to stand for all those who fought for the South in the war.

Oxford isn't the real Mississippi, I heard time and again. It's been called the Velvet Ditch. Apart from the bookstore and a number of good restaurants on the beautifully old-fashioned square, whose storefronts house law offices and high-end boutiques, there's no place to buy anything you really need. For that you must drive to the highway, where in addition to the Walmart you'll see signs for a fitness studio called Rebel Body, a guitar shop called Rebel Music, and a clothing store touting Rebel Rags. The University of Mississippi's venerated football team is called, of course, the Rebels, though in 2014 the chancellor decreed that "Dixie" would no longer be played at halftime. Many alumni were infuriated. None of them actually want to put their lives on the line to defend slavery, but the word *rebel* has a seductive sound. Besides, all those symbols belong to family tradition.

There's no question about it: the binding ties that every native Mississippian mentions are appealing. "Doesn't everyone love the place they were born?" asked one recent University of Mississippi graduate. "Not like this, they don't," I had to tell him. Curtis Wilkie, the liberal journalist who returned after decades of reporting from Boston to the Middle East, says people are kinder here. Lee Paris, the conservative businessman who founded an interracial church group, says he loves Southern culture for its gentleness. I couldn't help being touched by the sweetness of the drawl, the way strangers move to hold a door or pick up a fallen package, the genteel friendliness that greets you on the sidewalk or at the cash register. It's impossible to reconcile that sense of gentleness with the knowledge that more people were lynched here than anywhere else in the country, and *lynch* is a word that hides more than it shows. They were hacked to pieces, burned to death slowly, fingers and teeth sold as souvenirs to the mobs who drove for miles to witness and jeer. Mississippians' beloved Jesus, mocked as he hung dying, did not suffer more. It's hard to square with any definition of *gentle* I know.

Yet white folks are not the only ones drawn back and again to the place. "I am damned proud to be a Southerner," says Charles Tucker. He's a tall black man from a tiny Delta town who, when I met him, was working for the Winter Institute. Southern food is better, he told me; Southern people are warmer, whether black or white. "I've lived up north. You don't realize how starved you are for human companionship until you come from the North to the South, where people will actually look you in the eye and speak to you. People who haven't seen you for a while will hug you. They will ask after your family and actually mean it. The South has a ton of problems. Being human is not one of them."

Whatever fears I'd had as I crossed the Tallahatchie River evaporated the first time I walked into the Winter Institute. The welcome I was given stopped just short of a hug as a group of strangers, black and white in equal proportion, stood up to greet me warmly. Founded in 1999 by Susan Glisson, the institute enjoys the name and the patronage of William Winter, the most progressive Mississippi governor since Reconstruction.

> To outsiders familiar with only the Old South image of Mississippi, the William Winter Institute for Racial Reconciliation could sound like an oxymoron, at best a cosmetic effort by wealthy businesspeople to polish the image of the state. But the founders were committed people . . . [and] it became an example of the other Mississippi, a small but energized minority in the state that . . . poked holes in the caricature of the state as home only to rednecks, racists and demagogues.[3]

When she wrote the above, Carol George was describing the Winter Institute's first big victory, its key role in bringing the main killer of civil rights workers Chaney, Goodman, and Schwerner to trial. There were other successes: helping a Delta community honor the memory of Emmett Till, training Mississippi police chiefs to avoid racial profiling in the wake of Ferguson, smoothing discussions that led to the removal of the Confederate statues in New Orleans. Much of their work was done at the University of Mississippi, where the institute was housed until 2018. Given the university's central role in past civil rights struggles, as well as its centrality in present Mississippi power relations, the institute's efforts in Oxford had far more than academic significance.

The staff included people as different as Jackie Martin, a seventy-four-year-old black veteran of the civil rights struggle in McComb, Mississippi, and Jennifer Stollman, a fifty-year-old blond, blue-eyed Jewish historian from

Detroit who views her work as a form of *tikkun olam*—the Hebrew idea of repairing the world. Most of their work consisted of talk.

"They say talk is cheap," says Susan Glisson. "But only cheap talk is cheap. Honest, purposeful talk works."

Susan is a white woman who speaks with a sweet, soft drawl, slings a baseball cap over her long brown ponytail, and tends to wear overalls that recall the early staff of SNCC—the Student Nonviolent Coordinating Committee—one of the leading civil rights organizations of the 1960s. In her impoverished family in Augusta, Georgia, nobody imagined getting a Ph.D. in history. But she grew up in "something people think does not exist, a progressive Baptist church," and she remembers her pastor receiving death threats for inviting black children to the church Bible camp. She was finishing a dissertation on Ella Baker, the leading light of grassroots civil rights organizing, when she came to Mississippi and discovered the power of narrative. "We know all the facts we need to know about race, but facts alone do not heal. Narrative shows the myriad ways we are vulnerable." The guiding principles she developed can make academics cringe: Be present and welcoming. We are not here to set someone else straight.

"I hated the language when I first saw it," said Jennifer, whose own style is sharp, fast, and very funny. "But it turns out that the guidelines work."

"I didn't know what I was doing when I started," Susan added. "I was making it up in the car."

This is how she described the institute's tasks:

> . . . prosecutions against racist violence, public ceremonies that I term rituals of atonement, historical tours and markers that change the geography of memory, the creation and implementation of school curricula on human rights, healing work among previously segregated groups through community building to alter public narratives of communities known for racial violence, academic investigation and scholarship on patterns and legacies of abuse, and partnerships of advocacy and policy groups that seek new institutional reforms that undo the structures of oppression and replace them with equitable ones.[4]

None of those things can take place without the national conversation about race that has been so often called for and so rarely achieved. Talking about race makes everyone uneasy. If I mention race to an African American, am I reducing her to a category rather than meeting her as an individual? I certainly felt like a category during my first years in Berlin, watching Germans react to the news that I'm Jewish. Suddenly they felt an urge to mention the uncle who helped Jews emigrate just before the war, or to present me with an expensive book about Moses Mendelssohn. I've grown skeptical about the first claim, and I'm not all *that* interested in Moses Mendelssohn. At one formal dinner I was stuck between a couple who persisted in telling me how much they love Woody Allen, while I tried to turn the conversation to Mozart. I failed.

The centrality of race is so palpable in the South that it's impossible to ignore in conversation, however unsteady. The Winter Institute developed procedures for making those conversations honest and productive, and watching those procedures in 2016 made me feel more hopeful than I'd felt in years. Eight of them, to be precise. Susan, Jennifer, and I reminisced about where we were the night Obama was elected. After reading his books in 2007, I'd become a volunteer when my friends were still calling me out of touch: only someone living in Europe could believe that an African American intellectual might be elected president. Sitting in a Mississippi diner and hearing about the little victories of the institute and its allies brought back the brightness of the early Obama campaign.

What keeps them going, said Susan, is something she learned from her mentor, SNCC veteran Chuck McDew. "Mississippi is the Broadway of the movement, and you don't leave Broadway." Put less theatrically, if you can change Mississippi communities, you can probably change anything. Is it redemptive to stand on ground zero, knowing you're at the heart of America's worst? "I still think Mississippi holds the key for healing the nation," said Jesse Jackson. "There's something magic about Mississippi."[5]

Perhaps it isn't just the challenge: perhaps you actually like places where you feel a little fear. Not too much, just a little. It took me years, after all, to stop feeling fear in Berlin. I cannot say my fear of Mississippi turned into a deep love, but it did become the deep fascination that's a first step toward love. Everyone says it: you either get it or you don't, but the state exudes a kind of gentle seduction even in its hardest, harshest spots.

People in Oxford are tired of hearing Faulkner's quote: "The past is never dead. It's not even past." But it's true no matter how often it's repeated, and nowhere more so than in Mississippi. The historian Howard Zinn's remarks about the South make sense: it is "not the antithesis but the essence of American society which could therefore function as a mirror in which the nation can see its own blemishes magnified."[6] If the South is a mirror, Mississippi is a microscope.

After a short stay in 2016, I asked the Winter Institute if I could spend a sabbatical there the following year. I don't think they really believed I'd return, any more than the friends back home who asked, "You're going *where*? *Now*?" With a solid sweep of the South, Donald Trump had won the 2016 election. My apprehension returned, just a little, but my plans were already set. I had an office at the Winter Institute and a rented house, complete with front porch and rocking chairs from which to watch the townsfolk stroll between the university and the Square. If I wanted to study American *Vergangenheitsaufarbeitung*, there seemed no better base than an institute whose web page called its vision "a world where people honestly engage in their history in order to live more truthfully in the present, where the inequities of the past no longer dictate the possibilities of the future."

◆

Jennifer Stollman was raised in a Jewish community in suburban Detroit. What made her a social justice activist? "Serendipity" is part of her answer. She was born on Martin Luther King's birthday, in the year of his death. Her father and her aunt marched in Selma, two of the many Jews who believed that segregation was in conflict with Jewish tradition and decided to do something about it. When Jennifer describes her biography while she's training a group, however, she brings up something else. "I was adopted out of the foster-care system when I was almost five, so I remember going from eating onion-skin soup, when there was nothing else, to a purple organza bedroom." Being lifted out of the cycle of poverty into a life of privilege made her aware of the arbitrariness of social injustice at a very tender age. Racism was fierce and open at the University of Michigan in the '80s, where she became politically active while studying American history, eventually earning a Ph.D. with a dissertation on Southern Jewish women.

"I had done Hebrew school, studied and taught the Talmud, lived and worked in Israel. It was enough already. I didn't want to do a Ph.D. on Jewish history." But she was fascinated by the diary of the Jewish wife of a Georgia plantation owner. "Farrakhan's claim that Jews were the principal slaveholders is a lie. But Jews have to confront their history apart from these triumphalist narratives that say we treated our slaves well and we were all civil rights activists. We've got to tell the truth." She began to read letters of Jewish women who lived in the nineteenth-century South, appalled by what she found. "Women never beat their slaves, but they used the threat of sale." When she spoke about her work at her hometown Jewish Community Center, she was roundly attacked by the audience, among them a number of

Holocaust survivors. "I had this endless faith that my community was forth-right and self-reflective. 'Young lady,' said an older man who started to roll up his sleeve to show his tattooed number, 'do you know how dangerous this is, the story you're telling?' He accused me of sympathizing with Louis Far-rakhan, who has blamed the Jewish community for racism. I said, 'No, I'm trying to get you to see that we are part of this history; lying about it only expresses our anxieties. We are not fully Jewish in America if we're not fully telling the truth.' Only one woman in the room supported me. It was ten years of education in one night."

Stollman went on to teach at several colleges across the country, includ-ing a short stint at the University of Mississippi. She thought she was settled at Fort Lewis College in Durango, Colorado, where she learned Navajo in order to work with the large Native American student community, while ski-ing the Durango slopes in the afternoon. In 2013 Susan Glisson asked her to become the Winter Institute's academic director, promoting racial reconcili-ation at the university that was always a symbol of white supremacy. While knowing that her Northern Jewish background would make her an outsider in Mississippi, Stollman took up the challenge. After helping to develop the institute's procedures for confronting racism, she was soon on call as an ex-pert on moving through racial tension not only at the University of Missis-sippi but at campuses and communities across the South.

Jennifer became my Mississippi mentor. She was the first to take me to the Delta; I marveled at the way she pointed out crops that hadn't yet sprouted, where all I could see were fields of dead sticks. She got us out of a carjacking attempt in Clarksdale while I was distracted and dazzled by an elegantly derelict blues club. She was crucial in explaining the way things worked, and didn't, in Mississippi, translating the native tongue when necessary. *Bless your heart* sounds sweet, for example, but it's closer to a curse than anything else. A hypothetical sign that read, for example, KWIK KAR KOMPANY, was less likely to be a reflection of local illiteracy, high as it is, than a barely coded pledge of allegiance to the Ku Klux Klan. (A road trip made to count how many deliberate misspellings of this kind dot the roads could last quite a while.) The magnolia is not just any old state flower; it was chosen as an emblem of pure whiteness.

And she helped me read the Confederate iconography tucked into the pretty university. The Johnny Reb statue towers over the entrance to campus and is graced with a heroic quote from Lord Byron. There was a recent vic-tory, now marked only by absence. On the flagpole where a lone American flag flies, there had been a Mississippi one emblazoned with the Confederate emblem the state government refuses to change. An intense student campaign mentored by the Winter Institute led the university to take that flag down, though not without great dispute, national attention, and an appearance by the Ku Klux Klan. There is also, most controversially, a memorial statue to James Meredith.

Once a year during Black History Month, a group of African American students called Men of Excellence lead a tour around the campus in honor of Meredith. Roscoe, the guide I followed, had tied his long hair back into a ponytail, but like all his fellows, he wore a dark blue jacket and a yellow striped tie. The tour started at the Lyceum, where Meredith was taken for shelter when rioting students tried to attack him. "When I think of thirty thousand troops guarding one black kid, I feel honored by what he did for me," said Roscoe. We proceeded to the spot where a French journalist and an American jukebox repairman were shot dead in the struggle. The press was there in force, for everyone said the Civil War had come again. The students, aided by Klan members who had come from across the South, were no longer just fighting to keep Meredith out; they were picking up the banner of the Confederacy against the hated North, which insisted on enforcing the federal laws that gave Meredith the right to study where he chose. Curtis Wilkie, who was a student at the time, recalled, "I thought the university might close. There was even the thought that Mississippi might try to secede from the Union again. That's how intense the situation was." To this day, most black Mississippians prefer to study at one of the historically black colleges rather than venture onto the University of Mississippi campus, despite its better funding and facilities. "Our uncles and aunts ask us why we choose to go to a school known for its racism," said Roscoe. "Our answer is the same as James Meredith's: we're just exercising our constitutional right." We were standing next to the flagpole; high over the bare treetops, the Stars and Stripes waved with the wind. "Later we had to battle to tear down the Mississippi flag. Look at its absence and feel your heart sing."

The tour ends at the monument to Meredith, which was unveiled in 2006. It consists of a pillared marble arch on which four words are carved: COURAGE, OPPORTUNITY, PERSEVERANCE, and KNOWLEDGE. Before the archway, under the beam marked COURAGE, a bronze statue of the young James Meredith steps forward. It's an accurate rendering of the short, handsome young man whose resolute face, flanked by U.S. marshals, is set against fear. Meredith swears he never felt it. But how could he avoid it when the troops sent personally by President Kennedy to protect him were being barraged by Molotov cocktails and gunfire? Meredith answered that question in his 2012 autobiography. "As a black male living in Mississippi in 1960 I was already a walking dead man . . . It takes no great courage for a dead man to want to live."[7]

Roscoe asked the group to observe a moment of silence "for the sacrifice this man made for us." We should ask ourselves, he continued, "Are we simply doing the norm, or doing things to inspire others, to uplift others as James Meredith would like us to do?" The silence was observed; the group—mostly black students, with a sprinkling of white and older people—looked solemn, reflective, and satisfied.

The gratitude expressed by the Men of Excellence was noble and moving, but the exposition at the statue left out complications in the story. First of all, the university may have changed enough in half a century to devote central space, and money, to memorialize the man who made it infamous, but not all members of the university are pleased with the change. To put it mildly. In 2014 two drunken frat boys hung a noose around the statue's neck and draped the rest with a Confederate flag. They were expelled—national attention, outside pressure—but it was federal, not state law that prosecuted them for hate crimes, and the final sentence was extraordinary. One of the young men did serve six months in jail, but the other was given a year's probation and ordered to write a five-page report on chapter 19 of Faulkner's *Light in August*, which describes a lynching. It was a federal court in Oxford, after all. It's hard to know how anyone could understand that chapter alone, without context, but the judge must have thought that requiring him to read an entire book would be cruel and unusual punishment.

The more fundamental fact about the statue was left out of the tour entirely. James Meredith hated it. By 2018 he had softened, but for years he urged that it be not only dismantled but "ground into dust."[8] Susan Glisson told me the story. "We wanted to commemorate the struggle for equal access in education in Mississippi in a way that reflected the movement itself, which was grassroots. There was no desire to deify a savior." Susan and other progressive forces on the campus raised money, and recruited a national jury to judge the proposed design. The jury eventually selected the African American artist Terry Adkins, whose design involved two sets of doors inscribed with the words JUSTICE HENCEFORTH and EDUCATION FOREVERMORE." Between them, hurricane-proof glass panes were engraved with words inspired by Meredith's 1966 March on Fear: *"Teach in fear no more. Insist in fear no more. Unite in fear no more."*

The chancellor refused to accept the design; he found the word *fear* "too negative." Despite protest, the chancellor insisted on rejecting the original design, so a different committee settled on the statue of James Meredith. He has called it an idol, a graven image, a violation of the Second Commandment. He doesn't like to see himself rendered as a "gentle, solitary supplicant,"[9] and he is outraged that the monument includes a "butchered, out-of-context quotation from my 1966 book . . . expressing my love for the land of Mississippi but making no mention of my hatred of its ruling system of white supremacy."[10] The quote is a sop to local patriotism, meant to soften the hearts of those alumni who would object to any Meredith monument whatsoever—quite possibly because they were among the rioters fighting to keep him out. The carved plaque reads ALWAYS, WITHOUT FAIL, REGARD-LESS OF THE NUMBER OF TIMES I ENTER MISSISSIPPI, IT CREATES IN ME FEELINGS THAT ARE FELT AT NO OTHER TIME . . . JOY . . . HOPE . . . LOVE. I HAVE ALWAYS FELT THAT MISSISSIPPI BELONGED TO ME AND ONE MUST LOVE WHAT IS HIS.

What bothered Meredith the most, said Susan, was the knowledge that he was used. The Meredith statue, like the naming of countless streets after Dr. Martin Luther King, has been used to claim that we have turned a corner to make racism a thing of the past. At the University of Mississippi, that claim was reinforced by the ceremony at which the statue was unveiled, where Congressman John R. Lewis and Morgan Freeman, among others, made triumphalist speeches. Meredith himself, although invited to the ceremony, was not invited to speak—"because of time constraints," according to the university. *He's too volatile*, say some. *Unpredictable*, say others. *Nutty as a fruitcake* comes up often too.

The university is not averse to inviting controversial speakers on occasion, especially when they're outsiders with no plans to stay. On my first trip to Oxford I went to hear the black feminist writer Brittney Cooper speak to an audience of some hundred students and faculty, most of them white. She's a good speaker, and I liked the fact that she could express rage at America's systematic racism in that space, but I was disturbed by her answer to one white student's question. "What should we do?" asked the girl. "There really could be a President Trump." It was March 2016, and Trump was surging in the primaries. "Black folk have a long experience with crazy white racists," Cooper answered. "We've learned to keep our heads down, raise our children, and get on with our lives."

I waited till the students' questions were finished before approaching the speaker, disturbed that she'd missed a teaching moment. "Shouldn't we be telling students to get their asses moving and make sure everyone they know is registered to vote?" I asked, adding that as a writer who lives abroad, I'm painfully aware of how much the American presidency affects the whole world.

Cooper looked me up and down. "You keep saying *we*, but Trump is not my problem. He's a white people's problem. There's no *we* between us."

I swallowed hard before saying that I didn't even know anyone who would consider voting for Trump, but I was worried about disaffected voters.

"Disaffected white voters is also a function of white privilege," said Cooper.

I could have speculated about how different Congress would be if all the disaffected and disenfranchised black voters went to the polls, but I didn't want to argue, and conversation was clearly impossible.

"There's no space for a *we* yet," said Jennifer, standing beside me as I fumed. "I have to believe it won't be that way always."

There were any number of *we*'s between me and Brittney Cooper. We are both women, writers, humanities professors, Americans. Perhaps she's a mother too. We are certainly both human beings who could be blown to bits if an unstable commander in chief decides to play with the nuclear codes. Racial experiences divide us. But can't we use other experiences to try to bridge that gap?

The Winter Institute's signature program, the Welcome Table, proceeds on the assumption that we can. It brings together racially mixed groups of fifteen to twenty people, beginning with a weekend retreat. Thereafter they meet every month for a year and a half. Groups engage in a series of exercises designed to build trust between them, as individuals, before moving to confront more difficult questions about race. When was the first time you noticed that race is an issue? is a question that brings most everyone back to their childhood, however different black and white childhood experience will have been. Poetry is read about homes, about identities; participants are required to write and share their own. The group breaks into dyads and triads, then returns so that each can tell their partners' stories, not their own. Learning to listen. Learning to hear. All that takes place to create a mosaic of *we*, opening minds and hearts to face the harder stuff.

Once trust is established, the group moves on to information. The difference between systemic and deliberate racism, for example, and the ways in which we are all damaged by both. The ways in which intention does not matter—anyway, not always. ("The opposite of *good* is *good intention*," wrote the Berlin Jewish writer Kurt Tucholsky.) You may not mean to express a racist or sexist stereotype, but if you've grown up among them, you have to work to notice that they're there.

The Winter Institute's style made that work as pleasant as possible, insisting on the humanity of the perpetrator as well as the victim. "The limbic system is primed to distinguish between safety and danger, and takes in eleven million secondary cues every moment," says Jennifer. "We can consciously categorize forty or fifty of them; our unconscious work is done for us." Implicit bias is always operating. There's a reason I tensed up, some time ago, when I saw a tall, casually dressed young black stranger rushing toward me on a New Haven sidewalk. How could I know he was running to ask if I was the one he'd seen on Tavis Smiley's show? Though I succeeded in concealing it long enough to be gracious, my initial anxiety left me ashamed for years. "Learn to recognize it, not weaponize it," says Jennifer. "That way you can navigate it, and it's liberating." What we've learned about neuroplasticity shows that even unconscious processes can be changed.

They cannot be changed until they're acknowledged, and claims about being post-racial or color-blind do not help. As an African American woman in one of the groups put it, "If you say you don't see color, it means you don't see me." A friend had told her he'd just realized she was black. "I always knew *he* was a white man. What does he mean he just realized?" I remembered the German man who long ago rushed to tell me he wouldn't dream of noticing I was Jewish, as if the only decent thing to do with the unpleasant fact that I am Jewish is to overlook it altogether. This is what most white people do with race, and the implication is very clear: not being white is unpleasant, if only because it makes white folks uneasy, so the proper thing to do is ignore it entirely. "My job is to work with anxious white people," says Jennifer. "People who are so worried about saying something wrong that they say nothing at all." That lets racial resentment grow and fester, on all sides of the table. In some ways it's more poisonous than outright racist action.

The process of building the trust needed to talk directly about racism, past and present; learning the mechanisms by which we imbibe and inherit it; as well as discovering how to intervene to confront it in ourselves as well as others—all that can be done in programs of varying length. The Winter Institute has led such programs for criminal justice workers, teachers, corporations, and the Mississippi police department. In the final third of the Welcome Table program, the group develops a project it will complete once the process is finished. The first project was bringing Chaney, Goodman, and Schwerner's killer to trial. It could be developing programs for civil rights education and commemorating community heroes; using a coastal oil spill to set a program for environmental justice in motion; even creating a communal garden in a Delta community that normally runs on chips and

Twinkies. What's important is that each community decides on a workable task that meets its own needs, using the trust built in the groups to foster the even deeper trust that evolves when people work together on something that concretely furthers the common good. I know. It sounds either utopian or banal, and quite possibly both. But in its first two decades, the Winter Institute's programs served thousands of people, and I have seen it work myself.

I asked the staff member April Grayson what she did with the tension she must experience in the process.

"There's the private me and the facilitator me," she answered. "I might be outraged at something someone says, but I hold sacred their right to tell their story." The faith in the power of narrative—the belief that every story needs to be told—is not the belief that every opinion is equally valuable. Nonetheless the Winter Institute has been criticized for being too soft, giving too much power to racist white people by honoring their narratives. "We try to emphasize that our way isn't the only way, but our way is to uphold the sanctity of people's stories. When you're listened to, no matter what your identity is, you feel valued, and you're more open to engage in conversations that get deeper and deeper."

April is a small-boned, pretty white woman who was born in 1970 with four generations of Mississippi blood in her veins. "Their Confederate history was in the background, but it was never romanticized." Her father's family were considered oddballs; they were always reading poetry. "It took me years to do the math and realize where all the arrowheads came from. We found them while we were gardening. I had to acknowledge that this family land so dear to me belonged to Native Americans, and that one of the most infamous incidents in Mississippi civil rights history happened down the road." The home of Vernon Dahmer, a well-respected man whose independent store allowed him to be more outspoken than many other African Americans, was firebombed by the KKK. Dahmer fired back at the attackers long enough for his wife and children to escape into the woods through the back door, but he died of smoke inhalation a few hours later. "Every time I feel ready to leave Mississippi, I think of his wife," said April. "She's been asked so often why she didn't leave, and her answer is always the same: 'Cause I can't change it if I leave.' I figure if Ellie Dahmer can do it, I can do it."

April grew up in a progressive-minded family in Rolling Fork, a small town in the Delta. Her father was a dedicated superintendent for the county public schools at a time when most white people sent their children to "seg academies," private schools that were founded to avoid integration after it was clear that the federal government was serious about enforcing *Brown v. Board of Education*. In the little Methodist church that was the center of the social world in the community, many people thought her dad was the devil—simply for supporting good public education for white and black students alike.

Her family was never sure who they could trust. Did the nice lady at the corner grocery belong to the Klan? "People don't understand how much fear there was," said April. "I knew a family in McComb whose daughter was chosen to be Miss Mississippi. They were run out of the state after the father had the audacity to talk to a journalist about the need for integration." April considers herself fortunate; although she and her brother were among a handful of white students at the public school she attended, she had many African American teachers who had been involved in the civil rights movement, and she came out knowing more about civil rights history than most current graduates.

Like most reflective Mississippians, April left the state for years, working and studying documentary filmmaking in Seattle. "I loved Seattle, but it was so *white*," she said, incredulity still breaking through her words today. She returned to work at the Winter Institute, partly as an oral historian, filming many of the institute's events and subjects, later taking charge of the Welcome Table program. April is so gentle that even her outrage comes out in a sweet-tempered fashion, but when it comes, it's unmistakable. She is especially furious at the state's continued attempts to undermine integrated public education. "Once it was seg academies, now it's charter schools. It's still about race here, and there's an orchestrated attempt to sabotage public funding for education." None of her anger is visible at the meetings she runs with patience and skill.

The group I'd just witnessed had been discussing the Mississippi state flag. Most of the black participants said they didn't care much; questions of poverty and education were more important than symbols. It was the white participants who insisted that the Confederate symbol is parallel to a swastika. The black participants said it was different, but they didn't say why. One older African American administrator pointed to his gut. "It tears me up inside every time I see it," he said, "but I don't show that to others."

The discussion ended without resolution, and I don't know if the group ever achieved consensus. "This is not all happy touchy-feely stuff," said April. "It can get very intense. In New Orleans there was one man who was really malicious, out to prove that our process was ridiculous. Another one showed up wearing a hunting knife just to intimidate us, but we don't play to the drama. He could have snapped, but he just fizzled out." Despite detractors, so many communities ask the Winter Institute to set up programs that the small staff has to turn down many requests.

Recently, April started a Welcome Table together with a Catholic priest in Vardaman, Mississippi. The sign at the town's entrance reads

A LITTLE PIECE OF HEAVEN

WELCOME TO VARDAMAN

SWEET POTATO CAPITAL OF THE WORLD

Who picks all those potatoes? Central American immigrants, most of whom came in legally many years ago and overstayed their visas. They don't talk about Confederate insignia, but about less symbolic problems: separated families, abusive employers, children threatening suicide, people no longer going to church for fear of being picked up by ICE. April guided the group as good-naturedly as always. Only when we left did she say, heatedly, that she wished she were an immigration lawyer.

On the drive back to Oxford, I switched on American Family Radio, which was holding a discussion about whether Jesus supports restrictions on immigration. Of course he does, said the speaker, and he supports a border wall too. How do we know? Revelation tells us about the heavenly gates, and if there are gates to the heavenly city, it stands to reason there's a wall. He also says you must wash your robe in the blood of the lamb in order to enter. That means you have to assimilate.

The date was February 8, 2017, should you care to check the source. I couldn't make this stuff up.

◦∾◦

"What keeps you going?" I asked Jennifer.

"Dark humor is helpful."

"Boredom is never a problem?"

"It's never the same thing twice."

"There's fear and depression, but not boredom," said Susan Glisson.

"I've never seen you get angry," Jennifer said to her. "Even when they were beating the shit out of us in New Orleans."

"I've only screamed at two people," said Susan. I won't repeat the names.

"When he said he was supposed to be the fourth person in the car—and he's just a jackass. He started screaming at me, so I gave it to him. I wish I had a dollar for every person who said they were supposed to be the fourth person in the car."

The car in question held the murdered heroes Chaney, Goodman, and Schwerner. The claim reminded me of ones I sometimes hear in Germany: *my grandfather was a secret resistance hero*. Like any other significant movement, the civil rights movement created longing, exaggeration, and outright lies. When the shouting is all over, who doesn't wish they'd been a hero?

Jackie Martin, another Winter Institute staffer, was a real civil rights hero at the age of fifteen. She was born in 1946 in McComb, one of the most violent spaces in Mississippi, but she prefers to talk about the warmth of the self-contained black community in which she was raised. Though her mother had only an eighth-grade education and her father had less, they made sure that life would be different for their ten children. The segregated library was closed to black people, so the community bought and shared what books they could. Jackie cannot remember knowing any white people as a child, for she was allowed to cross the tracks that separated the communities only when accompanied by her mother. "Emmett Till's lynching was pivotal, and our parents used it as a teaching moment. 'This is why we are so strict. We need to protect you from the white community.'" Still, she says her parents didn't raise their children to be fearful, just cautious. Nor were they raised to hate anybody. They just didn't understand why the white community had so many rights and they so few. Black veterans returning from World War II had changed the temperature of the South. Lauded as liberators in Europe, they returned to a place where they had very little liberty themselves. "If I was man enough to fight the war, I'm man enough for everything else," said Jackie's uncle. Like many other black veterans, he left the South, embittered, in the '50s.

"In the summer of '61 Bob Moses came to town." The legendary civil rights activist asked McComb's young people to work with him canvassing for voter registration. "Kids are courageous; that's why they make change. We didn't think about the danger," Jackie recalled. SNCC set up a school to teach people how to interpret the Constitution, one test African Americans had to pass in order to register to vote. It was the year of McComb's first sit-in. Following successful sit-ins in North Carolina, sixteen-year-old Brenda Travis tried to desegregate the local bus station by ordering a hamburger. She was given a one-year sentence for trespassing. Released early, she was expelled from the local high school. Jackie, her older brother, and 112 other students staged a walkout in protest, marching down to city hall and drawing a crowd of onlookers shocked to see so many black students walking.

Already trained in nonviolent protest tactics, the students were orderly. They sang, and when told to stop before city hall, they knelt and prayed. Bob Moses and Chuck McDew—"the guys, we called them"—did their best to keep the students safe, but they couldn't protect the white SNCC worker Bob Zellner from being beaten senseless by the mob or the students from being arrested. "One jailer was nice, and brought us water. I wish I could remember his name. One girl started crying because it meant her mother would lose her job. But we were going on adrenaline and the good feeling that we could change the world."

Most of the students were under eighteen, so they were released the same evening. When they returned to school the next day, the principal demanded that they sign a promise never to engage in civil disobedience again. They refused, and their parents stood behind them. They knew the community could stand together, and they weren't going to let the school take away one more right from a black child. Besides, they were proud. "Maybe they hadn't stood up themselves, but they raised kids who could."

All 114 were expelled and barred from the Mississippi public school system. They couldn't have known what a blessing that was: they were taught by Bob Moses, who already had an M.A. in philosophy from Harvard, Chuck McDew, and others in Mississippi's first Freedom School. Later, private religious schools offered to take them. The Tennessee civil rights hero Diane Nash took Jackie to Atlanta, and then to New York, to tell the story of the high school students who'd stood up to terror.

Jackie too left the state for a time, but she returned to her hometown, where she worked in local government administration for nearly thirty years. After she retired, she began to work part-time for the Winter Institute, where she often leads Welcome Tables with April. "We have an opportunity to show what race relations can be like," she says. "Mississippi is one of the best-kept secrets out there." Jackie doesn't believe the country will get rid of every racial problem, but she believes it can get better; she has seen it happen. At seventy-four, she still has the zeal to continue to work for it. Her highest hope for Mississippi is that it could be a model for America.

I asked her why so many white Southerners hate President Obama. Her answer was swift; she had no need to speculate. "I've had two white men tell me they're afraid he'll take revenge for all the things whites did to black people."

"But he hasn't! And his mother was white besides!"

"They're still afraid."

"I suppose it is a wonder that more black people haven't sought revenge."

"We're better than that," said Jackie.

∾

When I returned to Mississippi in 2017, Donald Trump had just been inaugurated. No one was echoing Brittney Cooper; the new president was everyone's problem, and people from all walks of life were engaged in doing something about it. There were not enough of them, but the diversity of engagement was both comforting and uplifting.

By early February, the Haitian American law professor Michèle Alexandre had organized a gathering of local activists who met in a cupcake shop to discuss first steps. "Pushback is only to be expected," she said. "I know this, though my heart is not yet healed. But we now know there's a plan to create chaos in all the major agencies: justice, environment, education. The first thing Trump did was to fire people so he could replace them with foxes guarding henhouses. Litigation comes later, and they want to drive us out of our minds trying to protect the vulnerable."

"We have to keep reminding ourselves that the majority didn't want this," said Daniel, a white volunteer.

"People assume that the loudest group is the majority," said the Winter Institute's Charles Tucker. "We have to repeat the same message we've been saying, but louder."

"We're not demonizing anyone who voted for Trump," said Susan Glisson.

The Winter Institute operates as a nonpartisan organization, believing that civil rights are human rights, independent of party lines. I understand the impulse: they want to open the circle as wide as they can. There are political conservatives who hold all people to be equally deserving of justice; there's no principled reason they can't be opposed to racism, sexism, and homophobia. But historically, it turns out that conservativism and tribalism usually go together, and not only in America. It's not a necessary connection, but it's nevertheless very real. Yet I understand why the group wanted to emphasize moral rather than political language, even if it did initially result in the unwieldy name A Group of Concerned Citizens Against Fear and the Erosion of American Principles.

Not three weeks later, the concerned citizens could no longer fit into a cupcake shop. The town hall meeting was held in Oxford's largest theater.

A pretty blond woman representing Moms Demand Action explained how to call legislators to push for new gun laws. A Southern Poverty Law Center attorney explained how their organization sued and bankrupted the Klan in the '70s and how they were now tracking the new hate groups that sprang up after Trump's election. Two students asked for support for the labor drive they were organizing to form a union at Nissan, the largest factory in the state, which had moved to Mississippi to profit from cheap, nonunion labor in the poor and jobless Delta. A gray-haired former journalist vowed to organize other retired women to chase down their representatives who were avoiding constituents' demands to protect Obama's health-care reform. All these and other community efforts are ongoing. Like other groups that blossomed after the election, they focus on local action they hope will have national repercussions. It is too soon to tell, but as I followed many such meetings, I was buoyed beyond anything I'd expected. Had I spent the first half year watching Trump's presidency from New York or Berlin, I might have despaired. Instead I was watching from what is, officially, the least educated state in the Union, and I joined the local chorus: if there's hope for Mississippi, there is hope for anywhere else.

By the beginning of March, an organization called Mississippi Votes was preparing for the 2018 midterm election. As the SNCC heroes had understood fifty years earlier, it was clear the only way to uphold civil rights was to elect congresspeople who care about them. Mississippi Votes was organizing volunteers to knock on every door in the state. Since Mississippi is too poor to invest in data management, no one knew who wasn't voting and why.

"It's like your grandfather who refuses to get an iPhone," said Ella, a young black woman who had worked for the Obama campaign in Iowa. As the first state in the country to vote in the national elections, Iowa has experience collecting vast amounts of data. In a training session for volunteers, Ella explained the eighteen crimes that lead to disenfranchisement in Mississippi. Some of them are strangely anachronistic, like timber theft. But many ex-convicts who committed other crimes don't know they are eligible to vote, even while serving their sentences. The door-to-door canvassing is intended to educate those who might think they don't have the right to vote, and to get them registered.

"It hasn't been done on this scale since Freedom Summer," said John, a tall young white man who was working with Ella. Organized by SNCC, Freedom Summer drew nearly a thousand Northern white students to help black Mississippians register to vote.

Voter registration is one of the causes Adam Flaherty took up. His first engagement in traditional forms of political action ended in failure: the proposed state constitutional amendment to adequately fund public schools did not gain enough votes to pass. Adam described that as heartbreaking, but it hasn't dented his sense of duty to improve Mississippi rather than become part of the brain drain the state bemoans but does little to stop.

I first met Adam after giving a talk about the differences between German and American ways of working-off-the-past. The blond, mild-looking young man raised his hand tentatively to ask, "Do you think the difference is due to the difference between Habermas's discourse ethics and Rawls's notion of reflective equilibrium?" I don't, actually, but it was hardly the question I expected to hear from a junior studying at the University of Mississippi. I got to know this young man, who appeared more extraordinary with every meeting, quite well. He's the first in his family to attend university; his father, an occasional construction worker, has cussed him out for becoming a "college-educated prick." He escaped the troubles in his difficult family by immersing himself in literature and theater, eventually winning a Rhodes scholarship to study philosophy, politics, and economics at the original Oxford. Adam turned down the award when his ailing mother had a heart attack. Living at his grandparents' home just outside Oxford, Mississippi, he manages to keep faith both with his growing moral and political principles and with the family who rejects all of them. His father, Adam told me, finds Jefferson Davis to be a better American than Abraham Lincoln; his relatives all voted for Trump. Adam thought his way out of their worldviews years ago.

"Empathy has a way of eating at you. It's not enough to have a dialogue within the bounds of reasonable discourse. I will not sacrifice my autonomy for the sake of my father's redemption. But it's an area of my life where there's an opportunity for me to do good. It's entirely possible that the consequences will be nothing. But I think consequences aren't all that matter, you know? With philosophers"—here he paused, looking thoughtful—"the South is a perfect test case for moral and political theory," he said, hurrying off to register new voters. Adam is immensely concerned with the connections between reason and emotion, and whether it's possible to raise people's consciousness of injustice through rational argument. Surrounded most of his life by people who seem immune to it, it's small wonder that he clings to philosophy like a swimmer gripping a raft in a storm. Upon graduating, however, he chose not to pursue it professionally, but opted to teach mathematics in the Delta with the Teach for America program.

Buka Okoye stood out in the seminar on philosophy and social justice

that Jennifer and I taught together. Tall, dark, and handsome, Buka is the
son of Nigerian immigrants who live in Jackson. He was a senior majoring
in public policy, but he knew a lot of philosophy, and his comments in the
seminar were always measured, forceful, and completely serious. When he
had something to say, everyone else stopped talking. Still, I didn't fully appreciate him until we spent two hours talking philosophy during a Memphis march commemorating Martin Luther King's assassination. Slipping
toward the back of the line so we could hear each other over the resplendent
marching band, we went through Kant's idea of autonomy, Rousseau's notion of democracy, and were starting on the question of whether Heidegger
can be deconstructed when we reached the Lorraine Motel.

As president of the campus chapter of the NAACP, Buka led the university in reconsidering its Confederate symbols. The Charleston massacre set
a wave in motion that prompted many universities to examine the remnants
of white supremacy still glorified on their campuses. The University of Mississippi was no different. It took four months, and considerable student pressure, to remove the state flag from its entrance. "My school is finally taking
a stance," said the student organizer Dominique Scott. "Which side of the
war do you choose to be on?"

If it took the university 150 years to conclude it was not on the side of the
Confederacy, well, better late than never. There remained the question of
what should be done with its twenty-seven Civil War–related historical sites.
To no one's surprise, the university appointed a committee that originally
consisted of four retired white men. "Any wonder why their version of history came out so poorly?" said Buka. He led the student protest, supported
by many faculty, that succeeded in enlarging the committee on contextualization to include people of color, whose first focus was the giant Johnny
Reb statue at the university entrance. The first committee had proposed a
plaque that made no mention of slavery, a position that implicitly endorses
the common Southern view that slavery was not the cause of the war at
all. Instead, it promoted itself with the words "The university admitted its
first African-American student, James Meredith, in October 1962 and has
worked since to promote inclusiveness in all its endeavors."

With the exception of a building named for Mississippi's most racist
governor, James Vardaman, who openly advocated lynching as a means to
suppress black voting, the committee was not in favor of renaming buildings or removing statues and signs. Rather, it supported contextualization,
a process that simultaneously preserves offensive material by embedding it
in historical context and distances the institution from assenting to it. I'd

seen plenty of instances of the process in Berlin; the Academy of Science's decision to erect a plaque explaining that the swastika mosaic on the floor predated the Nazis was only one of them. So I was especially curious to hear it discussed at the town meeting called by the university after the committee had completed another version of its report.

The little Belfry church, oldest African Methodist Episcopal congregation in the county, was packed full that evening. The meeting was chaired by Don Cole, who began his career at the University of Mississippi as one of the black students expelled from it for demonstrating for more black faculty, and athletes, in 1969. Now he's a professor of mathematics and assistant to the chancellor for multicultural affairs. Cole opened the meeting by noting that the University of Mississippi is further along in the contextualization process than Yale, Harvard, and Stanford. Before submitting its final report to the chancellor, the committee—now in subcommittees, including a subcommittee that reviews the work of other subcommittees—wanted to call this meeting to ensure that the process was transparent and the community had input.

The parts of the community that showed up that evening were almost exclusively white, and very happy to offer input. One white man after another stood up in that black church and described himself as a proud university alumnus, naming the date of his graduation. For good measure, one alumnus added the graduation dates of his brothers and brothers-in-law. Their positions would be familiar to anyone who has followed recent American debates. *You cannot rewrite the past, you should not dig up old bones, what may be distasteful to us was just fine back then. Let things be, don't DESTROY Ole Miss TRADITIONS, things have already gone too far. For the sake of God, the state, and the university, do not take one step more!* One man came armed with a poster on which he had written tables and numbers. "I'm in economic development, and we know that sixty-five percent of all tourists seek travel experiences that retain their historical character. It's a 192-billion-dollar industry." He added that alumni donations could be affected by the proposed changes.

This ruckus was not raised, mind you, by a proposal to remove anything but the name of the lynching cheerleader James Vardaman. All that was up for discussion was the addition of a number of plaques.

Allen Coon, a tall, blond student who'd been active in the drive to take down the Confederate flag, questioned the distinction between Vardaman and other racists still honored with buildings in their names. "Vardaman talked the talk, but the others walked the walk. What's the difference between praising lynching and owning black bodies?"

"We hear your question," said Don Cole, looking uncomfortable. "We are still debating it."

Chuck Ross, a black professor of African American history who was also a member of the committee, looked ready to burst. "This is not a modern interpretation. People of the time were very clear about what they were doing. I cannot do my job as a historian without noting that these people left letters. They left memoirs. They were proud of what they did." One white alumnus rose to support him. He urged that what was at issue was not denying history, but expanding it. "Maybe when we have an Ida B. Wells Hall we could have a Vardaman Hall too." Wells, the courageous writer who fought against lynching, was born in nearby Holly Springs.

After several hours Cole concluded the town meeting by quoting Socrates: an unexamined life is not worth living. "This is what we do in academia," said Cole. "By putting everything on the table and examining it, we think the truth will come out. The committee members have devoted their lives to this university. They don't want to destroy it, only improve it." Cole walks a very narrow line every day.

In an article for *The Atlantic*, the historian Timothy Ryback compared the work of the committee on contextualization to recent events at the original Oxford University. Students who protested the statue honoring Cecil Rhodes were told they could love it or leave Oxford—in polite Oxbridge tones, of course. Ryback argued that the original Oxford could learn something from its namesake.[11] It's no surprise that the committee for contextualization posted the article on its website, but those behind the scenes in Mississippi were not so sure. A few days after the town meeting, I interviewed Chuck Ross. Did he think the whole effort was a matter of window dressing? Did the university want real change?

"That's a very complex kind of a question," said Ross. He paused, shaking his head slowly, deciding where to begin. "From the time that James Meredith got the opportunity to come here in 1962, many have argued that we as a university have been stripping ourselves of our Southern identity. They won't go so far as to say we lost something beginning with integration, but this institution has just been the standard for Southern pride. It's been a very effective and vital way of keeping classes of whites from challenging each other."

Ross is skeptical that real change will occur in his lifetime. There are people who want to move the university forward—if only to "make sure that people like yourself, the public media who come to scrutinize, can see signs of progress." On the other side are the alumni who identify with Ole Miss, the university as it used to be. "If you want them to donate money to support buildings like the one we're sitting in now, then they want to feel comfortable." After the town meeting, he'd spoken to one of the alumni who was opposed to changing anything, including the name of Vardaman Hall. The man's relation to the university was entirely nostalgic; he wanted things to be left as they were in his undergraduate days. Ross responded by suggesting that the university go back to having an all-white football team, which would mean "you would never have any chance of beating Alabama or the others, because the game has changed and African American athletes are doing all the heavy lifting." In Mississippi and Alabama, only God is more exalted than football; the alumnus was so appalled at the suggestion, he did not understand it. Nor did he understand Ross's point, which was that if you want black athletes to win the games for you, you shouldn't force them to parade around Confederate symbols.

"The university is so saturated with those symbols that many African Americans on campus just give up. Your grandmother, your aunt, your father, everybody's told you: you can't change white folk, it's their school."

For Chuck Ross, that attitude is not an option. He's at the university for the long haul, teaching history to black students and white ones. With his work on the contextualization committee, he tries to create, at the least, sensitivity to the problems those symbols invoke, even if he's doubtful about the possibility of deep change. Mississippi's governor declared April to be Confederate Heritage Month, a clear reaction to the fact that the federal government has declared February to be Black History Month.

I have always been wary of Black History Months and women's studies departments, believing they confine their subjects to reconstructed ghettos. *Of interest to black people. Good work for a woman.* Those are the unspoken but absolute assumptions such programs unintentionally reinforce. I want to live in a world where everyone who studies American history reads Frederick Douglass and everyone who studies English reads George Eliot—just to stay with the nineteenth century. If they are cloistered, another generation will grow up thinking they can learn American history without Douglass, English literature without Eliot. Intellectual segregation is no better than any other kind.

But I know the other side of the argument. Chuck Ross teaches African American history because the texts and the problems he wants to teach don't get the hearing they deserve in standard history departments. He can get discouraged because he believes that most white Mississippians he meets are still fully committed to the Confederate mentality that has dominated the Southern political world since Reagan was elected in 1980. Going to vote in 2016, he was struck by the huge number of white male voters. "They were looking at each other and connecting informally. I saw very few black males, I saw more black females, and I knew that if this is representative of America, it's not going to work. When you see that the most unqualified candidate ever won the election, it is a total backlash to Barack Obama."

I thoroughly agreed, but the young people I kept meeting in Mississippi made me more hopeful. It wasn't only Adam and Buka. Though I knew they were in a minority, I kept finding others who were outstandingly bright and outstandingly committed, thirsting for justice, hungry for change.

"I don't think you've had much of an opportunity to interact with the large number of people in fraternities and sororities," said Ross.

He was right. I tended to avoid the Square on Friday and Saturday nights when they come out. The boys flaunted expensive cars, the girls flaunted skintight designer dresses, and long before the stars began to twinkle, they all began to weave. Greek life, as they call it, is probably the most central part of their college experience, as it is in many state universities, North and South. Students who came to me have already chosen to be outsiders.

I asked Ross a final question. "What do you think the differences would be if you'd wound up teaching African American history in Ohio?"

"Oh, it wouldn't be as exciting. Here history is a living, breathing thing. It's not just something in the books you write and have students discuss. You have an opportunity to live it."

A year after our conversation, the committee had made its final recommendation, and the chancellor opened the ceremony at which the disputed plaque was unveiled. Rita Schwerner Bender, Michael Schwerner's widow, had suggested a simple solution for the Johnny Reb statue: just add the Mississippi articles of secession, which make plain that slavery was the heart of the Confederate cause. But Rita wasn't on the committee, which eventually came up with this:

> As Confederate veterans were dying in increasing numbers, memorial associations across the South built monuments in their memory. These monuments were often used to promote an ideology known as the "Lost Cause," which claimed that the Confederacy had been established to defend states' rights and that slavery was not the principal cause of the Civil War. Residents of Oxford and Lafayette County dedicated this statue, approved by the university, in 1906. Although the monument was created to honor the sacrifice of local Confederate soldiers, it must also remind us that the defeat of the Confederacy actually meant freedom for millions of people. On the

evening of September 30, 1962, this statue was a rallying point for opponents of integration.

This historic statue is a reminder of the university's divisive past. Today, the University of Mississippi draws from that past a continuing commitment to open its hallowed halls to all who seek truth, knowledge, and wisdom.

"I'm a trained historian," said Jennifer Stollman, who had been a member of the committee, "and I'm bored by looking at it." That's an outcome that might technically satisfy both sides. Spend months coming up with a statement that's historically accurate and put it in language so dull it's more likely to put people to sleep than to rile them up. It's not surprising that the solution was put together in an academic institution.

In 2019, student groups voted to remove Johnny Reb altogether. Whether the state will allow them to do so remains to be seen.

⌒

Local citizens in Oxford often oppose, more or less politely, the efforts made by progressive forces within the university to enlighten them. The love of local citizens for their idea of the university only redoubles their efforts to silence it. When the Winter Institute offered to conduct a Welcome Table for teachers of the local school district, some of the town turned out to oppose them. They were led by one Lee Habeeb, who works for right-wing radio star Laura Ingraham.

Habeeb had had his eye on the Winter Institute for some time, and on hearing of the planned workshop at his daughter's school, he went online. Three Winter Institute staff members had private Facebook accounts upon which they'd posted their immediate reactions to the 2016 election. Those reactions were typical for millions on each of the coasts, and indeed throughout the world. (*Die Zeit* and *Der Spiegel* are Germany's most respected weeklies. Days after the election, *Der Spiegel*'s cover depicted Trump as a malevolent comet aimed straight at the Earth. *Die Zeit* opted for a weeping Statue of Liberty and the words "Oh My God" in English.) In Mississippi, however, the vast majority of white voters supported Trump, and the comments of the Winter Institute staffers were unacceptable. Jennifer Stollman wrote about angry rural white voters and about taking a moment to weep and rest before getting up to continue the fight for equity. Jake McGraw retweeted Marine Le Pen and said the fascists of the world are uniting. Melody Frierson posted a notice offering a teach-in on resistance for Inauguration Day. All these were photographed, photocopied, and distributed by Habeeb under the heading "Should intolerant activists teach tolerance in our schools?"

Habeeb demanded a discussion at the town school board meeting, which was held in the Oxford Middle School auditorium. Like so many institutional spaces, this one was lit by ghastly, ghostly overhead bulbs. Apart from a large American flag and a small sign reading IN GOD WE TRUST, the only decoration that relieved the gray gloom was a small collage on the blackboard featuring a yellow star with the word *Jude*, decorated with tinfoil and string. Clearly the students had been learning about racism—far away, and in another country. The room was packed to overflowing, and the school board members were trying to keep order. They had imposed a limit of ten minutes on every speaker, which Habeeb challenged by demanding to add his wife's minutes to his own.

"We'd like to hear your wife speak for herself," said the school board chair, seeping Southern charm.

Several people stood to speak in defense of the proposal, and the Winter Institute. An Italian American who'd participated in a Welcome Table called it one of the most noble and uplifting experiences of his life. Speaking for the institute, April Grayson said they'd worked hard to find a model that enables people to discuss difficult questions. Her voice was shaking slightly as she told the packed hall that she welcomed this kind of dialogue.

Those who were angry refused to be calmed:

The Facebook posts prove they are a bunch of liberal extremists, however kumbaya their website appears to be.

Not one of those staff members is conservative, and they talk about tolerance. I don't want anyone teaching my daughter about race.

Nothing wrong with their plan, it's the people who teach it. Do you want Che Guevara or Stalin teaching your kids? One of the staff has a Che Guevara T-shirt on his Facebook page—the butcher of Cuba, they called him.

What the hell are microaggressions: fifty things my kid won't be able to talk about because of political correctness?

I'm a Christian, not just on Sunday, and these people come from the outside![12]

It was instructive to hear claims that, with minor variations, were made sixty years earlier in opposition to integration. *Anyone actively opposed to racism is an outside agitator disrupting a peaceful way of life, and an un-Christian communist to boot.* The atmosphere in the room was so tense that I was surprised when the school board voted, 6–0, to allow the Winter Institute to offer seminars for those teachers who chose to participate.

When the chairwoman announced the decision, her ambivalence was unmistakable. In honey-sweet tones she said, "What Mr. Habeeb said about Facebook posts by certain individuals is concerning to me, I'm not going to sugarcoat it. But the Winter Institute staff are all professionals, so they won't bring their personal views into the training. I talked to the Mississippi police chiefs who worked with Dr. Stollman, and they said they'd recommend her in a heartbeat." And with some general remarks about what's beneficial for our children, she closed the meeting. The victory felt Pyrrhic. True, my friends at the Winter Institute would be allowed to bring their program to the Oxford public schools. But how many of the assembled voices would continue, politely or not, to undermine it?

～∽∾

"You're doing the Lord's work," said Curtis Wilkie. We were seated at Square Books waiting for Richard Ford to begin a reading. I'd been introduced to Wilkie as a visiting scholar at the Winter Institute.

"*They're* doing the Lord's work," I responded quickly. "I'm just writing about it."

Curtis Wilkie's ties to Oxford go way, way back. Not only did he study here in the fateful year of '62; his great-grandfather, a Confederate soldier, was also a proud graduate of Ole Miss. Curtis was born in 1940, and his book *Dixie* described how, thanks to encounters with the black civil rights leader Aaron Henry, he went from being an ordinary Mississippian to a fierce critic of its racist policies. Curtis became a reporter who covered Martin Luther King in the Delta, Jimmy Carter in the White House, and any number of Jews and Arabs in Israel and Palestine. He returned to Oxford in 2002 as progressive policies were gaining traction in the South. He now teaches journalism and Southern history at the university, when he isn't working or sipping sweet tea in his exquisitely flowering garden. The Sunday afternoon I met him there, he was distressed by his home state.

"When I wrote *Dixie* nearly twenty years ago, I was very optimistic about where we were going, particularly racially. That's when I decided to come back home." Now, he says, Mississippi is regressing. Reliving battles that were fought in the '60s. White people "have an appalling record of voting against their interests because to do otherwise would help the blacks."

"You really think it's that simple?"

"In Mississippi, in the end, everything goes back to race."

For Curtis Wilkie, Lee Habeeb is a symbol of a national rightward turn. Though Curtis hadn't been to the school board meeting, he'd heard plenty about it. As a Southerner who never lost his drawl or his ability to defend the South against Northern condescension, and still had a place on the national stage, he counts as Oxford aristocracy: someone whose left-leaning views will be forgiven because he comes with pedigrees that make most things forgivable. He'd followed Habeeb since he first surfaced a few years earlier in discussions over the university's treatment of Confederate symbols. Curtis believed he was part of a shadowy group that receives money from the Koch brothers.

"Habeeb is smart enough not to embarrass himself publically," he said. But as a student, Curtis had known groups that went much further. "They were known as the Rebel Underground, and they would slide racist tracts under your dorm room door. Before Meredith. After Meredith. We had two chancellors in a row who stood up to those bastards." Chancellors Robert Khayat and Dan Jones were respected by most faculty and many students. Although Khayat's liberal views were hardly welcomed by the Institutions of Higher Learning—the governor-appointed body that oversees state universities—he raised too much money to be disposable. The IHL did fire his successor, Dan Jones, because they found his positions on Confederate symbols "too liberal." Curtis wanted to give the new chancellor, Jeffrey Vitter, a chance. "He's not as activist as we'd like, but so far he hasn't come down on the side of the demons." It was tepid praise, but whoever the chancellor might be in the future, Curtis believed that the forward movement at the university was impossible to stop. When he started teaching in 2002, the black student body was 4 percent of the total; now it's nearly 20 percent. There's a resolute LGBT movement that would have been unimaginable before. And the Winter Institute is doing the Lord's work—in Oxford, but also in the Delta, in Neshoba County, and elsewhere.

"I think we're all beaten down." Curtis sighed. "In part because of Trump, but also the governor, the legislature, the general mood in Mississippi. Things are not getting better here, but they are on the Ole Miss campus."

I asked him what he'd do if he were the governor of his beloved state. The thought experiment wasn't crazy; he had once been a governor's son-in-law. His answer was immediate: he would focus on improving education at every level. The current government, he said, is determined to do whatever it can to undermine it. He believes that the movement that supports charter schools as alternatives to public education is part of a very effective right-wing conspiracy.

Sooner or later, every Mississippian I met—black or white, progressive or conservative—raised the question of education. By most measures, the state of education in Mississippi is the worst in the nation. James Meredith says that education has always been the most important subject of his life. His autobiography concludes with a Challenge for America: "I challenge every American citizen to commit right now to help children in the public schools in their community, especially those with disadvantaged students" before listing a host of practical suggestions. Everyone, he argues, whether they have children or not, has a stake in the quality of public education.

I have always believed in what Jean Améry called the central truth of the much-maligned Enlightenment: "knowledge leads to recognition, and recognition to morality." Améry did not come by that belief lightly. After spending two years in Auschwitz, the Austrian philosopher wrote the most searing account of the Holocaust I ever read. There are more gruesome descriptions, but Améry's analysis of what Auschwitz did to the mind seems to leave reason damned. Yet he spent the rest of his life writing the twentieth century's strongest defenses of the Enlightenment, which he saw as the only power against the irrationalism at the heart of fascism. Even further, he believed that the only hope for fulfilling the one truly human task—giving meaning to the meaningless—lies in "the benevolent optimism of the Enlightenment with its constant values of freedom, reason, justice, and truth."[13]

Upholding that belief today is more than complex. It's a matter of combating false consciousness, the ways in which ideologies and advertisements blind people to their real human interests through a combination of propaganda and distraction. And so often, those who write and pay for the propaganda believe it themselves. *If all the people want is bread and circuses, what's wrong with giving it to them?* Claims like that are usually made by people whose own goals reach no higher than French pastry and box seats at the theater. You can't really call them deceptive; flooding the airwaves with mind-numbing entertainment instead of culture that challenges is hardly at odds with their own way of life. The tastes may be different, but there are classy ways to numb your mind as well as vulgar ones. Why shouldn't those who own the means of production peddle the same stupor to others?

But these are complicated ways of opposing the Enlightenment, and in Mississippi the opposition is a blunt force. I'd no idea that those who perceived educated African Americans as a threat were still explicit about it until a white waitress came up to the table in Jackson where I was eating dinner with Charles Tucker. They'd known each other for years. "See that table over there?" The waitress motioned, lowering her voice just a tad. "One of them just said, 'If we let them get educated, they'd figure out how badly we were screwing them,' and the others laughed." I was shocked that anyone would be this open in a public restaurant, perhaps just as shocked that they would admit it to themselves at all. But then Mississippi is a place where the resistance to the Enlightenment is out in the open, making it anything but obsolete. No wonder the place never failed to move me.

∾

There's another ghost drifting through corners and conversations in Oxford, and he isn't even dead. When people talk about the university, James Meredith is never very far away. I knew he lived in Jackson, and I wanted to meet him, but no one I knew was willing to introduce me. They'd all met him on one occasion or another, but said they didn't know him well enough to ask. He didn't come to Oxford often, he hated the statue, he's hard to talk to anyway. Or so I was told. With less than a week to go before I returned to Berlin, I'd given up hope of interviewing him.

Instead I went to Hernando, just south of Memphis, to interview Robert Lee Long, editor of the local paper there. I'd met him at a town meeting in Oxford, where he spoke passionately about his project to exchange the current Mississippi flag for an earlier one that was designed in 1817. Yes, he allowed, it has a magnolia, and that has baggage too, but "you're never going to get the good ole boys to give up their stars and bars without a shred of history. What the good ole boys rail against is this idea of political correctness." Curious to know how a seventh-generation white Mississippian came to champion such a project, I went to the office of the *DeSoto Times*, whose weekly edition was about to go into production.

With all the allure of Southern hospitality, Robert apologized for the fact that he could only give me an hour before his staff began to chafe. He was glad to talk about his cause, which he sees as the only realistic way to remove the Confederate icon. "Robert E. Lee himself said, 'Furl the flag, boys, take it down.'" Robert Lee Long is distantly related to Robert E. Lee's family, but it's not the only famous Southern family among his relations. He was not, he said, "necessarily" named for the commander in chief of the Confederate Army. His people were cabinetmakers on one side, cotton brokers on the other, and his great-great-grandfather, a member of the Dixie Boys of Company K, was captured in the Battle of Lookout Mountain and sent to a prisoner of war camp in Rock Island, Illinois. "He was there for over a year and weighed eighty-two pounds when he came out. I would have every right, if I wanted, to carry some kind of grudge, some kind of cross, had I not had an enlightened grandmother in Memphis."

Lucy Wilkerson, Robert's grandmother, used the family cotton money to go to university and thereafter to travel the world. "There's nothing like getting out and seeing how other cultures live to really change your world-view," Robert said. "She marched with Coretta Scott King, and she was a true Methodist minister's wife, embracing the humanity of man." Robert's father, on the other hand, was very much of the Old South. Robert said he became a newspaperman in the cauldron of political confusion that marked his family; he wanted to investigate and find some truth.

He began his journalism career in high school, when the school paper sent him to interview both James Meredith and Ross Barnett for the twentieth anniversary of what was called the Meredith Crisis. The principal warned him that the governor, who was frail, should be treated with caution, but after flattering the old man, seventeen-year-old Robert asked Barnett some tougher questions. Had he changed his views in the past twenty years? "He was deaf, but his secretary leaned down to his ear and said, 'He's asking about James Meredith.' It was like the old man had been struck by lightning. That was his legacy. With every ounce of fervor, and that chin just shaking and that turkey wattle just wattling, he said, 'Young man, I have not changed my views one iota, and you can put that in your paper.'" The ex-governor had a heart attack a few hours later, but Robert took no responsibility. "He had faced far tougher journalists than a high school kid. I asked the question that had to be asked because in the early eighties people still looked upon him with reverence."

Long wanted to continue to talk about Barnett, but I interrupted him. "What did James Meredith say at the interview?"

As it turned out, Robert Lee Long's relationship with Meredith went far beyond that high school interview. Just the previous year, he and Meredith had taken a train trip across the country, speaking against racism at five colleges in the West. Robert worried about protecting the man whose life had been threatened so many times, but Meredith was disarming—even to a man who came to threaten him. "Perhaps because he's a conservative himself, I don't know. He's just a free spirit. He doesn't espouse any particular line."

My head spun ever so slightly. I was leaving the country in four days, during which I'd already planned several meetings. I settled back in the tiny newsroom to listen to this paradigm of enlightened Mississippi, as he put it himself. Robert was arguing that it wasn't just the blood and agony of the civil rights workers that changed Mississippi; Mississippi had to change itself. "Believe it or not, it was Nixon's silent majority that had to have a soul-searching moment and say 'You know what? Racism is wrong. *I* have been wrong. I've got to change.' People like my own dad."

Robert turned back to an earlier question. "You asked me if I believe in collective guilt. Yes, well, I kind of sort of do." It was an interesting locution for an otherwise articulate man. "Because when you have the original sin of slavery in Mississippi, there has to be an atonement. I'm one of those sinners that will sip whiskey on a Friday afternoon, but I teach a Sunday school class." With the right sort of atonement, Robert believes, Mississippi can shine. In the endearing local patriotism I had come to expect, he began a love song to his home. "We've always been told *you're from Mississippi, you'll never amount to anything*, yet we have a state of overachievers in the arts, in music, in literature. I love the fact that we have Leontyne Price, we have Morgan Freeman, we have Elvis Presley. I remember seeing Miz Eudora Welty writing in her window. I want my state to be the best. We engage each other in conversation, we tell these stories, we enjoy our spirits, we enjoy good gospel music whether we're believers or not. I yearn for the day when we can truly embrace, as Lincoln said, the better angels of our nature."

Atonement, he believes, begins with acknowledging history. "I've got a thirteen-year-old, and I'm trying to inculcate in her the importance of history. Not from some textbook standpoint or to win prizes—no, it's so you won't make the same mistakes your grandfather or your great-grandfather made. You'll be able to look at yourself in the mirror and say *I'm a good person and I'm contributing to the world I live in*. I get passionate about it, and my daughter gets tired of me saying it, but it's true."

As a newspaperman, Robert follows international news more closely than most Americans. He ended by saying that he hoped Europe wouldn't make the same mistake with its Muslim immigrants that America had made with its people of color. He stood up, apologetically; it was a Friday afternoon and the paper was in need of printing.

"I'm wondering if I might ask you a favor," I said, rushing to get the question out before I faltered. "It sounds like you're pretty close to James Meredith. I've been wanting to meet him since I arrived. Could you possibly put in a good word for me?"

"I'll call Judy right now," Robert answered. "His wife makes all his arrangements."

Leaving his staff more anxious by the minute, Robert picked up the telephone. Judy Meredith didn't answer, but he left a long message asking her to call the woman from Berlin who was writing about what Americans, among others, might learn from Germany's responses to its racist past. In the time I had left, I was doubtful she would answer, but I thanked Robert profusely and happily agreed to take a selfie outside the newspaper office. He pointed to the road leaving town, where I could see the marker where Meredith had been shot. In 1966 Meredith had announced a March Against Fear, planning to walk some two hundred miles from Memphis to Jackson. His goal was to encourage black people to vote. A year after the passage of the Voting Rights Act, most were too frightened to register. If they saw a black man walking alone through the state, surely it would lay their fears to rest.

Sixteen miles into the march, Meredith was pumped full of buckshot by a white man in the bushes by the road. The press initially reported his death, but a quick operation saved his life, though some of the buckshot remains in his body to this day. Martin Luther King Jr. flew to the hospital in Memphis and vowed to continue the march. King was joined by a host of other civil rights leaders, and the march swelled into the thousands. By the time they reached the state capital, six thousand new voters had been registered. Later reporters would see the March Against Fear as Meredith's second blow against Mississippi despotism, which together with his integration of the university marked the end of Jim Crow everywhere in the South.[14]

I photographed the plaques that marked the spot as part of the Mississippi Freedom Trail and returned, rather glumly, to my car.

The gloom changed to elation the next morning when I got a call from Judy Meredith. Sure, I could visit. He's at home all afternoon. Would I like to come today?

Jennifer offered to drive me to Jackson, and she was insistent all down the highway. "This is an honor. He is an icon, and you're invited to his home. An icon, remember? Think about what you want to ask him, because we'll only stay an hour. Any more would be rude." Her well-meant admonitions left me more nervous by the minute. Two hours later, in the midst of a gushing rainstorm, we arrived at a house so modest we couldn't believe it was the right one, and we circled the block checking numbers.

Inside, a few reproductions of African art graced the walls, and Fox News was running on a large television. James Meredith looked more impish than imposing in white khakis, a button-down shirt to match, and a baseball cap that said OLE MISS. Four of his grandchildren were seated stiffly around the dining table in the living room corner. Ranging in age from about ten to sixteen, each stood up to shake our hands, looking shyly at the floor before sitting down again.

"I told you," Meredith said to them, "this lady's going to tell you something about Germany. I'm going to shut my mouth," he said, turning to me. "And maybe you can give me a summary of how Germany handled the problem you're talking about."

African Americans I met everywhere in the South were so fascinated to hear about Germany's transformation that I was almost sick of talking about it, but this was James Meredith. I wasn't prepared, but I had to oblige. I talked about how Germans after the war talked like Southern defenders of Lost Cause mythology: for twenty years they saw themselves as the war's worst victims, refusing to admit any wrong. How their children had erupted in the '60s, asking why they should respect the authority of people who committed one of the worst crimes in history. I talked about the way the working-off process had started from below, and how long it took the government to act. I talked about monuments, mentioning the stumbling stones that dot the sidewalks—

"Like the Hollywood stars?" asked Meredith.

"In a sense. Except they don't have just a name, they have a date of birth and the date they were deported to a concentration camp."

"Right on the sidewalk?"

"Yes, sir. The idea is that people should remember every day what was done to their neighbors and do what they can to make up for it."

"Get out of here," said Judy Meredith incredulously. She's a handsome professor of mass communications who had once been to Berlin herself as a member of the Fulbright Commission. "I really enjoyed the beer. But that was a while ago."

"They've been working on things like this on and off for fifty years. My interest is in figuring out how to translate that. Every place is different, but if they did it, why can't we do something like that here?"

"I can tell you," said James Meredith. "Because America never got their butt kicked. Besides, the problem is different. Black people built this country. They say cotton was like oil? It was bigger than oil. Cotton changed the way people dressed all over the world. I'm not trying to discourage you," he continued. "I'm trying to encourage you. I still want to read your book. But you may have a problem. I promised God I wasn't going to lie no more."

"I hope not" was all I knew to say. "I know you've told the story of how you integrated the university many times. You're wearing an Ole Miss hat. I want to ask what you think of the University of Mississippi today."

"I was very upset the last time I was there, when I saw the statue of the Confederate soldier. Last time I was there, they had my name on it two times. Do you know what they had the audacity to do? Take my name off. I wasn't shocked, I was stunned. I'll never forgive Ole Miss for that."

It was an odd kind of outrage, given the reason his name was taken off the plaque. Students and faculty had complained that the plaque as it stood was an attempt to absolve the university of everything that happened after 1962. *After James Meredith integrated the university, it has worked since to promote inclusiveness in all its endeavors.* It was a stance that failed to do justice to the violence and intensity that took place in Oxford at the time, much less the halting way the university continued to drag its feet on ending racism in the years thereafter. Meredith's indignation over the absence of his name was even odder, given that he'd often called for the destruction of the statue he has called a graven image.

In his autobiography, he cheerfully admitted to charges that he has both a Messiah complex and a colossal ego. I thought he'd be pleased to hear about the James Meredith tour I'd taken with the Men of Excellence months earlier.

"You know what I like best?" said Meredith. "The coats and the ties."

"You were wearing a coat and tie in all the pictures," I said. Clearly they were trying to look like him, despite their long hair.

"I do have a question for you," he said. "Do they know how bad a dude James Meredith was?"

The seventh of thirteen children, Meredith was born in 1933 in Kosciusko, Mississippi. One of his great-grandfathers was a white man. Given the incidence of rape on Southern plantations, that was hardly uncommon. More uncommon was the fact that this great-grandfather was "the founding father of white supremacy," who wrote the notorious Mississippi Constitution of 1890, which set aside every aspect of citizenship African Americans had gained with Reconstruction and established the notorious Black Codes that severely restricted civil rights. Another great-grandfather was the leader of the Choctaw Nation. James's father, whom he adored, owned a small timber farm and "was known as the hardest-working and most dependable man in the county."[15] He was the first, and for many years the only, black man to vote in Attala County. "Three years before I was born, my father and his neighbors borrowed $310 from the Merchant and Farmers' Bank to build a one-room schoolhouse," Meredith told us. "There was one teacher and eight grades. At three, I started at that school, and by the time I was six, I knew just about everything that was taught there. And because of that, every place I went where there was an opportunity, I was able to take advantage of the opportunity." When he was seven, his father told him he had a divine mission; he must bring together the best of the white and the best of the black and save the world.[16]

Like his father, who had no qualms about pointing a shotgun at an intruding policeman, James Meredith never believed in nonviolence. After finishing high school, he joined the U.S. Air Force, where he served, both at home and overseas, for nine years. He still considers himself a military man, whose purpose as a soldier was "to secure my country and its principles against any enemy. I saw white supremacy as one of the most powerful enemies the United States faced."[17] The issue, he believes, was not civil rights, but American citizenship. Meredith insists on military metaphors. His goal in 1962 was not to integrate the University of Mississippi, which he viewed as a minor and timid objective, but to "physically and psychologically shatter the system of white supremacy in Mississippi and eventually all of America, with the awesome physical force of the United States military machine."[18] In the two years when the state of Mississippi fought the federal injunction that granted him a place at the University of Mississippi, Meredith received enough credits to graduate by attending Jackson State, a historically black university. His object was not education. Rather, he sought to "drive a stake through the heart of the beast."[19] He was opposed to Dr. King's idea of nonviolence, believing that only overwhelming physical force applied by the federal government could overcome white supremacy. Meredith was averse to flooding the streets with brutalized bodies; far better, he thought, to flood the courts with lawsuits that would trigger American troops to enforce federal court orders.[20]

That's exactly what happened in Oxford in the fall of '62, though not without some foot-dragging by the Kennedy brothers. By all accounts, Attorney General Robert Kennedy was genuinely committed to the civil rights movement, but he and his brother were worried about losing Southern support in the next election. (As Lyndon Johnson later predicted, federal support for the civil rights movement did lead most Southern Democrats to join the Republican Party.) For almost two years, the Kennedys negotiated with Governor Barnett to find a solution that would allow them to enforce federal law while allowing him to save face. But compromise proved hopeless, and President Kennedy was under international pressure. The dogs and fire hoses and beatings and bombings that accompanied the civil rights movement had made world headlines, and the Soviet Union did not refrain from pointing them out. *Doesn't the violence against African Americans show that American proclamations about liberty and justice are nothing but hype?* This reasonable question became a problem for the Kennedy administration. Finally, it sent federal troops to put down the armed insurrection taking place in Oxford, and when the first set of troops proved insufficient to stop the riot, planes and jeeps brought in thousands more. The ensuing battle resulted in two deaths, more than three hundred military and civilian casualties, three hundred arrests, and the mass federal confiscation of hundreds of firearms.

Meredith's military metaphors will seem odd unless you know that the battle wasn't metaphorical at all. On campus he was guarded by three jeeps full of soldiers wherever he went, but his family's home in the countryside was shredded with buckshot, narrowly missing his sister. For himself, he insists, he was never afraid at all.

"There have been no accidents in my life," he told us. "Everything has been according to a plan. It's hard when you promise God you ain't going to lie no more. You have to think before you say anything."

"It's true," I said, waiting for him to think.

"Most of my life, when people say anything to me about Ole Miss, it's 'thank you for being so brave.' I ain't never wanted to be brave. I wanted to be considered smart. And now it looks like I'm going to have to tell you all. You ever see the way I looked when I walked on that campus?"

"I've been struck by those photos, and I've seen some newsreels."

"I practiced ten years on that. It didn't just happen. I had read all the great books of the Western world. And in one of them the historian wrote about the last time the pope conquered Rome. Originally the popes were military commanders. This historian described the way the pope looked. His troops stayed on the outskirts of the city, and he walked all the way from the outskirts by himself. It was designed to scare the life out of anyone who opposed him. They thought, this guy's got to be crazy. Anyone can kill him."

Meredith paused, sure of his impact. "Every day on campus, my goal was to look like that pope."

To see how intense the battle was, you need only read the speech Governor Barnett made to justify his defiance of federal law: "There is no case in history where the Caucasian race has survived social integration. We will not drink from the cup of genocide."[21] Genocide? According to arguments like Barnett's, it's a slippery slope. *Integrate the schools, and the kids will befriend each other. Let them befriend each other, they'll start to date. And before you know it, there will be mixed-race babies all over the South.* The fact that millions of lighter-skinned African Americans were products of a system that allowed white men to rape their black slaves—and later their servants—bothers no one who holds such views. The fear is of the mirror image of that fact, the fantasy of black men raping white women that was so often a pretext for murder. I cannot say if this image is a form of projection. Does white guilt at the knowledge that their ancestors took black women as they pleased fuel the fear that black men will do the same?

I have come to believe that part of the deep white hatred for Barack Obama is connected to it. Otherwise that hatred is incomprehensible. No white person I met in the South would say their distaste for Obama was a function of racism. *I don't agree with his liberal policies,* they'd tell me. But disagreement is not hatred, and a growing body of literature argues that racism was the deciding factor in the 2016 election. Still, the simple word *racism* needs to be unpacked. Jackie Martin told me that white Obama haters were afraid of revenge, but that didn't seem enough to explain the depth of their passion. Nor did the fact that the Obama family's behavior in the White House refuted every racist cliché. Their very presence undermined any excuse for white supremacy. *Blacks are stupider than whites? Lazier? Less honest? Less kind?* Say what? For those with neither Obama's intellect nor his character, his very excellences were a thorn in the side. But another, less visible thorn must have pained Southern white voters, whether they noticed the sting or not. Barack Obama was not just the first black man to become American president. He is the product of the phantasm that fed racist nightmares: a very dark man from Kenya who married a very white woman from Kansas. This must have fueled the incredible claims, still visible on the internet, that the forty-fourth president was the Antichrist. The president once called himself a mutt; Ross Barnett would have called him the first step to genocide.

"I wonder what you think about President Obama's impact," I said.

"He's clearly the smartest president," said Meredith. "Before he went to Harvard, he went to Columbia." Proud of his own degree from Columbia Law School, Meredith had earlier insisted that Columbia was superior to Harvard and Yale. "Beyond a doubt, Obama is the most important thing that's happened to blacks anywhere in the world."

The grandchildren slumped in their seats. One boy was thumbing through an atlas; the electronic distractions so ubiquitous elsewhere seemed to be forbidden in the Meredith household, with the exception of the television playing Fox News. "He says he's got to listen to all of them," said Judy, rolling her eyes just slightly. "I leave the room and get on my computer when he's watching." I wasn't sure that was the only reason Meredith went for Fox. He is known to enjoy flaunting expectations. His political views are conservative: God, family, and a good education are the pillars of his worldview. But he goes much further: he'd briefly befriended David Duke at a time when the Klan leader had disavowed racist ideology. Meredith now acknowledges that Duke has re-embraced it, but he makes no apologies for supporting him, nor for working for the archconservative Senator Jesse Helms. The former segregationist was the only congressman to respond when Meredith wrote to many of them in 1988, seeking a job on Capitol Hill. Was Meredith really just trying to know the enemy, or did he approve of the way Fox presents the news? It was very hard to tell when he was teasing, confounding, and when he was playing it straight. As Robert Lee Long put it, Meredith is a free spirit. He's perfectly aware that many call him crazy.

The doorbell rang, and the children brightened considerably as a delivery boy entered with two large pizzas. Jennifer and I took it as a signal to stand up.

"You've been very generous with your time," I began, remembering Jennifer's warnings. "We don't want to take up any more—"

"Now, that really bothers me," said James Meredith. "What makes you think I don't know how to run you all out when I'm ready?"

"It's a matter of respect, sir," said Jennifer. "I don't want you to have to run me out."

"Break bread with us," said Judy Meredith.

We had no choice but to help ourselves to the tiniest pieces of pizza in the box and stay for another three hours.

"I understand you are both focusing on education now," I said.

"Go to the car, boy, and get that brown folder on the seat," Meredith said to his grandson James.

"Isn't it still pouring?" I asked. "I don't want the young man to go out in the rain."

"He said get the folder out of his car," said little James. Clearly his grandfather had the last word on everything.

Little James returned, dripping, with a brown folder. Meredith opened it and handed me an essay. "It's the most important piece I ever wrote," he said. The essay was devoted to the importance of education.

"It's moving to meet someone who has done so much and can say at eighty-three that the most important thing is what he wrote last month," I replied, deciding it was time to bring out the gift I'd grabbed on my way out the door. "If it's not rude, I'd like to reciprocate. This isn't my best book, and you don't have to read it, but perhaps one of your children or grandchildren—"

"It's got English in it," said Meredith, thumbing the pages. "Why wouldn't I read it?"

"He reads everything," said Judy.

"I just suppose you have a lot to read."

"When I went to law school, I took a speed-reading course. If it took me longer than a day to read this book, boy, it would really be something."

Judy Meredith says she was glad I was looking at the Southern experience. "To be honest with you, I thought like everyone else. I never thought in my wildest dreams I would come through here, let alone move here or marry a Mississippian. The whole world thinks it's just awful here, but it's been good to me. People are so much nicer here."

"They are," I agreed again.

"I grew up in the fifties and sixties," she continued. "There was so much activity in terms of marches and King and Medgar Evers and James, all concentrated in the Deep South. There was little being done where I grew up in Chicago."

"Didn't Dr. King say he never saw as much hatred as he saw in Chicago?"

"I think I read that somewhere too. That's why it is better to live here than up north, even to this day. It was never cleaned up there."

"The grand wizard of the KKK is from Michigan," said Jennifer.

Judy Meredith teaches at Jackson State, where she says most black people don't care about things like statues.

"I know some students who care very much," I replied.

"That's up there at Ole Miss," she said.

"It don't sound like you understand what Ole Miss is," said James Meredith.

"That's why I'm here, sir."

"You think we want everyone up at Ole Miss? You got to be kidding."

"But you're still wearing a hat."

"You don't understand why, and I ain't going to tell you," he said with a smile.

"How many hats did they give him?" Jennifer asked Judy.

"Oh, you know that story? They give him hats every time we go up there."

"Boxes and boxes and boxes," said her husband.

"The first time he had on the Colonel Reb hat, that symbol they stopped using." Johnny Reb, the generic Confederate infantryman, still stood at the entrance to campus. But to the indignation of many alumni, Colonel Reb, the generic commanding officer who once symbolized the university, is no longer used as a mascot. Buy a hat or a mug or a tote bag today and it will say nothing more provocative than "Ole Miss." "Don Cole took us on a little tour and asked me, 'Judy, how can I get that cap off his head?' I told him to buy him another one and switch it out. That's what they did."

"That still ain't the reason I wear it," said Meredith. "But I ain't going to tell you why."

"We can't encourage you?" asked Jennifer. "You said you don't lie."

He took another piece of pizza and paused to eat it. "Have you ever seen that picture of Iwo Jima? With the soldiers when they conquered it?"

"Sure," I said.

"They put up the flag, but they could have put up anything they wanted."

"Yes."

"I captured the colonel."

"You sure did, Mr. Meredith."

"My established image was just a good guy who wanted an education. They put pressure on the chancellor, and he called me into his office. He wanted me to make a statement that all I want is an education. I said, 'Chancellor, you got to be crazy. I'd be a fool to go to all this trouble to get an education. I already had an education when I came here.'"

"You captured the colonel," I said.

"Well, you can say 'captured.' I said 'conquered.'" He hadn't, and I've got the recording to prove it, but no matter.

"You conquered the colonel."

"So the crown belongs to me."

"That's going in my book, sir."

5

Lost Causes

Just how much life is left in Confederate ghosts became clear to the world, at the latest, with the election of Donald J. Trump. The Southern Poverty Law Center, which documents hate crimes, reported a huge spike in the first ten days after the election alone. "I do not think there's any question that Trump is the cause," said Heidi Beirich, director of the SPLC's Intelligence Project. Suddenly it was acceptable to express the fury that had been rising since a black family moved into the White House. A church burned in Mississippi, a swastika sprayed on a Pennsylvania wall, Confederate flags defiantly raised from Florida to Colorado. No one who knew the South was surprised, for the ghosts had been present all along. Stored in some German attics are boxes of carefully wrapped china decorated with swastikas, but Southern homes display their Confederate memorabilia proudly, and Southern stores make considerable profits selling it.

Nor is the display of loyalty to the Lost Cause a private affair. It's part of the public arena. Consider Atlanta, which proudly anointed itself capital of the New South not long after the end of the Civil War. Today the city is home to two million African Americans, a series of black mayors, and a thriving hip-hop industry. In addition to the inevitable Martin Luther King Boulevard, Atlanta's streets pay tribute to less famous civil rights leaders: Ralph Abernathy, Hosea Williams, Donald Lee Hollowell. But just sixteen miles outside Atlanta is Stone Mountain, the world's largest piece of solid granite. At 1,686 feet, it dwarfs the pine and dogwood that surround it, compelling any human in its neighborhood to look up and feel small. Surrounded by a park featuring a steamboat, a petting zoo, and a chintzy recreation of a Wild West village, it is Georgia's premier tourist attraction.

There's no way to tell how many of the four million people who visit each year come for the bas-relief carved on the mountain's face. It's a feat of engineering that's hard to ignore entirely, but it's possible to enjoy the park's other attractions, like the miniature train that, somewhere along the ride around the mountain, gets attacked by swooping actors dressed as Indians. I remember whooping it up with the rest of them as a child of seven or eight. The steady, upright Confederate generals carved into the rock only cover, in the end, a fraction of the granite. The train ride was more interesting.

Trips to Stone Mountain were an occasional Saturday treat. My parents never talked about this monument to Confederate glory. The sculpture was first planned in 1915, in the heyday of that Lost Cause historical revisionism that rebranded the Civil War as a noble fight for Southern freedom, and Reconstruction as a violent effort by ignorant ex-slaves and mercenary Yankees to debase the honor of the South in general, and its white women in particular. If you can stand it, watch *Birth of a Nation*, shown in Woodrow Wilson's White House that year. A movie milestone, *Birth of a Nation* was the highest-grossing film ever made until *Gone with the Wind* came some twenty years later, and between the two of them, the myth of the Lost Cause was blasted throughout the United States. *Birth of a Nation* is technically and ideologically cruder than Margaret Mitchell's classic, which makes its message all the clearer. As one of the silent film's captions puts it, "The former enemies of North and South are united again in defense of their Aryan birthright." Even a non-Aryan may be swept, for a moment, by the combination of music, mob violence, and melodrama to feel a tinge of relief as the knights ride to avenge the maiden's death—just as you felt in your childhood watching the cavalry ride to rescue white settlers from what were not yet called Native Americans. That's the power of movies, even if you know how often the charge of rape was not only a trumped-up excuse for a lynching but a fantasy concocted to conceal the truth of sexual violence— that countless enslaved women were raped, and often impregnated, by their white masters. It wasn't a truth apparent to Woodrow Wilson, who wrote,

"The white men were roused by a mere instinct of self-preservation . . . until at last there had sprung into existence a great Ku Klux Klan, a veritable empire of the South, to protect the Southern country." Perhaps it's no surprise that Wilson made *Birth of a Nation* the first film to be shown in the White House. That quote, used as a caption in the film itself, was taken from Wilson's own *History of the American People*.

The United Daughters of the Confederacy originally planned for a Stone Mountain monument that would capture the full panoply of the Lost Cause story, with thousands of Confederate soldiers marching across the mountainside. The vision raised no objections in the Georgia of 1915. It was a year when the Klan celebrated the lynching of the Jewish Atlantan Leo Frank, and its own renewal, with a late-night ceremony atop the mountain itself. Nor was the rest of the country opposed to what was called a monument to reconciliation.[1] (If you find the word *reconciliation* an odd way to describe triumphalist sculptures, you've forgotten that reconciliation between white and black folk wasn't on the agenda. Reconciliation between white members of the opposing armies was to be achieved by valorizing the defeated, and ignoring the cause for which they'd fought.) Stone Mountain was intended to rival the Great Sphinx, but internal disagreement and funding problems led to the dismissal of the original sculptor, who went on to ply his grandiose trade at Mount Rushmore. Decorated only with the head and the horse of Robert E. Lee, the mountain was left untouched by human hands for decades.

Work on the monument, downsized to portray three generals without troops, was resumed in the 1960s. Ask yourself why, after nearly forty years of neglect, anyone would bother to raise the sums necessary to put workmen on precarious ledges in order to carve the image of long-dead generals. The first initiatives to finish the bas-relief were undertaken shortly after *Brown v. Board of Education* declared segregation illegal. By the time the civil rights movement had achieved further victories, money and men had been found to complete what was, in effect, a giant fuck-you to the new order. Stone Mountain was only the biggest of such gestures that flourished through much of the South. It was symbolic enough to merit mention in King's "I Have a Dream" speech, which expressed the hope that freedom will ring all the way from the curvaceous slopes of California to Stone Mountain of Georgia. Civil rights activists have proposed to set a large bell at the summit, using King's resonant words to counteract the message of the gray generals; some have called for blasting off the whole damn carving. To date they have yet to persuade their fellow citizens, some of whom still use the mountain for Klan rallies.

The bas-relief is unavoidable, but it's possible to overlook the worst features of the monument. My mother must have hustled us past the Stone Mountain Memorial Garden on the way to the train ride, so I was all the more disturbed to see it as an adult. It is dedicated to sacrifice and valor, words carved into the granite benches and underlined by quotes from Robert E. Lee, Thomas Jefferson, and Michel de Montaigne. Particularly striking is the quote from the American Founding Father Patrick Henry. Every American schoolchild knows his "Give me liberty or give me death"; chiseled into the Memorial Garden are the lines with which Henry preceded it: "Is life so dear, or peace so sweet, as to be purchased at the price of chains or slavery? Forbid it, Almighty God." Didn't the sons and daughters of the Confederacy notice the cognitive dissonance?

The makers of the Memorial Garden were not alone in turning truth upside down. One Southern historian wrote that "white youths found something to envy in the freedom of their [black] fellows' feet from the cramping weight of shoes and the freedom of their minds from the restraints of school."[2] Others went so far as to argue that caring for their slaves was such a burden for the slaveholders that "the negro was the free man and the slaveholder was the slave."[3]

Just to rule out any possible ambiguity, the space between garden and granite is traced by eleven paths, representing the eleven states of the Confederacy, leading down to the base like rays of a rising star. Each path is headed by plaques that purport to describe each state's reasons for joining the Confederacy and each state's contributions to it. Alabama blames the war on John Brown, whose "raid on Harper's Ferry in 1859 set off a wave of anger in the state."[4] Fierce-looking portraits of Brown accompany the description of Alabama's losses and hardships. The Mississippi plaque eschews threatening images in favor of a drawing of the state convention, at which 75 percent of the delegates voted for immediate and unilateral secession, for "The people of Mississippi viewed Republican victories in the 1860 elections as a threat to their rights and property."[5] The plaque omits the Mississippi Declaration of Secession, which spelled out what the abstract appeal to rights and property actually meant:

Our position is thoroughly identified with the institution of slavery—the greatest material interest of the world. Its labor supplies the product which constitutes by far the largest and most important portions of commerce of the earth. These products are peculiar to the climate verging on the tropical regions, and by an imperious law of nature, none but the black race can bear exposure to the tropical sun. These products have become necessities of the world, and a blow at slavery is a blow at commerce and civilization.[6]

Like the other plaques, the one dedicated to Mississippi forgoes any mention of the enslavement of black people, focusing instead on the suffering of white people.

If you want to make the Lost Cause narrative seem intellectually hefty, you call it the Dunning School of history. The beliefs that the war was not about slavery and that Reconstruction was a disaster were spread academically by W. A. Dunning, a Columbia history professor during the Jim Crow reign of terror, and his students. You might compare him to Ernst Nolte, who ignited the Historians' Debate by arguing that the Nazis gleaned every wretched trick they knew from the Bolsheviks, who really started the war. A monument in Germany with Nolte's explanation of the causes of war would never get off the ground. Yet here at the mountain, the Dunning School is literally written in stone.

Elsewhere, you need help to read some of the signposts. Plenty of evidence is written into the landscape: the statues of Johnny Reb raised before the courthouses that anchor a broad square in the center of every town, standing guard to preserve the legacy of heroic resistance to Northern tyranny. All those stately columns gracing mansion porticoes look elegant till you know what ideology was written into the architecture. The Greek Revival movement was not just an ode to the birthplace of Western democracy. It brandished a key claim of the antebellum South: great civilizations are founded on slavery. (The fact that Greek slaves' lives were considerably better than American ones was never mentioned.) Southerners were proud that prewar European visitors to America generally considered the South to be more civilized than the rougher regions of the North.[7]

You can find a shade of that civilization in Natchez, Mississippi, a national center of wealth in the days when cotton was key to the international economy. In 1841, Natchez was the richest town in America, and its perch on the bluffs overlooking the Mississippi River spared it from the Union bombardments that destroyed most of neighboring Vicksburg. As a consequence, it contains more magnificent mansions within a couple of square miles than anyplace else in the South, though the town itself now looks drab, almost shuttered. A couple of downtown blocks of brick and wood house a few antiques shops and an indifferent restaurant. Real life takes place in the suburbs and malls, except for the representation of life on display every year during the Natchez Spring Pilgrimage.

No one who has seen it can repeat the cliché that Americans don't care about history. The pilgrimage centerpiece is the Historic Natchez Tableaux, a performance of music, dance, and occasional storytelling highlighting scenes of the town's past, presented by enthusiastic locals. The clerk at my hotel said that four of her children were in it, and she told me to watch for her son. "His teacher says he's such a pretty dancer, he would have been the talk of the town before the war. Now I ask you: What sixteen-year-old wants to hear he would have been cool two hundred years ago?"

Seated in the auditorium, I had no way to make out which boy was her son, but I wondered what things were like in 1932, when the Natchez Garden Club began to organize these pageants. This one had clearly been modernized. All the white women and girls wore hoopskirts and bows as they danced round a maypole, and the soldiers in gray swung their belles to the tune of "Dixie," but the pageant did make an attempt to acknowledge the reality of slavery—though not without pointing out that Yankees were slave traders. One tableau depicted the wedding of Confederate president Jefferson Davis to a local beauty, which took place at a house that is now an expensive bed-and-breakfast proudly advertising that happy event. Just after that tableau, however, was a little skit that decried how hard it was for slaves to wed. It even acknowledged what often happened after enslaved people were permitted to marry: a black woman about to be sold away from her child sings a mournful version of "A Change Is Gonna Come." Other black women introduced themselves as "proud to work building up Melrose Plantation for twenty years, and we protected it when intruders wanted to take the fine furniture in the family's absence." The loyal slave who hid the family silver from marauding Yankees is an old Jim Crow trope, though it doubtless happened on occasion. Whether the Natchez tribe after which the town was named would have recognized themselves under the title "Two Cultures Collide" that marked the segment on Native American history is another question. The tableaux ended on a high note as former enslaved men, now Union soldiers, demolished the market where they'd been sold away from their families, though it was a white Union officer who gave the order to tear it down. The crippled Rebel in rags shook hands with the tall Yankee in dress uniform. The master of ceremonies directed the audience to rise and sing "The Star-Spangled Banner" along with the cast.

"The British use their history to comfort themselves," said Neil MacGregor.

Southerners who created the Lost Cause narrative set out to do the same. As the Confederate general Beauregard wrote in 1875, "I believe now, as I did when I fired the first gun in 1861 and one of the last in 1865, that the cause we upheld was a just and holy one" and looked forward to "after having taken as active a part in making history, to see that it is correctly written."[8]

The writing of that history portrayed the antebellum South as a sweet, slow place where planters' pretty daughters danced under moonlight and magnolias while placid, loyal slaves served iced tea, rocked their masters' babies, and sang soft spirituals. When this Arcadia was threatened by base and brutal Yankees, the fathers and brothers of those hoopskirted girls took up arms to defend it, much as their forefathers had done a hundred years earlier when declaring the colonies' independence from their British rulers. (Among many things left out of the story is the fact that few who actually fought in the Confederate army were slaveholders. The wealthier planters— those owning more than twenty slaves—were exempt from army service in order to protect the home front from possible uprisings of those happy, loyal enslaved people.) Despite the unmistakable words of the Mississippi Declaration of Secession, the Lost Cause narrative insisted that the war was not fought over slavery, but over the issue of states' rights—an abstract phrase that veils the question of what, exactly, Southern states thought they had a right to do. The valiant efforts of some million Confederate soldiers, the narrative continues, were no match for the greater numbers and industry the Yankees had at their disposal, and so the Cause was lost. The Yankees made defeat all the more bitter by imposing Reconstruction. As one Southern chronicler put it, "They were subjected to the greatest humiliation of modern times: their slaves were put over them."[9]

It's easy enough to understand the appeal of this story for a defeated Confederate general, and perhaps for his daughters and sons. More puzzling is the way the story, slowly and hazily, came to capture the hearts of the North. Weary of war, eager for reconciliation, and keen to get on with the business of industrialization that was changing the American economy, Northerners conceded most of the mythmaking to the South. Not many had been enthusiastic abolitionists anyway. The view that everything was tragic, and everyone was valiant, paved the way for the Compromise of 1877, when a disputed election was settled by a promise to withdraw the federal troops that had guarded the rights of newly freed African Americans. This effectively ended Reconstruction and began open season on those black men and women who were determined to exercise those rights that emancipation, along with three constitutional amendments, had proclaimed. But just as the foggy mantra *we were all tragic victims* made the compromise easier for Northern whites to swallow, once established, it reinforced that view itself. *Birth of a Nation* and *Gone with the Wind* were only the most famous block-busters that grabbed the nation's attention. Hollywood turned out hundreds of films suggesting that the war was a tragic misunderstanding, including two starring Shirley Temple, who made the Lost Cause look not only noble and valiant but incontestably cute.

In 1864, General Sherman's army laid waste to a wide swath of land between Atlanta and Savannah. The song "Marching Through Georgia" described the devastation as "a thoroughfare for freedom and her train." In the decades after the war, the song was so popular that Sherman swore, in 1890, never to attend another parade unless "every band in the United States has signed an agreement *not* to play 'Marching through Georgia' in his presence."[10] Nonetheless, the heroic Union narrative faded as war memories did. An immigrant today who wants to become a U.S. citizen must pass a multiple-choice test composed of a hundred questions about American history and tradition. Only one of them allows for more than one correct answer: Name one problem that led to the Civil War. Slavery? Economic reasons? States' rights? Check any one of them, and the Department of Immigration will count you right.

African Americans continued to insist that the war was a war of liberation, and as early as 1870 Frederick Douglass complained that Americans were "destitute of political memory."[11] "The South has suffered, to be sure," he said, "but she has been the author of her own suffering."[12] The war, Douglass continued, was not a sectional conflict, but "a war of ideas, a battle of principles . . . a war between old and new, slavery and freedom, barbarism and civilization." It was not a fight "between rapacious birds and ferocious beasts, a mere display of brute courage and endurance, but it was a war between men of thought as well as of action, and in dead earnest for something beyond the battlefield."[13] On Memorial Day 1871 Douglass spoke at the mass grave of the unknown Union dead at the newly created Arlington Cemetery: "May . . . my tongue cleave to the roof of my mouth if I forget the difference between the parties to that . . . bloody conflict . . . I say, if this war is to be forgotten, I ask, in the name of all things sacred, what shall men remember?"[14]

Black folk were not the only ones to remember. Abolitionists and philosophers insisted on speaking truth about the moral and political struggles of their day. The monuments over which Americans are now battling were raised after the war in a concerted effort to defeat truth itself. Curiously, the

Lost Cause narrative was partially revived in the work of historians in the 1970s who argued that the war was an economic conflict. By that time, the idea that wars may be fought for ideas and principles, so clear to Frederick Douglass and William James, was wholly out of fashion for anyone unwilling to risk the charge of naïveté.

By modernizing the Lost Cause narrative, Natchez preserves it. Though I never heard anyone use the word *evil*, modern Southerners agree that slavery was wrong. It's unlikely that the 1932 version of the tableaux featured, much less celebrated, the destruction of the slave market by black men in Union colors, but even the contemporary version of Natchez history highlights the breadth of the gap in white memory. Everything after emancipation is a blank, as if nothing else happened between the races at all. Now the war is over, we can unite as one big family in singing the national anthem and go our separate ways until next year's pilgrimage.

It's significant that Natchez's annual self-celebration, like that of other Southern towns, is framed in religious terms. A pilgrimage is a holy expedition, a journey to sacred space. Seeking meaning in suffering, Lost Cause theologians conceived the South as a nineteenth-century Jesus, innocent and martyred but destined to rise again. The pilgrimage to the past is a form of reassurance and prayer: that our sins will be redeemed if we present them with a dollop of remorse in a sea of innocence. The ritual combines pagan ancestor worship with Christian sacralization of suffering. There's even a faint smell of theodicy. With an advertisement reading "There is cotton to pick at Frogmore . . . DELTA MUSIC AND THE COTTON FIELDS THAT GAVE IT BIRTH," the Natchez Pilgrimage brochure urges the visitor to cross the river to Louisiana and view an old plantation. Tourists are invited to the working cotton plantation to "understand how the wealth was created in the Natchez District, and experience a thorough explanation of slave culture" before visiting the Delta Music Museum "to listen and learn about the music interwoven in the culture." Everything happens for the best, said the seventeenth-century German philosopher Leibniz. *If those cotton fields gave birth to an art form so rich that Mississippi now markets itself as the birthplace of America's music, wasn't it a blessing in disguise?*

❧

However warped the presence of history, the South does at least present it. This was reason enough for me to be there, even though Martin Luther King said that the hatred he saw on the faces of protesters outside of Chicago was fiercer than anything he'd seen in the segregated South. He was there to focus attention on the struggle to integrate housing, of which it's often said, "In the South they don't care how close you are, as long as you don't get too big; in the North, they don't care how big you are, as long as you don't get close."[15] Northern neighborhoods and Northern schools are still often more segregated than Southern ones. There, few white people get close enough to black people to have their stories seep into consciousness.

In the South, the street etiquette that takes place, or does not, every time black and white people meet on a sidewalk makes history inescapable. Do I flinch when a black man moves to let me pass, knowing that in earlier days that move was made in fear? Black men who did not drop their eyes and step into the street when a white woman passed risked a lynching. Or is the gesture simply Southern in a place where white and black men instinctively rush to open a door or pick up a dropped pen for a lady? Street dilemmas are so intense that the repercussions can be analyzed for hours. Any Southern space you pass through will force a reminder of racial history, even if it doesn't contain a signpost commemorating one or another battle site. Thousands of these sites stud Southern landscapes. Confederate armies never made it past Gettysburg, the one significant Northern space dedicated to Civil War history.

෨

Large and lovely houses, some still complete with the plantations that built them, dot the South. They are usually repurposed as bed-and-breakfasts, complete with servants in antebellum costume, and favored as wedding sites. The Whitney Plantation, an hour north of New Orleans, is completely different. *Smithsonian* magazine described it as America's Auschwitz. Whitney does borrow one feature from the U.S. Holocaust Memorial Museum. At the beginning of the tour, the visitor receives a tag with the name and imagined likeness of a former slave. On the back of the tag is a quote from one of the thousands of interviews from the federal WPA public works project. Like most of the New Deal programs, this was aimed at creating jobs during the Great Depression—in this case, jobs for writers. Unlike many of the programs, this one yielded long-term treasure, allowing us to hear forever the last voices of those who were enslaved. My tag represented Mary Ann John, who was eighty-five years old at the time she was interviewed. She was quoted:

I was ten years old when peace was declared . . . what I knows, I was borned with, for I never went to school a day in my whole life. I don't know A from B. One of my sisters was born right in de fields. Dey just dug two holes . . . She gets down in dat hole and gives birth to de baby and de baby just rolls out into de hole. Den de boss has someone to take de baby to de house, an' makes my ma get up and keep right on hoeing; I never will forgit.

Other features of the tour are designed to shift your identification from slaveholder to slave. The central focus of most plantation tours is the Big House, which invites you to imagine yourself as Scarlett O'Hara. At the Whitney Plantation, the Big House is visited last, through the back door, where house slaves would have entered. The tour is focused on enslaved people's lives: the rough cabins they lived in, the huge copper pots they used to boil and stir the cane into sugar that was taken down the river to New Orleans and thence to the world. They often lost limbs to third-degree burns received while pouring hot syrup from cauldron to cauldron. There are metal cells where slaves were kept before auction, often for months if it served market interests; the prices for black bodies always increased before harvest season. As grim as the rust-colored cells were, they often brought one advantage: to prepare them for market, the slaves were fed considerably better than they would be afterward, their bodies often greased with butter to make them glow with a healthy-looking shine.

There are artworks created for the museum: a memorial to the children who died on the plantation, a series of severed heads depicting the leaders of the 1811 uprising that took place nearby. It was the largest slave uprising in the United States. A plaque reproduces the court judgment handed down when the rebellion was suppressed:

The Tribunal decides that the death penalty will be applied to them without torture, and the heads of the executed will be cut off and planted on the end of a pike at the place where each convict will suffer the right punishment due to his crimes in order to frighten by terrible example all malefactors who might in the future make an attempt on the public peace.

The most compelling monuments are the slaves' own words, collected from WPA testimonies and etched on granite tablets placed in long rows. The descriptions of what was done to hungry children are so painful that I shed tears. I glanced at the other members of my tour group. There were some twenty of us, white, black, and Asian American, a couple from Holland. Several were families. The pretty, young guide was a knowledgeable black woman in running shoes who grew up a few miles from the site. None of us revealed very much.

The Whitney Plantation's owner has had to be more expansive. John Cummings is a retired New Orleans lawyer and real estate investor who spent sixteen years and $8 million to construct the museum. He had liberal leanings before that, for he successfully handled several civil rights cases, but when he bought the property as an investment, he realized he had no idea what slavery was. "And this is not black history, it's our history, my history."[16] He hired a Senegalese historian, Dr. Ibrahima Seck, as director of research while he spent years going to weddings and funerals in the surrounding community, explaining his vision until they accepted it. "It's people like me who started this mess, dealing in slaves. Why would it be a surprise if some white kid came along and tried to do something that would correct what his own ancestors did?" As Cummings pointed out when the museum opened in 2014, there are more Holocaust museums in the United States than in Israel, Germany, and Poland combined, but not one devoted to slavery. "By neglecting slavery, we have failed to acknowledge the most significant event in our collective history."[17] His mission is "to present the facts of slavery to all I could find, so everyone would understand how strongly the deck was stacked against African Americans. Plenty of people ask *why can't they get over it?* 150 years after emancipation. But unless you know what the 'it' is, you can't get over it. We're trying to define the 'it.'"[18]

John Cummings now spends most of his days at the plantation. Nearing eighty, he often crosses it in a golf cart. As research continues on the lives of the men and women who were enslaved there and on other Louisiana plantations, the museum has rightly received national acclaim, but the experience of reading that testimony on those grounds is more powerful than anything you can read about it.

Some smaller projects deserve equal attention. In 1934, five ladies of the Holly Springs Garden Club visited the Natchez Spring Pilgrimage and decided to start their own. The pretty little town in the hills of northern Mississippi was never as grand as Natchez, but it too has a wealth of intact old mansions that were spared destruction because Union troops occupied the town in the first years of the war. The annual Holly Springs Pilgrimage furthers tourism with talks, period music, and tours of town homes, some complete with Civil War reenactors playing a panoply of Confederate soldiers.

In front of the largest house on the tour, a group of five or six men dressed as different companies of Confederate soldiers was camped on the lawn when I arrived. A round-faced, clean-shaven man in his thirties, sitting on a horse, told me he represented the First Mississippi Cavalry. "Just think about those guys going into combat after coming all that way in the saddle from south Mississippi. There was freezing rain all the way. They had no supply wagons; all their supplies were what they could carry right here." He tapped the front of his saddle. "I just think it's a great honor to represent them. If we don't remember this history, it will come back and repeat itself."

I could honestly nod in agreement, until I asked what he meant.

"I'm afraid of what you see in the news, taking out this ancestry, tearing down statues in New Orleans, talking about taking down the statue of Nathan Bedford Forrest in Memphis—"

"We went to the Forrest birthday memorial," interjected his companion, a handsome gray-bearded man on foot. "We rode around, fired a musket in the air. Not a lot of space to do much in that park. What really grabs me is that the Forrest family donated that land to Memphis. He and his wife are buried there. They should leave it alone."

The Forrests were disinterred from the original cemetery where they'd been buried and placed in the elaborate monument-cum-tomb close to the Memphis city center in 1904, when Southern commitment to memorializing the Lost Cause was in full force. In 2015, however, following the Charleston massacre, the Memphis City Council voted to disinter them again and send the remains to their original burying ground, for Forrest was not just any old Confederate general. He first achieved renown for ordering a massacre of black Union troops who had surrendered at Fort Pillow, Tennessee. And though there are still historians arguing over whether he was guilty of war crimes, none dispute that he was a founding member of the Ku Klux Klan. Shortly before his death, sincerely or not, he did disavow the Klan. His funeral was the largest in Memphis history.

"They won," added a hard-faced, fiftyish mounted man.

"Who won?" I asked.

"All those universities pushing communism, socialism, the indoctrination that started back in the sixties. They won."

"They didn't win the White House," I countered. It was April 2017.

"I don't know about that yet," he replied.

The men were eager to reminisce about their fake battles. "We did Shiloh two weeks ago and there were one hundred seventy forces."

"Who plays the Yankees?"

"We do. Though when you get a real big battle like Shiloh, they come down from Ohio and Michigan. But we'll do it too," said the hard-faced one. "I don't mind putting on a blue coat. I'd prefer not to, but I will."

"It itches worse than the gray one," said his comrade. The men laughed.

"The funny thing is, we were in Gettysburg a couple of years ago for the hundred and fiftieth anniversary, and we saw more Rebel flags and bumper stickers with Pennsylvania license plates than you see down here. Everybody wants to play the Confederates. Guess they like a dying cause."

The young man on the horse teaches history in a high school in a small Mississippi town, and he asked what brought me to the Holly Springs Pilgrimage. When they heard I was a visiting scholar at the University of Mississippi, which they consider a hotbed of socialist indoctrination, they became wary.

"You faculty?" asked the hard-faced man.

I replied that I'd been teaching a little, but my main work at the moment was writing a book.

"What's it about?"

I reached for the formula I'd used before in situations where I hoped to keep my interlocutors talking about views I abhor. "I'm writing about the different ways Mississippians remember their history, all sides of it."

"But you're on our side, aren't you?" The question came from the man whose hard face grew harder.

I hesitated for a moment that felt very long. "Probably not," I said, exhaling slowly.

"What's that mean?" His cold blue eyes fixed mine as he stared down from his horse.

"Got our weapons loaded?" called another, to a general round of laughter. There were six of them, two on horseback, all heavily armed. Inside the mansion, the ladies of the garden club were preparing for the ball, but the afternoon had darkened, the other tourists gone.

"Look," I said finally, "I am not on the side of the Klan."

"We're not either. These aren't Klan uniforms."

"We don't dress up in some stupid sheets."

"I know," I replied. "But you were talking about honoring Nathan Bedford Forrest."

"Well, he wasn't Klan," said the older reenactor. "He was offered the grand wizardship and turned it down."

Checking sources later, I read that Forrest's relation to the wizardship is still a matter for historical dispute, but not his role in founding the Klan.

The young history teacher looked even more earnest than before. "I'd always taken history for granted," he told me. "But after the Charleston shooting, when they started attacking everything Confederate, that got me interested in learning more."

"Me too," I answered. I did not elaborate.

"There are more Klan members in Indiana than in Mississippi," added the history teacher. "Sure, money was made with slave labor, but the war was about taxes and federal tyranny." He prided himself on being a history teacher who shows his students all sides of the story. He'd shown them a film about the Klan in the 1920s, when its membership was highest. "And they weren't marching behind a Rebel flag; it was an American flag. So my students asked, 'Why aren't people calling to change the American flag?'"

"That's just it," said the hard-faced man. "They won. Who was Obama's friend in the Weather Underground? Bill Ayers? All that shit they started in the sixties, they won. They hate America. They hate everything we stand for."

∽◌∾

The ladies of the garden club do not exactly welcome local efforts to combat such views. Following the signs to the library, where tickets for the pilgrimage are sold, I was greeted with a warm Southern smile, brightly gleaming teeth, and a map showing the mansions that were open for the weekend. As the hostess was pointing out the biggest ones, her blond face froze. I'd told her the main object of my visit: the "Behind the Big House" project that is dedicated to restoring the slave dwellings with the care usually devoted to the mansions that depended on them. "We're not connected with they-em," she drawled, emphasizing *them* just enough to indicate disapproval, not enough to signal contempt. *It's not nice, dear. Why dig up those old bones?*

"Could you tell me where I can find them?" They were not listed on the map.

"I'm not rightly sure."

The town is so small that she must have known. Across the room, another of the garden ladies was selling tickets for a festive luncheon. She eyed me with the sympathy any decent local would feel toward a lost out-of-towner. "If you go up the street two blocks and look in at the house on the corner, I'm sure they can tell you."

No one inside the house on the corner wanted to talk about the rift with the garden club, with whom they had worked during the first year of their program. Behind the Big House began several years before the Whitney Plantation was restored. A very few citizens lobbied for a pilgrimage that told the whole story, including slave dwellings along with the homes of the slave owners. "We worked together for a year, but they decided they didn't want controversy; they'd rather talk about furniture," said one of the men who drives the project. He stopped short of criticizing his neighbors more sharply. In small Southern towns, the hope that not naming a problem might make it disappear still rules. In any case, you have to nod, smile, and chat with your opponents on the sidewalk. Even those committed to frank discussion are uneasy about spilling community secrets to a stranger.

Still, they told me quite a lot. David Person's grandmother was related to the people who owned Montrose, the house where I met the reenactors. It's the grandest house on the pilgrimage. "Alfred Brooks built that house as a wedding gift for his daughter, and then he took the whole wedding party to New York. Now, who paid for all that?" David speaks with a soft, slow drawl that cushions but does not mask his outrage. "It was all built on the institution of slavery."

David is a retired lawyer who was born in San Antonio—"My mother went and married a guy from Texas"—where he learned to feel at home as a minority in the majority Hispanic community. "You better understand where you are and make it work. I have a great comfort with color." But his extended family has been in Holly Springs "since they bought up all the cheap Chickasaw land in the 1830s," so the local people accept him despite his political views. After six years studying at the London School of Economics, he left London, bought an old house in Holly Springs, and set out to clean up the traces of the thirteen hunting dogs the last owner had kept in her house. He felt obliged to restore it faithfully, but he had no idea where restoration would lead him. It was David's neighbor, Chelius Carter, who set the project in motion.

While growing up in rural Tennessee, Chelius never questioned segregation. "The sun rose in the east, set in the west, that's just the way it was," he told me, though his ancestors were not big landowners, but "dirt farmers. If they owned any slaves, they probably worked alongside them." A restoration architect who specializes in antebellum houses, he'd decided at an early age that he wanted to live in one. When he bought the place in Holly Springs, the fact that there were slave quarters in town had been lost to living memory. Inspecting the storage shed behind his new house, he was surprised to find a stairwell. Before becoming an architect, he'd worked as a telephone installer, so he was used to fiddling around in people's attics. Under the insulation was a floor, and it dawned on him that this was where the slaves slept. He realized that this was culturally more important than the

Big Houses in the area, since so few slave dwellings remain. He and his wife, Jennifer Eggleston, whom he calls the brains and beauty behind the project, began to envision a way to use this to tell the story of the enslaved population that made the Big House happen. In 2012, there was no similar effort in the entire country.

Yet there was Joseph McGill, a South Carolinian whose ancestors were enslaved. In 2010 he began the Slave Dwelling Project, his mission to sleep in every extant slave dwelling in the country. When I met him in 2017, he had slept in ninety-four, writing a blog about the history of each one. McGill is a short, dark man in his fifties who has always been passionate about history, but it wasn't his work for the National Trust for Historic Preservation in Charleston that led him to the Slave Dwelling Project. McGill spent many of his weekends as a Civil War reenactor, acting as a member of the 54th Massachusetts Regiment, the first African American troops to serve in the Union Army. Tired of simply re-creating their battles, McGill decided to go further. Slave dwellings in America were rarely built with solid material, and those still standing were rotting from neglect. By calling attention to forgotten spaces, McGill hoped to call attention to those who lived and died within them.

McGill knew Eggleston and Carter, who were seeking to enlist other homeowners in showing the darker side of Southern history. Only two Holly Springs homeowners had joined them, but together with McGill and his friend Jodi Skipper, an African American professor of anthropology and archaeology at the University of Mississippi, they began to restore the dwellings that would illuminate the lives of those who lived in them. Carter's goal is to create dialogue. "The two races don't get together at church, at business, in school. We thought we could create meaningful dialogue over this terribly flawed and conflicted shared history. If me and my wife have a problem and put it in a box in a closet, that problem ain't going away. It's up in that closet waiting. This dialogue needed to happen generations ago. Not to talk about the people who contributed so much to Southern culture is basically cultural genocide."

Like the owners of the homes on the Holly Springs Pilgrimage tour, the three Behind the Big House owners open their homes and welcome the tourists themselves, albeit without the hoopskirts that are obligatory in the pilgrimage homes. Chelius created an exhibit of charts describing the history of the cotton industry in Holly Springs, which he patiently shows to every visitor, explaining how cotton was global currency. In the kitchen, Michael Twitty, a Jewish African American culinary historian from New Orleans, served a succulent stew whose ingredients he declined to name. In the back of the Big House, Jodi Skipper and her graduate students, whom the rain had stopped from excavating further that day, welcomed me into the slave dwelling. Her description of every feature mirrors the exactitude you hear on the Big House tours: the utensils are not original, but collected by the owners; the hooks in the ceiling held cooking pots; the open fire cooked the meals for every family, enslaved or not. The children slept upstairs, perhaps in rough beds, perhaps on the floor. The restorations are all works in progress. A pitchfork and plaster shards leaned against the rough wooden planks of the cabin wall. A yellowed photo showed a former enslaved couple who came dressed in round hats and long coats to visit the place in 1924. Most of the visitors are white, sometimes coming by accident if they mistake the house in front for part of the pilgrimage, but African American visitors have been increasing, and school groups now ensure that hundreds of students visit the project every year.

Back in the Big House, I asked Chelius what influenced him. Was there a book or a conversation that had moved him away from the easy soft racism of his youth? "Naw," he said. "It was just growing up." Pressed again, he allowed that a Mark Twain quote meant a lot to him, though he couldn't recall the exact words: exposure to other countries and other cultures is deadly to prejudice. He'd grown up in a family that was "about as fundamentalist as you can get—everything's literal," but had spent some time in his twenties as an archaeologist digging in the north Jordan desert. Exposure to other religions gave him a perspective he never found in the South. "You begin to see we're all trying to get to the same places. Maybe on different buses." Now he was raising his children to "be curious and question authority. Be the change in your world."

At the next stop, Joseph McGill stood in the slave dwelling, telling the history of the house. He admired the way its owner, Mrs. Burton, kept and increased her wealth after she divorced. "She had an entrepreneurial spirit. According to the 1850 census, she owned eight slaves, and by the 1860 census there were eighty. She was a phenomenal woman."

"Growing cotton?" I frowned. "We know how the cotton was produced."

"Well, there is *that*," he said, laughing. "But you've got to give her the fact that she was still quite a woman. And you've got to remember there were black slave owners too. Didn't make it right, but that was the business model."

McGill asks every visitor where they come from. A white woman from Olive Branch, Mississippi, asked him—gingerly—if he feels a presence in the cabins where he sleeps.

"If you're looking for a presence, you can probably feel one, but I don't look for the presences, because if communing with the ancestors was possible, I wouldn't want to. They lived a life no one should have lived, and I don't need them telling me about it. I'd be pissed off. I couldn't talk to the owners in that frame of mind. I'm asking them to let me sleep in these spaces, after all."

Mostly the homeowners are welcoming, often inviting him to dinner and asking about his travels. Whether moved by guilt or something foggier, they sometimes renovate the dwelling in advance of his visit. McGill is glad for anything that encourages the cabins' preservation. More recently, white people have asked to join him. "Why not? I thought. Everybody needs to know this." Now the people who join him to sleep in a slave dwelling are about equally divided between black and white.

Back at the Big House, David Person proudly pointed to the photos framed on the grand piano. His great-great-grandfather had been a U.S. senator in the 1840s and later a judge. He was against secession "but went along with it like everyone else." He and his sons fought in the war he thought was wrong, but he later raised his voice against the Black Codes introduced in Mississippi after the war to deny African Americans the civil rights that the Fourteenth Amendment had just granted them. "He died a broken man," says Person, pointing to a mournful photo in a bronze-colored frame. "The neighbors saw him in the street, muttering, 'All is lost. All is lost.'"

Person is relieved that his family did not own slaves, but the Burton family, whose house he lives in, is another story. "This house is built on cotton money." Even during the war, Malvina Burton lost only two crops: once when Union soldiers burned the harvest on the town square, and once again when they confiscated the cotton she'd managed to get to Memphis, hoping to send it downriver to New Orleans. "But those were the only failures. She made a ton of money. After the war, a lot of the slaves stayed on as sharecroppers—the second form of slavery." Person put some blame on Great Britain. Though it was proud of abolishing slavery in its own territory, 80 percent of its cotton came from the Deep South. "Eighty percent? They could have shut it down immediately," he says. "But they vacillated and compromised. Didn't want France and Belgium to take over the market."

While renovating the Burton house, Person hired a muralist to paint a history of Holly Springs in the parlor, which he patiently explains to visitors. Holly Springs is the capital of Marshall County, which in 1850 was the largest cotton producer, with the highest number of enslaved people, in Mississippi. As such, it is fertile ground for the Southern history sketched on the wall. "This man in the corner brought the cottonseed from Carolina, and here are freedmen building the houses. Finally we have our brethren the Chickasaw, who owned the land you're standing on." Person is as quietly passionate about telling the story of Native American genocide as he is about the story of slavery. "This is Delilah Love," he says, pointing to a downcast woman in a long green dress, her head crowned with drooping feathers as she uselessly reaches toward two small boys heading for a covered wagon. "This is her saying goodbye to her children; they had to go." Forty-five hundred Native Americans were forced to leave this part of Mississippi, escorted by federal troops who were ordered to shoot anyone who diverged from the prearranged route. History does not record whether Delilah ever saw her children again.

Person is working with the county to establish a Chickasaw park on land that was stolen from the tribe. It will be dedicated to the history and culture of the Chickasaw, some of whose descendants still live in the area. He hopes to organize a reunion of them along the lines of the reunion he organized for descendants of the Burton estate, white and black. No names of the latter were recorded by the census taker, who was interested in black numbers, not black persons. A descendant of the black Burtons went through cemeteries, church records, and family Bibles until she identified most of them. Now Person holds an annual reunion of about a hundred people. "The white descendants were not ready; they didn't come the first few times, but when they came last year, they were blown away. We talk about everything."

"Like guilt? Shame?" I asked.

"None of that," said Person. "We just talk about the truth of slavery, and how you use that for healing." How much shame is needed to talk about truth is a question that's still open for those Southerners working for reconciliation.

Together with Alisea McCleod, an African American professor at the local Rust College, Person founded the organization Gracing the Table, a forum that gives black and white citizens an opportunity for the frank discussion of racist history that we prefer to avoid. The group grew from the spontaneous discussions provoked by visits to Behind the Big House, and they went on to organize conferences, films, and training sessions on community mediation. "When people walk out of the Big Houses, they think about the pretty table that reminds them of one their grandmother had. When people walk out of here"—he gestured toward the slave dwelling— "they come out with a flow of emotions. Some are so upset we have to set out chairs so they can rest." Person is convinced that the unexamined history of slavery has done immeasurable damage to the white community as well as to the black one. "My people would be appalled at where Mississippi is now. It's almost a failed state."

I asked what led to his progressive politics. There was his father, a county judge who was sympathetic to the black community in San Antonio. There was the cousin who married "an ass-kicking Unitarian minister" in Holly Springs. There were his years studying government in the early '60s at the University of Texas at Austin, where he'd campaigned to desegregate the movie theaters. There was time spent in London, looking at his country from the outside. I always seek to understand what influences people to stand up for what's right, but in the end there may be no explanations. There are human beings who open their eyes, look at the evidence, and decide to devote their lives to persuading others to do the same.

"It's like pushing a giant stone," said Person. "You can get little chips off. It takes time and patience and sometimes a sense of humor. That's all I'm trying to do—make little whacks at the stone."

※

Diane McWhorter presents as a real Southern belle: forty years living in Boston and New York barely dented her drawl, and I've never seen her be anything less than gracious, warm, and sweetly attentive. Yet when she returned not long ago to her native Birmingham and greeted the mother of an old friend at a debutante ball, her greeting was returned with "There are about ten people in this room who would like to kill you tonight." No doubt it was said with a drawl as soft as hers. The homicidal urges resulted from the revelations about proper Birmingham society in her history of the city's civil rights struggle, *Carry Me Home*. The book was inspired by the fear that her father might be connected to the men who dynamited the church where four African American girls were murdered. Her work, therefore, is as good an example of homegrown *Vergangenheitsaufarbeitung* as you can hope to find. In nineteen years of research she found out a great deal about the city fathers' complicity with the Ku Klux Klan. "For black people, my book was reassurance that it wasn't as bad as they thought; it was worse," she says.

At the age when I was singing the plaintive civil rights song "Birmingham Sunday," Diane was getting ready for a prom or a debutante ball, the kind of thing real Southern girls did. She said there was no epiphany, no one moment when she looked at the structures that framed her childhood and said *this is wrong*. She does remember seeing the movie *To Kill a Mockingbird* and crying when Tom Robinson was shot, then worrying what her father would say if he saw her crying over a black man. She was ten years old. "That's about the age when people start deforming their consciences in order to accept something that's not just manifestly wrong but manifestly contrary to the religious beliefs that are front and center in their lives." Like Bettina Stangneth or Jan Philipp Reemtsma or David Person, Diane McWhorter cannot say why her conscience resisted attempts to deform it. Coming to understand the evil of segregation was a process that began when she went to Wellesley, where she first met African Americans in a social context. "Interracial socializing was simply not in the cards for a nice white girl in Birmingham, Alabama, where everyone had to be 'in your place.' It was an instant switch." The process culminated in the semester she spent in Berlin researching a book about Hitler's top rocket scientist, Wernher von Braun, who later built the Saturn V moon rocket for NASA in Huntsville, Alabama. She began to see her hometown through the lens of Nazi Germany. "Suddenly it dawned on me that the segregated South was a totalitarian society. Every aspect of life was organized around this one thing, race. It determined your emotional and social life, where you were born and educated, and it was enforced by a police state." It was acceptable for the state to kill its political opponents; Bull Connor organized—fortunately unsuccessful—assassination attempts against the civil rights leader Fred Shuttlesworth, a man of the cloth. "Maybe it wasn't the Night of the Long Knives, when Hitler massacred his opposition in 1934, but it was a criminal state nonetheless."

For black people, segregation was enforced by terror. For white people there was something more subtle though less comprehensible: shame. The richest black man in Birmingham would lunch with the president of the local U.S. Steel outpost when they were both in New York, but never at home. "Whites were more scared of ostracism by each other than they were of black people. It's a very childish thing: the same impulse that makes kids not want to be seen being nice to the fat girl at school." Now those Alabamans want to be seen as having been secret antisegregationists, just as a generation of Germans claimed they had been in "inner exile" during the Third Reich years. "Every time I give a talk, audience members have an irresistible urge to tell me about the small acts of subversion they practiced on behalf of their maids. I'm certainly not knocking that—it's better than not having the urge—but if everyone had acted on those impulses, segregation would have ended a lot sooner."

Diane doesn't minimize how hard it is to behave righteously under an evil system. "What we had in the South wasn't literal genocide, but it was sociopolitical and economic genocide, and it was conspicuous." White Southerners were presented with a moral quandary every time they took a drink from a whites-only water fountain, though few chose to face it. Northerners could spend a lifetime without having to think about racism; in the South it was daily. Children did not understand it, but they noticed the fountains, the maid's bathroom, the maid's cup.

"So did adults who opposed segregation drink from the colored fountains out of protest?" I asked. Another Alabama woman had told me she always wished to drink from the colored fountain, for as a child, she imagined it rainbow-colored, instead of the dull clear water she drank.

"Honestly," said Diane, "the colored fountains weren't usually refrigerated. You'd be getting lukewarm water."

All those hot Southern days.

She is adamant that if we're serious about working off the evils of racism, we should count time from the end of segregation, not the end of slavery. For slavery was constantly re-formed and renewed until segregation was legally ended in 1964. She thinks working off takes generational time. "My generation was raised in denial because our parents denied it. Unlike the German '68ers, we were barely awake at the end of segregation." Many of her parents' generation are still in denial. The desire for regional innocence is so powerful that every single Klan witness at the Birmingham bombing trial in 2001 said under oath that he never had any bad feelings about black people. Finally the accused church bomber's exasperated lawyer said: Martin Luther King's job would have been a lot easier if someone had told him my client was the only racist in Birmingham. "Do they believe it?" Diane asked. "I don't know. Do people change?"

They have changed their language. "The country club euphemism for black person is *Democrat*," she told me. *There are a lot of Democrats staying at our hotel.* Statistically speaking, the euphemism is accurate. Scanning color-coded maps after the 2016 election, I saw just one long swath of blue that was neither a coast nor a city. Eighty percent of the Mississippi Delta population is African American, and they colored that piece of the state Democrat. The rest of Mississippi? Like all but a few Southern cities, it has gone Republican, whoever the candidate, since the Civil Rights Act lost the South, as Lyndon Johnson predicted.

Not that the South today is willing to acknowledge it was their opposition to civil rights legislation that sent them into the arms of the Republican Party. "My father, who was a total racist, insisted he never had anything against black people. He was just against communism and the federal government. Which is absolutely a residue of Reconstruction grafted onto the Cold War." White Southerners tilt toward visceral martyrdom: "*Why is the national press always picking on us?* There's a grain of truth in that," said Diane. "The North had no opportunity to go bad in the same way."

She thinks the key difference between Germany and the South is that Germany unequivocally lost the war. Surely the loss prevents most any deliberate attempt to mourn a Lost Cause in Germany. Perhaps this is thanks to the length of the Allied Occupation. More likely it's because the generation of Germans born after the war accepted the international consensus that German behavior during the war was inexcusable. At the most, it could be forgiven.

"It's still not clear that the South lost the war," said Diane. "It's driving the national agenda, after all. You can see it with Trump; that's the same population who elected George Wallace."

∼∾∙

Growing up in the South of the 1960s, I couldn't help hear the cry "The South will rise again!" I never connected it with theology until I read Charles Reagan Wilson's *Baptized in Blood: The Religion of the Lost Cause.* Wilson argued that the Confederate defeat presented a theological problem: If God was on their side, how could they have lost the war? Wilson's answer is that the South replaced a dead political nation with a cultural identity whose heart was evangelical Protestantism. The South was an innocent victim crucified by superior political and economic forces. "You have to remember that the war was a total disaster for the white South," Wilson told me when we met for a bourbon in his favorite Oxford bar. "The death rates were comparable to those in Europe during World War I." What better way to recover from catastrophe than to identify with that long-ago innocent, tortured to death but destined to rise once again?

Wilson's work, from that first book through the editing of the *New Encyclopedia of Southern Culture,* made him the grandfather of authorities on Lost Cause mythology. He began his studies because he wanted to understand how a people could be so religious and so racist at the same time. His boyish grin and baseball cap belie the fact that he recently retired as director of the University of Mississippi's Center for the Study of Southern Culture. Wilson knows that the South's intense cultivation of history—its plaques and pageants and monuments, so much more evident than they are in any other part of the country—is a direct result of deliberate mythmaking. He's a historian with many interests, after all. "It's amazing that William

Faulkner and Muddy Waters lived seventy miles from each other in the same period." He'd be the last to object to Southern focus on its history, if only it were expanded. It's not only black history that gets lost in traditional narratives; so does the populist movement of the 1890s, which tried to make common cause between poor white and black farmers who shared an interest against the planters. Thanks to right-wing violence, economic pressure, and a considerable amount of vote theft, the Populists lost elections they were predicted to win. After that, racist politicians supported segregation with the argument that whites were superior because of the nobility with which they'd fought the Civil War. "That's why ninety percent of those monuments were built after 1890."

I'd been reading old books supporting the Lost Cause in an effort to understand how anyone with half a heart or a mind could defend it. I understand the nostalgia for simpler, softer times; I understand the resistance to a culture that enshrines speed and utility over traditional Southern values like honor. I just don't understand what is honorable about torturing, raping, and murdering people whose skin was darker than theirs. Further reading has yet to help me grasp how they navigated the contradiction, but it has produced some interesting facts. I asked Wilson what he thought about the argument of one Frank Lawrence Owsley.

"Ah, Owsley." He smiled ruefully. For scholars of the period, Owsley is notorious.

In the agrarian tract *I'll Take My Stand*, Owsley described the rise of Southern religious fundamentalism in response to abolitionist arguments that slavery was a sin. The abolitionists argued from reason: *Think of the prophets thundering about justice, think of Jesus's appeals to love and mercy. Look at Creation: if we're all descended from Adam and Eve, aren't we all brothers and sisters at heart?* The abolitionists could not deny, however, that there were slaves in the Bible, and that was the slave owners' focus. *If slavery was present in biblical times, why shouldn't it be present in ours?*

"Is that why Southern religious fundamentalists insist on literal readings of the Bible?"

Wilson paused. "As a historian, I'd have a hard time proving it, but my gut reaction says it's probably true. I think Southern whites are very literal-minded about the Bible, and the Constitution as well, because they are always searching for ways to read texts that would support their racial views. It goes beyond race to support a hierarchical worldview in which everyone has a place: slaves, children, women. A typical Sunday morning starts with a biblical text that gives legitimacy to whatever the preacher wants to say."

Yet he thinks the forward movement in Mississippi is undeniable, even since he arrived there from Texas in 1981. Black culture is recognized (and marketed) as a state treasure; there's a thriving African American middle class and business community in Jackson, which recently elected a mayor named for a hero of the African struggle against colonialism. Wilson enjoys the irony of the fact that the Trent Lott Leadership Institute at the University of Mississippi has used the staunch segregationist former senator's money to subsidize reconciliation projects that bring together students from Mississippi, South Africa, and Northern Ireland. As for the Black Caucus in the Mississippi State Legislature, "it seldom gets its way, but it's listened to," Wilson said. The caucus focuses on social projects such as education in rural counties that makes a difference to the communities where its members were born. "It's easy to portray the South as racist and retrograde, but that ignores all the people who are doing good work in local communities. The steps are incremental, but they matter in people's lives."

The South has felt besieged, Wilson told me, since the newsman William Lloyd Garrison began publishing his abolitionist paper *The Liberator* in the 1830s. "Southern whites became incredibly defensive, and they've been defensive ever since. They think they never get a proper hearing in the national culture; they're never taken seriously."

"They *run* the national culture, politically," I countered. It isn't just the originalism—religious and constitutional. I never met anyone in Mississippi who didn't own a gun, however progressive she might be. Indeed, progressives are especially careful to keep one in the glove compartment of their car. They know how many arms the other side has. And the insistence on small government and resistance to federal authority is emotionally fueled by buried memories of Reconstruction.

"What drives me nuts about Southern Republicans," said Wilson, "is the way they rail against the federal government while taking more federal tax money than any other part of the country."

"Do you think that stems from antipathy to Reconstruction?"

"Reconstruction reverberates," Wilson told me. In the '50s and '60s, racists like James Eastland and Strom Thurmond referred to Reconstruction all the time, but Republicans don't mention it today. Wilson finished the bourbon he'd been nursing and paused once more. "This is hard to talk about as a scholar, but it's like a vanished memory, almost subconscious. It would be hard to prove that, but I think it's still there."

"I am careful with neuroscientific claims," I told him, "but there's a lot of new evidence about intergenerational trauma. It does get passed down."

"Reconstruction was their trauma, for sure."

"Can we say that an unconscious memory of Reconstruction is one of the forces driving the worst of our national politics—all the way to resistance to Obamacare?" Historians are wary of speculation, but philosophers don't have to be.

"That's certainly where the hostility to the federal government was implanted. It's their original sin," concluded Wilson.

"You get the feeling that the newspapers themselves could explode and lightning will burn and everybody will perish," wrote Bob Dylan of the time he spent in the New York Public Library's archives, reading microfiche copies of Civil War journals. "The suffering is endless, and the punishment is going to be forever . . . Back there America was put on the cross, died, and was resurrected . . . The godawful truth of that would be the all-encompassing template behind everything that I would write."[19]

"We will always be fighting the Civil War," said Diane McWhorter. "It's just the basis of this country."

☙

Even towns that see themselves as enlightened can surprise you. A good place to see how Oxford prefers to preserve its Confederate history is the Lamar House, located near the center of town. The lovely white clapboard house, done in modest Greek Revival style, was built by Lucius Quintus Cincinnatus Lamar. Today it serves as a museum to honor nineteenth-century Mississippi's most important statesman. He represented Mississippi in Congress until he resigned in December 1860 to draft the Mississippi Ordinance of Secession. His contemporaries found him an exceptional writer and orator, and Lamar's support of the state that was founded to defend the institution of slavery was not confined to words. He also served the Confederacy as a lieutenant colonel and as Jefferson Davis's envoy to England, France, and Russia. His lugubrious, long-bearded gaze is preserved in a life-size bronze statue that stands before the house, not far from a flash of wisteria.

When the cause for which his heart and soul had burned was lost, Lamar set his sights on reconciliation, which is why he is honored today. After receiving pardon for his allegiance to the Confederate cause, he went on to serve in the U.S. Congress, Senate, and Supreme Court. In 1874, shortly after returning to Congress, he asked, and was allowed, to give a eulogy for Charles Sumner that made his fellow lawmakers weep. For Senator Sumner was a fiery abolitionist from Massachusetts who was nearly beaten to death on the floor of Congress by a senator from South Carolina who loathed Sumner's fierce opposition to slavery. For this eulogy, which ended with the appeal "My countrymen! Know one another, and you will love one another!," Lamar received a chapter in John F. Kennedy's *Profiles in Courage*. The Lamar House marks this distinction by placing Kennedy's book under a spotlight in the center of one of its ample rooms.

Why did Kennedy choose to honor this man? The president wrote that few speeches in American history had such immediate impact as Lamar's eulogy for Sumner, "the most significant and hopeful utterance that has been heard from the South since the war." But Lamar's speech was no *mea culpa* for the Confederate cause. In pleading for all sides to forget the strife, he was skillfully asserting that all sides were at fault. Even worse, he slyly managed to repeat all the Confederate arguments for slavery while professing to praise Charles Sumner. Sumner, said Lamar, was born with "an instinctive love of freedom," and to restrict anyone's freedom was "a wrong no logic could justify . . . it mattered not . . . how dark his skin, or how dense his ignorance . . . It mattered not that the slave might be contented with his lot; that his actual condition might be immeasurably more desirable than that from which it had transported him; that it gave him physical comfort, mental and moral elevation, and religious culture not possessed by his race in any other condition." Lamar's speech goes on and on, repeating well-rehearsed arguments in favor of slavery while ostensibly eulogizing its steadfast opponent. You needn't read far between the lines to come away with the impression that Sumner had been a decent, principled, wrong-headed fool. As the congressmen cheered and wept, Charles Sumner must have fumed in his grave.

Kennedy didn't quote the backhanded defense of slavery in Lamar's speech, only the nicer, conciliatory bits. But Lamar's plea for reconciliation had a clear purpose; his real goal was a plea for the end of Reconstruction and the removal of Union troops from the South. As he wrote to his wife just after the speech, "I never in all my life opened my lips with a purpose more single to the interests of our Southern people than when I made this speech. I wanted to seize an opportunity, when universal attention could be arrested, and directed to what I was saying, to speak to the North on behalf of my own people. I succeeded fully."

No one who has studied Reconstruction doubts that it was accompanied by abuse and corruption, just as no one who has studied it doubts that those Union troops were all that stood between the newly emancipated African Americans and the Ku Klux Klan. It's the latter fact that was obscured by the Lost Cause version of history that clearly shaped Kennedy's views. In the same chapter he described Reconstruction as "a black nightmare the South never could forget" and the Radical Republicans as "Congressional mob rule that would have ground the South . . . under its heel."[20] But Kennedy was a politician, not a historian, and Lost Cause mythology wasn't confined to the South. It crept into normal discourse without the flowers and the flourishes so impossible to miss in Mississippi—much like Lamar's own defense of the Confederacy snuck into his tribute to the Confederacy's most hated foe.

Representing Oxford's favorite way of eliding its history, Lamar House acknowledges that Lamar was the author of the infamous Ordinance of Secession, which directly linked the Confederacy to slavery without obscuring the cause of the war by reference to ambiguous states' rights. It avows its dedication to showing one slave-owning statesman's transformation, and it highlights—as does Kennedy's book, and most any other text about Lamar—his famous eulogy for Sumner. But it cannot be an accident that nothing in the museum points to the odd underhandedness with which Lamar buried a defense of slavery in an alleged plea for reconciliation. The reconciliation Lamar sought was a reconciliation between Northern and Southern white people that, by obscuring the causes of the war, would leave racism untouched. Without reflection or critical analysis of what the famous speech actually said, the museum leaves you with no model for facing the past except *let bygones be bygones*. It's a genteel sort of refusal to face up to history. I doubt that anyone in town belongs to the Klan, or even its more respectable cousin, the White Citizens' Council. They'd simply prefer to leave the past unexamined, cover it with honeysuckle, and go back to their bourbon. It's the kind of response that ensures no one will reflect on the ways that past seeps into present.

✧

For nearly forty years Mississippi activists had demanded a museum in Jackson, the state capital, that would tell the story of the local civil rights movement. It was finally opened in December 2017, just in time to fit into the celebrations of the Mississippi Bicentennial. The construction of the museum, which received $90 million in state funding, came at a price: Governor Phil Bryant and the legislature insisted that a museum devoted to the entire history of the state be built next to the civil rights museum. Since it was Bryant who initiated Confederate Heritage Month, expectations for the history museum were very low. Surely it would glorify the story white

Mississippi prefers to tell about itself, a story of well-mannered men and gracious ladies, a culture more kind and more civilized than any you can find up north. Thoughtful Mississippians sighed in anticipation. They had no choice but to accept the Museum of Mississippi History as the price of the civil rights museum, whose opening was eagerly awaited.

The Mississippi Civil Rights Museum is indeed a triumph. It tells the story of the movement in each of Mississippi's communities, with inventive and challenging exhibits showing the best that contemporary museum design can offer. It's easy to spend hours there, sunk in stories of those heroes who risked and sometimes lost their lives in the struggle for justice. And justice is done to Medgar Evers, James Meredith, Fannie Lou Hamer, Bob Moses, James Chaney, Andrew Goodman, Michael Schwerner, and many others whose names resound less loudly in the history books. In addition to a trove of interviews and films, the artifacts can be chilling: a charred cross, a re-created jail cell, shards of glass from a bombed-out church, the rifle that killed Medgar Evers. I left the museum feeling lightened and raised. Though I knew many of the stories, it was impossible not to be inspired by the courage and wisdom that is honored there.

Yet the museum has few surprises for anyone who has seen the National Civil Rights Museum in Memphis or the Center for Civil and Human Rights in Atlanta. Mississippi's museum is no better or worse than these, and all three are important. What is truly surprising is the Museum of Mississippi History. Instead of the whitewashed story so many had expected, the museum is organized around the heading "One Mississippi, Many Stories." It begins with a gallery devoted to the Choctaw and Chickasaw Nations, sparing few details about the laws that forced them to abandon their homes. The director, Rachel Myers, is determined to show what Mississippi looked like from the perspective of Native Americans, enslaved people, women, and others whose stories are often obscured. "It's the only way to do justice to the richness of Mississippi," she said, smiling innocently. You can compare the dwellings of wealthy planters, yeoman farmers, and enslaved people, all of whose homes have been carefully reconstructed. There is, to be sure, an exhibit of the many flags used during the Confederacy, but there are also the tools used during Reconstruction by African American blacksmiths, information about the evils of the sharecropping system, and several damning quotes of the Ku Klux Klan. The final gallery, devoted to the years from 1946 to the present, begins with a SNCC symbol showing white and black clasped hands. "However did you get away with it?" I asked the young director. She smiled and said there wasn't much oversight. Politicians had too much to do to examine the content of the museum they'd demanded. The result is an honest portrait of a very complicated place that is indeed able to face up to its history—at least as long as it's inside a museum.

The grand opening was marred by Donald Trump's decision to crash the party, causing black activists—from Jackson's mayor, Chokwe Antar Lumumba, to Congressman John Lewis—to boycott the occasion. But Trump came and left quickly, and his appearance could not overshadow the power of Myrlie Evers-Williams, who spoke that day. Evers is the widow of the murdered civil rights hero Medgar Evers, an activist in her own right, and an eighty-four-year-old woman whose strength and beauty would be formidable in a woman half her age.

"I stand before you saying I believe in the state of my birth," said Evers-Williams. "And that is something I never thought I would say."[21] She had been skeptical about the concept of two museums, she continued, fearing that Mississippi was returning to the old idea of "separate, and possibly equal." Former Governor Winter, standing frail on the podium at ninety-three, convinced her that both might be necessary. "Going through the museum of my history, I wept," said Evers-Williams. "I felt the blows. I felt the bullets. I felt the tears. I felt the cries. But I also felt the hope that dwelt in the hearts of all those people." The two museums, she concluded, are not separate. "Both buildings share the same heart, the same beat. My hope is that people will come here from all over the world to study humanity, to see how we made progress." If that's not the voice of Enlightenment, nothing is. Evers-Williams's voice climbed in cadences that grew headier with every sentence. "Make use of these jewels that we have here. Walk through the halls and put your finger in the bullet holes, hear the sounds of the gospels, the cries and the tears. Lead the way throughout America, because we are being challenged almost as much as when Medgar Evers was alive. This is my state! This is my country! And I refuse to turn it over to anyone who challenges that." The unnamed object of that remark had already boarded Air Force One, though I doubt that Myrlie Evers-Williams would have hesitated to say it to his face. "Stand tall," she concluded, "and go tell it on the mountain that Mississippi has two museums linked together in love and hope and justice. If Mississippi can rise to the occasion, the rest of the nation should be able to do the same thing."

Reacting to the murder of Medgar Evers, even John F. Kennedy changed the views he'd had when writing the tribute to Lamar.

"I'm coming to believe that Thaddeus Stevens was right. I had always been taught to regard him as a man of vicious bias. But when I see this sort of thing, I begin to wonder how else you can treat [the Confederates]."[22]

6

Faces of Emmett Till

For it is always the face that matters. When his mother, Mamie Till Mobley, insisted on leaving his body unretouched, his casket open, what everyone remembered was the face. What was left of the child's visage after hours of vicious torture is so gruesome I will not describe it in these pages. If you really need to see it, you can find it on the web. If you have seen it already, you never want to see it again. When Till Mobley—a tough civil rights activist before there were many—insisted on showing it at his funeral, she hoped it would produce wrath. With wrath, just possibly change. She couldn't imagine that the image would become the spark that lit the smoldering civil rights movement. African Americans of a certain age remember exactly where they were when they first saw that photo.

What is the decent way to represent it? The Emmett Till Interpretive Center, across the street from the Sumner, Mississippi, courthouse where the boy's murderers were acquitted by an all-white jury, chose not to use that picture. It doesn't appear at all in their storefront museum. Instead they chose a picture of one of the cuter ten-year-old boys you ever saw, grinning in overalls. "We want to remind people it was a *child* that they murdered," says the center's director, Patrick Weems. Seventeen miles down the road is ETHIC, the Emmett Till Historic Intrepid Center. It is owned and run by John Thomas, the mayor of tiny Glendora, where Till's body may have been found. Mayor Thomas, whom everyone in Tallahatchie County calls Johnny B., has taken the opposite tack. His museum has a life-size wax reproduction of Till's coffin and body, along with a replication of the storefront of Bryant's Grocery, where Emmett Till's trip to buy a piece of candy turned out to be fatal. Again it is the face that compels you to look—and look away.

For many who knew little of civil rights history, New York's 2017 Whitney Biennial was the first place they encountered Emmett Till's face. Dana Schutz, a successful white artist, exhibited a painting called *Open Casket*. It is vaguely expressionistic, the face itself a wild blur. Hannah Black, an Afro-British artist based in Berlin, wrote a Facebook post that went round the art world and beyond. She argued that the painting should be destroyed, for it was another attempt made by white people to capitalize on black pain. Others went further and called not only for the picture but for the artist to be burned. It didn't happen, but a strong young black artist, Parker Bright, stood in front of the painting to prevent its being viewed. Some called *that* performance art. *What have they done to that face?* it was asked. The discussion provoked a debate about cultural appropriation that is unresolved to this day.

∽

"In the South, particularly the Deep South, courtesy is more important than truth," said Frank Mitchener. We sat in his sunlit office in Sumner, overlooking the muddy bayou. Mitchener spent much of his life as a cotton planter. "Not many people left who still have a grandfather who fought in the Civil War," he told me as he showed me a picture of a ramrod-straight soldier in uniform, cigar in one hand. "He carried the flag." Mitchener is also proud to be one of the last people alive who went to the Till trial. "That trial was a catalyst for the civil rights movement." He's the president of the National Cotton Council, which makes him a powerful man in these parts. That enabled him to raise the money to renovate the courthouse, the base of the Emmett Till Interpretive Center, where Mitchener serves as cochairman. "The best thing about the Emmett Till trial," he told me, "is that it happened sixty years ago."

You would think after sixty years, thousands of pages of scholarship, and an FBI investigation, everything about the death of Emmett Till, and the trial of the men who murdered him, would be known. But there are still questions open that leave people bickering in the Mississippi Delta today.

Here's what is certain.

Emmett Till was a fourteen-year-old boy full of life and dignity. His short time on this earth was not easy. His parents' marriage ended before he could know his father. Complications at his birth left consequences so severe that doctors feared he would never walk. After he overcame that hurdle, a bout with polio left him with a mild speech impediment. But he was raised by a tough and loving mother who was utterly devoted to bringing him up right and a grandmother who was there for support when his mother went to work to pay the bills. They lived just outside Chicago, part of the Great Migration that left the violence and oppression of the South for cities up north, where they could find decent jobs and raise their children to hold their heads high.

Emmett developed a strong sense of responsibility early on, doing the cooking and household chores to relieve his mother's struggles. That didn't stop him from being a boy who loved baseball and made everyone around him laugh. Besides his mother and grandmother, he had a large extended family, some who came from Mississippi for visits, some who came to stay for good. Kin were always welcome. So when his great-uncle, Mose Wright, invited him and his beloved cousin Wheeler to come down south for a vacation, Emmett wanted to go. Wheeler Parker was his idol, his other half.[1] There would be farming and fishing and plenty of open space. And there was something else, as his mother wrote later:

> When Emmett crossed over into Mississippi, there surely must have been something familiar to him. Not something he recognized with his eyes, but something he felt deep within his soul. Mississippi had always been a part of his life . . . Even in Argo, even in Chicago, Mississippi was still a place we were desperately trying to escape. Why had my son wanted to go back there so badly? What was this deep longing he felt? It was like he had been programmed at birth to return to the soil of his ancestors, at this time, in this way, and for a purpose he could not possibly have recognized.[2]

His mother said no. Absolutely not. His grandmother concurred. They prayed on it. Emmett argued, Emmett pleaded. Papa Mose Wright, a respected preacher who sharecropped a small plantation, gave assurances. "In a curious kind of way," his mother continued, "a way that only makes sense to a fourteen-year-old boy away from home, away from the familiar world of a doting mother and grandmother, to that boy, Mississippi represented free-dom."[3] In the end they said yes. It was the worst decision they ever made.

Not that they failed to prepare him. *Don't talk to white folks unless they talk to you first. If they do, say "Yes, ma'am" and "No, sir." If you see a white woman coming, you step off the sidewalk. Don't look her in the eye.*

"'If you have to humble yourself,' I told him, 'then just do it. Get on your knees, if you have to.'"

"It all seemed so incredible to him. 'Oh, Mama,' he said, 'it can't be that bad.'

"'It's worse than that,' I said."[4]

She repeated her lessons. In the relatively safe Illinois world he'd grown up in, she'd never had to talk to him about race. He was raised with a sense of confidence and pride. Everything he'd learned all his life had to be unlearned to prepare for the trip. But "how do you give a crash course in hatred to a boy who has only known love?"[5]

You can't, not really, but the first week of Emmett's vacation was delight-ful. When he wasn't helping pick cotton, he and his cousins went fishing or swimming in the Tallahatchie River, dodging water moccasins in the day and listening to *The Lone Ranger* around the radio at night. For boys from the city, the Delta was idyllic. All that wide-open space. Wheeler Parker was proud to pick one hundred pounds of cotton in a day, which was too hard and too hot for Emmett, even with a hat on. "Mississippi is home," said Wheeler Parker half a century later. "Ain't nothing wrong with the land. Ain't nothing wrong with the dirt. Some of the people aren't too cool."

I was awed by his understatement. For Wheeler Parker was there, pray-ing for his life, when some of those people barged into Mose Wright's house at two in the morning, looking for the boys from Chicago. The men's names were Milam and Bryant, and they were half brothers. Bryant was the owner of Bryant's Grocery and Meat Market, the only store in tiny Money, Missis-sippi. While Papa Mose was in church, the boys had driven the few miles uptown to buy some treats. Bryant himself was fetching a load of shrimp from New Orleans. His young wife, Carolyn, was minding the store when Emmett went in to buy two cents' worth of bubble gum.

Emmett left the store with his gum. He whistled. Was it a wolf whistle? Or the whistle his mother had taught him to use when his stuttering threat-ened to get the better of him? No one will ever know. Turns out that a whis-tle, any whistle, was reason enough for a death sentence in that place and that time. In the dark of his home, Papa Mose pleaded. If Emmett had done anything wrong, he would take care of it. Even whip him if it came to that.

Mose's wife, Aunt Lizzy, offered the intruders money if only they'd leave the boy alone. They were armed and undeterred, and they took Emmett out to the back of their truck, where at least one other person was waiting. Milam told Papa Mose they would kill him if he ever identified them.

Everyone who saw what happened next is dead now, so no one alive can say for sure. What's certain is what Bob Dylan, at the age of twenty, put so delicately: "They tortured him and did some things too evil to repeat."[6]

Emmett Till was probably dead by the time they threw his body into the river, but they tied a seventy-five-pound cotton-gin fan around his neck just to make sure. They failed to weigh down his feet, so a fisherman found his body a few days later. Mose Wright was called to identify the corpse, which was so mangled he could do so only by the ring on Emmett's finger, which had belonged to the father the boy never knew. Hoping to destroy any evidence that might bring trouble to his county, Tallahatchie County sheriff Clarence Strider ordered Mose Wright to get the body in the ground immediately. It took several courageous black Mississippians to prevent that from happening and send the body back to his mother on the *City of New Orleans*. It was the train she'd put him on two weeks before.

The face she had to identify, she wrote, was much worse than the face that the rest of the world saw three days later, though she'd asked the funeral director not to retouch it. She knew she could have described it in detail, but "people still would not get the full impact. They would not be able to visualize what had happened, unless they were allowed to see the results of what had happened. They had to see what I had seen. The whole nation had to bear witness."[7] She was right, and they did. Tens of thousands filed past the body that lay in a Chicago church, and millions more saw the photograph. Men cried, and women fainted.

It became national, even international news. Writing from Rome, Mississippi's own William Faulkner said, "If we in America have reached that point in our desperate culture when we must murder children, no matter for what reason or what color, we don't deserve to survive, and probably won't." The pressure was on Mississippi to act this time, so Bryant and Milam were locked up in a Delta jail. They confessed to kidnapping Emmett, though they claimed they'd let him go. In preparation for the first time in Mississippi memory that white men would be tried for killing a black boy, the state began a slow campaign. Sheriff Strider said the body had been too long in the water to be positively identified. Anyway, he said, there was evidence that the NAACP had plotted the crime. The jury was carefully selected to ensure that the murderers would likely be acquitted.

And they were. In September 1955, after a five-day trial, despite the unshakable evidence of brave African Americans who risked their lives to testify against white men, the jury took one hour and seven minutes to pronounce the murderers not guilty. Mamie Till Mobley came down from Chicago to dispute the claim that the body found in the water was not the body of her son. She stayed with T.R.M. Howard, a wealthy black doctor and activist who provided her with bodyguards. And in a moment so dramatic it's been turned into a play, Mose Wright became the first black man in Mississippi to accuse and identify the killers in public. "Dar he," said Wright of the man he'd seen kidnap his grandnephew. The photograph taken by the *Chicago Defender* shows an unswerving white-haired farmer pointing straight to the accused. That photo too went around all the wire services. Later civil rights heroes like Medgar Evers and Ruby Hurley worked with the black reporters who sat in separate side seats, along with Mamie Till Mobley. Like everything else in Mississippi, the Sumner courthouse was segregated. None of their strategies were enough to change the verdict, but with hundreds of journalists attending the trial, the story became known to the world. Mose Wright, who had never lived anywhere but the Delta, did not wait long. He left the cotton in the field, sold his farm animals, and, with the help of Dr. Howard and Medgar Evers, left for Chicago. His life was worth less than nothing in Mississippi anymore.

You cannot be tried twice for the same crime in America. Knowing this, Milam and Bryant were happy to take the $4,000 *Look* magazine offered for their story. It was a lot of money in that place and time. Four months after the trial was over, they confessed what most people knew: they killed Emmett Till. They said they hadn't meant to go that far, "but that boy showed no fear. What else could we do to keep *those people* in their place?"[8]

◦◦◦

Those are the facts that were proved over and over. Most people born in America before about 1970 knew them. Mamie Till Mobley spent the rest of her life speaking about it, fanning the spark until the civil rights movement was truly burning. Rosa Parks said it was the thought of Emmett Till that made her refuse to leave her seat on that bus in Montgomery. You couldn't avoid knowing about it. Unless you lived in the Mississippi Delta, where no one wanted to talk about it for a long, long time.

"Not even at home?" I asked several black Deltans. "Something grandparents passed down to their grandchildren, perhaps as a warning?"

Most of them said no. Benjamin Salisbury, who works at the Interpretive Center, said some of his teachers did mention it, especially during Black History Month. "None of them said 'If you don't watch out, you'll wind up like Emmett Till.' I think the ones that talked about it wanted us to understand that the history, the stuff in the book, got there because it happened outside of the book first." But Benjamin went to school in the twenty-first century, and his mother is a community organizer. Many other young African Americans who came from the places where the murder happened learned about it first at the summer seminar the Winter Institute gives for high school students across the state. The institute plans carefully to avoid traumatizing them.

White people in the Delta lived with silence too. Maudie Clay grew up just across the bayou from the courthouse, and she didn't hear the name of Emmett Till until she was twelve. Even then, her teacher's view of the story was, well, peculiar. "She explained that a bunch of outside agitators came into Sumner, and when she was in West Tallahatchie High School, they couldn't get off the bus and go to the drugstore and drink Cokes because their parents said the town was full of outside agitators. It was all those reporters who came for the trial."

It's not unlike the silence that reigned in Germany in the first decades after the war. In both German and Jewish families, anything connected to the war was off-limits. Neither side could bear to talk about it, one side afraid of facing its own guilt, the other afraid of succumbing to pain and rage.

If you wanted to know, you could find out a lot. The facts I just listed have been confirmed now for decades. Patrick Weems told me about the matters that scholars still debate. He was born outside of Jackson in 1985 and began his political life as a right-wing Republican. Hurricane Katrina began to change his views. Sometime during his studies at the University of Mississippi he underwent a crisis of conscience, interned at the Winter Institute, and began to volunteer in Sumner, where he's now the director of the Interpretive Center. After showing me the meagerly funded memorial park in Glendora, he took me to the red, rusting bridge over the river where Till's body was found. That's the official story.

"The problem with the story is that it's not a river, it's a bayou. The water moves very slowly—too slowly to carry a body all the way from Leflore County, where he was murdered. And the water's way too low." We looked out over the grimly named Black Bayou, which is studded with cypress trees. Though they were bare and bleak at the time of year I first saw them, I loved the way they stood straight in the water. They are all over the county, and I never saw them without humming the old civil rights song "We Shall Not Be Moved."

"Look at the lines on the trunks," I said, pointing. "The water used to be several feet higher. And wider as well; those trees on dry land have watermarks too."

The land was not really dry when we scrambled down to look at it, pushing our way through tangled bramble. I turned back when the mud began to squelch through my boots, watching as Patrick continued to investigate the trees. "You're right," he said. "The water could have been high enough back then." I couldn't share his excitement. The question mattered a great deal at the time when it was a question of jurisdiction. Had the body been found in Leflore County, the trial would have been held there; the prosecution might have had a chance. Some say that Sheriff Strider purposely brought the body to Tallahatchie County, where a hostile, poor white jury was easy to ensure.

Given that the distances are a matter of a few miles, I couldn't see why these unresolved questions mattered. For the rest of the world, Emmett Till was murdered in the Mississippi Delta, like so many African Americans before him. What I wanted to understand was the present: What does Till's murder mean in the Delta today? How is it remembered? How is it repressed? What do local people, black and white, think about the efforts to commemorate it now?

But nowhere is Faulkner's claim more fitting: in the Delta, the past is not even past. Patrick is working on a tourist trail that will tell different versions of the story. They are all still alive there.

∽

The Most Southern Place on Earth is the title of one book about the Delta. "The Delta is to Mississippi what Mississippi is to the rest of the country," says another. It's a place of myth and poverty, and it probably always was. Even after every song and story you may have heard about it, the Delta hits you viscerally. Some people cannot stand it. "I don't want to be part of a poverty safari," said my son as I took him down Highway 61 to New Orleans. "It's all right for you," he added. "You're doing work here." Some people cannot let it go. As we stood in line at the Clarksdale Juke Joint Festival, a white woman from Greenwood told me,

> There's a magic, an aura about it. Watching that sunset over the Delta, you've got people that will look at it and say "There's nothing here" and you're going

"No, it's all right there, you've just gotta be open to looking at it." And when you see those colors shot across the sky, you just feel it. Feel the humidity when your hair stands out like crazy. There's just no way to explain it unless you were born and raised here.

I told her I got it, even though I wasn't. I even get why many black people feel that way too. Morgan Freeman, who was born and raised here, now spends most of his spare time in Clarksdale. He's got a home, a restaurant, and a blues club there, and he is often the man behind anonymous donations for local causes—private kindergartens, signs commemorating Emmett Till. He once paid for a fancy high school prom, on the condition that the students agreed to integrate it for the first time in Clarksdale history. But even black Deltans like Wheeler Parker, who are unprotected by fame and wealth, call the place home.

It's a harsh kind of home, and probably always was. When white Americans who'd exhausted the soil in Georgia or Alabama came out to settle the Delta in the nineteenth century, it was wilderness in every direction. More panthers, bears, and alligators lived there than human beings. Millions of trees had to be cleared before the land was ready for farming; the rich black soil is considered the best in the world, with the possible exception of the delta surrounding the Nile. Trouble is, what makes the land so rich is what also makes it menacing. The Mississippi floods frequently, and while it spreads fresh fertile topsoil all the way from Illinois, it also washes out crops, and lives, on a regular basis. Even when the river isn't flooding, the weather is extreme. All that flat space makes tornadoes and lightning easy to see at a distance, but they hit real fast. Summers are maddeningly hot, mosquitoes huge and fierce. The bears and the panthers are gone now, but you have to watch out for poisonous spiders and snakes.

The harshness of the land was compounded by the harshness of the settlers. A great deal of violence shadows those wide-open plains. As white settlement expanded with black slavery, Native Americans were slowly pushed from their lands. Andrew Jackson's 1830 Indian Removal Act drove most of the Choctaw and Chickasaw, who'd populated the Delta, westward on the Trail of Tears. The soil they had lived on is so rich that for a good forty years the Delta was the place where America's greatest fortunes were made. White planters took black earth and black bodies and forced into bloom the crop that would fund their lavish lives. Weeklong house parties with hoopskirts and hunting and plenty of whiskey. Mansions with Greek porticoes and marble bathrooms. The field hands who generated the product that created the wealth were truly dirt poor. At a time when cotton was America's most valuable export, hundreds of thousands of slaves (and later sharecroppers, whose lives were only marginally better) toiled to produce the white gold. Picking cotton is hard, says everyone who ever tried it, and it has to be picked in late summer, when the fields offer no shade from the relentless sun. Slaves were tortured to keep up the vicious pace.[9]

You can still see fields of cotton all over the Delta, along with soybeans, alfalfa, and rice. But as agriculture became increasingly mechanized, most of the field hands became superfluous. Their luckier grandchildren find work today as guards at one of several huge prison complexes. Those who are unlucky tend to sit on the desolate stoops waiting for something to change. Most of their houses are in desperate condition.

In an attempt to fight the destitution, the state of Mississippi has encouraged tourism by trying to market the region's highlights. You can take the Blues Trail from Memphis all the way down to Yazoo City. It's studded with metal signs marking the birthplace of John Lee Hooker or the crossroads where Robert Johnson sold his soul to the devil. You can see Charlie Patton's grave and B. B. King's birthplace. There's a sign for a Juke Joint Chapel in Clarksdale that reads

THE GOOD LORD MUST LOVE THE BLUES
ELSE HE WOULDN'T HAVE MADE LIFE SO DAMNED HARD

There are several creaky blues museums to visit, and a host of annual music festivals. The Shack Up Inn has renovated sharecroppers' cabins; you can pay $95 to spend a night in two funkily dilapidated rooms. "The Ritz We Ain't," says its website.

The second initiative is the Freedom Trail, sometimes called the Civil Rights Trail, set up by the state of Mississippi in 2011 "both as a visitor attraction and an educational tool."[10] Surely some of those who constructed it genuinely admire those men and women who risked and often gave their lives to bring justice to the state. The trail marks the grave of Fannie Lou Hamer, the homes of Amzie Moore and Medgar Evers, the place on the highway where James Meredith was shot, the parks where Martin Luther King held rallies, and many spaces devoted to Emmett Till. The markers are reverential, but their supporters also care about revenue. Mississippi is the poorest state in the nation, and the Delta—two hundred miles long and eighty-five miles wide—is its poorest space. There are very few jobs there. The Blues Trail and the Civil Rights Trail, which cross at several points, can feel awkward and eerie. They are evidently a way to commodify suffering, but they are also a major source of income for the rural black community. Buy a meal or a tank of gas in the Delta, and you're helping some family get by. It's a moral dilemma the young may find easy to resolve. I don't.

Sumner, Mississippi, is a good case in point. Its population of about four hundred is literally divided by the train tracks that separate black from white. Like many a place in the Delta, freight trains still blow that lonesome whistle as they pass by. Like many a place in the South, it's centered on a square anchored by a courthouse, with a Johnny Reb statue guarding the front. Surrounding the square are a row of storefronts, about half of them empty. Around the back are the remains of what used to be juke joints. There is no grocery store. Despite all that good earth, the Delta is called a food desert, since the fields are devoted to cash crops. You can go two miles down to Webb and buy junk food at the Dollar Store, or you can ride twenty miles to Clarksdale and get something better. Like many a place in the Delta, the town was on the verge of dying until it decided to own, and own up to, Emmett Till.

It's only seventy miles from genteel, wealthy Oxford, and another world entirely. That's the right amount of space for a day trip, but after a day trip to Sumner, I wanted a whole lot more. There's no hotel near Sumner, but Patrick found me something better. His in-laws, Maudie and Langdon Clay, have a gorgeous Victorian on the bank of the bayou, brilliantly funked up with offbeat statues grouped ironically with signs like HELL HURTS. They also have a cousin who owns a building on the square. It's occasionally used as an art gallery, and there's a small apartment on the second floor. When I went to get the key at Maudie and Langdon's place, Langdon had cooked up a fine dinner. They are both internationally known photographers, and they told me they're the only Democrats in Tallahatchie County.

Maudie is as local as it gets, though unlike anyone in these parts, she spent ten years in New York City, where she met and married Langdon. A fifth-generation Mississippian, she was born in the house where she lives. Her mother was born there as well. Her grandfather owned ten thousand acres of cotton plantation in neighboring Sunflower County, where the family spent their summers. It was "a pretty bucolic childhood. We never did a damned thing. My brother and I tried to pick cotton one time, and I don't think we lasted more than a couple of hours," she said ruefully. "Having grown up here as a white person of some means was kind of like winning the lottery, but I didn't quite know how lucky I was until later."

She grew up with books and *The New Yorker*, both a rarity in Sumner even among families of wealth. Maudie always wanted to get out of Sumner, until she had children of her own, when she returned to raise them in the small town she knew. "And then they could leave it. Can't really say why, except that I just had a very deep connection to this town and this Delta. I have a real mission here. I've taken some photographs in other places, but this is the place I wanted to reveal, just by keeping a record of what it was like here." Her haunting book of Delta images is dedicated to the memory of Emmett Till. Born in 1953, she is too young to remember the trial, but she read most of what was written about it. Like the time a *New York Times* reporter was approached by "kind of a country guy who said 'Why are y'all so interested in Emmett Till? There are hundreds of dead niggers in the Tallahatchie River.'"

That's just why Emmett Till matters, of course. That's what Black Lives Matter marchers mean when they chant

Michael Brown, Emmett Till
How many black boys will you kill?

When Maudie came back to Sumner, she thought "in my insane youth" that she could change people. "I thought people can listen to reason, understand that there's a big world out there, and that this sort of insular thinking is wrong. But it turns out I didn't have many allies out there." Because her family has long, deep roots in Sumner, she and Langdon are tolerated "as token liberal artists," though her neighbors never talk to her very deeply. She has seen some progress. "When I was a kid, a black person had to jump off the sidewalk and tip their cap, and I didn't even know there was anything wrong with that." The biggest change in her lifetime came when African Americans were allowed to vote, though she noted that it took death and destruction to get there. Sometimes Maudie engages in local politics, even running for alderman. Mostly she takes powerful, poignant photographs and looks forward to leaving for Europe whenever she or Langdon has a show there.

"Are there enough towels over there?" asked Maudie as I rose to leave for the apartment they'd lent me. "Be sure to shake 'em out." The brown recluse spider, she continued, has a bite that can kill an old man or a baby. "They've been living in this house for a hundred years, so we try to coexist with them."

I found no spiders, and with its airy ceilings and exposed brick walls, the apartment would delight anyone seeking space in Greenwich Village. What buoyed my heart the most was the view overlooking the square out to the courthouse, where, despite an expensive renovation, the clock kept no time. Everything moves so slowly that it doesn't much matter. After the Sumner Grille shuts down at nine p.m., there isn't a soul on the square, and my car was the only one parked there. There was a bit of a glow from a streetlight, and no noise but an occasional hound barking into the darkness.

◦~◦

The Emmett Till Interpretive Center began with an apology. Jerome Little, the first African American president of the Tallahatchie County Board of Supervisors, believed that the town of Sumner should apologize to the Till family for the murder and trial. Little, who grew up on Frank Mitchener's plantation, couldn't move the most powerful person in town by himself. But he knew Susan Glisson, the director of the Winter Institute, because of her work in Philadelphia, Mississippi, where she had helped move the community through the process that brought the murderer of Goodman, Chaney, and Schwerner to trial. When Susan turned to Governor Winter for advice, he urged her to contact Betty Pearson, a fierce and fearless plantation owner in Sumner who had been radicalized by witnessing the trial. With Little, Pearson became cochair of the committee that eventually constructed the apology that was read on the steps of the courthouse in 2007. When Pearson retired to California to be near her children, Mitchener took her place.

Over dinner with Susan and her partner, Charles Tucker, I asked him what Susan's contribution to Sumner had been; I knew she was too modest to tell me herself.

"She moved the biggest boulder in Tallahatchie County."

"Boulder?"

"Frank Mitchener," said Charles.

"Susan's a peacemaker," Frank Mitchener told me later.

For years, some in the African American community had pushed for a monument, but without white support they got nowhere. The early meetings were contentious. They fought over the word *apology*. Mitchener refused to agree to one. He had nothing to do with the murder and he opposed the outcome of the trial, so why should he apologize for it? He was willing to agree to the word *regret*. The compromise was to call it "The Apology" but to use the word *regret* in the text itself. Frank thinks the process worked because they agreed to the Quaker model of ruling by consensus. "It takes a little longer, but it works." But the committee didn't just want an apology, it wanted to restore the courthouse, and many in the community objected.

"'Why in the damned hell are you trying to fix that courthouse? Why do you want them to remember how it was in '55? We want to forget about that,'" Mitchener quoted.

Mitchener didn't get to be a boulder without learning how to negotiate. The town was dying. The courthouse provides a couple of jobs, but its significance is primarily symbolic. A courthouse is the anchor of every town in Mississippi; it's the center of Sumner, such as it is. Without a working courthouse, a town is likely to expire.

"Frank loves his community," said Patrick. "Jerome called him the godfather of West Tallahatchie. Maybe even Tallahatchie County. People say that if Frank believes it should be done this way, he probably has a good reason for it, and we should go along with whatever Frank thinks."

"I'm one of those white people who wanted to save the courthouse," said Frank. Even if it meant opening old wounds. He described his childhood as idyllic: raised in a little town where he could walk to school and back home for lunch, play football at recess, ride horseback in the country. Like most white people in Mississippi, he began by telling me that the North was racist too. "We in the South get criticized for having segregation until the sixties. Yet Princeton University was segregated." He'd had an offer to study at Princeton, but his father refused to let him go north of the Mason-Dixon Line. "And the United States Army was segregated until 1949." On the whole, Frank told me, the Delta was a cosmopolitan place. "We had three or four Jewish families, the Italians had grocery stores, and the Lebanese, who we called Syrians. In Cleveland they had three school systems: Chinese, whites, and blacks."

Aside from a stint in the army, Frank has spent his life in the Delta. You can see his love for the place in the way he sweeps his arm over toward the muddy bayou that passes, slowly, just feet from his office. "You've heard the term *earmarks*? That's a dirty word now, but that's where we got our money from." Frank asked Senator Thad Cochran—"a moderate Republican like myself"—to set aside $850,000 to renovate the courthouse. The renovations took several years, and the renewed courthouse did contribute to a small revitalization of the town. There's a good restaurant on the square now, and a brand-new beauty salon. Both are black-owned and -operated small businesses. Race relations are better now, most people say. There's a little bit of tourism; even buses come by regularly to tour the courthouse.

Patrick, or one of the volunteers from the Interpretive Center, begins the tour by reading the apology.

THE APOLOGY: RESOLUTION PRESENTED
TO THE FAMILY OF EMMETT TILL

We the citizens of Tallahatchie County believe that racial reconciliation begins with telling the truth. We call on the state of Mississippi, all of its citizens in every county, to begin an honest investigation into our history. While it will be painful, it is necessary to nurture reconciliation and to ensure justice for all. By recognizing the potential for division and violence in our own towns, we pledge to each other, black and white, to move forward together in healing the wounds of the past, and in ensuring equal justice for all of our citizens.

Over fifty-two years ago, on August 28, 1955, 14-year-old Emmett Till was kidnapped in the middle of the night from his uncle's home near Money, Mississippi, by at least two men, one from Leflore County and one from Tallahatchie County, Mississippi. Till, a black youth from Chicago visiting family in Mississippi, was kidnapped and murdered, and his body thrown into the Tallahatchie River. He had been accused of whistling at a white woman in Money. His badly beaten body was found days later in Tallahatchie County, Mississippi.

The Grand Jury meeting in Sumner, Mississippi, indicted Roy Bryant and J.W. Milam for the crime of murder. These two men were then tried on this charge and were acquitted by an all-white, all-male jury after a deliberation of just over an hour. Within four months of their acquittal, the two men confessed to the murder.

Before the trial began, Till's mother had sought assistance from federal officials, under the terms of the so-called Lindbergh Law which made kidnapping a federal crime but received no aid. Only a renewed request in December 2002 from Till's mother, supported by Mississippi District Attorney Joyce Chiles and the Emmett Till Justice Campaign, yielded a new investigation.

We the citizens of Tallahatchie County recognize that the Emmett Till case was a terrible miscarriage of justice. We state candidly and with deep regret the failure to effectively pursue justice. We wish to say to the family of Emmett Till that we are profoundly sorry for what was done in this community to your loved one.

We the citizens of Tallahatchie County acknowledge the horrific nature of this crime. Its legacy has haunted our community. We need to understand the system that encouraged these events and others like them to occur so that we can ensure that it never happens again. Working together, we have the power now to fulfill the promise of liberty and justice for all.[11]

It meant a lot in Sumner, and it didn't come easy. But like Richard von Weizsäcker's speech in Germany, it stated only what the rest of the world thought obvious.

The makeshift museum tells the story of Till and the trial, but the center's main focus is the present, leading small groups of visitors through discussions before they tour the courthouse itself. As at the Winter Institute, discussions begin by asking participants to recall the first time they noticed race. "We actually had a Rockefeller," Patrick told me. "David Rockefeller told his story of recognizing that race existed while he was at Harvard because he had a black roommate. Then Bill Foster, a sharecropper's kid, told his story. It's really good to see people integrate their own stories into Till's story and this national story."

You can't quite say the town has prospered since it acknowledged its history, but it is no longer moribund. Frank's connection to Senator Cochran provided a lifeline. I'm loath to say his involvement only stemmed from pragmatic motives. He has a sense of justice that led him to attend an NAACP meeting back in 1959. "I just felt like I needed to. They weren't getting much white support, and they needed my support." Ninety-nine percent of white Tallahatchie County was against any form of integration. Three white faces at the NAACP meeting in Clarksdale couldn't change things on their own; it was federal intervention that forced it. Still, the support of a few white Mississippians—Betty Pearson at the forefront—was important.

But Frank's sense of justice is tempered by loyalty to his own family history. It was his grandmother, a member of the United Daughters of the Confederacy, who built the Johnny Reb statue on a pedestal that reads OUR HEROES in front of the courthouse. He doesn't want the statue taken down, but he was crucial in the decision to erect the plaque that stands on the other side.

EMMETT TILL MURDER TRIAL

IN AUGUST 1955 THE BODY OF EMMETT TILL, A 14-YEAR-OLD BLACK YOUTH FROM CHICAGO, WAS FOUND IN THE TALLAHATCHIE RIVER. ON SEPTEMBER 23, IN A FIVE DAY TRIAL HELD IN THIS COURTHOUSE, AN ALL-WHITE JURY ACQUITTED TWO WHITE MEN, ROY BRYANT AND

J.W. MILAM, OF THE MURDER. BOTH LATER CONFESSED
TO THE MURDER IN A MAGAZINE INTERVIEW. TILL'S
MURDER, COUPLED WITH THE TRIAL AND ACQUITTAL
OF THESE TWO MEN, DREW INTERNATIONAL ATTENTION
AND GALVANIZED THE CIVIL RIGHTS MOVEMENT IN
MISSISSIPPI AND THE NATION.

A Mississippi magnolia marks the sign as official state property. I don't know how many committee meetings it took to agree on the statement, but I know that each word was considered over and over. If you want an emblem of the state today, you cannot do better than face that courthouse. In the front, the American flag waves over the Mississippi one, which still has a Confederate flag in its upper-left corner. On each side, a memorial: one to the "deathless dead" who fell serving the Confederacy from Tallahatchie County, the other to Emmett Till. In the current debate over Confederate monuments, many in the South argue that they should stay and be complimented by monuments to others: civil rights heroes or victims of racist terror. But in Sumner, as elsewhere, the monument to the Confederacy towers over everything else.

That marker is made of very thick metal. The purple ones that dot the county, marking different steps of the Till saga—the grocery store, the funeral home, the cotton gin, the place where his body was (perhaps) found— are not so solid. They were damaged very early. "Jerome said this is what you get when you have national leadership like George W. Bush," Patrick told me. "This is what happens on the local level when people at the top are giving them cover." One sign was knocked down. One was smeared with the initials KKK. And one was shot up. It was replaced. And shot up again. And again. Seven times. Patrick let it lie in his parents' garage for a couple of years before he put up a new one. Just five weeks later, in July 2018, four bullets pierced it anew. The sign is located two miles down a gravel road outside of town. This is not a matter of chance.

Not every white man in Tallahatchie is as torn between justice and loyalty as Frank Mitchener. When pushed to choose between them, most will favor loyalty, even if it means violence. But there are conversion stories too. When the thick metal sign first went up before the courthouse, one white man was enraged. He marched into the courthouse, screaming at a black woman who worked there. She called the police, who came but didn't help. Then she called one of the white board members of the Emmett Till Memorial Commission, who came down to the courthouse to speak with the man I'll call Bobby.

"What's the matter?" asked the board member.

"Why are we bringing this Emmett Till thing up again?" He kept on; she listened; and when he was done ranting, she asked just one question.

"Bobby, how old is your son?"

"He's about to turn fourteen."

"Well, Bobby, we're not trying to force anything on anybody, but we think this is an important story to tell so this kind of thing doesn't happen again."

Bobby went home and thought about it. The next day he went to the board member's house. She was anxious until he spoke. "Look, my wife is a seamstress. We think we need to have a proper unveiling the day of the apology. I think she could put something together so we can have a proper cloth on top of the sign."

And she did.

Not every conversion happens so quickly, and it's hard to know how deep Bobby's conversion went. It was a start, however, and it's the kind of thing that gives Patrick hope. He sees the Interpretive Center as a place "to incubate new stories." He wants not to dwell on Till's murder, but "to use this space not only to reflect on this community's journey toward racial reconciliation, but to point the finger back at the tourist and say 'What are you doing on your own?'" This would be, he says, a pivot from dark tourism to reconciliation tourism. "Which might be out of bounds for what a museum on a shoestring is supposed to do, but I don't care." Patrick hopes for a grant that will allow him to develop an Emmett Till trail, renovating all the spaces and accompanied by an app that explains and raises questions about the story. In the meantime, there are occasional art exhibits, poetry readings, drama and film performances.

Two evenings a week the space is open to Baby University, where Mae Ruth Watson, who trains Head Start teachers for a living, lectures on what she calls positive parenting. All her students are African American, in their late teens or early twenties, and most of them are obese. It is almost impossible to eat well in the Delta. She teaches them to replace corporal punishment with discipline, and television with interaction. At every session they receive a free case of Pampers and a box containing a healthy meal of chicken salad and fruit. Mae Ruth bowed her head to say a quick grace before opening her plastic container. "You have to break bread with us," she told me, for I'd hung back, unwilling to take anything from this impoverished institution. "There's plenty for everyone," she assured me.

Mae Ruth was scathing on the subject of education in the Delta. When she first entered community college there, she told me, she couldn't speak a whole sentence. A trim, silver-haired woman with grace and authority, she worked her way up till she could train Head Start teachers herself, turning the program into one of the best in the state.

✑

I thought about Mae Ruth's claims about the Delta school system while I was talking to Benjamin Salisbury. He's the only person who has worked at both Emmett Till museums, giving tours, doing clerical work and odd jobs. Born in 1985 about a mile from Sumner, he graduated from West Tallahatchie High School, then went to a Delta community college. "I majored in music. I didn't think I was good at anything else." He taught music in elementary school, but he "did a horrible job" and decided that teaching was not for him. I can understand that. Benjamin is a warm and friendly young black man with very little self-confidence. His inarticulateness has nothing to do with vocabulary; he doesn't quite believe he has a right to speak, at least not with force. He was clearly surprised at my own way of talking when we spoke about national politics. He seemed to agree with everything I said about Obama and Trump; he'd just never heard anyone speak so decisively. Before you can learn anything else, your teachers must have taught you that your voice matters.

Ben was raised by a single mother who works on community development for an NGO. "She works in trying to help people, in a nutshell. It was always something she . . . I wouldn't even say 'made time for,' it's just what she did." So it's no surprise that Ben wants to give something back to the community. "Tallahatchie County is my home, good and bad, or what I perceive to be good and bad." He volunteered for the one Emmett Till center before getting a paying job at the other, for he believes that learning the story can help the community. "Because we live one day at a time. So you're trying your best to ensure that if you saw the beginning of that day, you'll see the end of it. But we're connected to those things that guide us to the day we're in."

Ben insisted that he wasn't taught the Emmett Till story as a way of scaring young black people into compliance. "But growing up here, there were certain things you were taught about how to carry yourself to minimize the likelihood of being targeted or accused of something. In my house we were told the importance of just doing such and such and avoiding such and such."

"What were you supposed to do, and what were you supposed to avoid?" I was interested in specifics, but how can a young black man in the Delta—

told all his life to watch what he says—feel at ease with a strange white woman who walks into life here for a very short time?

"The way my mother described it was: Carry yourself like a child of God. Carry yourself like a person who knows God for themselves and that intel should prevent some things from happening. Sometimes bad stuff happens no matter what, but there's a difference between those instances and those where you bring unnecessary attention to yourself." In other words: Don't stand out. Don't talk too loud or too forcefully. Australians call it the tall poppy syndrome, but down in the Delta it's not just flowers whose heads get cut off.

I asked Ben what he'd like to do with the center if money were no problem. Suppose a big grant came through: What would the Interpretive Center do with it to help the community? His answer was immediate: he would like to offer scholarships for youths in the community so they could take steps to be self-sustainable. "For black people, it was a dream come true to be able to go to college." Now the cost of an education, even at a small local college, has made that dream unaffordable. Who from the Delta can afford to graduate with debt? He'd also like to have a computer lab that gave the community access. Tablets are getting cheaper, but most people have no internet access. The internet connection in the apartment where I was staying, right on the Sumner square, was so hopeless that I'd taken to using the wireless at the Interpretive Center.

"Contrary to popular opinion," Ben continued, "most folk in this community don't disregard the ability to learn. There are things that—I don't want to say hinder, but there are things that stand as obstacles to them taking certain steps to be a little more informed and engage with the world outside the one they know."

It would take so damn little. College scholarships, broadband access. They'd create a community where people felt they had to know what was happening in the world simply in order to talk with their neighbors.

Ben has decided to stay in Mississippi—for now, he says. "I know that just as we all have the capacity for bad stuff, we also have the capacity to do good. There is that hope that resides within myself, my family and friends. So that's why I guess I love this place. Mississippi is special because it's a surprisingly accurate reflection of our country. It's good and bad."

&

Bill Foster was always ashamed that he was born in Mississippi, and grateful that his family moved to Illinois when he was six years old. He still remembers his teachers, and he's grateful for the education he got there. I noticed the difference immediately. Unlike Ben, who is still struggling to find his voice, Bill was educated to believe he has the right to speak boldly and clearly about anything under the sun. As a child, he made fun of Mississippians. He was astonished that his cousin Jerome Little wanted to stay in Sumner. "He loved it here, always had animals. He was happy to go out and slap the hogs." Bill's family came down from Chicago to visit their kin every summer—through 1955. He still remembers the rules of the day. "Face down if you see a white person coming; you move to the side. At no time did you have any interaction with females. That was really taboo." After Emmett Till was killed, there were no more summer vacations in the Delta.

Like Jerome, who would be the driving force behind the Emmett Till Interpretive Center until his death in 2013, Bill was born on Frank Mitchener's plantation, where his father worked chopping cotton. When they moved up north, he found work digging graves. Bill himself worked for the railroad, laying track in the Chicago cold until he joined the air force, which he called his lucky break. If he'd joined the army, he would have been sent to Vietnam. Instead he got to see the world: five years in Germany, another year in Korea.

Bill preferred the summers in the South to the winters in the North. When he first retired to Sumner, he wondered what the hell he was doing there. If anything feels like home to him, it's Chicago. Yet there are times when he appreciates the smallness, the neighborliness of Sumner. Like the time he got a prescription at the pharmacy and later ran into the owner, who said he owed him some pills. He'd counted them wrong the first time.

Bill Foster's original connection to the Interpretive Center was through his cousin Jerome, but he began volunteering because of Patrick Weems. Initially Bill thought Jerome was mistaken, stirring up all that painful history. Let the past be past. Then he read the apology. "And I got to understand what they were trying to do here. A lot of it was for the courthouse; it's not because they're so good inside. In the South people are more concerned about monuments. I never thought about leaving my name on something."

Now he leads tours there. However many mixed motives were behind the restoration, he thinks people should know the history. He's disappointed that people from outside the community seem the most interested; locals, whether young and old, don't care as much. There are some, he allowed, but Patrick seems to be better at reaching them.

Bill Foster remembers the first time he saw the Emmett Till photo. He was eleven years old, standing with his cousins, and he cannot describe the look on their faces. "I thought: Why would they show the body like that? It was a powerful, powerful moment." For a long time he thought the murderers were monsters. "They had that much hatred in their hearts?" Now he thinks they were "just people, and that's what people do." He has seen people "turn into animals" in gang wars in Chicago. "They weren't any worse than the guys that I know."

Later I asked Patrick how he won the community's trust.

"Slowly," he said.

Everyone in the county, black and white, greets him warmly, even if it's just with a wave from a car window. He is friendly and respectful, and he remembers all the names. He joined the volunteer fire department. For years he worked without a salary to build up the center. That made an impression on the black community, which was suspicious of a white boy from Jackson. But he learned everything there is to know about Emmett Till and got to know the surviving Till family. Being a student of Susan Glisson, who was well respected in the black community, surely helped. And it didn't hurt that he was courting Maudie and Langdon's daughter, Anna Booth, and got married in the Sumner church.

It's easy to see why Patrick feels a rapport with his in-laws. His own parents are "pretty supportive" about his work at the Till Center; his mother has donated to it, but they've never taken a tour and they don't really understand it. His grandfather ran a gas station—"just a step above the Bryants." This meant they weren't classy enough to be invited to join the White Citizens' Council, and they didn't join the Klan. His mother claims she didn't know anything about the racist terror going on in Mississippi and Alabama; she was caught up in joining a sorority, not knowing what was going on in the rest of the world. Or around the corner. "My mom made sure my dad didn't say the N-word around us, but it slipped out from time to time." Some of those memories are vivid and painful. Like the rest of his family and friends, Patrick was a die-hard Republican who got his information from Fox News. He was enthralled by Bill O'Reilly. He was still a Republican when he started interning for the Winter Institute in 2006. "We didn't understand civil rights and human rights as a political issue. We were of a mindset that things were post-racial. They were rough around the edges, but we just needed to make this last push and we'll integrate everything. Then we can finally have black Republicans." Susan Glisson and the Winter Institute opened his eyes; so did a black preacher in Oxford who listened to his story and gave him books to read. Desmond Tutu. Henri Nouwen.

"He uses the language of a beloved child of God, and he means that. I didn't know I was a beloved child of God, and to really claim that means that you have self-worth and you can also give that self-worth to other people."

As we drove along the two-lane highway, Patrick asked if I could smell it. "We've been crop-dusted. They call it the Delta crud." He pointed to a small yellow plane flying low over the soybean fields. "What you're smelling now is poison." It stank. We rolled the windows tighter. In addition to many health problems born of poverty and poor nutrition, cancer rates in the Delta are high. That's one result of the crop dusting on those long, lonely fields.

Patrick's cell phone rang; it was a Chicago newspaper doing a story on the memory of Emmett Till. "It's not guilt that drives me," he told the journalist. "It's a sense of responsibility." When he hung up, I told him that's the slogan of the best postwar Germans: no to collective guilt, yes to collective responsibility.

The granddaughter of Sheriff Strider, the man most responsible for fixing the trial, bent over backward to help the center. Patrick is grateful for her help, which also led him to think about the differences between guilt and responsibility. Responsibility, he says, is more powerful "because guilt like that is not sustainable. It's not systematic. It's not helpful." Responsibility, on the other hand, is something that can drive you for a long, long time. "I might not be at the Emmett Till Center forever. I might have to take a job that pays more bills, but my true work, my passion, will always be this kind of work."

I'm not sure his distinction between guilt and responsibility works. It's true that guilt can twist you, turn you lame. If that happens, it makes everything worse, turning remorse into resentment. When your soul is the thing that matters most, it can leave you seeking redemption without regard to the souls you left behind. There's a lot to be said for the Jewish tradition around Yom Kippur. That's the day we read a plaintive list of our collective wrongdoing and ask God to forgive us. *We* have sinned. *We* have lied. But you are not meant to sing the prayer without first going to everyone you've wronged during the past year and making amends. Otherwise God will not hear you.

I doubt that guilt can be entirely separated from responsibility. What makes a young white man from Jackson feel responsible for this corner of the Delta? Isn't it at least partly the fact that members of his own family, though never veering into murderous racism, had been the sort of softly angry racists whose views helped shape the world that would acquit a child's killers?

I'd heard a lot about Johnny B., one of the first black activists in Tallahatchie County, before I met him, but I never heard the same thing twice. "One of them guys who started to fight for whatever rights people had." A sonuvabitch? A shyster? A racist? A black Donald Trump? A convicted felon? Asking around, I never got the same two stories about what he did to deserve six months' jail time—during which he continued to serve as the mayor of Glendora, conducting business by phone. Embezzling the federal funds earmarked for his town? Bootleg whiskey? Whatever it was got him kicked off his original post as treasurer of the Emmett Till Commission. Once the foundations looked at the website and saw that a man convicted for messing with money was the treasurer, the commission could forget about raising any more funds. They allowed him to stay on the board, but Johnny B. is still fuming about the fact that their public museum gets more funding than his private one, ETHIC—the Emmett Till Historic Intrepid Center— seventeen miles down the road.

One thing no one disputes about Johnny B.: his father was an accomplice in Emmett Till's murder. He worked for J. W. Milam, and what Milam told him to do, he did. Hold the boy in the back of the truck? Drive the truck itself? Burn the boy's shoes? Wash the blood that flowed from the wounds into the tin slits of the truckbed that carried him to the river? No one alive knows exactly what his tasks were. What's certain is that Sheriff Strider kidnapped Johnny B.'s father, Henry Lee Loggins, and another black man who had been there. Strider locked them in the Charleston jail under assumed names for the whole of the trial so they couldn't be subpoenaed as witnesses. It was almost like being the son of a kapo, I thought, those concentration camp prisoners selected by the SS to supervise others. Their choice was to help brutalize or be brutalized themselves, and few people choose the latter. Still, it's hard not to feel guilt for the sins of the father. Even if it's not the guilt that Sheriff Strider's granddaughter feels. Patrick told me he had more sympathy for Johnny B. than most of his colleagues did, "even when he does things that are, well, Johnny B. Go make up your own mind."

In his office at the Emmett Till museum he built in Glendora, Johnny B. was suspicious, though I'd been careful to buck local custom and call him Mayor Thomas. He wanted to know whom I'd talked with, and when I described the book I was writing, he wanted to hear more about Germany, like everyone else in Mississippi. *They really talk about it? Acknowledge, apologize, repent, renew?*

He was the first interviewee to balk when I asked for permission to record our conversation. "What for?"

"My memory is terrible." Which is true. "If I don't record it, I won't remember the half of what you tell me."

Johnny B. played for time. He is writing a book of his own about the murder, he told me. It will highlight the stories his father told him, stories no one else ever heard. Since Henry Lee Loggins was the only real witness to the torture and murder of young Emmett Till, Johnny B. thinks his book will be a sensation. He's been working on it for years.

"How's your book gonna affect my book?"

I assured him I wasn't there to steal his story. I would not ask about the secrets his father told him. Perhaps my book might even help raise interest in his. "I'm only devoting a chapter to the commemorations of Emmett Till. It could make people curious to hear the whole story."

There was an old clock ticking on the dull brown wall of the office and foyer to his ETHIC museum. Johnny B. hesitated a moment longer.

"Okay, let's tape," he said.

He began by complaining about the museum in Sumner. In Glendora, by contrast, "you have an institution that is the first in the country recognizing the situation with the child who was fourteen years old. In 2005, two years before they did anything in Sumner. Yet we've been totally left behind. We spent four hundred thousand dollars and are barely able to keep the lights on, which is how this free state of Tallahatchie works. I've been trying to correct that since '75, being the first African American elected to office in this county since it was founded in 1833."

He was also angry about losing the fight with Frank Mitchener, who refused to apologize for the murder and trial ten years earlier. "We asked for an apology and received a regret. 'We regret what happened,'" he repeated with disdain. "It's too late now."

He went on. "They don't show the kid's body as we display it here. I think it should be the full treatment, as Mrs. Till said. In Sumner you won't find the casket or the body display, which I think is a crucial part of everything."

I asked him what he would do with a bigger grant if he had one. It's a fantastic sort of question, so his first answers were understandably vague. He'd like to get the community engaged in its own history; they don't care enough. He's an advocate for charter education and hopes the other building on his land could be converted to an educational facility. That would lead to jobs, if people only cared about the history of the community. "We should have our own documentary. You should be able to get a DVD. Have our Trail of Terror tour or the Glendora walking tour, which includes all the sites involved in the murder of Emmett Till."

Though I kept my promise not to ask about his father, he wanted to talk about him anyway. "The African Americans that were engaged in this heinous act are now being called accomplices. They were directly under the duress of J. W. Milam, who lived just over there." Behind the wall where Johnny B. was pointing lay a long tract of bare field.

"He doesn't sound like a man you could say no to."

"He wasn't. When you pass this building, there used to be a crossing. A train was coming, and J. W. Milam told one of his fellows, 'I don't like this truck here. Take it and run it into the train.' He did. End of story. That's how much clout J.W. had here."

Glendora is frighteningly poor. Its two hundred citizens are all African American. It's hard to call it a town, just a few flimsy houses and a ramshackle row of stores alongside the train tracks. Only one was open, selling fishing tackle, chips, Wonder Bread, and beer. Otherwise there's just ETHIC, Johnny B.'s museum in an old barn. Outside it is a rusting wagon wheel and a cotton-gin fan. There are weeds pushing through the cracked brick path. Patrick once took me here to look at the river site. Everywhere else in the county, people give him a friendly wave, but in Glendora, a young black man, eyes full of despair and anger, rolled down his window to spit. Nobody seeing the state of the town could blame him.

I asked Johnny B. how his father's story affected his life. His answer was indirect; he said he was destined to be where he is today. "Milam once said there would never be a nigger running this town as long as he lived. Because I was a year, eight months, and twenty-eight days old at the time, he couldn't stop me."

Johnny B.'s father told him Milam was a good man, as far as it went, well-regarded in the community until the crime. Were standards of goodness so low that they didn't notice? In the introduction to *Blues for Mister Charlie*, James Baldwin's play based on Emmett Till's murder, Baldwin wrote that he feared he would never be able to draw a valid portrait of the murderer:

> In life, obviously, such people baffle and terrify me and, with one part of my mind at least, I hate them and would be willing to kill them. Yet, with another part of my mind, I am aware that no man is a villain in his own eyes . . . But if it is true, and I believe it is, that all men are brothers, then we have the duty to try to understand this wretched man; and while we probably cannot hope to liberate him, begin working toward the liberation of his children. For we, the American people, have created him.[12]

Worried about possible attacks on his family, Johnny B.'s father went into hiding after the crime. Whether attacks from a white community still fearing he could reveal something that might do them harm or attacks from a black community unable to let out its rage on the real criminals, Johnny B. wouldn't say. For six or seven years his mother raised eight children on her own. He was the only one in his family who couldn't pick cotton.

"Couldn't or wouldn't?"

"Couldn't. My older brother could pick two hundred pounds by three o'clock and barn it and go home. I got to be out here all day, and I wound up with twenty or thirty pounds. Fifty years later a writer brought me a book about the lynching, and that's where I read about my mom talking about if they were sick, J.W. would come in the house and beat them and make them go to the field. I must have been there when all of these things were taking place, that's why I couldn't pick cotton. Just couldn't pick it."

Johnny B. said his father was never the same after Emmett Till's murder. As far as he's concerned, "He passed away with the killing of Emmett. He had to, he and the other African American who was there. I don't see how they could ever survive in the right sense with such an incident taking place."

He was done talking about his father. Wanting to change the subject, I pointed to the invitation to attend President Obama's 2009 inauguration, hanging framed on the wall, and said I was jealous. I'd been one of the two million people freezing out on the Mall. Johnny B. thinks Obama didn't do enough for African Americans. He allowed that he'd be in the grave if it weren't for Obamacare, but he didn't have much good to say about the former president. "I didn't get a chance to get any closer to him than the first inauguration and that was the Fallen Hero ball I was invited to as a result of my son committing suicide in the military after two tours in Iraq."

His son had enlisted for a career in the military and served seventeen years, the last few as a medic. Somewhere along the line he developed PTSD. "My daughter-in-law recognized the situation and tried to get him to go in for treatment, but he knew that any time they go in for treatment, that was it. No more promotion, no more advancement."

I was quiet for a long time. There were no windows in the big tin barn to stare out of, and it would soon be time for both of us to move on. I asked him what he thought Emmett Till's story can do for us today.

"I'm a believer that if you don't remember the past, then you don't know where you're going. You just stumble back over the same thing. So Emmett, as we use him here, is the beginning of healing. I think that case, at some point, will be a shot heard round the world. I've had Russians, Ukrainians come here. Everybody."

I am still trying to understand how the story can heal. Heal whom, in fact. Doesn't the image of Emmett Till create pain? Rage on the one side, shame on the other? "Racial reconciliation begins with the truth" is the first sentence of the Sumner apology. That's a fine beginning. Now what?

Johnny B. thinks the white community has to step forward for healing to work. African Americans have been too reactive. "I can apologize for my father being involved, and that's what I did. That's when we got the family down here—we held Emmett's seventieth birthday here in Glendora with his family. Because I wanted to apologize on behalf of my father as well as this community. It was this community that it all took place in, from pre-meditation to the end of the day when the blood was washed out on these grounds."

He is proud to own the grounds. Their original owner had told him, "'Johnny B., you ought to be floating down the river behind this town.' Just like they did Emmett. I looked at him and said, 'You ought to be in front of me.'" This is, Johnny B. told me, the reason he worked so hard to buy the place. I understand his desire for revenge. I understand the youth who spit at a car full of white people on the Glendora tracks.

Not six weeks after our talk, a big storm hit the Delta and a tree fell on Johnny B.'s house. The roof collapsed on the bedroom where he was sleeping with his wife. That's Delta weather, and Delta housing. His wife was killed. Johnny B. survived.

∾

I was not the only person driving around the Delta listening to stories about Emmett Till in the spring of 2017. Long before the Dana Schutz painting, Black Lives Matter brought the case back to the fore. The North Carolina–based historian Timothy Tyson had just written a book, criticized by the local people and lauded elsewhere. Its singular feature was Carolyn Bryant's confession: contrary to what she'd said at the trial, Emmett Till never tried to touch her. Most people thought she was lying back then, so what difference did her late confession make? At least three films about the case are in production, one of them produced by Jay-Z and Will Smith, another by Whoopi Goldberg. There were also Darryl and Brandon, documentary filmmakers who had already made a film about racial terror in Florida. Like me, they were less interested in the Till trial itself than in its impact on the local com-

munity. Over first-rate hamburgers and fries at the Sumner Grille, Darryl
was telling me about his work covering juvenile (in)justice for *The New York
Times* when he spotted his quarry on the other side of the room.

"That's John Whitten sitting at the bar. He's the son of—"

"I know who John Whitten is." His father was one of the lawyers appointed to defend Milam and Bryant. I'd even been shown, during a quick
drive-by, the military arsenal he keeps in his backyard, but I'd never seen
him up close. He looked like a caricature of a good ole boy: big belly, small
eyes, short white beard, a sort of hunting cap on his head. It was the first time
in the Delta that I felt a shiver of fear.

Darryl wanted to interview him very badly, and he spent much of the
dinner wondering whether he should introduce himself. Should he walk over
to the bar and buy him a beer? Would it be rude to interrupt him in front of
his wife and friends? Maybe not, but would the fact that his friends' backs
might be turned signal disrespect? After eyeing him all evening, Darryl decided against approaching him; he had the man's phone number, and he'd be
returning to Sumner again. That's when Whitten, weaving slightly, walked
straight up to us. "What a good-looking table! Y'all ought to stay here."

Darryl says that Southern men are taught to be gracious to ladies. That's
one way of putting it. Meanwhile, Darryl played his hand with the ease of a
good actor. "No! You're John Whitten? I've heard so much about you." Leer-
ing at me all the while, Whitten asked what we were doing here. In a town of
four hundred, every stranger gets noticed. I said I was writing a book about
how Mississippi remembers its history.

"Here they just defecated on it." Whitten gestured toward the courthouse
a few steps past the door. "The Emmett Till thing. I saw it, and I know what
I know."

Asked what he saw, he noted that he was seven years old at the time of the
trial, so what he saw was the television cables coming from the courthouse.
"You had to slow down or they'd bounce the fillings out of your teeth." As
an adult, however, he had talked with Sheriff Strider and an FBI agent when
an investigation was opened many years afterward. "Tallahatchie County
didn't have a damn thing to do with it, other than the sheriff missing his
guess on the county line by about one hundred fifty feet, which put it in our
court system here." He promised to tell us more if we came to his place the
next afternoon.

Sumner feels so safe it is hard to imagine a crime taking place here. Except the one that made history, and that was long ago. Whitten, however,
believes the place is full of criminals, and he keeps up his target practice,

though he doesn't hunt anymore. Preparing the deer is too hard, and he doesn't believe you should shoot anything you're not going to eat. "But if you can't defend yourself and your family, you shouldn't be here, 'cause they're going to kill you." He didn't say who *they* were, but that was his excuse for the giant arsenal he showed us the next day. The yard is very large, but most of the tanks are parked in the garage.

"Not a tank," he told me. "That's an armored personnel carrier."

"He showed you his arsenal?" exclaimed Frank Mitchener later. "Oh, Lord."

He showed it off proudly, along with his shed labeled MAN CAVE and DANGEROUS. Most of the signs inside were advertisements for beer, but one poster was remarkable. It pictured four Native Americans in full regalia, each carrying a rifle. TURN IN YOUR WEAPONS! read the caption at the top. Below, in smaller letters, were the words THE GOVERNMENT WILL PROTECT YOU. It sits behind the table that held the largest electric train set I ever saw.

"In a lot of places, the Civil War is real abstract," he told me. "Here it's close to home." His great-grandfather was a lieutenant in the Confederate Army. Whitten's grandfather's grandfather had a farm outside Atlanta when Sherman's crew went through. When they started to torch his house, he argued with the soldiers. They shot him. His widow loaded up what valuables they had. Of the twenty-four slaves they had owned, twenty-two came with them on the shambling wagon train to Mississippi. Of their own free will, emancipated. At least that's what Whitten said.

As he told it, he was in college when a black man came to his door asking to see his grandfather. "'I know you?' asked Grandfather. "'No, Dr. Thaxton, you don't. I'm doctor so-and-so. I'm sure you knew my mother, so-and-so.' My grandfather said, 'Lord's sake, man, why didn't you tell me?' and hugged him. Told me to get a couple of Cokes and cookies so they could sit on the porch swing." The man's mother was one of his grandfather's former playmates. "She was the daughter of one of the former slaves, and the families were still on good terms at least as late as the sixties. You hear all the garbage about how badly the slaves were treated. Well, some of them were, but I don't know any." Whitten opened another beer. "Why should we mistreat our slaves? A slave cost one or two thousand dollars. Cheaper than a tractor today, but you wouldn't mistreat your tractor, now would you?"

With the sky turning gray, the sun had receded; I started to shiver. Even the Delta can get cold in February.

"We've got a damp cold down here," said Whitten.

I could not find the moral line between shutting up and listening for the sake of information, and being a coward. He knew I was not on his side. When I'd said I was based at the University of Mississippi, he'd replied, "I wouldn't piss on it if the whole place was burning." Given what I'd come to know about the University of Mississippi, it felt ludicrous to imagine it as a hotbed of liberal thinking, but that's how it appears to much of Mississippi. I suppose it's the difference between the gentility of the White Citizens' Councils and the brutality of the Klan. Some say the Klan never took hold in the Delta, if only because the planters depended entirely on black labor. Finding truth is so hard when you stand on foreign ground. Though I didn't really think the man would harm me, I didn't think anything I could say would possibly change his views. I decided to keep my mouth shut and listen to him talk. To this day, I don't know if I should have walked away.

His version of the Civil War was the one I'd heard talk about, but never quite so directly. *Nobody in the South was in the slaving business. They just bought what was sold to them by those northeastern sea captains. Slavery had nothing to do with the Civil War. It was all about taxes. The South was carrying the burden while the North was getting rich.*

"By the time the war broke out, folks in the South had already started a program trying to educate the slaves and trying to repatriate the ones that wanted to go back to Africa—"

"I thought it was illegal in most places to teach slaves to read," I interrupted. "Or did I get that wrong?"

"I don't know," said Whitten.

"But in Mississippi?"

"I don't know," he repeated.

"You're saying people educated their slaves here?"

"As far as I know, they did. I wasn't there."

I had circled around my main interest, the Till trial. What had his father told him?

"It's difficult to make a conviction on something as serious as murder when (a) nothing happened in your county, (b) the folks aren't from here, (c) the deceased was not from here, though he had some kin. People here had no connection with it. It may not have happened at all."

"You think the murder may not have happened?"

"Well, they don't know. They didn't have DNA back then. They had a fella who'd been laying in the river for weeks and he wasn't in real good shape when they pulled him out. Who knows? As a former prosecutor myself, I tell you it's difficult to convince people to convict two guys who were well thought of, former military people. Fought from D-Day all the way to the end of the war. You can't get twelve folks to think too badly of men who will fight for their country."

Unless they were black men, many of whom were lynched when they came back home to the South after fighting for their country abroad. But that conversation was not going to happen. Instead I pointed out what everyone knew: Milam and Bryant confessed to the murder just months after they committed it.

"True," said Whitten, "but that's not a standard setup in a court of law. Once they were found not guilty, that's forever."

"I wonder what your father might have said about that."

"It bothered him."

"They did confess it."

"That case bothered him the rest of his life."

"Did he ever talk to you about it?"

"Not a whole lot."

Had we left it right there, I could have left with some pity. Not a whole lot, but some. Few people are brave enough, and farsighted enough, to stand up to the conventions of their times, even when those conventions are rotten. In the Mississippi Delta. On the wide Prussian plane. It takes heroes to do so, when most of us prefer to be victims nowadays.

But we didn't leave it there. "This whole Emmett Till situation, it wasn't a hate thing here," Whitten continued. "Just like Trump says, folks from New York came down and wrote every backwards slant they could. But all you've got to do is have one guy say it, and it's put on the internet as truth."

I suppose anyone who challenges the framework you live in will be accused of lying, at least for a while. Especially when a leader is making you doubt the possibility of truth itself. "I am just trying to understand you, because Milam and Bryant confessed it. It seems clear they killed that child. You don't think it is?"

"I can tell you what I know. I know they got paid a lot of money by *Look* magazine. And I know they told *Look* magazine what *Look* wanted to hear, or they wouldn't have paid them. We're looking at two fellows trying to eke out a durn living in two small country stores. That's why they were gone when the fuss started up in the first place. They were gone down to the coast to bring back a load of seafood to sell."

No one disputes this.

"All I know is, I wasn't there and I didn't know either one of them and it happened somewhere else. It wasn't here. The only thing we had here was the big, thick cables across the street and a half-length tractor-trailer truck that ran all the time the reporters were out there."

The pale light was fading. Whitten said it was time to go out to feed his coons.

"Your what?" Had I heard wrong?

"My raccoons. I love coons, keep one in the house. We're big on pets. The other nine are out at my place in the woods. I go to Charleston once a month and bring back a ton of dog food for them."

The word *coon* is a racial slur. Looking up its origins later, I learned there's a debate about its origin. Some say it's short for *barracoon*, Portuguese for the cages where Africans were held, often for months, before being shipped off as slaves to America. Whatever its origins, the word *coon* is now second in offensiveness only to the word that begins with an N. In this light, Whitten's obsession with his coons could be called extraordinary. I'm not a psychoanalyst, but I believe in the unconscious even for those who don't believe in it themselves.

"Y'all wanna come out and see?"

Had Darryl and Brandon not been there, I wouldn't have gotten into his truck, but they were set on the trip and I was curious about the raccoons. We drove out through the Delta, all lead-gray and brown, till we reached a shed on a plot that was run-down and dirty. A small American flag served as a curtain for one window, a large Confederate flag for the other. A little farther on was a rusting motor home, and yet another military vehicle.

"Automatic fake dog feeders," said Whitten, pointing to five containers that looked like trash cans. "You put the food in the top, they use their noses to push it open."

I took pictures of the desolation I didn't want to forget and returned to the car, pleading cold. Whitten said the raccoons come out after dark; he wouldn't expect a woman to haul those bags of dog food anyway.

Eating dinner back in Sumner a few hours later, I saw Whitten at the bar with his wife.

"I'm here every night," he said cheerfully. "Paid for these seats myself. Got my name on it, so nobody else ever takes them."

I wondered how Vanessa, the African American chef and owner of the Sumner Grille, can take it. She looked tough, patient, and weary. Like everyone else in town, she knows who he is. Away from Darryl and Brandon and their camera, Whitten talked more freely.

"Carolyn Bryant's as senile as an old goat," said Whitten. "More squirrels in her head than most people have in their attics." He insisted her confession was worthless. "Why else would that happen to him if he hadn't done nothing?"

Instead of talking about Emmett Till, he said, people should be talking of a black-on-white murder that happened in the neighborhood more recently. One of the criminals is on death row, but he isn't dead yet. "They oughtta take him out and burn him. Or at least shoot him. State executioner is a friend of mine. He's a real nice guy. I think he does it as a volunteer. Somebody's got to protect the community."

I finished my tuna salad, returned to the apartment, and locked the door, trying to understand how men like Whitten think. Or don't.

- Emmett Till must have done something to deserve it.
- Maybe it wasn't Emmett Till at all. That body was in the water for a long time.
- Milam and Bryant were fine men who served their country.
- I don't know them at all.
- They were paid a lot of money to confess it, so who knows if the confession was true?
- Carolyn Bryant is senile, her confession counts for nothing.

These claims contradict each other completely; they cannot all be true. Yet Whitten seemed to hold them in his head all at once. That must have been how the defense worked at the trial. Here it seemed to work to defend Whitten from truth itself.

Earlier in the day I'd asked Whitten why he thought people outside the state were afraid of Mississippi. His answer was telling. "They think it's a big, dark morass. We like it that way, 'cause we've got plenty of people here. We don't need any more."

❧

Thank God the next day was Sunday, and I had an invitation to Willie Williams's church. To tell the truth, I was fishing for an invitation the first time I met Willie Williams, who has been the treasurer of the Emmett Till Commission since Johnny B. had to resign.

"What I always say, and he laughs about it, I say he's a preacher, so he's not gonna steal," said Mitchener.

Reverend Williams is the preacher of a small church in Tutwiler, the tiny town a few miles from Sumner, but he supports his family with his day job at the auto body shop he owns down the road. "I love messing with cars, so I went to a trade school and learned how to do auto body work." Before he could open his own shop, he spent ten years as a security guard at Parchman Farm, the notorious Mississippi State Penitentiary. The violence there, which extended to murder, affected him deeply. He went back to school at Millsaps, a progressive Methodist college in Jackson, and was ordained as a pastor in 1998. The auto body shop is small enough to manage while still doing the work of a preacher.

Willie Williams's answering machine takes calls for customers and parishioners alike. It ends with the message "Have a blessed day, and don't forget who gave it to you." When I finally reached him, he was gracious and pleased. Willie's face is noble and handsome, and there are bits of gray in his short Afro and beard. We were both born in the year Emmett Till was murdered.

As a pastor in Tutwiler, he feels "blessed, just to live here." Working to build the community, he looks to help people "find their passion. Whether it's tutoring a kid or trying to make life better for someone else. Why did God give you the creativity you have? You can spend your life, or you can invest your life. You just have to make a decision."

One of his decisions was to join the Emmett Till Commission. He told me he was honored when Betty Pearson asked him to join and asked him to call her Betty. "It was hard, not because she's white, but because she's old enough to be my mother." I didn't quite believe that. Patrick had told me of another black board member who wanted to use the back door when invited to a party at Frank Mitchener's house. It was 2015. But he'd grown up on Frank's plantation, and, well . . . Willie doesn't want to talk about anger, and perhaps he doesn't feel it. He did speak of fear when John F. Kennedy was murdered. "The black neighborhoods said we were going to be sent back to Africa. They said this president was for black people, and that's why they killed him."

"I can imagine I'd be pretty angry if I'd been raised here, with those stories," I said.

Willie replied by quoting Martin Luther King. If you hate, you make the person you hate too powerful. Hate isn't sustainable, not without hurting yourself. The Emmett Till Commission, he thinks, is a way to make something healing out of the ashes.

He is carried by faith, but he is also the kind of person who makes that faith come alive. Willie exudes it. I know perfectly well what Marx said about opium. I know how many times Christianity was used to deflect African American attention from the hell they lived on earth. But talking to Willie Williams, you sense the ways in which faith can be a buoy, not an anchor. I'm still not sure why he'd told me earlier that I had to meet John Whitten.

"I know him a little bit," said Willie. "We talk."

"Now, how do you get along with somebody like that?"

"Well," he said slowly, "the thing is, people are different. I don't know. John is married, has two boys. He's an attorney; his dad was part of the defense—"

"I know."

"But being a person of faith, I pray for people. I believe that God can intervene in people's lives."

Could I pray for John Whitten? It was a moment when I was glad I'm not a Christian. But Christian or not, I stand by the Enlightenment. Doesn't that mean believing every single soul is redeemable, one way or another?

I was very happy to step into Willie's small brick church that Sunday morning. Half the women embraced me when I entered, and all of them did so when I left. In between, the reverend gave a strong, slow sermon. It was called "A Biblical Answer to Racism."

"I really want to be sensitive to the pain and hurt that the sin of racism has bestowed on our nation, but God is a healer. This morning let us look at Acts chapter seventeen. Here's what I want to ask you: Is God a racist? He's not. Racism is a sin against God. There's only one race, and that's the human race. There's different tribes and nations and tongues and the Bible never refers to the word *race* as applied to people. Always nations, and tribes, and tongues."

Amen, said the congregation.

"Acts chapter seventeen, verse twenty-six, look at it. 'And he made from one blood every nation.' Lord, help us now. Even knowing all you know about us, yet you say 'Come and let me reason with you.'"

Uh-hunnh, said the congregation.

"What I'm trying to tell you, don't allow bitterness to enslave you. We're not the only people—the Jewish race have been through things too. I was watching something last night about the Holocaust, the ovens and things. What kind of person does that to another human being? But it happened. We have all fallen short of the glory of God. Ask God to give you courage, to be able to see people as he sees people, amen!"

Amen, they repeated.

"It bothers me when people say we haven't made any progress in this issue of racism. We have made some! There was a time when Susan couldn't even be in our congregation."

I blushed.

"Not that she'd be threatened by us, but people of her own ethnicity would say, What are you doing down there with them black folks? God is not like man. He said whosoever will, let him come. I want to give a shout-out for our congregation—we love people, man. This place has been full of all kinds of folks from all over this country. You'll never hear me minimizing the pain of racism. But in the civil rights movement people were killed on both sides. It was one black and two whites who lost their lives in the civil rights movement right here in Mississippi . . .

"Give God some praise! We are fearfully and wonderfully made. Some of us tall, some of us short, some of us got good hair, some of us got nappy hair. Some of the folks with the good hair, they want to have nappy hair; the folks with nappy hair, they want to have good. God likes a variety; we all bring something to the table. God says come to me and I will give you rest. Now bow your heads in prayer. Lord, I pray for the healing in the area of biracial relationships."

The congregation prayed.

There was more, and collection plates were passed. Reverend Williams was trying to raise enough money to take the teenagers to the Lorraine Motel and the Civil Rights Museum in Memphis.

"We do want to recognize our guest, Dr. Susan Neiman. All the way from Berlin, Germany, what about that? She's been doing some work with the Emmett Till Commission—and I really appreciate you coming, it meant a lot to me."

Trying not to stammer, I could only say that I appreciated the warmth of their welcome. "God bless you," said the men and the women, coming up to shake hands or embrace, as they chose. I could not stop thinking of Dylann Storm Roof, for I was sure this is how he was treated that Wednesday night in Charleston. It was unspeakable enough to murder nine strangers, however often the phenomenon repeats itself throughout America. But to murder nine strangers who have welcomed you with openhearted love? The capacity to return hate with love wipes reason off the map, at least for a while. I cannot understand it any more than I can understand how, knowing that story, black churches across America continue to open their doors and their hearts to white strangers again and again. What love and courage. What courage and love.

❧

The second morning I woke up in Sumner, I saw a white man in his fifties put a bag of rice on the hood of my car. "You're a foreigner," he said. In Sumner I'd count as a foreigner if I'd come from Jackson. "Have some rice."

I was touched, for this was the Delta hospitality of which I'd heard tell. Then again, I doubted he'd be so hospitable if my skin were another color. It took me a moment or two to reply. "Thank you," I said, "but please give it to someone who needs it more. I don't eat a lot of rice."

Days later I felt I'd been churlish to refuse. Mike Wagner is a member of the Emmett Till Commission. He truly cares about racism and poverty, and he gives away tons of rice every year. And as it happens, his rice turned out to be delicious, even for someone as indifferent to rice as I am.

Mike's family has farmed for ten generations: rice and cotton and soybeans. His grandfather was considered progressive, inviting his black workers to sit at table with him. "If they're good enough to work with me, they're good enough to eat with me." Mike Wagner was offered a job working for the Pearsons, the most liberal and engaged family in the county. "I think part of the job was being their son. Betty was way left of anyone around here." Betty Pearson influenced him deeply. He started to buy land of his own; in a depressed economy, they were practically giving it away. "I probably have the closest thing to a plantation around here in terms of the land supplying the needs of the farm. We grow our own food." But he specializes in rice, thousands of acres of it. One afternoon he took me to the rice mill he'd built, full of all the colors rice can bear. He hopes his son will take over the business.

Mike is proud of using methods he calls sustainably organic; he uses a few chemicals but not the massive poison that wafts through the Delta. He prefers to spray at night, when the wind is down, so he doesn't hurt his neighbors. "He's cutting-edge," said Frank Mitchener. Mike is convinced the Delta will be "a splendid place someday. We've got the best land in the world and we've got brainy people. Now if we can only fix this damn educational system, we'll be all right."

In the past thirty years, he said, there's been wonderful progress. When he first came to the Delta from Missouri, he thought it would take three more generations to solve the Delta's problems with race and poverty. "We're about one and a half generations into my thesis. We have way more problems on this planet than the color of your skin," he said with some passion. "We've got water problems, we've got resource problems. But I digress."

Mike was asked to join the Till Commission after Betty retired. He tried to refuse, but he was, he said, the last guy there. I suppose that means the last antiracist white guy; the commission is committed to having an equal number of blacks and whites on its board. He's glad they restored the courthouse. "It's one of the best examples of Romanesque architecture in the South, and it's right here on this pretty little bayou." Had the courthouse been condemned, it would have destroyed the town. Now there's a little civil rights tourism, and the restaurant he opened and Vanessa took over. He got involved "selfishly, because I want my kids to have the best damn community in the United States. You don't need to live in an urban area to enjoy what the best is." Part of that means engaging with the memory of Emmett Till. "That event is what started the civil rights movement. That was huge."

After showing me how the rice mill worked, Mike took me back to town the long way, past Bryant's Grocery in Money, Mississippi, where the crime against Till began. The grocery has long been abandoned; one side, overrun by kudzu vines, looks ready to cave in. The Till Commission wants to buy and restore it, but the owners would prefer to consign it to oblivion. In front there's a plaque marking the shuttered store as part of the Mississippi Freedom Trail, but it's been badly scratched up. Nobody is working on figuring out who defaced that sign, nor who shot the thinner one full of holes. Mike Wagner is a gentle man. He does not want to believe that any of his neighbors could have done it. "Maybe it was just some hunters messing around," he said helplessly.

"Seven times?"

He could not answer.

⟋◯⟍

I'd left my perch in Sumner but drove the seventy miles back there often enough from Oxford, as I did for a reenactment of the trial. A high school teacher from West Virginia proposed to take his students to Sumner, where they would read the entire transcript in the courthouse where it happened. Was it a good idea? Wheeler Parker wanted it, and Patrick never says no to the Till family. The reading would take up three evenings; Jennifer Stollman and I went to the first.

It felt excruciating. Not because the kids evoked the pain, but because they could not. The mostly white students took their places in the courtroom—this was the witness stand, that's where the jury sat—but they read without affect. Sometimes it seemed they had trouble reading at all. Was it their first rehearsal? The answer turned out to be no, but in the near-empty courtroom it felt appallingly flat. They read the description of Till's beaten body the way one might read a description of how to build a house or fry an egg. Jen and I exchanged unhappy glances.

"I'll stay if you need to for your research," she whispered.

"Let's go," I answered. "I can't take any more."

I'd wanted to sit out the reading in order to meet Wheeler Parker, Emmett Till's favorite cousin, but the reenactment was so disturbing it felt impossible to stay. Anyway, I had Reverend Parker's phone number. When I reached him, he said he was leaving for Chicago the next day, but if I came to his hotel in Greenwood early, he was willing to talk. I explained my project in the hotel lobby. Wheeler Parker was interested; he'd been stationed in Germany in the '60s.

"The thing I've noticed," he said, "is that there are so many similarities between Hitler and Trump. I'm not saying Trump is as bad as Hitler, but—what did he say? The bigger the lie, the more they believe you. People want to be liked, so most people go along. You have to stand up with that fire in your belly and speak the truth in love, not in hate. The people who didn't stand up in Germany, they've got to feel terrible when the truth comes out."

"And their children hate them, mostly."

"Do they talk about it?"

"All the time."

"They recognize where they went wrong?"

"Yes, sir, they do."

Wheeler Parker is kind, and the longer he talked, the kinder he grew. His wife joined us in the lobby. She thought the reenactment was "awesome. The first time I saw it, my husband and I left in tears. This put us right in the courtroom."

"You've seen it performed by these kids before?" I asked, skeptical.

"In West Virginia. In fact it was our idea they should have the opportunity to perform it here. Some of the students were better than others."

Who was I to criticize a reading that had left Reverend and Mrs. Parker in tears? No one was closer to the story than Wheeler Parker. He'd planned the trip with Emmett, ridden together with him on that train, changed cars when the *City of New Orleans* reached the segregated South. Knelt on the floor that hot night in August, praying that Milam and Bryant would not take him too. I trod very carefully. "My friend and I didn't feel it was respectful enough. When they got to the graphic descriptions—"

"Well, that's what you want," said Reverend Parker. "You want it raw. As they talked, the description was clear in your mind. Took you right down to the river. It affected me emotionally."

He told me about the preparations for the reenactment. The students wanted some props—in particular, a cotton-gin fan. They couldn't carry one all the way from West Virginia, but they figured they were going to cotton country and could easily rent one there. They called one shop that sold agricultural equipment. Yes, there were gin fans. "Wait a minute," said the white man on the phone. "You doing that thing over in Sumner? Well, you just go straight to hell." The second call was even worse. "The last time we had a gin fan in these parts, we hung it around a nigger's neck." The man on the phone laughed when he said it, just like the man they'd called first.

I was almost too shocked to speak.

"I'm not," said Reverend Parker. His face expressed a fine combination of sadness and savvy. "Some places are covert and some are overt. Here, they just come out and tell you what they feel."

If that's the kind of sentiment still buried so close to the surface, then what the students had done was right, even righteous. Only an aesthete, I thought, would complain about how well they'd performed.

"We know their attitude toward black boys," Reverend Parker continued. "What's happening now is kind of like during the civil rights era, when they put it on TV. Then the rest of you all saw it. We experience it all the time."

Yet he called his years in Mississippi very precious. When he was coming up, everybody got to know each other, everyone shared. At the time of year when his family slaughtered the animals, Wheeler was always told to take a piece down to Mrs. Jones's house. If somebody was in trouble, somebody else was there to help them. They didn't need a whole lot, just enough to get by.

Now that chattel slavery is over, he thinks we've become slaves to riches. As a soldier in Germany, he'd been impressed that people there took time to take walks in the woods, and he swore he'd keep up that pace when he got back to America. Slow, he said, enjoying life. "I didn't last three weeks before I went back to the rat race."

Reverend Parker thinks greed is at the heart of America's troubles. "If you've got money in America, we'll look up to you. We don't care how you got it, whether gangster or dope seller. Look at Trump." He sighed. "I tell people, read the Bible. Rich people in the Bible are miserable people. Read the stories."

He thinks Obama, by contrast, was a godsend, and he has little patience for young people who say he made no difference. "They have no idea of the price we paid to get an African American president. I never thought I'd see that in my lifetime." Of course one man couldn't change everything; we expected miracles from him like we expect miracles from doctors. Think they can fix everything. Still, Obama made a difference. "I like his spirit. What they say? When they go low, we go high."

It is, in fact, the only righteous way to go. So easy to say, so hard to maintain. Yet it must have been this kind of a thought that sustained Wheeler Parker in that night of terror, and in all the nights thereafter.

"You can tell I come from a mix," he said. Like most African Americans, he is brown but not black. "So who was doing the raping? Starting back with the president, what's his name?"

"Jefferson."

Though the reverend thinks the Great Migration was mostly driven by economics, his father-in-law left the South for another reason. "You couldn't protect your wife or your daughter from the man." White men want black women, but they fear black men. He believes that's because when black men are free, they rise to the top. And the greatest fear is of black men taking white women. "People got killed for a reckless eyeball. Look at Emmett Till." He sounded weary; he is not young. "I'm trying to get some philosophy and make sense of it," he continued, "but I get so far and I can't go any further. It just doesn't make sense."

I asked Reverend Parker what he thought about Dana Schutz's painting, hanging at that moment very far from Greenwood, at the Whitney Biennial under massive protest.

"I've heard a little something about it," he said, "but not enough to comment."

"You're talking about that painting in New York?" Mrs. Parker asked, looking disgusted. "She made him look like an animal. An elephant."

That hadn't been my problem; I found the painting too decorative. Hard to tell what was being represented on that canvas, but if you hadn't seen the title, you might hang it on your wall. No one, ever, could imagine hanging up the photograph it was meant to interpret. It's too harrowing to look at for long.

"Our attorney spoke to a group of people in New York regarding it," said Mrs. Parker. "Call Chris," she told her husband. "Ask him to come down."

Christopher Benson is indeed an attorney, but that's just the beginning. He's an author, a professor of journalism and African American studies, and, most important in this context, the coauthor, with Mamie Till-Mobley, of *Death of Innocence*, her account of Emmett Till's life and death. He has also written a play, *Inheritance*, about an encounter between the daughter of Amon Goeth, the concentration camp commander made infamous by the film *Schindler's List*, and the Jewish woman who had been Goeth's personal slave. Benson sees them as part of the same story as Emmett Till's. It happens ever again. "I try to focus on the intimate story that has a much larger meaning. You focus on the traumatic memory of the survivor, but now you have an interesting story because the children of the perpetrators have also experienced some trauma."

As one who knew Mamie Till-Mobley's story so well—he was the one to help her write it down in the last six months of her life—Benson was asked by *The New York Times* to write about the controversy stirring up the art world. What would Mamie have thought about it? For her, wrote Benson, what happened to her son was not just an African American story. It was also an American story about "fulfilling the promise of freedom, justice and equality for all. She welcomed the megaphone effect of a wider audience reached by multiple storytellers, irrespective of race. Mrs. Till-Mobley opened that coffin to force us to cast our eyes on a shared national responsibility." Benson believes that Schutz's intentions in developing the painting were good ones. "Here she is in conversation with Mrs. Till-Mobley, who wanted to develop the universal themes of family love, tragic loss and a journey to justice. Still, Ms. Schutz inadvertently reminds us of a traditional expression of white power through imagery. Mrs. Till-Mobley flipped the script on the spectacle of black death . . . It is for these reasons that the image occupies such a special place in black collective consciousness." Mrs. Till-Mobley, Benson concluded, would have supported a more robust kind of engagement, perhaps even organized by the Whitney. "As a public school teacher and activist, she would have seen a teachable moment here. And so should we."[13]

Benson's call for dialogue was heard by the Whitney Museum, which invited him and others to organize a public event. Watching a video of the discussion much later, I was disappointed with all the presentations but his. Many were disjointed, dogmatic, and far away from the real world that gave rise to the story. I didn't think the painting was a good one, but it's a far cry from that to the view that any white artist's attempt to portray black pain was exploiting and commodifying that pain itself. If white people have a

254 LEARNING FROM THE GERMANS

responsibility to examine white racism, isn't an evocation of the violence it created a start? It's insulting to call this an American problem, said one panelist. For me, that turns thought upside down. How hard did the heroes of the civil rights movement fight to make Americans see that racism wasn't "the Negro problem," but something concerning us all? That if black people were murdered and degraded by white people, it is white people, precisely, who must face that problem as our own?

People fought to get the blues played on mainstream radio stations; earlier it was called "race music." As blues and gospel and R&B and soul and hip-hop took over the airwaves, there was plenty of exploitation of the musicians who created it. But shouldn't the first step be to recognize all that music as *American* treasure, then to thank the African Americans who created it by fairly distributing the spoils? *There's no fair way to do it*, some say. *That music was born from black pain and struggle, and it ought to remain in black hands.* But I know of nothing more moving than Paul Robeson's rendering of the "Partisan Lied," written in Yiddish as response to the Warsaw ghetto uprising in 1943. And the fact that he sang it in 1949 in Moscow, as Stalin's anti-Semitism began to sweep the Soviet Union, shows he knew exactly how to use it. I don't think a Jew could have done it better. It was Robeson's use of that song, in Yiddish and Russian, to express a universal fight for justice that made it all so poignant.

There is a sense in which only an African American can understand the pain that photo of Emmett Till produced. Would it be the same sense in which only a Jew can understand the Holocaust? Here the ground starts to slip. I'm inclined to agree with Jean Améry that only a Holocaust survivor can understand the pain of the Holocaust; I do not think I can.[14] Not by standing on the bone-white stones of Dachau or in the cold fog of Buchenwald. Not by reading memoirs, for even the best of them, like Améry's and Ruth Kluger's, leave me staring into a void I cannot fathom. Not by visiting a Holocaust museum that gives you a name on a tag to insist you identify with someone's true story. Jews around the world were raised in the shadow of the Holocaust, but so much was drenched in myth that, for me at least, it always felt far away. Even when I sought the truths, the myth overshadowed. Even in Berlin.

If Améry is right, the Holocaust is only comprehensible, if at all, to other survivors. Born later to the same tribe, I am not one who will ever share the understanding of which Améry wrote. At best, I share understanding of what it meant to grow up in the wake of the Holocaust with Jews like myself—those who have tried to turn that wake into something alive and universal.

Those who could grasp the Holocaust itself are not us, but survivors, be they Jewish or Roma or communist or gay. Understanding isn't tribal, the stuff that flows in your veins. It demands either shared experience or very hard work. And even then there's a gaping black hole that surpasses understanding in its heart.

Can a white woman understand the pain of Emmett Till's mother—or Eric Garner's, Trayvon Martin's, Tamir Rice's? If we cannot entirely understand it, aren't we obliged to try? "All men are slaves till their brothers are free" rang the words of the now-forgotten "Medgar Evers Lullabye." African American history in all its torment and glory is American history, and we cannot move forward until all Americans see it that way. Isn't that why Mamie Till-Mobley opened the casket to begin with?

You cannot hope to understand another culture until you try to get inside a piece of it and walk around there for a while. You know you'll never get it the way someone who was born inside it does. The songs you heard as a baby matter. The glances between your parents that could mean either joy or fear. How could you know? But they affected you the way cries in the night affected you, stirring up nightmares that went back generations. The stares and the slights you could not understand. The kinds of warnings other children didn't have to hear. Beatings too, sometimes. How many black parents beat their children, hard, so they wouldn't get beaten up worse by the man?

Those things you cannot learn later. But you can get quite a lot, actually, if you let yourself be touched by a piece of art. Made by cultural insiders for each other, to start with, but from the perspective of watchful outsiders too. Both inside and outside perspectives matter. We are not alone in this world. The arts are the only thing that have the power to shake you up. All the facts in the world don't matter until they move you, and the arts, broadly speaking, can do that better than anything else.

Anselm Kiefer became Germany's greatest postwar painter through his giant ravaging paintings that floodlit German crimes—and the tragedies, both Jewish and German, that they caused. Heinrich Böll and Günther Grass became Nobel laureates for doing the same. The light they provide is very different from that which Jewish artists evoke, but it's light that we need all the same. All three are incomparably better artists than Dana Schutz, for Mamie Till-Mobley opened the casket to make the world see something concrete. In moving to the abstract, Schutz may fairly be said to obscure it.

So this is not an argument for Dana Schutz's painting, but an argument for cultural appropriation—the only way we can begin to understand each other's worlds. As Kwame Anthony Appiah argued in his powerful book *The Lies That Bind*, we've been doing it so thoroughly for so long that it makes no sense to speak of a pure cultural product at all:

> All cultural practices and objects are mobile; they like to spread, and almost all are themselves creations of intermixture. Kente in Asante was first made with dyed silk thread, imported from the East. We took something made by others and made it ours. Or rather, they did that in the village of Bonwire. So did the Asante of Kumasi appropriate the cultural property of Bonwire, where it was first made? Putative owners may be previous appropriators.[15]

Appiah presented a host of examples that make it impossible to maintain an idea of essential cultural identities. He also offered an even more devastating argument: the problem is less that we can rarely decide who owns a piece of culture than that the very idea of ownership is the wrong model to impose on culture. "Unfortunately," he wrote,

> the vigorous lobbying of huge corporations has made the idea of intellectual property go imperial ... To accept the notion of cultural appropriation is to buy into the regime they favor, where corporate entities acting as cultural guardians "own" a treasury of intellectual property, extracting a toll when they allow others to make use of it.[16]

This is not to deny that producers of culture are often exploited and underpaid, or that cultural traditions that have value—sometimes sacred value—to those who were born into them are trivialized and disrespected. But, Appiah concluded,

> those who parse these transgressions in terms of ownership have accepted a commercial system that's alien to the traditions they aim to protect. They have allowed one modern regime of property to appropriate *them*.[17]

The hotel lobby in Greenwood wouldn't stop playing Muzak, so when Chris Benson arrived, we looked for another place to talk. "The Magnolia Room," he said with a grin. "Very Mississippi." He had talked at length to Dana Schutz, and he thinks she had every right to express her relation to the Emmett Till story. He found her well-intentioned but naïve, failing to understand the pain caused by the photo for "people who have struggled against the negative images that have been portrayed by white people taking ownership of it." He thinks provoking discourse is crucial; otherwise we cannot move forward. But he knew from his own experience how hard interpretation can be. "Each time you interpret something that already exists, whether it's a text or an image, you have to ask yourself 'What can I add to this story?' A white perspective certainly adds something." But he didn't think the painting was successful, perhaps because the softening of the photo was wrong. "I want to know the white perspective on this story," he said. "How does this affect a white mother, a white person generally? What can you bring to help me understand you better? That's more meaningful."

Because I am Jewish, Chris called me a special sort of white person. "There is a commonality between the Jewish experience, the history of oppression, and the African American experience." I was brought up to believe that, but I am no longer sure. Too many Jews have forgotten it, too many African Americans have denied it, seeing Jews as just white folks and exploiting ones at that. In the South there is still faint memory. Not just Goodman and Schwerner, but one-third of all the Northerners who came down in support of the civil rights movement were Jewish, whether they were religious or not. It's all in the Prophets, and old gospel songs. But who remembers that?

"Reverend Parker and I were talking about it over breakfast this morning," Chris continued. "That commonality is deeply rooted."

It is certainly rooted for him; that's why he's working on a piece about the Holocaust. He has talked to Holocaust survivors and Jewish intellectuals, none of whom object to an African American telling their story. "But they do want me to do it right. So it's fascinating; they embrace me and tell me stories. It's like, we're going to keep feeding you this information to make sure you understand us."

Who has a right to Emmett Till's story? Who has a duty to it? Horrific crimes were committed in the name of white women all over the South. As a member of that tribe, I surely have a duty to remember that violence and to act in ways inspired by it. But if I have a duty to a story, don't I have a right to it?

Nor do black and white exhaust the perspectives we need. I've told this story from multiple standpoints: that of the loving relative who was with the child at the time; that of the son of a man who was forced to participate in the killing; that of the son of the man who most viciously argued for the murderers' acquittal. Each has a perspective we need if we want to try to comprehend the whole. We need to know what resonates, and how generations who never knew the story are impacted by it, as well as the impact on those who were right next to it in the Delta. Looking at an event from multiple angles is the only way we can approach something like truth. As a Jew, I want to know more about W.E.B. Du Bois's visit to the ruins of the Warsaw ghetto, Paul Robeson's thoughts about growing anti-Semitism in the Soviet Union, Christopher Benson's interpretation of an encounter between the daughter of a Nazi concentration camp commander and his Jewish slave. I am enriched, not diminished, by the reflections of others. Some things you see best from a distance.

One lesson from my time in the Delta: motives are always mixed, and in the end it is not motives but deeds that matter, as Arendt showed in *Eichmann in Jerusalem*. It doesn't matter what moves you: it's what you do, and leave behind, that counts.

The scions of Sumner were saving the courthouse by nodding to history, but it was more than a nod, and it wasn't easy to achieve. The Emmett Till Commission required very hard work. And of course a mayor wants to bring funds and tourism to his destitute town, a place so poor that many shantytowns in the global South look acceptable by comparison. Johnny B. shines a light on a forgotten hellhole, and it brings some results. And if a German scholar is looking for a job and a German institution is looking for good public relations, isn't it better that there be solid historical records of how often most institutions in Germany were entwined with the Nazi state?

What is certain: it's good that those deeds have been marked and preserved. Imagine a world where the greatest crimes ever committed were consigned to dust. Where nothing acknowledged racist terror of any kind—the Holocaust, the genocides, the lynchings were left without a trace. Whatever helps us escape oblivion is welcome.

"You can't possibly understand the civil rights movement without knowing the Emmett Till story," concluded Chris Benson. "It's an American story, but it is the story that affects African Americans in a much deeper way. Tell your story and how you relate to our story. Tell your story in ways you've been inspired by our story. Tell your story in ways you've been politicized by our story and how you're now going to move forward to do your part in breaking down this system. We still see the residue of that. We haven't had that moment of reconciliation." That's just what I'm trying to do, I thought. I do not know if I will succeed.

PART THREE

Setting Things Straight

7

Monumental Recognition

There was a time when American philosophers brought passion and clarity to the major social and political events of their day. Without the words of Thoreau and Emerson, the great abolitionist John Brown could have gone down in history as a deranged terrorist.[1] Nor did the two men confine themselves to giving speeches that argued for Brown's heroism and his cause. They actively, and illegally, helped his coconspirators escape to Canada. (Emerson lent the horse; Thoreau drove the wagon.) At the age of seventy-eight, John Dewey went to Mexico to preside over the tribunal that absolved Leon Trotsky of Stalin's allegations. Dewey received death threats for his pains. In 1897 William James gave the oration at the dedication to Augustus Saint-Gaudens's monument to Colonel Robert Shaw and the 54th Massachusetts Regiment. Brought back to recent memory in the movie *Glory*, the 54th was the first company of African Americans to fight in the Civil War. Half of them lost their lives in the brave attempt to capture Fort Wagner. James's youngest brother, Wilkie, was gravely wounded in the battle.

James's speech is worth reading, for it illuminates what matters in contemporary debates about historical monuments. Some insist that those debates are about "heritage, not hate." In fact they are about neither. Few of the people who support retaining Confederate monuments actively hate black people. This is partly because you needn't be a Freudian to know that not every emotion is conscious. Even more important, the debates are not really about affect at all, despite all the emotion they raise. They are about the values we deliberately choose to hold—though emotions will inevitably attach to those values, as they should. James's speech reveals, with great passion, why monuments are made.

> The war for our Union . . . has . . . but one meaning in the eye of history And nowhere was that meaning better symbolized and embodied than in the constitution of this first Negro regiment.
>
> Look at that monument and read the story . . . There on foot go the dark outcasts . . . State after state by its laws had denied them to be human persons . . . The bronze that makes their memory eternal betrays the very soul and secret of those awful years.
>
> Since the 'thirties the slavery question had been the only question, and by the end of the 'fifties our land lay sick and shaking with it like a traveler who has thrown himself down at night in a pestilential swamp and in the morning finds the fever through the marrow of his bones.[2]

James continues with thoughts that could have been expressed yesterday.

> Our great western republic had from its very origin been a singular anomaly. A land of freedom, boastfully so called, with human slavery enthroned at the heart of it . . . what was it but a thing of falsehood and horrible self-contradiction? . . . But at last that republic was torn in two, and truth was to be possible under the flag. Truth, thank God, truth! even though for the moment it must be truth written in hell-fire.[3]

At the time James was writing, that truth was beginning to be obscured by legions of historians and popular fictions deliberately constructed to destroy those gains that still remained after Reconstruction. Since the violent protests over the planned removal of a statue of Robert E. Lee in Charlottesville, contemporary historians have filled pages of newsprint with information many of us never knew. Most of the statues that commemorate the Confederacy were built some fifty years after the war, as the sons, and particularly the daughters, of the Confederacy worked to create the myth of the

Lost Cause. The second wave of monument making occurred in the early 1960s, in response to the success of the first desegregation campaigns. The monuments were not innocuous shrines to history; they were provocative assertions of white supremacy at moments when its defenders felt under threat. Knowing when they were built is part of knowing why they were built.

James emphasized that the monument he praised was not only a tribute to the military values that Shaw and his soldiers upheld as they fought to the death on a lone Carolina beach. Shaw had, James wrote, civil courage.[4] Blessed in his life, happy in his former regiment, the white officer Shaw nevertheless accepted command of the first black company. "In this new Negro soldier venture, loneliness was inevitable, ridicule certain, failure possible." Yet "Shaw recognized the vital opportunity; he saw that the time had come when the colored people must put the country in their debt." For "our nation had been founded in what we may call our American religion, baptized and reared in the faith that a man requires no master to take care of him, and that common people can work out their salvation well enough together if left free to try."[5]

The civil courage that led Shaw to give up an easy berth in order to take on an assignment that he believed embodied those American ideals is, James continued, a lonely sort of courage. It is

> the kind of valor to which the monuments of nations should most of all be built . . . The deadliest enemies of nations are not their foreign foes; they always dwell within their borders. And from these internal enemies civilization is always in need of being saved. The nation blest above all nations is she in whom the civic genius of the people does the saving day by day, by acts without external picturesqueness; by speaking, writing, voting reasonably; by smiting corruption swiftly; by good temper between parties.[6]

James's speech makes it clear: monuments are not about history; they are values made visible. That's why we build memorials to some parts of history and ignore others. They embody the ideals we choose to honor, in the hopes of reminding ourselves and our children that those ideals were actually embodied by brave men and women. What is at stake is not the past, but the present and future. When we choose to memorialize a historical moment, we are choosing the values we want to defend, and pass on.

The 2017 demonstrations against the planned removal of the Robert E. Lee monument in Charlottesville, Virginia, established one thing beyond doubt: Nazis are not just a German problem. You may prefer to call the demonstrators white supremacists, but that's a distinction without a difference. The deliberate use of Nazi symbols—swastikas, torches—and slogans—*Blood and Soil! Jews will not replace us!*—leaves no room for doubt. Not everyone who wants to preserve those symbols is a Nazi. But American Nazis' embrace of the Confederate cause made clear that anyone who fights for those symbols is fighting for values that unite Nazis with racists of all varieties.

One argument for removing Confederate statues is that they hurt some people who have to walk the public space in which they're displayed. A descendant of enslaved people will feel injured when she walks by a bronze paean to a person who fought to keep her ancestors enchained. I think I understand how she feels. Germany has no statues of Nazis, but I've tried to imagine how I'd feel if it did, lining those streets I have come to love. Would I think, This is a statue of someone who would have killed me if given half a chance? Would I get used to the statue and simply walk by, suppressing fear and resentment all the while? I am certain I could not have stayed, or chosen to raise children, in a place where every town chose to erect a monument to Johnny Reb—call him Hans Wehrmacht—for all those who died serving the Nazi regime. But why is that?

I think it is more about reason than emotion. A hypothetical Germany still valorizing soldiers who served a murderous cause would have failed to reject that cause itself. No matter that many soldiers who fell were not true believers, but men convinced they were fulfilling a duty to protect the Fatherland, or even poor fellows who were drafted without any conviction at all. A somber, valiant figure dignified in bronze or stone has a way of lending dignity to the cause itself. Placing it in public space reflects, at the very best, ambivalence about the values for which that soldier died, whether or not any particular soldier shared them. How much more when the figure is a general whose allegiance to the cause was clear!

Germany has no Hans Wehrmacht statues, and certainly none to Rommel, usually considered the least noxious of Hitler's generals. Like most of my German friends, I thought it had no monuments to German soldiers at all, until an expert on German memory alerted me to the exception. In Friedland, a small town near Göttingen that had served as a transit camp for German refugees and soldiers, Adenauer laid the foundation stone for a monument in 1966. It is completely abstract; only its size has heroic dimensions. The monument doesn't valorize Wehrmacht soldiers who returned from POW camps in the Soviet Union, but it does place them in the center of

suffering, along with those Germans who lost their homes to Allied bombers or the Polish takeover of East Prussia. The committee that designed it
refused to mention survivors of concentration camps. All that hints at the
suffering Germans caused is a reference to the fact that "fifty million lost their
lives in the war," with no indication of how or why.[7] The memorial, wrote
Aleida Assmann, was already outdated when it was finished in 1967, and it
is virtually unknown in Germany today. The children of the former POWs,
who were instrumental in creating the monument, have learned another set
of values. They recoil from the thought of honoring men who fought for the
right to eradicate other human beings. As a matter of value, we should recoil from a monument to honor men who fought for the right to own them.
So much for Robert E. Lee.

This is about principle, not personal pain or tribal loyalty. In *Eichmann
in Jerusalem*, Arendt argued that Eichmann should have been tried for crimes
against humanity, not—as the indictment read—crimes against the Jewish
people. In the days before competitive victimhood became a major sport,
she may not have realized what an important distinction she'd drawn. Still,
she was prescient; the distinction becomes more important every day. The
murder of millions of Jews is a crime not only against a particular tribe but
against the very idea of humanity, and it is principally as human beings, not
as Jews, that we abhor and remember it. The crime we call the Holocaust—
an attempt to wipe out a slice of humankind simply for belonging to a particular tribe—was an attack on the idea of humankind itself, which is part
of the reason why so much of humankind, Jewish or not, recognizes it as the
standard of evil.

The images of cattle cars, gas chambers, and ovens are seared into whatever collective memory we have, but we don't need them to acknowledge
a crime against humanity. I support Black Lives Matter not from tribal
loyalty or even tribal guilt, but because the killing of unarmed civilians will
always be a crime against humankind itself. This is a universalist position.
At the same time, I reject the empty and misleading universalism of groups
upholding the slogan "All lives matter." They do, of course, but to say this
is to substitute a banal and trivial truth for an important empirical one. It
thereby distracts from the fact that African Americans are seven times more
likely to die from police brutality than anyone else in America—according
to the lowest estimates.[8] To understand this, of course, we need to understand the difference between universal and particular truths. In the present
age, it may be enough to hold fast to the ideal of truth at all.[9]

There is no hard data on the relations between the occurrence of violence and monuments to racist values. They are distinct, and violence can occur even when a state explicitly rejects racism and builds monuments to warn against it. Since 2000, German law has rejected the connection between German citizenship and German blood. The country is sprinkled with state-sponsored monuments to victims of racism, yet some of these monuments have been defaced, and right-wing racist sentiment has recently grown. Still, violence is more likely to occur when states subtly and suggestively support racism by supporting the valorization of those who fought and fell to maintain it. In Britain, an unprecedented rise in hate crimes has been documented since the Brexit vote, and the same is true in the United States since Trump took office.[10]

You're more likely to notice a monument when you find yourself in a strange city. You might rub Pushkin's nose for luck in Odessa or sit down next to Albert Einstein in Sedona—just to name two non-martial heroes honored in bronze. You may strain to remember what Admiral Nelson did that merited so high a column flanked by so many pigeons. Maybe you wonder when westerners began collecting obelisks, those phallic Egyptian mysteries thought worthy of venerating the first American president. Mostly you walk by in a hurry on your way to the office or the supermarket, hoping you'll finish all the tasks on today's agenda without getting too distracted to write the delicate email or pick up a loaf of bread for the morning. Living just outside Boston for eight years, I never saw the monument that William James so gloriously described.

If monuments are values made visible, it's likely you ignore the ones around you. Values are most visible when they're under threat. Otherwise they are precisely the things you take for granted, like the monuments themselves. All the more reason you may become attached to those that surrounded you as you grew. What you remember is less the monument itself, but the moments of your life that happened around it: the time you hid behind it while playing hooky or kissed in its shadow. The monument you barely noticed becomes a physical reminder of home, and you feel homeless, just a little, when it's gone.[11] Let us grant, for the sake of argument, that what residents of New Orleans miss, when they miss the now-absent Confederate statues, is not a symbol of Confederate ideology, but the feeling of being at home in the world. They'd walked, or more likely driven, right past it all their lives. But they are also missing a symbol of an ideology that refused to allow that feeling for others—who were literally not wanted, except as servants, and who could never be at home while it stood.

❧

Participating in Southern debates about Confederate monuments led me to try, over and over, to imagine a Germany filled with monuments to the men who fought for the Nazis. My imagination failed. For anyone who has lived in contemporary Germany, the vision of statues honoring those men is inconceivable. Even those who privately mourn for family members lost at the front, knowing that only a fraction of the Wehrmacht belonged to the Nazi Party, know that their loved ones cannot be publically honored without honoring the cause for which they died.

The German language occasionally uses the word *Monument* (emphasis on the last syllable) for the English word *monument* (emphasis on the first), but terms that have no English equivalent are more common. A *Denkmal* commemorates an event that needs to be thought about. If the event was particularly horrendous, a *Mahnmal* (warning sign) may be erected. For monuments to horror that are large—a restored concentration camp, for example—*Gedenkstätte* (place of reflection) is the likely term. The root word is *denken* (to think), and it signals the enormous amount of thought devoted to the question: What do we remember in matter, and how?

When William James was writing, it seemed clear that monuments were only raised to heroes. History was written by history's winners, and its losers merited no immortal attention. It's the itch for eternity that makes us remember in marble and bronze. They may not last forever, but they will last much longer than we will. In recent years, Germany has raised monuments to World War II's real heroes—those who risked or gave their lives to oppose the Nazis—as well as to the war's victims. There is also a set of monuments focused on the perpetrators as well as their victims: the concentration camps, for instance, the House of the Wannsee Conference, or the Gestapo torture chambers in Berlin. They are meant to honor the victims by showing how their tormentors functioned. All told, since 1945 Germany has spent more than a billion dollars building monuments to commemorate the Holocaust and many millions every year to maintain them. What's absent is any monument to those who created and fought the war.

Germans find the death penalty unconscionable because of the way it was used during the Nazi period. "That consciousness comes from an understanding that the Holocaust was shameful," said Bryan Stevenson. "We would not respect or work with Germany had they erected hundreds of Hitler statues throughout the country. If they were romanticizing Nazism, creating a narrative about World War II that said it wasn't really about Jews, it wasn't about world domination, it wasn't about Aryan supremacy, it was about something else—which is what we've done in this country—I certainly wouldn't have gone to Germany."

Stevenson is an African American lawyer who founded the Equal Justice Initiative, which has saved hundreds of prisoners from death row. He is also the creator of the National Memorial for Peace and Justice in Montgomery, Alabama, informally known as the National Lynching Memorial. After reading his stunning book *Just Mercy*, I was hesitant to ask for an interview: Wouldn't whatever I took of his time be better spent saving someone's life? "Thanks for coming to spend time with us" was his gracious reply to my apology for interrupting his work. Stevenson is the only national figure on record who took German confrontation with its bloody past as a model for what Americans should do with ours, and I wanted to know how he got there. An exceptionally busy man, Stevenson was kind, almost serene, when I entered his office in Montgomery.

"We're sitting in a building that's on the site of a former slave warehouse," he told me. "A hundred meters from here is the river where tens of thousands of enslaved people were brought by rail and boat. The slave auction site is literally a hundred meters up the street. If you came here three years ago, you'd find fifty-nine markers and memorials to the Confederacy, and not a word about slaves, in the public landscape." The difference between the United States and Germany, says Stevenson, is leadership. In Germany, "There were people who said 'We can choose to be a Germany of the past or a Germany of the future. We cannot do it by trying to reconcile the Nazi era with what we want to be. Either we're going to reject that and claim something better, or we're going to be condemned by that for the rest of our existence.' That was something that never happened in the United States."

Besides leadership, Stevenson thinks that what's missing in America is shame. Recent backlash notwithstanding, there is an American consensus that slavery was wrong. But even among descendants of slave-owning families, shame is hard to find. Regret is there, sometimes even remorse. Meetings between descendants of slave owners and descendants of people their forebears owned have taken place in several states. Some descendants of slave owners are appalled by the oppression their ancestors maintained. But the national sense of disgrace that led so many Germans to pass themselves off as Danish or Dutch is entirely absent; it is not the American way. Americans are inclined to believe in American exceptionalism, although those who insist the country is the greatest on earth are usually those who've never stepped outside its borders. They believe the country may have made some . . . mistakes in its past, but nothing so severe as to damage national pride. Stevenson believes that the mere recognition that slavery was wrong is not enough. "Without shame, you don't actually correct. You don't do things differently. You don't acknowledge." Guilt, it's been argued, is directed inward, and no one need know if you have it. Shame, by contrast, is what you feel when you see yourself reflected through others' eyes and you cannot bear to let that image stand. To overcome shame, you must actually do something to show others you are not inevitably caught in your, or your forebears', worst moments.

"What's fascinating to me," said Stevenson, "is that the Charleston shooting did something few things have done in the last half century. It actually made many white people ashamed. They increased the shame quotient because someone cloaked in a Confederate identity goes into a church and slaughters nine black people while they're praying. If he had gone into the projects and killed nine people, the flag would still be standing." But Stevenson has no illusions about the breadth of that shame. "It was just a moment." He doubts that Nikki Haley would have been reelected in South Carolina after directing the flag's removal, nor does he think the governor of Alabama, who followed Haley in removing that Confederate symbol, would have been removed from office for a sex scandal had he left the flag standing.

Initially, it was neither leadership nor shame that assured the absence of Hitler statues in the landscape of Germany. For that we can thank the Allies, and the fact that the Third Reich was so short-lived. A 1945 joint Allied directive outlawed "the planning, designing, erection, installation, posting or other display of any monument, memorial, poster, statue, edifice, street or highway name marker, emblem, tablet, or insignia which tends to preserve or keep alive the German military tradition, to revive militarism or to commemorate the Nazi Party, or which is of such a nature to glorify incidents of war."[12] But apart from street names and iron swastikas that studded some buildings, the Allies had little to remove. No statue of Hitler existed. He preferred to have himself enshrined in names of streets and squares, which were promptly renamed after the war. The giant architectural projects the Nazis had planned were largely incomplete; the empire that was meant to last a thousand years was defeated after twelve. Still, there might have been a wave of reaction decades later, like the one that left Confederate statues all over the South. Instead, Allied troops remained in Germany for nearly half a century, while the federal troops that prevented the South from glorifying the Confederacy withdrew after ten years. Yet fear of the Allied Occupation was hardly all that prevented postwar glorification of the Nazis. Shame played a major role, and it led not only to the absence of Nazi monuments but to the erection of thousands of monuments to their victims.

With the rise of the AfD, shame has become a subject of recent German discourse. In 2017, Björn Höcke, one of the AfD's more radical members, shocked Germany by criticizing the Holocaust Memorial that covers the huge piece of prime real estate next to Brandenburg Gate. Höcke, long associated with neo-Nazi publications, said, "We Germans are the only people in the world who have planted a monument of shame in the heart of our capital." He went on to say that the reeducation begun in 1945 had robbed Germans of their identity, and he attacked Weizsäcker's famous 1985 speech as a "speech against his own people."

Reactions to Höcke's speech were swift and sharp. Even the AfD considered throwing him out of their party, though they dropped the motion after some debate. Höcke had broken the taboos that have become foundational for the reunified German state. During the 1984 controversy over Chancellor Helmut Kohl's joint visit with Ronald Reagan to the Bitburg cemetery where members of the Waffen-SS were buried, the chancellor claimed he had the "mercy of a late birth." The suggestion was that he, like anyone born just before or after the Nazis came to power, had no responsibility for their crimes and hence no particular relationship to them. Even in the '80s, the suggestion was roundly criticized, and the phrase "mercy of a late birth" became a black-humored trope. No one believes that anyone like Kohl, who was three years old when the Nazis came to power, should be held responsible for them. But the German nation as a whole recognized a collective responsibility to remember, and do what it can to atone for their crimes.

If this idea, like Weizsäcker's speech expressing it, was already common in liberal circles in the 1980s, it became national consensus in the 1990s. That's why the giant Holocaust Memorial was built. Although I, like a number of critics, am no admirer of the form the memorial took, I admire the impulse behind it. A nation that erects a monument of shame for the evils of its history in its most prominent space is a nation that is not afraid to confront its own failures.

Höcke is right about one thing: no other nation in the world has ever done so. Britain's erection of a statue of Gandhi in front of the Houses of Parliament could be considered a start, as it implicitly suggests that Gandhi was right. But there's no monument remembering the victims of colonial famines and massacres, although a monument to the victims—or heroes, as they are called in Kenya—was erected in 2015 as part of an out-of-court settlement in which Kenyans sued the UK government for compensation for its bloody suppression of the Mau Mau rebellion. It stands, however, in Nairobi, where it's rather unlikely to be seen by a British schoolchild. Even so, those are steps ahead of French practice, which still has no public marker remembering the Algerian War. Though an African American museum and a Native American museum now grace the Washington Mall, no monument to the victims of slavery and genocide can be found there. ("The African American museum is wonderful," said Stevenson, "but most visitors go straight to Michael Jackson's glove.") No one erected a monument listing at least the numbers, if not the names, of more than a million Vietnamese slain in what they call the American War, next to Maya Lin's memorial to what we call the Vietnam one. Lin's decision not to valorize, but simply name, the American troops who fell was so politically controversial at the time that no one, apparently, thought of going further. Traditionally, after all, monuments are not built to remember failures.

Germany's unflinching memorialization of its failures is not a panacea. The rebuilding of Berlin that took place throughout the 1990s was a mind-numbingly discursive process in which historians, politicians, and citizens debated for a decade. Some choices, like the number of glass walls in new government buildings, can seem clumsy. But even if you grow weary of the seas of glass, you may admire the aspiration behind them: democracy should be transparent. No one, least of all a German, would claim that the rebuilding and renaming eradicated the roots of racism and militarism. Old resentments die slowly, though they do eventually die, unless demagogues deliberately revive them. The city was not rebuilt to reflect what is, but what ought to be. Berlin's public space represents a conscious decision about what values the reunited republic should commit itself to holding. The understanding that those values can only be truly embraced if we acknowledge the times when they were flouted is an understanding that real pride entails facing up to shame.

This kind of understanding fueled the furor over Höcke's speech, a furor that included not only verbal critique but a material response. The Center for Political Beauty, an activist group whose earlier performance pieces supporting refugees gained national political attention, rented a property directly facing Höcke's house in a Thuringian village. Supported through crowdfunding, the group stealthily built replicas of twenty-four of the pillars that make up the Holocaust Memorial—directly visible from Höcke's front windows. They offered to remove them if Höcke would take a leaf from Willy Brandt, kneeling before the world in apology for German crimes. Some critics called the action bad taste, Höcke called it terrorism, and the little field where the pillars stand was closed to the public after the artists received death threats. Still, they stand, as of this writing, as an example of creative possibility in confronting the rising right. I don't expect them to change Höcke, but the Center for Political Beauty was not interested in conversion. They believed that a provocation as deliberate as Höcke's should be answered in kind.

❧

There are monuments in Berlin that I prefer to the Holocaust Memorial. Besides the moving memorial to the Red Army at Treptow, there's a monument in the Rosenstrasse that is usually empty, though it stands on a side street just off busy Alexanderplatz. The monument consists of a little park with three reddish sandstone sculptures carved by Ingeborg Hunzinger, a Jewish artist who grew up in East Germany. A tall, round column beside the park tells the story of the largest and only successful nonviolent protest that took place in Nazi Germany.

It was February 1943, one of the darker moments of the war. Since 1936, when marriages between Jews and non-Jews were forbidden by the Nuremberg Laws, the Nazis had exercised considerable pressure to force those mixed couples who married before the laws to get divorced. Promotions were denied, jobs were terminated, rations were cut. Still, some couples remained faithful, and the government could not decide what to do with them. In the midst of a war that was looking less winnable every moment, should the government risk possible unrest by deporting those Jews still married to Aryans? They decided on a trial run, rounding up hundreds of Jewish men at their workplaces and holding them for deportation in a former office of the Jewish Community in the Rosenstrasse. Thousands of Jews had already been deported without protest.

This time was different. When the wives of the missing men found out where they were being held, they came, spontaneously, to the Rosenstrasse and insisted on having their husbands back. Having already endured considerable hardship and scorn for standing by their Jewish men, those women were as heedless of the Gestapo's guns as they were of the icy wind. They remained at the site for more than a week. The government backed down; the men were released. And nothing bears witness to this little-known protest but the starkly simple clay-colored figures on the sculpture, acting out terror and triumph. The inscription on it reads:

THE POWER OF CIVIL DISOBEDIENCE AND THE POWER OF LOVE
OVERCAME THE VIOLENCE OF THE DICTATORSHIP
WOMEN STOOD HERE
DEFYING DEATH
GIVE US OUR MEN BACK
JEWISH MEN WERE FREE

I have been to this monument many times and taken many guests there, sometimes in tears. It's often said that the tactics of Gandhi and Martin Luther King Jr. were successful because their oppressors were civilized. The British and the Americans could be moved by the moral courage of their opponents; totalitarian governments simply kill them. The women of the Rosenstrasse tell another story: even in the darkest moments of the Third Reich, right could overcome wrong with no weapons at all. What is tragic is not so much that the story is hardly known, its heroines' names unremembered, but that nobody followed their example.

What stopped others from doing so was not only the fear of Nazi terror but something else as well: the belief that heroic action is futile, and usually ends in death besides. This is the not-so-subtle message suggested by the many monuments to the Scholl siblings, Germany's most famous resistance heroes. Hans and Sophie Scholl, students at Munich's university, were arrested and guillotined for printing anti-Nazi leaflets. There is no contesting their courage, but the only consequence of their actions was to console later generations of Germans that not *everyone* capitulated to Nazi terror. Their story, like that of the other West German resistance hero, Count Stauffenberg, and his 1944 coconspirators, provides another and more sinister source of consolation: that resisting the Nazis achieved nothing but the deaths of those who tried. For millions of Germans who capitulated, that idea, however conscious, reinforced the idea that capitulation was the only rational thing to do. Unless you happened to have a taste for martyrdom.

Streets and schools named after the Scholl siblings dot the land, much as most Southern towns have a street called Martin Luther King Jr. The monument to the women of the Rosenstrasse, by contrast, inspires even as it provokes shame. The fact that their story could humiliate the millions of Germans who failed to follow their example may be part of the reason why several historians have recently tried to deconstruct the story, arguing that it wasn't the women's protest, but internal political considerations that led to the release of the men. The story remains under-researched, but no one disputes its basic truth: women dared protest, their men were freed, and all of them lived to tell the tale.

What about the memorial at the train station in leafy suburban Grünewald, from which fifty thousand Berlin Jews rode to their deaths? One track has been turned into a monument, forever closed to train traffic in acknowledgment of German railway complicity in their murder. Before the entrance is a large concrete wall studded with negative imprints of human bodies, symbolizing the absence of those who were deported. Absence is also the message of the Israeli artist Micha Ullmann's memorial to the book burning that took place on Goebbels's orders in 1933. You cannot see it until you are about to step on the glass panel that covers it. Underneath stand rows and rows of empty white bookshelves, just below the glass on the wide-open central square. Above them is a plaque quoting the nineteenth-century poet Heinrich Heine: *That was just a prologue. Whoever burns books will eventually burn people.* Another plaque states that Nazi students burned books on this spot, but the words are too sparse to convey what thousands of tourists passing by need to know: it wasn't an unwashed, unlettered mob, but hundreds of well-off and well-read students, and their professors, who gleefully followed the Nazis' first orders. There are photos showing their faces beam as they toss books into the flames right in front of the Humboldt University. We'd like to believe that illiterate masses are responsible for right-wing nationalism, but the numbers tell another story.

Most Berliners continue to insist that Germany face its own shame, even at the expense of other public goods. In 2001 the city of Berlin announced plans to build an underground parking lot in the vast space surrounding Ullmann's monument. Berlin has good public transportation but a dearth of downtown parking space. Places for 458 cars, it was argued, would fill a genuine need. Since the underground garage wouldn't displace the monument, but only fill up the empty space around it, this was an argument I accepted, especially since I'm wary of turning every reminder of terror into sacred space. But thousands of Berliners disagreed, and mounted a campaign against the parking lot, arguing that it would profane the monument. Their protests did not, in the end, prevent the garage, but it was delayed for several years, revealing the depth of citizens' engagement in preserving these hallmarks of shame. It is hard to imagine similar engagement anywhere else.

The German government agency for political education produced a meticulous report in 2000 documenting every monument to Nazi crimes in the

country. Berlin alone has 423, but some think there should be more. In particular, some people argue that the places where Nazi crimes were planned
and carried out should be preserved and remembered. There are two such
prominent places in Berlin. One is the House of the Wannsee Conference,
a villa on the city's outskirts where the Final Solution was prepared. You
can take a ride in the elevator Eichmann used, see the room where the Nazi
bosses drank cognac after lunch. At the entrance to the villa stand a pair
of graying stone angels with sheepish faces. The other is the site of the
Gestapo torture chambers, which have been partially unearthed in the city's
heart. Both sites include museums and educational centers. On the 2017
anniversary of Kristallnacht, in the lecture hall of the torture chambers,
known as the Topography of Terror, I heard a discussion on the differences
between monuments in the East and the West. On both sides, said the
historians, there was little interest in the sites of the perpetrators. Why was
Adolf Eichmann's office torn down to make room for new buildings in the
West? Shouldn't there be at least a plaque on the spot? Why was the house of
bureaucrats responsible for deportation left unmarked in the East? Doesn't
this show that both sides of the city were unwilling to confront Nazi crimes?

I think two sites of terror—one a fancy villa, the other a repellingly ugly
series of dug-up ruined cellars—are enough. The phenomenon has given rise
to dark tourism, a ghoulish curiosity to view all the places where humankind reveals its worst. There are many reasons people seek out sites of horror, and not all of them are morbid, but I don't believe they should proliferate.
Reminders of our susceptibility to evil are needed, but they need not be
overdone. There's a fine line between honoring victims and paying tribute
to their murderers—even by paying too much attention to the latter. There
is wisdom in the old Yiddish curse calling on God to give the cursed the
worst of all fates: may his name and every memory of him be forgotten. It's
an unhappy paradox: every time you remember a victim of the Holocaust,
you are keeping alive the memory of an SS officer. Like most paradoxes, this
one cannot be resolved by force. We can neither decide to forget the victims
for fear of perpetuating the memory of their torturers, nor to memorialize
every single site where evil was done for fear of forgetting how it happened.
Like most important questions, this can be settled only by judgment that
takes every particular into account.

In 1966 Berlin's mayor rejected the first proposal to turn the Wannsee
villa into a memorial museum, fearing it could become "a macabre cult
object." He wanted to tear it down. Even back then, thousands of citizens
insisted that it remain. If you're going to tear down reminders of dark history,

they argued, you'd have to tear down half of Berlin. Shortly after reunification, the monument and museum opened. It now serves thousands of German groups, who can research the Nazi history of their own professions, as well as visitors from overseas hoping to learn how to confront their own historical crimes. Delegations from Iraq, Chile, and the Congo were among those who visited the villa and met with its director in 2016. The House of the Wannsee Conference provides important services, as does the Topography of Terror, but a plaque on every building that served the Nazis would be a grim daily reminder of the worst of humanity. Far better to remember those who revealed the best of it, like the women of the Rosenstrasse.

Bryan Stevenson suggests that Southern buildings be renamed after white abolitionists and antilynching activists. He tells critics, "You should be proud of those white Southerners in Mississippi and Louisiana and Alabama who argued in the 1850s that slavery was wrong. There were white Southerners in the 1920s who tried to stop lynchings, and you don't know their names. The fact that we don't know their names says everything we need to know." If those names were commemorated, the country could turn from shame to pride. "We can actually claim a heritage rooted in courage, and defiance of doing what is easy, and preferring what is right. We can make that the norm we want to celebrate as our Southern history and heritage and culture."

There were not many white Southerners who had that kind of courage; there were not many Germans who had it in Berlin. Some would argue that elevating them creates a false impression. In commemorating its resistance heroes, for example, East Germany seemed to suggest that most of its citizens had been antifascist fighters. Once again, it's a line that only good judgment can draw. As Stevenson suggested, commemorating heroes is less a question of history than morality: these are the men and women who lived by the norms we choose to embrace. Heroes close the gap between the ought and the is. They show that it's not only possible to use our freedom to stand against injustice, but that some folks have actually done so.

In addition to the other monuments in Berlin, there are the nearly ubiquitous stumbling stones—small brass plaques recording the names and the dates of birth and deportation of Jews, gays, Sinti, and Roma who lived in the houses before which they stand. When the artist Gunter Demnig began the project in 1995, there was quite a lot of opposition, and not only from the Aryans. Charlotte Knoblauch, president of the Central Council of Jews in Germany, complained that the mini-monuments merely repeated the humiliations the victims suffered during the war, which she survived in hiding. "People murdered in the Holocaust deserve something better than a plaque in the dust and street filth." After her statement, the city of Munich refused to permit the stones, a ban still being protested today. Yes, it is true: you can step on the stones, as the people they commemorate were stepped on in life and in death. Far more often, pedestrians step around them, many stopping to pause, read, and hold in their breath.

The stumbling stones document what larger memorials cannot show: that the terror began not in far-off Poland, but in the heart of a city full of clubs and cafés, spaces where you can still buy a lottery ticket or go to the dentist. Each four-inch square recalls an ordinary human being, in the midst of her life, who was deported and murdered with little notice and no protest from the other ordinary human beings who surrounded her every day. The terror was here. Is that what the city of Munich, serenely rich and self-confident, doesn't want to face as it goes about its daily business? Did it justify its desire to be left undisturbed with deference to the opinion of one local Jew?

Whatever they may think in Munich, the stumbling stone project caught fire. It is now the largest decentralized monument in the world. As of 2018, almost seventy thousand stumbling stones have been laid across Europe, from Poland to Spain, with more applications arriving every day. Gunter Demnig has received a host of prizes, including Germany's highest honor, the Bundesverdienstkreuz. Now seventy years old, Demnig still lays nearly all the stones himself, his longish gray hair spilling out beneath his trademark broad-brimmed hat. His foundation takes care of requests and logistics. Most of the requests come from different towns in Germany. They are usually made by the children and grandchildren of the murderers, not of the victims, though the victims' relatives often come to watch the stones being laid. Those making the request must get permission from their local mayor to lay a stone in public space. Since so many German sidewalks are made of cobblestone, not much space is physically disturbed. Normally Demnig takes a cobblestone out and seals a stumbling stone in, but the political and psychic disturbance can be significant, as the controversy in Munich showed. That is, of course, the point: the stones are meant to disturb, make your head and heart stumble. In addition to obtaining municipal permission, applicants are expected to research the person being commemorated. Is the house before which the stone is to be laid the last place the deported chose to live freely, or was it in a ghetto to which she was banished? Is it possible to determine the exact cause and date of deportation? The word *suicide* is never used; Demnig insists on the phrase *escape into death*. Nor will he accept applications for stones commemorating mass murder: every victim should be remembered individually; every stone bears one name. The cost for laying a stone is 120 euros, a sum most people can afford.

Bryan Stevenson was profoundly affected by the stumbling stones. "They reminded me of the iconography of the Confederacy. You can't go anywhere in the South without running into some sign or some street or some name that is designed to remind people of this era, which they take great pride in." The stumbling stones do the same thing in reverse. Instead of pride, they are designed to evoke shame. "What I found interesting is that they have a kind of beauty and a kind of sobriety that makes it not inane. They are meant to disrupt your experience of space. For me, that was really, really powerful." Elements of that disruption appear in Stevenson's National Lynching Memorial. Located on the highest spot in Montgomery, the memorial consists of more than eight hundred columns, each representing a county in which the Equal Justice Initiative has documented a lynching. Where the victims' names are known, they are recorded on the columns. Outside the memorial is an identical field of columns intended to be transient: EJI has invited each of the counties represented to come and take one home. If the iconography of lynching could become as deep a part of the Southern landscape as the iconography of the Confederacy, truth—and, after that, reconciliation—about the nation's history would be served.

American slavery did not end in 1865. As Stevenson put it, the Thirteenth Amendment ended servitude, but slavery evolved. "We had a brilliant civil rights movement, but we didn't win the narrative war." The racial terrorism known as lynching was the most powerful instrument of white supremacy as late as the 1960s. James Meredith began his March Against Fear to combat the terror of lynching that permeated everyday life for black people, especially in the South. Despite two autobiographies, Meredith wrote that he could not put into words the sinking feeling in the stomach that came over every black American alone on a road. All this, he said, was the excess baggage in a black man's mind, whether in Scarsdale, New York, or Philadelphia, Mississippi.[13] The EJI has documented more than four thousand lynchings across 816 counties. Unlike the murder of Emmett Till, whose mother's tenacity and courage ensured that it was remembered, most of those murders were never publicly commemorated. The memory of them, however, has successfully intimidated many African Americans to this day. (The movie Get Out is a brilliant sci-fi meditation on that fact.) The spots where the murders took place have lived on in community memory even when the names of the murdered have been forgotten. "That was the hanging tree," a young white Mississippian may point out to his college sweetheart on her first visit home.

Even before the larger memorial was finished, the EJI worked to mark those spots throughout the South. Sometimes they place markers documenting a murdered person's story, a counterweight to the highway markers that document every damn skirmish in Confederate history. Even more strikingly, the EJI collects dirt. Aided by volunteers, they have shoveled earth from hundreds of lynching sites into tall glass jars displayed in the EJI's office, marking them with a label naming the date and place of the lynching and, where possible, the name of the victim. It is harrowing to see how many jars are labeled UNKNOWN where a name ought to stand.

"For me," said Stevenson, "the soil was important because I think the soil is the repository of all the suffering. We wanted it to create a tangible relationship to this legacy. In our narrative, the soil contains the sweat of people who were enslaved, the blood of people who were lynched, the tears of people who were humiliated by segregation."

My only problem with the exhibit—it is very, very beautiful. One jar, one name, one place, one date: the soil within may be mixed with bits of straw or stone, but it stands by itself as a reminder of a crime never punished, a death mourned in silence and fear. Put them all together and you have a vision of a rainbow, if rainbows came in brown. Red-brown, green-brown, almost black, caramel, cinnamon umber and taupe, chocolate and copper, mahogany and chestnut. I was born among the red hills of Georgia, but I never knew that Southern dirt came in so many shades. Lined up to the ceiling by the hundreds, the jars compose a stunning still life. The beauty felt distracting.

Standing in the office of the Equal Justice Institute, I thought of Adorno's declaration: writing poetry after Auschwitz is barbaric. I disagree with Adorno, but this much is clear: if you're memorializing massive crimes, you should be very, very careful not to aestheticize them. I mentioned my worry to Stevenson: "We've talked about the fetishization of violence. If we're worried about that, shouldn't the jars evoke more horror than grace?" The soil, he answered, was the site of blood, sweat, and tears. "But it still possesses the possibility of life."

The memorial itself merits the overused word *awesome*. While the starkly modern slabs are reminiscent of the Holocaust Memorial, the monument is constructed so that the slabs evoke hangings as the visitor descends. They are made of rusting metal that drips red when it rains, evoking blood but not insisting on it. Maybe Stevenson has solved Adorno's problem.

◦◡◦

In a fine and subtle essay, Jan Philipp Reemtsma asked about the purpose of such monuments.[14] It cannot be remembering for its own sake, for both remembering and forgetting are human activities that are neither good nor bad in themselves. "The historical past," wrote Todorov, "like the natural order, has no intrinsic meaning, and by itself it produces no values at all." The injunction to "Never forget!" should thus be unpacked. Reemtsma described the purpose of traditional war memorialization: "to send future generations into battle with a light heart, as is claimed for the fallen hero, or at least to assure them they will be remembered too."[15] But that cannot be the purpose of memorializing concentration camps. They are, first, instruments of history against those who seek to deny it. By preserving the space in which they took place, they document in order to prove to any would-be Holocaust denier that these crimes are undeniable. This was particularly important during the first years of the Federal Republic, where concerted resistance had to be overcome in order to preserve and document Dachau, the first of such memorials in the West. But proof, wrote Reemtsma, is no longer needed. The only people left unconvinced by the facts today are those whom no fact could convince.

Nor can the purpose of these spaces be hopes for conversion. In the light of rising right-wing nationalism, as well as Muslim anti-Semitism, some German politicians have proposed that visits to concentration camps, often a part of high school curricula, should be made mandatory. But why should the site of a concentration camp produce an epiphany? There is little reason to suppose that this happens, and some reason to suspect the opposite. "Why wouldn't someone who enjoys tormenting other people find such spaces attractive?" asked Reemtsma.

No visit to a concentration camp ensures you will identify with the victims rather than the perpetrators. Something about these spaces is always abstract, and anyhow, you know beforehand which side you're on. Peter Eisenman, the architect who created the Holocaust Memorial, once spoke of his hopes for it. "If a Japanese tourist who knows nothing about the Holocaust comes in fifty years, he'll feel something when he goes into the monument. Maybe he feels what it's like to go into a gas chamber." Eisenman's hopes were painfully immodest. Even if said tourist weren't distracted by hawkers and selfies, nothing about a monument could evoke the terror and despair of someone about to face a wretched death. The same is true of the memorialized concentration camps themselves. They cannot—nor are they meant to—put us in the place of those who toiled and died there. At most, the camps evoke their shadows, and remind us that our lives are not like theirs at all.

And yet, Reemtsma wrote, the concentration camps are sacred spaces. This is partly because they are always also graveyards, and human beings learn early to show respect to their dead. Some people cover their heads in a cemetery; everyone knows not to shout. Is it a feeling of reverence? A hint of superstition? Reemtsma, a resolute atheist, suggested that sacrality is something else: "A sacred space is not our object, we are its object. It doesn't have to justify its existence to us; we have to justify our ways of living before it."[16] The tendency to turn the Holocaust into a sacred religion is one I've criticized elsewhere, and I am chary of using religious language to describe its sites. I believe reverence should be saved for goodness and glory. So I wasn't prepared for what hit me one cold day in 2017, when I visited Dachau for the first time in thirty-five years.

Back then I'd been a graduate student on a government fellowship. It was my first trip to Germany, and I did what most Jews do. I visited the nearest concentration camp. I remember trying hard to feel moved, or shaken, or whatever combination of emotions seemed appropriate, and failing entirely. Later I chafed at the tenacity of Jewish tourists who view Europe as a vast Jewish graveyard, dutifully checking off death sites and noticing little else. Still, it seemed foolish to finish this book without visiting one again.

Though I didn't think there would be anything I needed to learn at Dachau, a map in the museum taught me something important. I knew that most large concentration camps had subsidiary camps to hold the overflowing numbers of prisoners as the regime wore on. I just didn't know how many there were, nor how widely they were sprinkled all over the country. The names of the large camps are burned into our brains, but whoever heard of Gmund? Utting? Gablingen? Saulgau? All these small towns, and many, many more, held small camp outposts where political prisoners, Jews, and later Russian POWs were worked and usually tormented to death. The postwar German claim that "we didn't know what they were doing in our name" might just barely work for Poland, but the subsidiary camps were right next door in blissful, bucolic Bavaria. You'd have to be blind, deaf, and dumb not to notice.

My visit to Dachau was meant to be a meta-visit. I rented an audio guide from the friendly curly-haired youth at the desk. For half an hour I tried to take meta-notes: What kind of people come to this site, and how? The schoolchildren were well behaved; the middle-aged Turkish couple, she in a hijab, were quietly holding hands; the Latin American family was ignoring the sign before the auditorium warning that the film is unsuitable for children under the age of twelve. The film is relentless, like the rest of the large museum. There are dimly lit panels devoted to each group of prisoners. There are examples of the haunting art they made: an ink drawing of a nighttime roll call, a watercolor of a hanging. Mostly there are photos that spare no detail. Paint peels from the walls where the SS once stripped prisoners of the last of their possessions, leaving them naked to walk to the bathhouse. Once you've withstood the museum, you can walk across the grounds where roll calls were held and enter a reconstructed barracks. You can also walk farther to enter the crematorium. Almost one million visitors view the site each year.

After a few minutes I put my notebook in my backpack and turned off the audio guide. I wanted to be alone with my own voice, or voicelessness. The space took me over. It wasn't about learning, even less about analyzing; for a couple of hours I was no wiser than anyone else. As the sun began to set, the glimmer of pink sky seemed to reproach the gray of the pebbles, the gray of the walls, the iron of the monuments erected to honor all the dead. Tears filled my eyes. At a steel cube containing the ashes of unknown prisoners, I said Kaddish. Did I say it? It welled up out of me, the way the Shema did as I stood in the Jewish monument, dark but for the word YIZKOR—remember—engraved at the entrance in Hebrew, and a thin ray of sunlight that forced itself through a hole in the ceiling. I thought I knew, and I knew quite a lot. I'd written a book about modern evil from Lisbon to Auschwitz. Yet there was something that had been absent—whatever it was that now made me nauseated, staring at all those pictures in the midst of all that ground.

The feeling of utter powerlessness in that vast, empty space didn't last long. It began to fade in the bookshop, where the gray-haired saleswoman ringing up my purchase commented on a writer we both loved. This was, for me, familiar ground: talking about books, weighing and praising. It didn't matter that the books in question were written by Ruth Kluger, who entered Auschwitz at the age of twelve. I was back in my normal world, doing what I know how to do.

Yet the memory of emotion remained after the emotion itself had faded. I understood what Reemtsma meant about sacred space. We are its object, not the other way around. These monuments of horror are absolutely necessary. One shouldn't go to many, and certainly not often; that would dull their force. But without them, all the reading and studying in the world could be lifeless and lame.

Reemtsma's essay acknowledged that only a minority is interested in such memorials, only a minority fought to have them erected and thinks about their meaning and their future. "But the minority made sure that its interests prevailed. That is what counts." He concluded:

> It is not a matter of memory, but of consciousness of danger that we know since we've known it was an illusion to believe that civilization is irreversible. The danger will always remain pressing. And it is a matter of something I will call shame. A shame that, detached from the question of guilt, seizes anyone who lets themselves be seized. To waken and practice consciousness and shame—that is the reason for these monuments.[17]

Let us stop for a moment to think about distance. Once, history was a matter of consolation or pride: *just see how far we've come from barbarism.* Now it's a matter of warning and shame. The modern subject of history evolved as a substitute for Providence. Since language began, peoples have recorded their histories in everything from songs to tax records, but the systematic study of history began with the process of secularization. The idea of Providence was the idea that the problem of evil is no problem at all, for an unseen and all-seeing God will turn the wheels of fortune so that every wrong is eventually righted, every righteousness rewarded. That idea was mortally wounded by the Lisbon earthquake of 1755, and it could not be revived.[18] By the end of the eighteenth century, Kant knew that this promise of justice could not be kept by theology, so he set history in its place. His critical philosophy allows us to believe that the human race *may* be progressing to a better state. If we cannot believe this much, we will never maintain the fortitude we need in order to make it true. That's why Kant calls this belief rational faith.

Hence history was studied for signs of progress within it. The discipline flourished in the nineteenth-century Prussian Academy, where faith in history as an exact science was so unshaking that it gave historians lavish funding that their colleagues in natural science envied at the time.[19] As Nietzsche later summarized, "It put history in the place of the other spiritual powers, art and religion, as the one sovereign: inasmuch as it is the 'idea realizing itself,' 'the dialectic of the spirit of the nations,' and 'the tribunal of the world.'"[20] The idea must have encouraged the empirical toilers: all those hours in the archives were not devoted simply to finding information, but to proving we live in the best of all possible worlds.

There was a notable jump from Kant to Hegel, who argued that history always tends toward justice and freedom.[21] Kant believed that progress is *possible*. Hegel and his student Marx believed that progress is *necessary*. The twentieth century left little room for belief in the latter, notwithstanding temporary Hegelian outbursts like those of Francis Fukuyama. One consequence was a turn from studies of history to studies of memory. Memory makes no claim to meaning beyond itself. Those who insist on the importance of preserving memory are, often enough, deliberately anti-messianic. We should, they believe, preserve historical memory not as source of hope or comfort, but as warning. *This is how fragile our civilization can be.*

∾

"You're meeting me in my post-optimistic phase," said Volkhard Knigge, longtime director of the Buchenwald Memorial. I had written to ask for an interview, and he offered me something better. Would I care to have his assistant show me around the camp and its new exhibit, then meet him for dinner in Weimar? The contrast is legendary. Weimar was the center of the German Enlightenment, where Goethe was a state functionary and Schiller built a theater; later it was the home of the Bauhaus, and Germany's first republic. The town has been beautifully restored. You can walk through cobblestone streets past graceful, gaily painted houses and think about the best Germany ever had to offer. Goethe's house, now a national museum, provides a surprisingly poignant picture of the great man's life. In the Anna Amalia Library, founded in 1691, the stunning rococo hall permits a glance into the collection of nearly a million works, many of them priceless.

Five miles down the road is the site of Germany's most central concentration camp. The citizens of Weimar had no objection when the SS announced its plan to build a huge concentration camp in the neighborhood; they were happy to cheer Hitler on his frequent visits. But they did object to the camp being named Ettersberg, for the wood was well known as a place where Goethe loved to walk, and somehow that was too much for the denizens of the town that Germany's greatest literary hero made famous. Though every other concentration camp was named after its location, the SS reacted quickly by inventing another name: Buchenwald. Now

Weimar and Buchenwald are eternally linked, the best and the worst of German history.

If Weimar and Buchenwald are emblems of German tradition, the Hotel Elephant is its quintessence. Originally built in 1696 on Weimar's central square, it has housed most every luminary of German culture. Goethe, Schiller, Wieland, and Herder were regulars; Liszt and Wagner later stayed there. Thomas Mann set a novel in it, and the hotel hosted foreign guests from Leo Tolstoy to Patti Smith.

Volkhard Knigge told me what few tourist guides will: the hotel was also Hitler's favorite. He stayed there thirty-five times and ordered it renovated from top to bottom in 1937. Apparently the order to build the most modern hotel in Europe was occasioned by his annoyance at having to walk down the hall to the toilet. By the time the renovations were done, the sign of an elephant over the front door had been replaced by a Prussian eagle, and a special balcony had been built so the Führer could greet the crowds assembled on the square. "In the 1990s, people regularly asked to stay in the Hitler suite," Knigge told me, "and the new management recognized it as a problem. So in 1997 we organized a concert on the square by Udo Lindenberg, and we had him stay in Hitler's suite—which we renamed the Udo Lindenberg suite." The provocative rock star must have enjoyed chasing out the ghosts. Not long after that was the fifty-fifth anniversary of Buchenwald's liberation. "We invited all the survivors and filled the hotel; the staff did everything they possibly could for them. Many survivors are very poor, especially those from Eastern Europe. Some of them have nothing. So a week in a luxury hotel was—wonderful. We did it again for the seventieth anniversary."

"A small culinary start to your evening," said our waiter. "This is a sesame cracker with chive cream and trout caviar. On the spoon is salmon tartar. And in the glass is potato foam soup topped with Parmesan risotto." There was already a bottle of Champagne next to the table. Knigge is a frequent and honored guest in the Michelin-starred restaurant.

I was glad to know that the remaining Buchenwald survivors had enjoyed a whole week of this, but I wasn't sure how to navigate one evening. Knigge's assistant, Dr. Michael Löffelsender, had just given me a four-hour tour of the camp. When I descended from the bus that took me to Buchenwald from the Weimar train station, the fog was so dense it was hard to make out anything at all. That seemed fitting. The new exhibit, opened in 2016, is quite different from that of Dachau; it contains little gore. There are portraits of inmates who survived and inmates who didn't. Their stories endure. There are strikingly lit collections of prison uniforms, tin bowls and ladles that capture the hunger better than photographs of starving prisoners. There is evidence of the lengths they went to preserve shreds of dignity through music and art. There is even an exhibit devoted to Schiller's furniture. As the air raids drew closer, the furniture was moved from Weimar to Buchenwald, where prisoners built copies to place in the Schiller museum while the originals were safely stored in the camp. The Nazis knew that no Allied air raid had targeted a concentration camp, so they could be sure the relics of German high culture would be safe there.

That exhibit is one of several that document the museum's current focus: to show that Nazism emerged in the middle of Germany, and Germany in all its glory, not on its margins. At the entrance to the museum is an old film clip of happy blond children in an amusement park not far from the place where the camp was being built. Next to the film are photos of Hitler greeting the masses from the balcony of the Hotel Elephant, along with photos of those masses filling up Weimar's central square with their cries. *Lieber Führer, komm heraus, aus dem Elefantenhaus. Lieber Führer, bitte bitte, lenk auf den Balkon die Schritte.—Dear Führer, please come out to the balcony so we can see you!* Also in the museum is a 1945 letter from Weimar city dignitaries written to the American command.

> Your news media suggests that the residents of Weimar had knowledge of the cruelties at Buchenwald and kept silent, so now they are morally complicit . . . The mayor of this city and the other signatories of this letter appeal to the world's sense of justice when we ask you to remove this undeserved stain from the great old cultural capital Weimar.[22]

Everything in the museum is designed to refute that letter.

"An exhibit that says 'suffering is suffering' is not enough," says Knigge. "Not unless you ask who wanted it. How did they justify it? How did they realize it? Why was there so little resistance?" Knigge says that's one reason he's become skeptical about German working-off-the-past.

"The real question," said Knigge, "is not 'What would I have done in '42, '43, '44?' Our memories are narrowed by the Holocaust, which shields us from the history of its causes. The real question is 'What would I have done in '32 or '33?' Then it's a question about courage, but not a matter of life and death. And it's not one you can answer by saying there was no chance for effective resistance."

There were plenty of chances. What the Buchenwald exhibit shows: the vast majority of comfortable, cultivated citizens of Weimar had no desire to take them. They were perfectly happy to have on their outskirts a camp that eventually held a quarter of a million inmates. Local companies used their slave labor; Hitler Youth groups took tours. The only objection Weimar made was to the idea that the camp's name be associated with its beloved Goethe.

There is something profoundly eerie about that objection. In making it, the townspeople implicitly acknowledged that the existence of the camp would defile something. Their moral compass was partly intact. Did they love Goethe—a.k.a. classical German culture—so much that they'd rather sully their name than his? As the Weimar mayor's postwar plea to the American command shows, they never thought that far; when the war was all over, they simply denied what they'd known. Arendt was right to argue that much evil results from sheer thoughtlessness. The kernel of moral care that made the citizens of Weimar want to keep Goethe's ghost clean suggests that most of us could think our actions through if we tried.

I share Knigge's view that what's important for the future is to think about the causes of evil, not to dwell on its results. "Obama just broke an American taboo," I said. "Because *Nazi* in America just means *the devil incarnate*." If that were the case, there'd be no need to think about causes. In December 2017, without mentioning his successor's name, Obama said,

> We have to tend to this garden of democracy or else things could fall apart quickly. That's what happened in Germany in the 1930s, which, despite the democracy of the Weimar Republic and centuries of high-level cultural and scientific achievements, Adolf Hitler rose to dominate. Sixty million people died, so, you've got to pay attention. And vote.[23]

"Which is why," I added, we need to acknowledge our history in America."

"I speak with people from authoritarian societies all the time," said Knigge. "From South America and Africa and Eastern Europe. I understand why they find German working-off-the-past a reason for hope. Barack Obama grasped it immediately. He came to Buchenwald shortly after his speech in Cairo. There was a state visit with all the protocol, and Chancellor Merkel was not particularly enthusiastic; she would have preferred to have him longer in Dresden. So he had breakfast with her in Dresden and spent most of his time here, and he broke protocol and stayed much longer than expected. There was a moment when we were alone in the crematorium, and he was looking at a large photo of corpses taken just after liberation. He asked me, 'What would that mean for a slavery museum in America?'"

"How did you answer him?" I asked.

"I confirmed that his question was the right one," said Knigge. "He had a speech already prepared, but he threw it away and improvised. He didn't say *And tomorrow I'm going back to lay the foundation stone for a slavery museum.*"

"He couldn't have done that if he'd wanted to."

"He couldn't. And he didn't say *And now I'm building a museum to commemorate the massacres of Native Americans.* But he understood the core of Germany's work to create this self-critical look at our history. Older forms of memory focused either on celebrating a nation's own heroes or mourning its own victims. We've developed a different paradigm that, when it's serious, asks about the perpetrators and their motives and the social conditions around them. That all comes from the awareness that neither victims nor heroes fall straight from heaven. Of course people have the freedom to make moral decisions. But we have to understand the structures within which they do so."

"I still don't understand why you're post-optimistic."

"Because this model of self-critical memory is coming under pressure from so many sides."

Knigge helped create that model. He never set out to be the director of Buchenwald. He was raised in a West German Pietist family—"authoritarian Protestantism, but with a certain fundamentalist resilience against the worst of Nazism." His father was drafted in 1943. Had the war continued, he would probably have had a major Nazi career, but fortunately, he was stationed in Paris. "My Francophilia is a reaction. For my father and grandfather, the French were the eternal enemy. They were filthy, erotically overheated—"

"Not the Russians?"

"Oh, the Russians in any case. But the French as well. My father spent half a year with his garrison in Paris until the city was liberated. He didn't mind shooting, but it wasn't war, it was Paris." The catastrophe, for those like Knigge's father, came afterward. After the Ardennes offensive, the German troops had to flee all the way through Germany before the eyes of their countryfolk. For his generation, the shame was unbearable. Again, Knigge's father was lucky; he landed, unwounded, in an American POW camp. Still, the psychological damage was undeniable. That generation was too young to have any responsibility for the Nazis but old enough to be entirely dominated by them. If you started school when Hitler came to power, you had no intellectual resources to resist the indoctrination that permeated the educational system, the youth groups, the culture as a whole. All those were directed toward cultivating troops of fanatical Nazis. When 1945 brought total defeat, what could you possibly say?

The silence broke with the first wave of teachers born after '45. "Suddenly the air was fresher," said Knigge. "You could breathe. We discovered film and theater and books. We got words for what we experienced—not this sticky silence." He decided to study psychoanalysis, which was a further revelation. "I'll never forget my first supervision. That's when I realized: For heaven's sake! There are words for emotions. You can express what you feel inside and be better for it."

Whatever reserve German families may have shown before the war was infinitely compounded after '45. Knigge's desire to study psychoanalysis was politically motivated. "To be a doctor in this society means you have to study history. I suppose I was euphoric, a little naïve, but the combination gave me a lot. My question was always: How does history stalk the subject? How does large, world-shaking history affect small individual biographies?" He went to Paris to study Lacanian analysis but found it "dreadful." When he returned to Germany, he became engaged in the struggle that was just beginning: to recognize and restore the sites of Nazi terror.

In 1990, West Germany had only a few pathetic monuments. Sites were hidden behind overgrown weeds; many had become trash dumps. "Those of us who were seeking were called unpatriotic nest foulers," said Knigge. "All that has been erased through the state-sponsored commemorations we fought for, but at the time, no one was interested in the camps. They were crime scenes in the middle of society."

"Would you like the wine menu, Herr Knigge? Or shall the sommelier choose for you? He understands your taste."

"I'll take the menu. Red or white?" Knigge asked me.

"Red, in this weather." The fog in Weimar was not as thick as it was in Buchenwald, but the night was cold and clammy.

When Knigge looks back at milestones of postwar German history, he begins with Adenauer's exchange: reparations were not called reparations, but they were the price for acceptance into the Western community, and the price was relatively cheap. "At the time, Greece was demanding reparations too, and the Foreign Office considered the matter quite coolly. We have trade relations with the Greeks: tobacco, grapes, a few other things. Israel was different, with enormous symbolic character." Reparations were paid in exchange for world recognition and the opportunity to keep silent about the quantity of Nazis, and Nazi thinking, that permeated the Federal

Republic. What was left of Christian and left-liberal tradition moved some to reflect about guilt, but most of the population did not. Artists and intellectuals insisted on confronting the nation's crimes. "As a historian, one must say these were all processes that made the accusations irrefutable. And Weizsäcker's speech was liberating. Suddenly we weren't just nest foulers, we had support from the government itself."

But the decisive event, according to Knigge, was reunification. Suddenly the Federal Republic had to do something with the mass of monuments left in what had been the German Democratic Republic. "Buchenwald, Sachsenhausen, Ravensbrück. And however they were politically instrumentalized, whatever historical inaccuracies they contained, they were damned big." In 1990 Dachau had a staff of five. Buchenwald, in the East, had more than a hundred employees, with an archive and a library and a structure, and unlike the institutions in the West, it had all been financed by the state. Suddenly the Federal Republic was helpless. They knew they had to do something with those sites, and they had no idea what. "That's where I came in," said Knigge. "There was a vacuum and a crisis. West Germany had no experience with concentration camp memorials. They saw that the questions were politically charged and decided to let academics solve the problems. To exaggerate only slightly: the politicians wanted the historians to navigate the minefields, let *them* burn their fingers. When the historians had removed the mines, the politicians could take over again."

Knigge is soft-spoken and determined—above all, determined to find truth. The demand to memorialize the Holocaust came from movements within civil society, of which he was a part. But it was the center-right chancellor Helmut Kohl who turned the demand into a political program. Before him, the Christian Democratic Union saw every demand to commemorate the Holocaust as a left-wing political threat. Yet "without Kohl there would be no national memorials. That's the bitter truth, and his own party attacked him for it. He wasn't particularly interested in concentration camp sites; he was focused on the national Holocaust monument in Berlin. But he got it. He was an opportunist, but not a cynic; he wanted the next generation's blessing." In the negotiations leading up to reunification, Kohl agreed to the East German demand that Buchenwald be recognized as a monument of national significance. If Knigge is right, it's not unlike Lyndon Johnson's role in the civil rights movement. He may have begun his life as a Texas racist, and his behavior at the 1964 Democratic Convention undermined the painfully hard work of civil rights workers in the field. His insistence on seating the all-white delegation of Mississippi Democrats instead of the Mississippi Democratic Freedom Party, whose members had risked their lives to vote, was a major blow to the activists. But they pushed him to move toward the right side of history, to insist on civil rights legislation that finally broke the back of legal segregation. You never know beforehand who's going to get things done.

Knigge was the seventh director of Buchenwald within four years. One GDR-appointed director resigned of her own accord when it became clear she'd been close to Margot Honecker, wife of the East German party leader. Other directors were simply overwhelmed by the political chaos surrounding their task: to overhaul the museum so that it was historically accurate and politically neutral, untainted by Eastern or Western agendas. Knigge himself was attacked by all sides. "The communist press headline was 'Adenauer's Grandchildren, Under the Leadership of Herr Knigge, Are Shredding Our Antifacism'. The right-wing press wrote 'West German leftist is preserving the national monument of the GDR, and with it the GDR itself.' I could only say 'Sorry, I cannot be both.'"

Volkhard Knigge was bound to antagonize both sides, for part of his task in reconstructing the museum was to deconstruct two potent political myths. East Germany memorialized Buchenwald as the center of communist resistance. And there *was* a communist underground in Buchenwald, but it was far too small to create the rebellion East Germans imagined. "One hundred guns and a dozen hand grenades? Against a thousand SS men, it would have been suicide." By April 1945 the SS was in panic, for they knew American armies were approaching. They'd been given orders to evacuate or even liquidate the camp, but the camp commandant wavered, sending some prisoners on a death march, leaving others alone. The SS finally fled, leaving a power vacuum that the communist camp organization filled. American troops came in almost by accident. "Unfortunately, it was never a strategic or tactical goal to liberate the camps. The troops did it if they happened to be there. That contributed to the communist legend." But what the GDR depicted as a heroic, well-organized rebellion was in fact the resistance takeover of an unguarded camp, with some American help. Undermining the myth that the camp liberated itself was part of Knigge's job.

The other myth came from the right. It was based on one fact: after Buchenwald was abandoned by the Nazis, it was used as a prison camp by the Soviets. From 1945 to 1950 some twenty-eight thousand Germans were imprisoned there. One-quarter of them died from hunger and disease. The fact of this camp leads many to insist on the equivalence of two totalitarian systems. Those making that claim leave out just one thing: those initially imprisoned in the camp were Nazi functionaries. Not the really big function-aries, who were hiding or imprisoned elsewhere. Under Soviet occupation, Buchenwald held the smaller cogs who kept the Nazi machine turning: the *Blockwart*, who watched every neighbor on the block to see who failed to hang her flag properly or who might be hiding a Jew; the lower echelons of editors who kept the propaganda running. "They were morally guilty," said Knigge. "Absolutely awful people. But they didn't kill anybody, so legally—it's a problem. Then there was the question of luck: one Nazi *Blockwart* might be sitting in Buchenwald while others were happily living their lives. Contingency played a big role; the Soviets weren't interested in exam-ining individual guilt." The overwhelming majority of postwar prisoners had a Nazi past, but not every one.

Still, many today insist on equating the camps, among them the former German president Joachim Gauck, whose father, an early and committed Nazi, was interned by the Soviets. When Gauck made a state visit to Bu-chenwald, Knigge told me, they had to have the old debate all over again because Gauck wanted to have the same ceremony for those imprisoned by the Nazis and those imprisoned by the Soviets. Buchenwald was to be a cen-tral place for revitalizing Cold War ideology. "For that you'd have to have a concentration camp without communists and a Soviet camp without Nazis, and we refused to offer either," said Knigge. "The West legend holds that all those interned in the Soviet camp were democratic opponents of commu-nism. The East legend holds that they were all major Nazi war criminals. It turns out that neither is true."

"Do you see the talk of two German dictatorships as a form of exonera-tion for the Nazis?"

"I do, which is one reason for my skepticism about German memorial culture. Enlightenment is a tough business."

Another reason for his skepticism is the pedagogical model used in most Holocaust education. "Students are told to imagine they were a German cap-tain ordered to shoot Jews and then asked *Would you do it or not?* It's a ridiculous exercise because you get only socially acceptable answers. Even neo-Nazis know what to say. And it's ridiculous because it involves no dis-cussion of the framework in which the Nazis developed: the breaking of the social constitution, the destruction of individual rights, and so on. All you get are the crude clichés: *oh, it was horrible.* And it *was* horrible, but that's not going to get young people thinking. Simple remembering is empty."

When Knigge works with youth groups, he asks them to be detectives. "I don't demand that they break out in tears or identify with the victims. I ask them, as detectives, to figure out why it happened. We have objects and witnesses, just like in ordinary crimes, and I ask them to sift through the material evidence and ask why. And for the first time—after all the moralizing *Never agains!* and *Oh how awfuls!*—for the first time, they pay attention."

It doesn't work with everyone. In most guidebooks, Buchenwald is now a must-see stop on a trail. Some of those who come are what Knigge calls Horror-Disneyland tourists. There are also committed Nazis who come to Buchenwald because they view it as a model. They are anti-Semitic, but they know that's unacceptable, so they talk instead about Muslims. And they'd like to round them up and gas them all.

"You can work with Holocaust deniers, because that's a matter of truth and lies. You can take them into the archive and show them documents. It's almost impossible to work with neo-Nazis. Often, they have very exact knowledge of the Holocaust. But in order to find something evil or inhuman, you have to begin with moral assumptions that knowledge can only strengthen. You can tie knowledge to a moral framework. But for hard-core neo-Nazis, I cannot assume that an ethical a priori exists."

"What do you do?"

"Call the police."

Knigge has tried to work with the hard core. There was a group of six or seven youths, all of them underprivileged high school dropouts, already under the care of social workers. In the day he spent with them in Buchenwald they all repeated Nazi claims. *Yeah, it was war and the prisoners were enemies. It may not have been pretty, but there was no alternative.* "At some point I was desperate and thought there must be a way to shake them up. So I said, 'Look, we see things differently, but I just want to understand you. What would you get from a society like the one you prefer? What would you gain?' Their answer was astonishing. They didn't think they'd be rich or powerful. They knew they'd still be at the bottom of the heap. But they said they'd have more dignity, simply for belonging to a higher race."

Longer-term programs might permit a breakthrough, but the people they're intended to change are usually disinclined to come. Nor does Knigge have the funding that long-term education would require. He has a hostel with seventy beds and seminar rooms for reaching those young people who are uncertain, not yet committed to the radical right, but it's hard to find the resources that would make such programs work. "As in any museum, politicians look at quantitative results: How many people walked through the door this year? Sometimes I sound cynical and tell them it doesn't take rocket science to drive up the numbers. All we'd have to do is stage burnings at the crematoria every Thursday evening. Someone always winces. I'm afraid there may come a day when nobody winces and somebody asks *Why not?* They often ask why I don't reconstruct the barracks, with holograms. It's a purely sentimental, historically shallow commemoration. And it drives young people away in droves."

Still, I pressed, didn't he think something has been achieved by all the work he and others have done?

"We need a double view. Every democracy has a right to ask about its successes. Here that means, what have we understood, what have we worked off? But we also need to ask, what has persisted? How many racist structures still survive? That was Adorno's question. He wasn't asking us to remember the past; memory by itself has nothing to do with enlightenment. He was asking us to confront the past. That's different."

"In Adorno's day, a great deal of Nazi thinking still survived."

"It survives today as well. There's much to do before we can pat ourselves on the shoulder."

"I've never met a German who thinks she can pat herself on the shoulder."

"Not exactly. But the young people think the work is all done. And I meet many people who still seek pseudo-anthropological explanations. *Man is evil, that's just how it is.*"

"What do you tell them?"

"I remind them of Freud, who said human beings are neither good nor evil. They can be formed."

⌘

"How do they know to put stones?" I asked Leroy Clemons, the bighearted, tough-minded alderman of Philadelphia, Mississippi, and president of the NAACP in Neshoba County, long infamous as one of the meanest, most racist places in the state.

Christians lay flowers at monuments and gravesites; the day I went to Dachau, three huge wreaths of still-fresh roses lay under the main memorial. Jews lay small stones, and I doubted there was a Jew in all of Neshoba County. I was standing in front of Mount Zion Church, just outside Philadelphia, pierced by a sharp sense of connection and loss. Carved into marble were the words THIS MEMORIAL IS PRAYERFULLY AND PROUDLY DEDICATED TO THE MEMORY OF JAMES CHANEY, ANDREW GOODMAN AND MICHAEL SCHWERNER, WHO GAVE THEIR LIVES IN THE STRUGGLE TO OBTAIN HUMAN RIGHTS FOR ALL PEOPLE.

"I do a tremendous number of groups every year from all over the world, so a lot of Jewish groups too," answered Leroy. "They come in big numbers, and they put the rocks down pretty much as soon as they come in."

As cochair of the Philadelphia Coalition, he helped bring Edgar Ray Killen to trial in 2005. Killen was the Klansman who organized the deaths of the three civil rights workers, and for forty-one years thereafter he lived his life undisturbed—because he was also a preacher, and no jury in Mississippi would convict a man of God. The memorial to Chaney, Goodman, and Schwerner resembles a tombstone, as does a similar one on the other side of the church. But no bodies are buried beneath them. The families of the murdered men wanted them buried together. In 1964 this was illegal, for Chaney was black, and Goodman and Schwerner were white, and in Mississippi even the graveyards were segregated.

It's a very long way from Buchenwald to Neshoba County, and some readers will balk at any connection between the two. Thousands of people died in Buchenwald, and in Neshoba there were only three. But Jewish tradition compares saving a life to saving the world, and oh what lives those three men could have led. Their deaths became symbolic, for better and worse. Like more massive murders, these were organized and carried out by the state where the Klan, the police, the sheriff's departments, and highway patrol officers were often one and the same. I kicked through the dirt in search of a suitable stone to place with the others, glad to know I wasn't the only Jew to whom Chaney, Goodman, and Schwerner had been heroes for longer than I could remember.

They were killed during Freedom Summer, the project I'd been too young to join. All I could do was admire a distant cousin from Chicago who'd spent a night at our home in Atlanta on his way to the heart of the iceberg, as Bob Moses called Mississippi. Freedom Summer was Moses's brainchild. Convinced that desegregating the ballot boxes was more important than desegregating lunch counters, Moses had launched a drive to register black Mississippians to vote. Not only during Reconstruction but for some time afterward African Americans in Mississippi had voted in large numbers and even held a variety of public offices. The Jim Crow laws put in place around the turn of the century dismantled every civil right that had been gained in much of the South.[24] Moses and his colleagues at SNCC had worked for several years to restore them. They had little success. Blacks who attended SNCC Freedom Schools, whose first order of business was teaching eligible citizens to pass the draconian voter registration tests, were hounded, beaten, and in several cases murdered. "I didn't know it was against the law to kill a

296 LEARNING FROM THE GERMANS

black man," said one young white man from Neshoba. "I learned that when I joined the army. When they told me, I thought they were joking."[25] Even the murderers in widely publicized cases, such as that of Emmett Till or Medgar Evers, were embraced by their own communities, who manned the juries that declared them innocent. Should SNCC continue a voter registration drive whose main result, until then, had only been an increase in the terror and torture of black bodies?

Freedom Summer was to be a solution. Mississippians might kill black people with impunity and without national attention, but what if a battalion of white people from the North came down to help register voters? The Ku Klux Klan might harass them, but surely they'd hesitate to kill them, and their presence would draw the nation's attention to the Mississippi battles it was inclined to ignore. Some SNCC members worried that the proposal could lead to a white takeover of an African American–led struggle. Others worried about the ethics of deliberately putting young people in harm's way. But the situation in Mississippi was growing desperate, and it wasn't hard to find one thousand idealistic students willing to go.[26] Though they were trained in the techniques of nonviolent activism, most of Mississippi viewed them as an invading army, not unlike the Union soldiers who'd descended on the state a century earlier.

Twenty-year-old Andrew Goodman from New York City was one of them. Mickey Schwerner, a twenty-four-year-old social worker, had come to Mississippi from New York with his wife, Rita, half a year earlier; they were the first full-time white civil rights workers in the state. James Chaney was a talented twenty-one-year-old local activist who had worked with Schwerner—"like Siamese twins."[27] Chaney and Schwerner had visited the Mount Zion Church several times in the hopes of persuading the black congregation to house a new Freedom School in Neshoba County, where no blacks had voted for years. In their half year in Mississippi, the Schwerners' work had been bold enough to attract considerable Klan attention. Plans to kill Mickey, whom Mississippians called Goatee because of his unfamiliar beard, had been brewing since April. In mid-June, the KKK saw a chance to carry them out.

They noticed a meeting at Mount Zion Church that they considered suspicious. This is what it looked like from the perspective of Philadelphia Coalition member Jimmie Jewel McDonald, who was just seventeen on June 16, 1964: "There was a collection meeting, and you would be at church forever, counting your little pennies, and you would want to get out and see your boyfriend under the tree someplace." Jewel, as she's called, told me she would have been at that meeting had she not been babysitting her niece. Jewel's mother and brother went to church—and came back beaten bloody, along with two other congregants. "*Where are the white people?*" the Klan members shouted while beating Jewel's brother with brass knuckles. They were looking for Schwerner, whom they knew had visited the church, but Jewel's brother didn't know who they were talking about.

"Well, I can tell you just by instinct," said Leroy. "You jump on a black woman's child, you gonna have to whip the black woman too."

Which the Klan promptly did, breaking her collarbone before ordering the two to go home. Jewel's mother refused to call a doctor. "I don't know who I'm going to see. A doctor might have been the one who hit me upside the head." That night the Klan burned Mount Zion Church to the ground. The church bell, all that remained after the blaze, still stands there. It was hardly the first black church the Klan had set on fire; at least thirteen were destroyed in Mississippi that year.[28] But their goal in burning this one was specific: they knew Mickey Schwerner would come to investigate the crime. Schwerner rushed back from a training session in Ohio, looking for information and affidavits he knew the local law enforcement would never seek. He was accompanied by James Chaney and Andrew Goodman. Goodman had just written his parents a postcard to say he'd arrived safely.

"They got it after he was dead," said Jewel. "He talked about how good the people in Mississippi were, and I know it just tore her heart out."

On their way back from the church the young men were arrested for speeding, a common enough way to harass civil rights workers and black people in general. But realizing he had "got Goatee," the sheriff kept them in jail long enough for his fellow Klan members to organize a lynching party. Shortly after their release on the dark two-lane highway, three cars of Klansmen forced the civil rights workers' station wagon to stop. Chaney, Goodman, and Schwerner were taken to an even emptier road that ran by the ringleader's property, and they were shot point-blank.

"You know why they wanted to do it here?" asked Leroy as he showed me the woody spot by the road where the killing was done. "Edgar Ray Killen said he drove by there every day, and he wanted to be able to look at the place and laugh."

The crime was so well planned that the bodies, placed inside a newly built dam, would never have been found without the $25,000 reward the FBI later paid an informant. "They had them buried so deep you never would have smelled them," said Jewel. "No bugs or no kinda bird would have found them." In the intervening months, the local community insisted that the boys' disappearance, and even the burning of the church, were a hoax cooked up by the civil rights movement to make Mississippi look bad. Meanwhile, the disappearance of two young white men was having the effect that SNCC expected. National and international press descended on the county. Unintimidated by anyone, from local police to President Lyndon Johnson, Rita Schwerner demanded that the federal government take immediate action to find her husband, while pointing out the injustice of the media attention he received. "If Mr. Chaney, a native Negro Mississippian, had been alone at the time of the disappearance, this case, like many before it, would have gone unnoticed."[29]

By the time the bodies were found, they only confirmed what most had suspected: the young men had been killed shortly after they disappeared. In the meantime, their story helped lead to the passage of the 1964 Civil Rights Act as well as the Voting Rights Act the next year. Ninety-six percent of Mississippi voters opposed those laws. In Neshoba County, white concern about the murders was concern for the local reputation, for the crime had put the place in the national spotlight. If the black or white communities in Neshoba ever spoke about it, they spoke behind closed doors. Jewel, who married and went north for a time shortly after the murders, said she learned more when she left Mississippi than she learned there in the months after it happened. The Mount Zion community rebuilt its church quickly. A plaque inside the door reads

OUT OF ONE BLOOD GOD HATH MADE ALL MEN
This plaque is dedicated to the memory of
Michael Schwerner
James Chaney
Andrew Goodman
WHOSE CONCERN FOR OTHERS AND MORE PARTICULARLY
THOSE OF THIS
COMMUNITY LED TO THEIR EARLY MARTYRDOM.
THEIR DEATH QUICKENED
MEN'S CONSCIENCES AND MORE FIRMLY ESTABLISHED JUSTICE,
LIBERTY AND BROTHERHOOOD IN THIS LAND.

The community also established a memorial service every year on Father's Day, the anniversary of the murders. When Martin Luther King Jr. made his way through a violent mob to speak at the second anniversary, he called

Philadelphia "a terrible town, the worst I have seen. There is a reign of terror here."[30]

While the black community remembered, the white community did what it could to forget. In the North, tributes to the three heroes were made in speech, song, and literature, but just days after the bodies were unearthed, the white people of Neshoba County were engrossed in preparations for their annual fair, one of the biggest in the nation. The Neshoba County Fair calls itself "Mississippi's giant house party"; the magazine *Southern Living* calls it the "sweet spot of all that's sacred in the South."[31] Before the 1964 murders it was the only thing outsiders ever heard about Neshoba County. Between the bands and barbecues and horse races that go on for the hottest week in the summer, Mississippi politicians arrive to recruit votes and the Klan to recruit members. In 1980 Ronald Reagan made headlines as the first national politician to appear there. By declaring "I support states' rights" just miles from the spot where the civil rights workers were murdered, Reagan revealed—to those who knew anything about dog whistles—that behind his grandfatherly pose he was a strong supporter of white supremacy, as his actions during his presidency would prove. His opposition to civil rights legislation, escalation of Nixon's war on drugs, and support for apartheid South Africa were prefigured at Neshoba. Every Mississippian could decode the message.

The crime of the young men's murder was compounded by the crime that took place thereafter. Though much of the town, as well as the FBI agents who investigated for months, knew the identities of most of those responsible, no one expected a local grand jury to issue an indictment for murder. On the night of the crime, the Klan chief Sam Bowers said to those present that no one who talked would live. Even forty years later, local citizens called to jury duty for the trial that finally took place said they would have to leave their jobs, their churches, or the county itself if they were part of a jury that found the ringleader guilty of murder.[32]

The federal justice system has no jurisdiction over murder cases, but in 1967 it did indict seventeen men for conspiracy to deprive the three slain activists of their civil rights. Back in Neshoba County, Florence Mars, the white woman righteous enough to testify, was forced to retire from teaching Sunday school, and her cattle ranch was subject to a Klan-instigated boycott so severe that she was forced to close her business.[33] But despite the fact that the presiding judge called the murdered men "one nigger, one Jew and one white man," seven of those charged were convicted of conspiracy, though their sentences were relatively short. It was, at least, an improvement on the trial of Emmett Till's murderers.

By 1989, Mississippi had moved further. Its secretary of state, Dick Molpus, made a public apology to the families of the slain, who had come to Neshoba County for the twenty-fifth anniversary of the crime, faithfully held on Father's Day at Mount Zion Church. A wealthy lumber merchant from Neshoba County, Molpus became the first local white man to publicly acknowledge the crime. Most Mississippians think that's the reason he lost the governor's race the following year.

It would be another fifteen years before the main organizer of the murders, Edgar Ray Killen, was brought to trial. He was eighty years old. The trial was one of the goals of the Philadelphia Coalition, the first tri-racial community organization in the county since Reconstruction. It included black, white, and Choctaw citizens, the last descendants of a large tribe forced to leave the county in 1833. The coalition's immediate goal was to prepare for the fortieth anniversary of the murders, when hundreds of people were expected to arrive in Philadelphia. "We were actually just trying to organize and see what we needed for the fortieth," Jewel explained. "Did we need Porta Potties, did we need to get phone lines set up in the church so the media could communicate?"

In the coalition, however, were a number of white lawyers and doctors. They knew who organized the killings, and they believed it was time to bring him to trial. The group met weekly—sometimes at city hall, sometimes at a local church—and, aided by Susan Glisson of the Winter Institute, its mission began to coalesce. Some members objected to working with a group located at the University of Mississippi, an institution well known for its racist history. Some people outside the coalition, such as James Chaney's younger brother, Ben, even accused the coalition of harboring Klan members. Mickey Schwerner's widow, Rita Schwerner Bender, distrusted the process from the start. She feared there would be nothing but a show trial, an empty attempt to clear the town's name. "I remember her saying 'All these people want to do is get their books written,'" Jewel told me, "'and I'm not helping them.'"

I took a long sip from the bottle of water on her kitchen table, and winced.

But the Winter Institute has a gift for helping diverse groups of people come together in ways that are honest without being brutal. And the now-retired Dick Molpus had said, "Until justice is done, we are all at least somewhat complicit in those deaths."[34] The coalition decided to push for a retrial, and they were successful in interesting a resolute and progressive state attorney general, Jim Hood. The case would be difficult. Key witnesses were dead, and much of the proof would rely on old testimony. Many people would balk at sending an eighty-year-old man—and a preacher, at that—to jail. Any local jury would resent the efforts of outsiders, including Jackson-based Jim Hood, to judge their affairs. As one Philadelphia resident put it during Killen's trial, "It was like when the North came into the South after the Civil War and told us *you have to do this, this, and this.* We didn't want to be told what to do."[35] Nevertheless, after a six-day trial on June 21, 2005, forty-one years to the day after the deaths he masterminded, Edgar Ray Killen was convicted. To the disappointment of the coalition and the victims' families, who had come to testify at the trial, the evidence was only enough to convict for manslaughter. Still, the judge gave Killen three consecutive twenty-year sentences, one for each young man whose murder he ordered. He died in prison in January 2018.

"The Killen verdict was a real landmark," said the historian Charles Reagan Wilson. "There have been a lot of civil rights murders and cases, but this one was particularly dramatic because it involved northerners and southerners, Jewish Americans as well as black Americans. This verdict will help the healing process, without question."[36]

Would it? Or would it allow Mississippi to rest in the self-satisfaction that the horrors that stigmatized the state all belonged to the past. Certainly, healing took place between individuals. Jewel McDonald, for instance, described how she was approached anxiously by a white member of the coalition. "She grabbed my hand and she says, 'I have to tell you: my ex-husband's family is the one that beat your mother and brother.' I said 'Oh my God.' Tears just started—she grabbed me and I grabbed her and we were just there a-boohooing and stuff. She says, 'And I'm so sorry.' I thought, well my Lord, that's the first person to apologize to me. That's how we became friends. I call her my soul sister, and she answers to it."

What I learned at the Winter Institute: national reconciliation begins at the bottom. Very personal encounters between members of different races, people who represent the victims as well as those who represent the perpetrators, are the foundation of any larger attempt to treat national wounds. What I also learned at the Winter Institute: such encounters are only the foundation. They can lead to the reconciliation of communities built on them, using the trust thus developed to work together confronting the injustices that remain. Group by group, community by community, state by state, nation by nation. It is a long and weary process, but it is hard to see an alternative.

Shortly after the trial ended, Rita Schwerner Bender wrote an open letter to Mississippi governor Haley Barbour:

> I am writing this letter because of recent and past actions of yours which are impediments to racial justice in Mississippi and our nation. Recently, after the verdict and sentencing in the Edgar Ray Killen trial in Neshoba County, you indicated your belief that this closed the books on the crimes of the civil rights years, and that we all should now have "closure" . . . There is yet much work to be done. As the governor of Mississippi, you have a unique opportunity to acknowledge the past and to participate in ensuring a meaningful future for your state. Please don't squander this moment by proclaiming that the past does not inform the present and future.[37]

The Philadelphia Coalition announced that the trial was only the first step on the road to "seek the truth, to insure justice for all, and to nurture reconciliation." Three brave young men were murdered not by a shotgun, but by the concerted efforts of an entire state, while "decent people remained silent while evil was done in their names. These shameful acts have been little understood by Mississippians."[38] The coalition concluded that their work had just begun.

Shortly thereafter, they were instrumental in pushing for the legislation signed by Governor Barbour to establish a civil rights curriculum for all grades in state public schools. Back in Philadelphia, the coalition created a Chaney, Goodman, and Schwerner Freedom School, now run by Leroy Clemons. As he showed me around the two large rooms that serve as his schoolhouse, we talked about fear.

"People outside Mississippi are afraid of being here, but in my generation it wasn't passed on. People always say it's a shame we didn't know about the history, but I always say I'm glad. I'm afraid if they passed the stories down, they would also pass the fear and the hatred down."

As a result, he said, he didn't grow up being afraid of white people, even if they belonged to the Klan, which regularly burned crosses on the hill up the street from his home most Saturday nights.

"You saw the fires?"

"Yeah, and it didn't faze us. On Sunday evenings we'd be up there on the same field playing softball. I can remember taking some of the charred wood and making bases."

Leroy, the first of nine children, was born in 1957 to a single mother who became an alcoholic. When she was on a bender, he took care of his siblings, keeping them busy and away from the moonshine sold in the woods across the road. That's how he explains his calling; he's been taking care of kids ever since. "The Philadelphia Coalition was never about convicting an eighty-year-old man. It was about changing the narrative in this city and helping the young people to move forward." Every child in the Freedom School knows the story of Chaney, Goodman, and Schwerner, but Leroy works to understand why it happened. "You can't go back and unring the bell once it's been rung, but you can choose what to do with the aftermath of it. I want them to understand the conditions that allowed these things to take place and what they can do to eliminate those conditions and remove those obstacles, not only for themselves but for the next generation."

Leroy exudes a nearly bottomless optimism. It's easy to see how the seventy-eight high school students who trek to his after-school program each semester are inspired. In addition to the inspiration that's usually missing in public schools, they also get discipline. Far too often, teachers approach black students with the lowest of expectations, refusing to expend energy helping children they believe will never learn. As a result, the children drop out or coast through school having learned next to nothing. Leroy is critical of many other programs. "Their philosophy is, we don't teach kids how to read, we teach kids the love of reading. My thing is, if you can't read, how can you love it?" Sometimes he places barely literate teenagers with younger children; while they think they're teaching the youngsters, they improve their own skills. "They know Mr. Leroy don't play. I'm going to let you have a little fun, and I'm going to feed you, but your purpose for being here is to learn. Life is not going to sugarcoat them, and I want them to be prepared." As a result, the number of students in Philadelphia who graduate from college has skyrocketed, while the number of teenage pregnancies has dropped by 40 percent. The drug, alcohol, and crime rates there are very low. "It's critical thinking," says Leroy. "We teach them through the lens of history to deal with the issues of today." Leroy makes education look not only cool but missionary. "I tell them, what we do in this room is not to be kept in this room. You have to share it with your friends who are not here. This room is where you learn to lead, and you don't let other people control the narrative."

Leroy grew even more buoyant in the room full of photos showing past and present students. WHAT SUCCESS LOOKS LIKE heads one poster board, over pictures of students in graduation robes. Many college students return to teach at the Chaney, Goodman, and Schwerner Freedom School in the summer. Pointing out pictures, Leroy glowed. "This young lady is planning to go to Ole Miss. That young lady played Rosa Parks in a skit. She's a real performer." Every year, the school prepares a short play for the National History Day Contest. One year they acted out the Mississippi Burning case—as the story of the murders in Philadelphia have come to be called—at the competition in Washington, D.C. "See that young lady?" asked Leroy, pointing. "That child was my biggest challenge." Her mother got eight years in prison for shooting an abusive boyfriend; the child had witnessed the event. "I talked her into joining the group. She played the role of Jewel McDonald, and she did an outstanding job. They were on *The Oprah Winfrey Show*. The fact that I got her across that stage . . ." He paused, head shaking. "She's graduated, too."

Leroy Clemons, beaming in a small Mississippi town, is as resolute a defender of the Enlightenment as I ever met. He thinks racial hatred results from the ignorance that allows people to be manipulated. Edgar Ray Killen, for example. "He said the reason why the children came down for Freedom Summer was to train African American males to go out and rape white females."

"Do you think he really believed that?"

"I do, because I've met people his age who still talk that way. That's what drove them. I don't fault them for their ignorance. I tell the kids all the time—when you're ignorant, people can convince you to do anything."

I've spent most of my adult life speaking up for the much-maligned Enlightenment, but even I can't share Leroy's infinite faith in it. Is it ignorance, for example, that drives the defacing of public monuments meant to teach people about history? I had seen the stones that Jewish visitors reverently place on the monument to Chaney, Goodman, and Schwerner, but I also saw the steel marker next to it that local people knocked down with a truck. The coalition got a stretch of highway named the Chaney, Goodman, and Schwerner Memorial Highway, but more than once the sign has been splashed over with paint. I toured Martin Luther King Jr.'s parsonage in Montgomery, led by an ardent Southern belle who said she'd volunteer to clean the toilets in the house if there was no other work to do. I walked out to see an empty pack of baloney, thrown onto the porch by an Alabama good ole boy we never saw. Is it just ignorance that drives the reaction? A Harvard education was clearly of little use to Chief Justice John Roberts in his 2013 decision to gut the Voting Rights Act. "Why take the Voting Rights Act away now when it's working?" asked Leroy. Passed in 1965, the Voting Rights Act authorized federal oversight of election regulations in those states that had been known to suppress black citizens' right to vote. Since the Supreme Court overrode the legislation, Republican state governments from Arizona to Virginia moved quickly to make voting more difficult for those poorer, largely minority citizens most likely to vote Democratic.

A year after that Supreme Court decision and fifty years after the murders, President Obama awarded the nation's highest civilian honor, the Medal of Freedom, to Chaney, Goodman, and Schwerner. Chaney's daughter, Goodman's brother, and Schwerner's widow came to the posthumous ceremony at the White House. Obama's citation read "James Earl Chaney, Andrew Goodman, and Michael Henry Schwerner still inspire us. Their ideals have been written into the moral fabric of our nation." Reporting on the ceremony, *Time* magazine said that their names would be unfamiliar to most people today.

Speaking after the ceremony, Rita Schwerner Bender said that the best honor Congress could give these men would be to reinstate the Voting Rights Act and aggressively enforce it.

❧

In the United States, debates over memorialization are raging. With the towering exception of the National Lynching Memorial, there are no large monuments remembering the victims of racial terror or dedicated to educating the public about the forces that led to those crimes. Small, local initiatives to remember and to educate, such as those devoted to Emmett Till or Chaney, Goodman, and Schwerner, are precariously supported. In addition to being woefully underfunded, the sparse monuments they build are often subject to violence.

"It's so much healthier to have a marker that is desecrated than to have no marker that no one needs to desecrate," said Bryan Stevenson when I mentioned that the Emmett Till marker had been shot up many times. "It expresses something about who we are. That even creates a little bit of change to some people in Mississippi."

The same, I suppose, could be said of the far vaster monuments in Germany. Before the design for the Holocaust Memorial had even been approved, the federal government had already budgeted millions of marks to clean off expected graffiti. And while the stumbling stones may be funded, and cherished, by thousands of Germans, they are loathed by many others. On the 2017 anniversary of Kristallnacht, sixteen stones were dug up and destroyed by far-right activists. This matters, but so does the fact that hundreds of Berliners immediately responded with donations to replace the vandalized stones.

Before agreeing about appropriate ways of memorializing the victims of racist terror, Americans must come to agreement about the other monuments to white supremacy that remain standing. The 2015 massacre in Charleston created momentum. Among others, New Orleans mayor Mitch Landrieu announced a week later that the city's major monuments to Confederate heroes ought to go. In preparing for their removal, he sponsored a series of community dialogues in which a cross section of New Orleans citizens met monthly for more than a year. The William Winter Institute was invited to New Orleans to facilitate the discussions. Director Susan Glisson said, "If the process is democratic, respectful, and equitable, the outcome will be the same." Some of the discussions focused on clarifying questions surrounding the controversy: *No, the monuments were not erected after the war but a generation or two later, by white supremacists who sought to rewrite history by glorifying, and obscuring, the Confederate cause. No, the statues would not be destroyed, but put in a suitable museum.* After nearly two years of discussion, public hearings, and judicial review, the New Orleans City Council voted 6–1 to declare four of the most egregious monuments a public nuisance. Mayor Landrieu gave a speech that was widely praised for its clarity and eloquence. Though it deserves to be read in full, I shall quote it in part:

New Orleans is truly a city of many nations, a melting pot, a bubbling cauldron of many cultures . . . But there are also other truths about our city that we must confront. New Orleans was America's largest slave market: a port where hundreds of thousands of souls were bought, sold, and shipped up the Mississippi River to lives of forced labor, of misery, of rape, of torture . . . So when people say to me that the monuments in question are history, well, what I just described is real history as well, and it is the searing truth . . . These statues . . . are not just innocent remembrances of a benign history. These monuments purposefully celebrate a fictional, sanitized Confederacy; ignoring the death, ignoring the enslavement, and the terror that it actually stood for[,] . . . [and were] erected purposefully to send a strong message to all who walked in their shadows about who was still in charge in this city . . . Relocating these Confederate monuments is not about taking something away from someone else . . . This is . . . about showing the whole world that we as a city and as a people are able to acknowledge, understand, reconcile and most importantly, choose a better future for ourselves, making straight what has been crooked and making right what was wrong.[39]

Nevertheless, the monuments were removed at night, under guard, to prevent the violence that the monuments' supporters threatened. And shortly after the statues were removed from New Orleans in May 2017, the state of Alabama passed a law banning "the relocation, removal, alteration, renaming, or other disturbance of monuments, memorial streets, memorial buildings located on public property for more than forty years." The state of Mississippi had no need to do so; its legislature had already passed a similar bill in 2004. In both states, Confederate Memorial Day is celebrated as a public holiday.

Such positions are under fire, as the racist demonstration at Charlottesville provoked the media to turn to a multitude of historians who had long ago shown the Lost Cause narrative to be baseless. The Civil War was fought not over states' rights, but over slavery, as William James well knew. Should the historians' consensus continue to sink into the general public, the conflicts over Confederate monuments will be laid to rest.

Bryan Stevenson isn't waiting for an end to that conflict before beginning to do the work that comes next. His goal is no less than changing American identity—as, he argues, German identity has been changed by its own confrontation with its horrendous past. "We are not doomed by this history. We are not controlled by this history. But we cannot deny this history."

8

Rights and Reparations

No material payment can compensate for the suffering slavery inflicted. No one who has read a thorough description of slavery, in Auschwitz or Alabama, would prefer it, no matter the compensation, to never having been enslaved at all. This is part of what led Jean Améry to refuse to apply for reparations, though his financial situation after the liberation of Bergen-Belsen was hardly secure. With no formal schooling beyond the age of twelve, Améry found work as a freelance journalist in Belgium, writing on anything from NATO to Marilyn Monroe. His breakthrough came in 1966, when he released a series of essays, published in English under the title *At the Mind's Limits*, reflecting on his experience as an Auschwitz survivor living in Europe during the twenty years that followed the war.

What could possibly heal the damage? To answer that question, Améry rehabilitated the idea of resentment, which Nietzsche decried as the attitude of sick, small-minded, slavish natures. Their "souls squint," Nietzsche sneered. Unable to cast off the wounds of the past, they are fixated on a wish that is as inconsistent as it is unnatural. Absurdly, resentment demands that the irreversible be reversed, the event undone. Améry turns Nietzsche on his head, proudly including himself among those whose morals Nietzsche despised as slave morality, since "every genuine morality was always a morality for losers."[1] It may be natural to think of time as flowing only forward, but that thinking is not only extra-moral but anti-moral.

> Man has the right and the privilege to declare himself to be in disagreement with every natural occurrence, including the biological healing that time brings about . . . The moral power to resist contains the protest, the revolt against reality, which is rational only as long as it is moral. The moral person demands annulment of time—in the particular case under question, by nailing the criminal to his deed. Thereby, and through a moral turning-back of the clock, the latter can join his victim as a fellow human being.[2]

The only thing that could truly make up for those crimes would be turning back time and undoing them. Améry knew this is impossible, but he insisted that we recognize the depth and the morality of the longing for it. He also insisted on its sanity, arguing against the psychologists who were beginning the field of trauma studies; his resentment, he said, was a form of the human condition that is "morally and historically of a higher order than healthy straightness." He rejected the "morally impossible thought" that the survivor's wounds could be healed by the death of six million Germans. The only way to solve the problem, he concluded, was "by permitting resentment to remain alive in the one camp and, aroused by it, self-mistrust in the other."[3] If this took place, Germans would have integrated Auschwitz into their natural history rather than allowing it to be neutralized by time.

When he wrote in 1966, Améry was sure this would not happen. "Germany will not make it good, and our rancor will have been for nothing." He believed the Nazi era would be understood as an accident of history, and no German would hesitate to hang a portrait of her great-grandfather in SS uniform in the parlor. At the time, Améry's pessimism was justified. Reparations had been paid, but they were not accompanied by any process of *Vergangenheitsaufarbeitung.* Former Nazis held powerful positions in government, the justice system, the diplomatic service, the schools. The Auschwitz trials recently completed in Frankfurt were considered a failure by the prosecutor, Fritz Bauer, for the media portrayed the guards on trial as freakish sadists with no connection to the German people as a whole. Hannah Arendt wrote that the majority opinion was manifest in the behavior of the defendants—in their laughing, smiling, smirking impertinence toward prosecution and witnesses, their lack of respect for the court . . . It was manifest in the behavior of the lawyers who kept reminding the judges that they must pay no attention to "what one will think of us in the outside world," implying over and over again that not a German desire for justice but the world opinion influenced by the victims' desire for "retribution" and "vengeance" was the true cause of their clients' present trouble.[4]

It was a time when Améry could be assured by a German businessman that bygones were bygones, since Germans no longer bore a grudge against the Jewish people—just look how magnanimous they'd been with reparations! Although Améry acknowledged that intellectuals like Hans Magnus Enzensberger declared that Auschwitz would remain Germany's past, present, and future, he believed theirs were minority voices, without influence.

Half a century after his book was published, what Améry regarded as an "extravagant moral daydream" has largely come to pass. It would be hard to find a German today who does not wish to turn time around and undo Nazi crimes—if only to avoid the decades of national shame that followed. The German government has so thoroughly integrated Auschwitz into its school programming that even many responsible citizens believe the Nazi era has been given too much historical weight. In 1966 Améry wrote that it would be dishonorable for German youths to cite Goethe and ignore Himmler. In the intervening decades there were times when many young Germans wondered whether it was honorable to cite Goethe at all. For years, it was argued that the whole of German culture was irreparably tainted. On the seventieth anniversary of the founding of Israel, even the AfD felt compelled to make a public commitment to Germany's historic responsibility to support the state. "Some of my constituents resented that," one party leader told me. "They asked if it meant that their children would still be paying for it." He felt the party was bound to make the commitment nonetheless. This is not to suggest that the AfD has overcome its racism—reducing both immigration and Vergangenheitsaufarbeitung are central to its platform—but that Germany has reached the point where open expressions of racism are politically ruinous. This may be the best outcome we can hope for, and it may also be enough. The seventeenth-century author La Rochefoucauld wrote that hypocrisy is the compliment vice pays to virtue. Who knew we would long for hypocrisy? Now many national leaders no longer feel the need to pay such compliments at all. Contra Kant and common wisdom, honesty is not always the best policy. Very often, social change begins with lip service. As the slow progress of German *Vergangenheitsaufarbeitung* showed, public postwar expressions of Nazi sentiment were legally unacceptable; by the 1980s they were socially unacceptable; now most people find them morally unacceptable. Recent backlash does not undermine the fact that this kind of progression is usually necessary. Moral revolutions do not happen all at once. As Kwame Anthony Appiah showed in *The Honor Code*, social ideas of what is shameful are crucial in creating genuine shame.

My central thesis stands opposed to much of what Améry wrote in "Resentments," but the essay remains enormously valuable for the light it sheds on the victim's moral psychology. It also underlines what the author Ta-Nehisi Coates called the crucial element of reparations: a revolution of national consciousness, a spiritual renewal.[5] Imagine an America where people were ashamed to hang portraits of their Confederate ancestors in uniform or to cling to the statues that honor them. Imagine an America where the raw and brutal truth of slavery and racial terror were integrated into historical narratives of American exceptionalism. The first condition of such a transformation would be profound: sincere apology for the torment that nonwhite Americans suffer.

It's revealing that the U.S. Congress did not even issue an apology for slavery until 2008: until you grasp the reach of your sins, you cannot really apologize for them. The congressional aides who wrote the 2008 resolution had clearly learned their history, for the apology didn't stop with emancipation but included remorse for most of the racist crimes that followed it. The House of Representatives concluded by expressing its "commitment to rectify the lingering consequences of the misdeeds committed against African Americans under slavery and Jim Crow and to stop the occurrence of human rights violations in the future." That rectification is yet to come. As Israel recognized when it demanded an apology from Germany before even entering into negotiations over reparations, reparations without apologies are blind. But apologies without reparations may be empty.

Outside of Germany, only scholars of contemporary German history know much about the country's efforts to work off its past, but the fact that it paid reparations is sufficiently well known to be the precedent for every argument that America owes compensation to descendants of enslaved people.[6] At first glance, the case for American reparations for slavery has little in common with the case for German reparations for the Holocaust. The Allies and the not-yet State of Israel began to discuss the latter even before the war was over, and the treaties signed at Potsdam affirmed the principle that Germany owed compensation for the destruction it had wreaked on the world. The destruction was so massive that the Allies acknowledged that Germany could not truly compensate for it without being ruined. Those initial discussions were less about compensation for individual victims of the Nazis than about compensation for the destruction of the Allies' respective territories. There was no need for argument or a complex verification process. Wehrmacht soldiers had been ordered to lay waste to a gigantic swath of territory, and lay waste they had. Immediately following the war, the Soviet Union began to dismantle factories and rolling stock from the eastern sector as payback for the devastation Germany had inflicted on Soviet territory. "Nobody was enthusiastic about the fact that the Russians deconstructed the train tracks," said the writer Daniela Dahn, "but most people expected worse. There had been plans to turn the whole country into potato fields. And we knew who started the war." She never heard another East German say the punishment was exaggerated. "The resentment was less directed toward the Russians than to West Germany, because they were originally supposed to pay reparations to Russia as well."

They did not. But only a few years later, West Germany signed an agreement with the State of Israel and the Jewish Claims Conference—organized to represent those Jews not living in Israel—to pay compensation to Holocaust victims. At the time, it was crucial to avoid the word *reparations*. The reparations demanded by the Versailles Treaty after World War I helped to undermine the German economy between the wars. Even more important, Germans felt they were unfairly blamed for what was, in the end, a mad scramble for power and colonial territory in which none of the actors was blameless. As the economy worsened, those feelings turned into deep resentments that fed the rise of the Nazi Party.[7] The demand for reparations for the First World War played a part in fueling the second, and nobody wanted to make the same mistake twice. Instead, West Germany got the Marshall Plan, and the question of further reparations was tabled until a final peace treaty could be negotiated. By the time a treaty was signed, in 1990, the question was considered obsolete.

West Germany had already paid some 80 billion marks to victims of the Holocaust, including payments made to individual survivors and hundreds of millions to the fledgling State of Israel. The toxic word *reparations* was replaced by one that had little history but was all the more problematic: *Wiedergutmachung*, which literally means "to make things good again." It was a word Arendt used to describe the resolution of ordinary injustice and enmity. But in describing her shock at the revelation that the stories of mass murder were true, she said, "It was really as if an abyss had opened. Because we'd always believed that everything else could be *made good again*, as everything must be able to be *made good again* in politics. Not this. This should never have happened."[8]

No wonder so many Israelis found the prospect of accepting reparations noxious. The new state considered forbidding all contact with Germany, and Germans, by law. Israeli passports were stamped, in English, with the words NOT VALID IN GERMANY, and *Ha'aretz* instructed its readers to avoid even the sort of casual contact with German nationals that might occur at a hotel in Switzerland.[9] Few Israelis needed instruction. Rage at the nation that had murdered their parents and children ran so high that some survivors declared that only the murder of six million Germans would be adequate redress. The idea that Germans could make things good again by offering money in return for lives ended—or, at best, wrecked—by Nazi crimes led many Israelis to protest the very idea of negotiations. Those protests turned violent in 1952, when the future prime minister Menachem Begin led a demonstration that ended with broken windows in the Knesset, where the matter was being debated.

Israel's legendary prime minister David Ben-Gurion was more pragmatic. Israel and West Germany needed each other: "The United States and other countries were endeavoring to bring Germany back into the family of nations just as Israel was battling for its international position against the efforts of the Arab countries to isolate the Jewish state."[10] As the Cold War intensified, U.S. scruples about allying with former Nazis waned. Despite a strong domestic movement in support of postwar demilitarization, plans for the Federal Republic to join NATO were already in motion. There was a small window of opportunity in which an Israeli demand for and a German offer of reparations would serve both countries' geopolitical interests. Ben-Gurion opened it.

In secret meetings he initiated, representatives of Germany and Israel discussed every aspect of a possible agreement, each constrained by the knowledge that his own nation was uneasy with the idea of reparations at all. The actual amounts were debated, of course, and the bargaining followed a process familiar to anyone who ever set foot in a souk. Each side demanded more, and accepted less, than the sum that was finally agreed upon in closing. (The Israelis began with a demand for $1.5 billion, Adenauer with an offer of $2 million. In the end the agreement was signed for a sum of $820 million in 1952 currency, 70 percent of which would be paid in German goods.) More interesting than the expectable haggling over sums was the wrangling over words. Was the Holocaust an injustice or a crime? In his first speech to parliament in 1949, Adenauer had lamented the wartime suffering of a long list of Germans—those who lost their homes to annexation or bombing, those interned in POW camps, those who were widowed or crippled. His failure to mention any non-German whose suffering was caused by German war crimes provoked criticism at home and abroad. Before entering into talks about concrete sums, therefore, Israel insisted that Adenauer make a formal statement to parliament admitting German culpability for crimes against the Jewish people. The statement was virtually drafted by the Israeli government.[11] The Jews wanted more acknowledgment of guilt, the Germans wanted less, and what emerged was a compromise. Still, the president of the World Jewish Congress, Nahum Goldmann, who was chiefly responsible for the success of the final negotiations, described Adenauer's speech as follows:

> What happened on that day in the German federal parliament was a novel departure in political history. In contrast with customary political practice, which always seeks to justify its own point of view and to make moral demands only on its opponent, the German people . . . freely and of their own accord acknowledged their guilt for past events and assumed responsibility for them. This suddenly opened an entirely new dimension in politics.[12]

Despite their opposition to compensation, a majority of West Germans acknowledged the justice of returning property that had been stolen from German Jews. But that was a matter of restitution, not reparations. It was much harder to claim that money was owed to a state that hadn't existed when crimes were committed against its citizens. Israeli negotiators argued that the money was needed to absorb the half-million refugees the German state had made homeless, whose health had been so decimated by German crimes that they could not contribute to the development of a poor and precarious state. It was a claim on which all sides could agree because its truths were undeniable. When Germany offered to make part of its payments in shipments of butter, Goldmann replied that Israelis could only afford margarine.[13] At a time when anti-reparations demonstrators in Jerusalem carried signs reading WHAT ARE MY MURDERED PARENTS WORTH?, the cost of integration was also the only thing that could decently be quantified.

Adenauer's decision to offer reparations was unpopular among most West Germans, which is part of what leads many historians to believe his motives were sincere. In addition to wanting membership in NATO and fearing harm from "Jewish banking circles" and "Jewish economic power," Adenauer seems to have believed that some compensation for the Holocaust was due.[14] Nonetheless, both then and thereafter, the process that survivors had to endure to receive reparations was mean-spirited and arduous. There were legitimate concerns about fraudulent claims, but they hardly justified the ways that Auschwitz survivors had to document the circumstances under which they arrived at the camp, find two sworn statements from witnesses confirming their presence there, submit their tattooed numbers for cross-referencing, prove that medical injuries were sustained there and remained debilitating—and finally demonstrate that their incomes were unacceptably low.[15] At the end of the process, the survivor who successfully documented her claims could receive $450 for each year she spent at Auschwitz. Although $450 was worth somewhat more in 1953 than it is today, it was still significantly less than the pensions paid to former SS guards and their widows.

However stingy the payments and stonehearted the process for attaining them, Nahum Goldmann was right: the reparations marked a historical shift. Traditional reparations were something that victors imposed on the vanquished, whose treasure and territory were taken as spoils of war without any appeal to right or wrong. Germany was indeed vanquished, but the reparations agreements were made voluntarily, albeit in the conviction that they would improve postwar Germany's miserable standing in the world's court of public opinion.

Those who oppose American reparations for slavery are quick to dismiss the precedent by pointing out the differences between the two cases. Their arguments turn on the justice as well as the difficulty of assessing claims made on the basis of a crime that occurred generations ago. Is slavery responsible for the enormous wealth gap between average white and black Americans 150 years after the Emancipation Proclamation, or the fact that young black men are more likely to land in jail than in college? And even if it is, how on earth should we determine who's entitled to relief? Slaveholders' records were rarely as systematic as those of the Nazis. Most Americans today believe that slavery was a crime. But after so much time and so little clarity, most also believe that any attempt to compensate the victims is hopeless. Besides, as the African American linguist John McWhorter and others have argued, hasn't affirmative action been an appropriate form of compensation?[16]

"The belief that blacks have been given too much is made possible by the refusal to countenance how much was actually taken away in the first place," wrote the author Jelani Cobb.[17] Affirmative action has been under attack since it was introduced, and whatever its limited successes, it could not serve the purpose that reparations are meant to serve. If affirmative action programs speak of the need to level the playing field, reparations claims seek justice for a crime. The need for affirmative action was grudgingly accepted and meagerly implemented, but it's easier to swallow a sports metaphor than to acknowledge an atrocity. Ta-Nehisi Coates is right to argue that "the idea of reparations is frightening not simply because we might lack the ability to pay. The idea of reparations threatens something much deeper—America's heritage, history, and standing in the world."[18]

Many—perhaps most—countries have rapacious and violent histories that they cover, in time, with a fuzzy blanket of benevolence. *We brought the natives religion, or railroads. The natives were no angels either, and besides, our neighbors were worse.* In the end, the attempts at justification come to little more than *everybody does it, and we weren't as bad as some.* American sins are not worse than those of other nations. They are simply more jarring because, unlike the foundation of other nations, America's took place amid a fanfare of ideals. Other nations commenced by believing in nothing but themselves; only America began its morning by pledging allegiance to a set of principles.

That Native Americans had a right to life, and African Americans to liberty, was a truth whose self-evidence eluded the Founding Fathers. From its inception, the United States of America insisted on ideals it refused to realize. Yet those ideals refused to fade. Sometimes they merely served the cause of self-delusion, but sometimes they retained enough weight to guide every progressive movement from abolition to the present day. Given that fact, recognizing the justice of reparations is a recognition of the need to rethink American history.

Over decades, such rethinking has taken place in departments of history and postcolonial studies; only occasionally has it penetrated popular consciousness. Very simple truths, like the fact that the Civil War was fought over slavery, need to be reestablished again and again. Descendants of Confederate soldiers have self-serving reasons for denying that their ancestors fought and fell in service to a criminal enterprise. It's natural to defend the honor of your forebears, if only with arguments so facile that a well-educated child could see through them. *He fought for states' rights.* States' rights to do what?

Sadly enough, the view that the Civil War was not fought over slavery has also been supported by intellectual trends on the left; in recent decades, we've become cynical about any claims suggesting that people take risks on behalf of moral principles.[19] Not conservatives, but people who call themselves progressive are often most intent on deconstructing the heroic Union narrative of the Civil War upheld by William James. It's easy to show that, unlike James's youngest brothers, the majority of those who fought for the Union were not in favor of emancipation. It's easy to point to Lincoln's statements denying racial equality. John Brown he was not, though Lincoln came to echo Brown in his somber Second Inaugural Address. Before the war began, preserving the Union was paramount. Only as it came to its bloody end was emancipation a central goal—partly due to the courage of two hundred thousand African American soldiers who fought for it.

The cause of the Civil War lies in the logic of slavery itself. When the war began in 1861, the slave system provided much of America's wealth. During the political battles of the 1850s, only slavery's expansion into the new territories was explicitly contested, whether in the halls of Congress or on the plains of Kansas. Just a minority demanded abolition, but because cotton production exhausted soil quickly, the slave system could not continue to enjoy massive profits without extending west of the Mississippi. The need for more land meant that the system had to expand or end, a fact recognized early by those who fought so hard, in the 1850s, to establish slavery in Kansas and California.

⌒

Any serious discussion of American reparations for slavery must acknowledge two facts:

1. America's wealth is intrinsically bound up with profits from slavery, from the plantations of the South to the factories of the North.
2. Chattel slavery was abolished in 1865, but it was replaced by other forms of subjugation that were not just a function of custom and prejudice but a matter of law.[20]

Earlier histories of slavery portrayed it as a premodern, agrarian institution, "fundamentally in contradiction with the political and economic systems of the liberal republic . . . inevitably the contradiction would be resolved in favor of the free-labor North. Sooner or later, slavery would have ended by the operation of historical forces."[21] Recent historical work has shown, however, that slavery was a major engine of economic growth, becoming ever more efficient until the outbreak of the Civil War. That growth was not confined to the Southern states where cotton was picked, though they were seven of the eight wealthiest states in 1860. As the nineteenth century's most traded product, cotton produced by enslaved people was directly or indirectly responsible for the growth of American and British economies.

Cotton was as central to the nineteenth-century economy as oil is to the economy today. "Cotton is King," said South Carolina senator James Hammond shortly before the Southern states seceded from the Union, "and no power on earth dare make war on cotton."[22] At the time, cotton made up 60 percent of U.S. export revenues, and the United States produced 60 percent of the world's cotton. It wasn't just the raw material for the nineteenth century's most successful industry, the textile mills that were as profitable in Manchester, New Hampshire, as in Manchester, England. Cotton also drove increasing demand for iron goods, rope, furniture, and shoes.[23] Apart from the products produced by their labor, enslaved people themselves made up 20 percent of America's wealth. Given the ease with which they could be sold on the market, enslaved men and women were also the most liquid form of wealth. The historian Edward Baptist showed that the owners of the nearly one million slaves who were sold from the Upper South to work the cotton and cane fields of Alabama, Mississippi, and Louisiana were less likely to be paternalistic planters fallen on hard times than remorseless entrepreneurs. As cotton production boomed, the separation of enslaved families became central to the slave system. Slaves were torn from their families because they fetched twice as much in New Orleans as they did in Virginia. Less obvious but more insidious was the way that bonds using those slaves as collateral enriched investors all over the world.

Sometime in elementary school I learned that a white farmer from Massachusetts named Eli Whitney invented the cotton gin. I learned that his invention made it easier to harvest cotton and was thus important for the Industrial Revolution, though without any understanding of cotton economics, I could hardly understand why this little piece of American history deserved attention in a textbook. I learned nothing about torture. Whitney may have invented the machine, but the men and women who served it were regularly and brutally whipped in order to increase production. In the absence of torture, a free laborer could pick some hundred pounds a day, the average rate to which production fell after slavery was abolished. At the height of the cotton industry in the 1850s, many enslaved cotton pickers averaged more than two hundred pounds every day.[24] The overseers' ledgers recorded the amount of cotton picked and the number of whippings administered next to each slave's name. Whoever failed to meet the constantly rising quota of cotton was subject to lashing with a ten-foot whip. Baptist showed that this form of torture was not the product of accidental sadism nor even a matter of punishment for alleged infractions. It was a central factor of production, forcing enslaved men and women to labor at inhuman speeds. "The whip," he concludes, "was as important to making cotton grow as sunshine and rain."[25]

As the Civil War drew to its bloody close, there was considerable discussion about what would become of four million emancipated African Americans. There was initial support for the idea that they were owed some compensation for generations of forced labor. General Sherman and Secretary of War Edwin Stanton met in Savannah with twenty black freedmen, most of them ministers, to ask what they wanted for their people. The answer was clear: they wanted to own the lands they had formerly worked for others, divided into plots large enough to support their families. Asked whether they would prefer those plots to be scattered among white people or to live in colonies by themselves, Reverend Garrison Frazier, the group's chosen leader, replied that Southern prejudice against blacks would take years to disappear; blacks would prefer, for the time being, to live by themselves. Four days later, Sherman issued Special Field Order 15. It set aside the islands south of Charleston, the abandoned rice fields along the rivers, and the county bordering the St. Johns River, Florida—a total of four hundred thousand acres—"for the settlement of the negroes now made free by the acts of war and the proclamation of the President of the United States."[26] Each family was allotted "not more than forty acres of tillable ground" and no white people, with the exception of military on duty, would be permitted to settle there.

The mules were promised later, but not by any binding order. The proposal to grant forty acres and the means to farm them seemed a matter of good sense and justice, not only to freedmen and -women but to officials of the Freedmen's Bureau and many other white Republicans. Had it been realized, it would have been an act of reparation for the thousands of acres those African Americans had worked, under the lash, without pay. Moreover, the vision of small, independent farmers exactly fit Jefferson's conception of the ideal conditions for a democratic republic. A few months later, the Freedmen's Bureau controlled nearly a million acres set aside for this purpose—0.2 percent of land in the South.

But Jefferson's vision had been replaced by reveries of profit in the world cotton market. Both North and South preferred large plantations producing for export to self-sufficient small farmers.[27] Moreover, President Andrew

Johnson was keen on restoring the rights and properties of the Southern planters who'd always had his sympathy. Not half a year after Lincoln's murder, Johnson overturned every order that had granted land to freed people and returned it to the planters who had started the war. As Martin Luther King Jr. said in 1968:

> At the very same time that America refused to give the Negro any land, through an act of Congress our government was giving away millions of acres of land in the West and the Midwest, which meant it was willing to undergird its white peasants from Europe with an economic floor. But not only did they give them land, they built land grant colleges with government money to teach them how to farm. Not only that, they provided county agents to further their expertise in farming.[28]

African Americans working the land could no longer be returned to prewar slavery, so sharecropping, a form of serfdom, was put in its place. Under the sharecropping system, the sharecropper worked the owner's field in exchange for a percentage of the crop. Sharecropping families were forced to buy everything they needed, from seed to salt, at the plantation store. They usually had to buy necessities on credit, at exorbitant interest rates, at the beginning of each season. The possibilities for cheating and outright theft were rampant, and generally exploited, for the owners were still seething at the loss of the people they regarded as property. The amount of cotton the sharecroppers picked was regularly underestimated, the price of goods was regularly inflated, and most sharecroppers never got out of debt. Though no longer in shackles, they could not leave the land.

Through enormous effort and self-discipline, some newly freed men nevertheless managed to become businessmen, teachers, lawyers, and even congressmen during the brief period of Reconstruction. Then Reconstruction was followed by the period commonly known as Jim Crow, named after a blackface minstrel caricature. Several writers now insist that the term is too innocuous to capture the horror of life in the South after Reconstruction. The journalist Douglas Blackmon proposed the term "Age of Neoslavery," arguing, "Imagine if the first years of the Holocaust were known by the name of Germany's most famous anti-Semitic comedian of the 1930s."[29] Bryan Stevenson calls it the Age of Racial Terror, bell hooks calls it the age of apartheid. Both neoslavery and terror were instruments white Southerners used to wipe out the gains of Reconstruction. In the absence of federal troops and Northern engagement, Southern states fiercely enforced the laws known as the Black Codes, which were largely successful attempts to evade the Thirteenth Amendment:

> **Section 1.** Neither slavery nor involuntary servitude, except as a punishment for crime whereof the party shall have been duly convicted, shall exist within the United States, or any place subject to their jurisdiction.
> **Section 2.** Congress shall have power to enforce this article by appropriate legislation.

The most systematically pernicious of those attempts turned on a clause in the first section of the amendment itself. It outlawed slavery and involuntary servitude "except as punishment for a crime whereof the party shall have been duly convicted." In the warped justice system of the postwar South, nothing was easier than inventing crimes and duly convicting African Americans of them.

Blackmon argued that the system of neoslavery, which persisted into the early years of World War II, explains more about contemporary American life, white and black, than antebellum slavery. Neoslavery was even more brutal. Under the old system, a chattel slave was the owner's property. Having made a considerable investment in a black human being, the enslaver had an economic interest in preserving that investment by upholding minimal standards of nutrition and health. Under the new system, convicts were not owned but merely leased by state prisons to private corporations that mined coal, forged steel, or built bricks. In some Alabama prison camps the mortality rate was 40 percent. If a convict died from malnutrition, lashing, overwork, or disease, the corporation could always get another. The price was trivial for the business owner, though the revenue was crucial for government coffers in states notoriously unwilling to levy taxes. Besides, the workers in question were criminals, weren't they?

Blackmon's devastating research shows they were not. Most were arrested under deliberately obscure vagrancy laws, according to which black persons unable to immediately prove they were currently employed by a white person could be charged, convicted, and sentenced to hard labor. Offenses such as spitting, selling produce after dark, walking next to a railroad, and talking loudly near a white woman could also result in prison terms. Under the new laws, it was no accident that 90 percent of prisoners in Southern jails were African American. Rather than reflecting on the legitimacy of the laws, however, most whites used the rise in African American crime rates to argue that blacks were inherently criminal. The resulting image of African Americans was even worse than it had been under antebellum slavery: people who'd been formerly viewed as loyal, albeit inferior, were now seen as dangerous. The increasing number of blacks in jail was used to support the old argument that they were not yet ready for freedom. In fact, Blackmon showed that the timing and scale of arrests were repeatedly correlated with the demand for cheap labor. Just before harvest time, for example, the number of arrests increased dramatically.

State officials responsible for arrests and convictions cooperated closely with the businesses to which convicts were leased. In some cases, business and law were controlled by the same person. Rounding up black men, and occasionally women, and putting them in the chains from which their parents were so recently freed served two purposes well. Along with the fear of lynching, fear of arrest kept Southern black people in a permanent state of intimidation. Many who were seized and sentenced never saw their families again, despite those families' appeals to federal authorities for help in finding the prisoners. Convict leasing was as effective a means of enforcing white supremacy as any ever devised.

The other purpose of the convict lease system was even more far-reaching. The growth of convict leasing coincided directly with the growth of the international labor movement. Access to a limitless supply of dirt-cheap labor allowed business to depress wages for free workers, break early strikes, and suppress the drive for unionization in the South.[30] Southern business literally had a captive workforce. In a 1911 letter to the state board of inspectors of convicts, the president of Tennessee Coal and Iron, a subsidiary of U.S. Steel, wrote "The chief inducement for the hiring of convicts was the certainty of a supply of coal for our manufacturing operations in the contingency of labor troubles."[31] In the conflicts between business and labor that often became battles during the early twentieth century, convict leasing was a potent weapon. Business had no reason to accept workers' demands for decent labor conditions as long as it could force many thousands to work under indecent ones. The system thus damaged working white people as well as black ones, though only the latter were actually subject to whips and chains. Not until America's entry into World War II did Attorney General Francis Biddle order the FBI director J. Edgar Hoover to investigate a case of involuntary servitude. The reasoning behind the government decision was breathtaking. As Biddle's assistant wrote, the case was but one of many instances "in which members of the Negro race have been the victims. Enemy propagandists have used similar episodes in international broadcasts to the colored race, saying that the democracies are insincere and that the enemy is their friend."[32]

Blackmon is no radical, but a white man from the Mississippi Delta who was Atlanta bureau chief at *The Wall Street Journal*, which makes his Pulitzer Prize–winning book all the more damning. His research shows that "the prolonged economic inferiority and social subjugation of African Americans that was to be ubiquitous . . . was not a conclusion preordained by the traditions of antebellum slavery."[33] The freedmen were poor, and often illiterate, but so were millions of white Southerners after the war. By the mid-twentieth century, most of the latter had joined the middle class. Black people suffered a series of reversals.

Shortly after Blackmon's book was published, Michelle Alexander, in *The New Jim Crow*, and Bryan Stevenson, in *Just Mercy*, argued that the mass incarceration of young black men, usually for trivial nonviolent offenses, is a continuation of the convict lease system.[34] For possession of marijuana, an eighteen-year-old can be locked into a brutal prison where he is likelier to acquire expertise in lawbreaking than anything else. Even worse, should he seek an honest job after completing his sentence, a felony conviction will deter most employers from hiring him. In most states it will also result in the loss of such basic civil rights as the rights to vote, serve on a jury, receive government financial aid for education, or own a firearm. Study after study has shown that black and white youths are treated differently for breaking the law.[35] Despite the 2010 Fair Sentencing Act, the crack that is smoked on a Bronx stairwell is still punished more harshly than the cocaine that fuels long hours in the kitchen of a high-end chef or the office of a Wall Street broker. The injustice is not limited to those who are actually sent to prison. As Stevenson argues, the knowledge that one in three black boys born today is likely to enter the penal system diminishes the hopes and expectations of all of them.

As a result of the war on drugs begun in the late 1960s, the prison population grew from 300,000 in 1971 to more than 2.2 million today. The United States has the largest prison population in the world, far exceeding that of China or Russia. Eighty percent of those prisoners are black or brown. Systemic racism contributes to the perception of those people as likely to be criminals, and that is no accident. The criminalization of African Americans was deliberate and intentional. Here's a quote from the diary of H. R. Haldeman, Nixon's chief of staff:

[The president] emphasized that you have to face the fact that the whole problem is really the blacks. *The key is to devise a system that recognizes this while not appearing to* . . . [He] pointed out that there has never in history been an adequate black nation, and they are the only race of which this is true. Says Africa is hopeless. The worst there is Liberia, which we built.[36]

The war on drugs was a war on black men initiated by Republicans as part of their Southern strategy to appeal to formerly Democratic white voters alarmed by the gains of the civil rights movement. The Democrat Bill Clinton further institutionalized that strategy through mandatory sentencing policies that appealed to white working-class voters across the country.

As Blackmon argued, commercial sectors of U.S. society were never asked to account for their role in supporting white supremacy, though "it was business that policed adherence to America's racial customs more than any other actor."[37] While he marshaled compelling arguments for the idea that industry should pay for its long use of slave labor, Blackmon did not demand that it do so. But the case for reparations received another boost in 2014, when the young writer Ta-Nehisi Coates published an article in *The Atlantic*.

Coates focused on a form of injustice called redlining, which excluded black neighborhoods from the mortgage support that was part of the New Deal. This support, which insured private mortgages, leading to lower interest rates and down payments, helped millions of white Americans enter the middle class after the Great Depression. A government "could have required compliance with a nondiscrimination policy," wrote the urban studies expert Charles Abrams. "Instead, FHA adopted a racial policy that could well have been culled from the Nuremberg Laws."[38] As a consequence, black families were subject to predatory landlords and loans, and locked out from acquiring what is, for most people, the primary source of wealth. Small wonder that the Pew Research Center estimates that white households are worth roughly twenty times as much as black ones. Since African Americans earn, on average, 77 percent of white Americans' salaries, the gap in wealth is much greater than the gap in income.[39]

Worse still, even those who managed to buy their own homes were damaged by the neighborhood segregation that mortgage policies underlined. It isn't necessary that public schools be supported by local property taxes. In Germany, for example, school funding is supported by state and national appropriations without regard to neighborhood. In the American system, a child born in a wealthy neighborhood will automatically have smaller classes, more equipment, and better-paid teachers than one born in a ghetto. Since well-educated parents tend to raise well-educated children, these are damages that persist across generations. As the philosopher Elizabeth Anderson showed in *The Imperative of Integration*, segregation is not only the root cause of inequality, but a significant force in undermining democracy.[40]

The development of segregated neighborhoods was not a matter of local prejudice; it was underwritten by federal law. Clauses in FHA mortgages granted to white people explicitly prevented resale to blacks. Redlining was not outlawed until 1968, and some of its victims are still alive. Focusing on them removes the first objection raised concerning reparations for African Americans: How can anyone determine to whom reparations are owed? Here there's no need to trace lines back to slavery. There are clear enough ways to establish who was left out of the New Deal that made white America a largely middle-class nation, just as they were left out of Social Security, the other lasting New Deal success. In order to sell the New Deal to Southern voters, Social Security was not made available to farm and domestic workers, which excluded 65 percent of African Americans working at the time.

In "The Case for Reparations," Coates showed that legally sanctioned economic injustice persisted until 1968, and he also showed that some early Americans found the idea of reparations natural. Long before forty acres were promised to liberated families, some Quaker communities made membership contingent on compensating one's former slaves.[41] In 1810, Yale president Timothy Dwight wrote, "It is in vain to allege that our ancestors brought them hither, and not we . . . We inherit our ample patrimony with all its incumbrances, and are bound to pay the debts of our ancestors . . . To give [slaves] liberty, and stop here, is to entail upon them a curse."[42]

You cannot choose your inheritance any more than you can choose your parents. You can only choose your relationship to them. Bernhard Schlink, the author of the best-selling book *The Reader*, has argued that breaking with them entirely is the only way for a German to escape her Nazi parents' guilt.[43] I disagree, and admire those descendants who attempt both to maintain clear antifascist positions and to honor those fathers and mothers whose actions were thoroughly dishonorable. But if you maintain a relationship, and especially if you assume any part of a legacy, you should be bound to acknowledge its context. Most states require that debts be paid before deceased people's assets are distributed to their heirs. It's an aspect of law that is based on intuitions about fairness: you have no right to enjoy the benefits of an inheritance without assuming its liabilities as well. There is no corresponding moral rule; unlike personal property, historical debt can rarely be quantified. Yet the intuition embodied in the law is one we preserve.

Coates's argument is as simple as it is eloquent. Slavery was, among other things, the theft of black labor that produced enormous wealth. For some early white observers, honor and justice demanded that at least part of the wealth be given to those whose labor produced it. If it can be proved that legal measures created to subjugate African Americans persisted a century after slavery was abolished, the debt that was owed to enslaved people should be paid to their heirs. The evidence for those claims was overlooked only because, for too many Americans, the period between the Emancipation Proclamation and the Montgomery bus boycott is simply blank. Recent research allows us to fill in that blank. Yet even earlier, Martin Luther King wrote, "The South deluded itself with the illusion that the Negro was happy in his place; the North deluded itself with the illusion that it had freed the Negro. The Emancipation Proclamation freed the slave, a legal entity, but it failed to free the Negro, a person."[44]

Reparations, Coates argued, would be the full acceptance of our collective biography and its consequences. It's dishonest to appeal to national pride without acknowledging national shame. If you'd be appalled by a German nationalist who boasted of Beethoven and bratwurst while ignoring Buchenwald, you cannot confine your vision of America to the words of the Founding Fathers or the deeds of the Greatest Generation. You must own American evils as well. Doing so, Coates wrote, would initiate a national reckoning that could lead to spiritual renewal. "More important than any single check cut to any African American, the payment of reparations would represent America's maturation out of the childhood myth of its innocence into a wisdom worthy of its founders."[45]

From myth to wisdom: it's a matter of growing up. In his argument for reparations, Coates reveals a remnant of faith in American ideals that is at odds with the pessimism for which he's been criticized. Some African American writers, like Cornel West and Thomas Chatterton Williams, have charged that Coates's later writings essentialize race and fetishize white supremacy; they argue for a more universalist vision that attends to the dynamics of class and power. Without such a vision, Coates's singular focus on white supremacy leaves both black and white people without agency, or hope of transcending tribalist conflict. For Williams, white supremacy and Coates mirror each other: "Both [white supremacy and Coates] mystify racial identity, interpreting it as something fixed, determinative and almost supernatural . . . So long as we fetishize race, we ensure that we will never be rid of the hierarchies it imposes."[46] To hold that ideals are ethnically and genetically determined is to cede the floor to a materialism that leaves human beings without power and ideals without force.

In "The Case for Reparations," however, Coates's appeal to American ideals struck transcendent notes that resonate with some of Obama's most stirring speeches, including the one he gave in Selma, Alabama, on the fiftieth anniversary of Bloody Sunday:

> What enormous faith these men and women had. Faith in God—but also faith in America . . . What greater expression of faith in the American experiment than this; what greater form of patriotism is there than the belief that America is not yet finished, that we are strong enough to be self-critical, that each successive generation can look upon our imperfections and decide that it is in our power to remake this nation to more closely align with our highest ideals? . . . To deny this progress, this hard-won progress—our progress—would be to rob us of our own agency, our own capacity, our responsibility to do what we can to make America better.

❧

The small town of Selma (population: 18,000) devotes the first weekend in March to celebrating the event that put it on the map in 1965: the march across the Edmund Pettus Bridge that was so brutally suppressed it led Lyndon Johnson to propose, and Congress to pass, the Voting Rights Act that protected all Americans' right to the ballot. Although that right had been established in 1868 by the Fourteenth Amendment, Southern states were resourceful in finding ways to get around it. The milder ways involved poll taxes, and tests full of unanswerable questions: How many bubbles in a bar of soap? How many feathers on a chicken? How high is up? When those tests failed to discourage resolute black voters, state authorities turned to terror.

The voter registration drive that claimed the lives of Chaney, Schwerner, and Goodman was no less violent in neighboring Alabama. Half a year after the murders in Mississippi, an Alabama state trooper shot Jimmie Lee Jackson, a black veteran and Baptist deacon who had joined others in a peaceful demonstration after five futile attempts to register to vote. It was a time when civil rights workers were told to stay out of Selma—the whites were too mean and the blacks too scared—but Jackson's death was galvanizing. Organizers led by Martin Luther King Jr.'s Southern Christian Leadership

Conference decided to march to the state capital with his casket. The first march, on what came to be known as Bloody Sunday, ended when state troopers spilled the blood and smashed the bones of marchers, including twenty-four-year-old John R. Lewis, now a long-serving Georgia congressman, as well as a number of young girls and grandmothers.

Reporters captured the violence on camera, and the nation was appalled. Two days later, Martin Luther King Jr. came from Atlanta to lead the marchers across the bridge, but he stopped to kneel and pray at the foot of a line of armed state troopers. Unknown to most of those who followed him, King had promised not to march without the permit that civil rights attorneys were working to secure. That night, a white Unitarian minister named James Reeb, who had followed King's call to come to Selma, was bludgeoned to death outside a local café. Reeb's death accelerated the pressure to allow the final march to proceed, and on March 21, 1965, thousands of people trekked fifty miles through the mud to Montgomery. This time, nineteen hundred state troopers were under orders to protect them. Arriving in the Alabama capital, the marchers were treated to a campsite rally that featured Harry Belafonte, Pete Seeger, Odetta, James Baldwin, Nina Simone, and Joan Baez.

Since 1992, the march across the bridge—still named for the Confederate general and Klan leader who became a U.S. senator—has been repeated every year. When I arrived at the church where the original march began, the civil rights leaders Jesse Jackson and Benjamin Barber were speaking to the crowd from the steps. I bought a T-shirt that read I MISSED IT IN 1965 BUT I WAS THERE IN 2017 from a young vendor wearing long dreadlocks. Both Jackson and Barber denounced the Supreme Court decision that had gutted the Voting Rights Act that people had died in Selma to achieve.[47] In the churchyard, someone passed out printed signs reading STOP VOTER SUPPRESSION! in red, white, and blue. We were there to honor a struggle that took place half a century earlier because it is one that still needs to be fought.

> Ain't gonna let Donald Trump, no
> Turn me round
> Turn me round
> Turn me round

As the march began, I positioned myself behind the woman with the best voice, singing along with others as she improvised and led. Pushing a stroller where her daughter sat smiling, wearing a lavender bow that covered most of her head, she sang with ringing determination and perfect pitch. The man singing "I ain't gonna study war no more" the loudest was wearing a U.S. Marine uniform. Maybe it wasn't as incongruous as it seemed: for many black Americans, military service is not only a decent job but an emblem of full citizenship—one reason why waves of lynchings were directed at black veterans returning from both world wars.

Looking up at the ironwork balconies like the ones I'd seen often in New Orleans, I could tell that some of the boarded-up storefronts were grand in their day. Though cotton made it wealthy in the years before the war, today Selma is as poor as the Delta—without the uncanny beauty of a Delta landscape. The church where the march began is now a national landmark, but the house next to it was abandoned, all of its windows broken, with paint peeling off most of the siding. Across the street a smaller house had simply imploded, spilling planks across what once was a yard. Selma is also racked by gang violence. "Proportionally speaking, we're the eighth most violent city in the country," one resident told me with a hint of pride. It isn't even really a city; as another told me, "We don't even have a chain restaurant like McDonald's."

Selma does have a small museum devoted to African American history, enslavement, and resistance. Housed in one of the storefronts on Water Street, its entry shows a rough mural of men and women bowed over cotton bolls. Above them is the lash-scarred back of a black man and the words *Never Again*, painted as if written by the blazing sun. At the end of the block is the Old Depot Museum, a large brick building that once was a train station. Now designed to show the history of the region, its main exhibits take up two rooms. The larger one is devoted to civil rights history, showcasing the four martyrs who died in Selma's voting rights struggle. The other room is devoted to the Confederacy, complete with canon, cannonballs of varying sizes, a clean Confederate flag, and a pair of worn crutches. The day I visited, a woman was setting up chairs in the civil rights room in preparation for the monthly evening meeting of the Sons of Confederate Veterans.

"It's the best room," she told me. "Of course, I could just move that cannon and they'd all fit into the Confederate room."

"So why do it this way?" I asked.

"I'm just a bitch"—she laughed—"and I think it's funny to make 'em sit there."

She was not at the march, but thousands of others were. There were old men and women aided by wheelchairs and walkers; there were children on shoulders and on foot. Three young white women wore Black Lives Matter T-shirts; one young black woman carried a handmade sign reading THIS COUNTRY WAS FOUNDED BY IMMIGRANTS. A grand lodge of African American Masons were dressed in stiff suits and black bow ties. There were two Buddhist monks in long saffron robes who come every year from Japan. A young white girl held a sign that said I WILL VOTE IN 2028. Three Jews wore T-shirts reading MONTGOMERY COMMUNITY in English and Hebrew. As we neared the bridge, the black woman with the wonderful voice struck up "We Shall Overcome." When she reached the verse that begins "Black and white together," I turned around. Everyone behind me was singing. It was all still possible: solidarity, hope, and even "America," which she sung out next, with even more gusto. *God shed His grace on thee.* Do you hear it as a statement about the past or a prayer for the future?

On the other side of the bridge stand memorials to civil rights leaders and martyrs, named or unknown. That day they were flanked on either side by smiling black families posing for pictures. Behind them the live oak trees were as gray as the Spanish moss that draped them under the cloudy March sky. Rows of outdoor stalls selling everything from cheap dashikis to neon-colored toy dogs flanked the highway. The Bridge Crossing Jubilee that commemorates the march is the town's largest annual event. Yet the city council is unable or unwilling to devote funds for the extra fire and police teams needed to remain on duty for the weekend that draws thousands to this forsaken place.

I'd signed up for a workshop connected to the jubilee. In four days, if I wanted, I could be certified as a Kingian Nonviolence trainer by Dr. Bernard Lafayette, one of King's assistants who was injured on Bloody Sunday, and his multiracial team. The participants were housed at a local black college. When I arrived there after the long drive down unlit back roads from Oxford, I felt chastened. One bathroom in the shared apartment had no mirror; in the other, the toilet was perpetually flushing, and a little force could knock down most of its walls. The building called the president's house was reserved for special guests; it only hinted at the desperate underfunding of the other college facilities. But the Healing Waters retreat center, site of the workshop, lay on a lovely spot of land overlooking the river. From the deck you can see the bridge where the battles took place.

Like the Winter Institute, the Selma Center for Nonviolence believes in the power of storytelling, the necessity of building relationships in order to get community work done, but in the Selma training there was little mention of race. Although Selma is 80 percent African American, Ainka Jackson said that few people, white or black, were interested in talking about it. "This isn't New York," she told me. "If I said we were holding a panel on race, I would hear 'There they go again.'" She finds it more effective to focus on community problems—education, homelessness—even though they affect far more black than white people. Even in Selma, she told me, nobody talked about Bloody Sunday until Ava DuVernay's movie *Selma* appeared.

Ainka is the director of the Selma Center, and her biography is impressive. She comes from an extraordinary family, who are largely responsible for organizing the jubilee, the center, the African American Museum, and most of the progressive community building that takes place in Selma. Her father, Hank Sanders, was the second of twelve children born in a three-room shack in the Alabama Black Belt. A scholarship took him to Harvard Law School, where he met his wife, Rose, who later changed her name to Faya Rose Touré to erase the names of her ancestors' enslavers. They moved to Selma and opened a law office. In addition to practicing law, Hank became a state senator while Faya Rose became an artist, a songwriter, and a community activist whose impatience has annoyed or inspired most everyone in Selma. She wears exquisite African clothing that looks more suited to Cambridge or Cape Town than to Selma. Together they raised three children, four foster children, and an uncountable number of homeless people, including one from Japan who showed up at their door.

All three of their children became activists and lawyers—"because people listen to lawyers," said Ainka, who had earlier been a teacher and a social worker. All three of them were onstage for the mock trial that takes place every year in the Dallas County, Alabama, courthouse, where so many African Americans had tried and failed to register to vote half a century earlier. In 2017, the subject of the trial was reparations for slavery. Sanders and Touré had been lawyers for the class action suit made by black farmers against the U.S. Department of Agriculture, which systematically denied black farmers the loans easily granted to white ones in the years between 1981 and 1995. Each of the plaintiffs received compensation, capped at $50,000 apiece, in 2013. Although that was often less than the actual damage they'd suffered, the $1.2 billion settlement was the largest ever paid as reparations for racist discrimination.

Now Touré was arguing a harder case. The fifteen thousand black farmers were still alive, the damages they suffered possible to trace. In the mock trial, she represented all those whose ancestors were enslaved in the United States of America. She called for compensatory damages for the work that was never remunerated, punitive damages for the harm done to succeeding generations. A woman called Sister Youni played the part of a slave, describing the Middle Passage, the labor, the hunger, the master who came most nights to have his way with her.

"So we add unpaid child support, Your Honor," said Touré to the mock judge. "How old are you?" she asked the witness. "Are you living in the nineteenth or the twenty-first century?"

"How can I know if I was never allowed to read or write?"

The next witness was Ray Winbush, a psychologist who wrote two books about reparations. He spoke of the damage done to descendants of enslaved people, arguing that the wounds of black women had always been underestimated. "Look at our skin color, look at our hair. All of us have an ancestor who was raped." Arguing for the straight line between that history and the fears of African Americans today, Winbush said, "Look at how we lower our voices when we say the words 'white people' even when there are no white people in the room." The audience laughed.

The lawyer for the defense was Touré's oldest daughter, Malika, heavily pregnant with her seventh child. As lawyers do, she argued about precedent: courts give compensation only for direct personal injury. There was no precedent for this kind of compensation. In 2013 the United Kingdom paid 20 million pounds to five thousand elderly Kenyans who endured torture during the Mau Mau rebellion, but that case was settled rather than tried, and those who'd been damaged were still living. Any court would say that the plaintiffs demanding reparations for slavery had no legal standing.

Any court would also deny the right of a witness to connect with his ancestors before answering a question. "You hear voices?" asked a cross-examiner.

But this was a mock trial, and Touré replied that connecting with ancestors is an African tradition, so moments of silence were allowed. With contempt, she dismissed the argument that African Americans wouldn't know how to spend reparations responsibly. "If you hit someone's car, would anyone argue he didn't deserve reparation because he's too stupid to spend it?" The defense argued that the case could be decided only by Congress, as courts only have jurisdiction over immediate personal injury, while it undermined any hope of congressional action by pointing to the budget deficit. Still, the verdict was unsurprising: the mock judge awarded $10 trillion in compensatory and $30 trillion in punitive damages. The courtroom cheered.

The mock trial was part of an all-day Southern Reparations Summit, where I was usually the only white person in the room. A couple of visits to black churches aside, it was an entirely new experience for me, and I ached for black friends who experience the reverse situation all the time. You cannot fully trust, and you do not really belong, leaving everyone floating in an air of uncertainty we politely pretend is normal. I took my seat, sat up straight, and listened. In addition to the Sanders-Touré family, the discussions were led by the leaders of N'COBRA, the National Coalition of Blacks for Reparations in America, founded in 1987. Senator Sanders began the summit by saying that the black farmers' lawsuit, though limited, had established a principle: the U.S. government has a duty to act when people were wronged by its actions. Although legislation as well as litigation would be needed for further justice, he hoped the success of the farmers' suit would encourage those who continue to work for comprehensive reparations. A loose set of arguments followed, punctuated alternately by humor and anger.

"Sherman didn't mention mules when he promised forty acres, but land came with mules those days. Otherwise it'd be like offering you a Lexus without an engine."

"The Jews got reparations for what happened between 1939 and 1945. What we suffered was worse and longer. Only what happened to Native Americans is comparable."

"White folks ask: Should Oprah get reparations? Nobody asks the Jews if Steven Spielberg should get reparations."

"When a white man tells me his grandfather wasn't a slave owner, just a smart engineer, I say that's just like a gambler who makes a bet on a pile of stolen money. Even if he didn't steal it, it's still stolen."

"Not all white folks were slave owners, but they didn't say a mumbling word."

"There were white people who died in the struggle right here in Selma."

"Just three. But white folks' fear of us is profound; they know the debt is enormous."

"Whites are happy to tell you their grandmother was Choctaw, but not that she was black—though sixty percent of Southern whites have black blood."

"Education is the problem. In a culture that emphasizes STEM subjects over the humanities and social sciences, we're cutting out the disciplines that teach critical thinking. That's deliberate."

"Once we integrated, we adopted other people's values—individualism, materialism—and left African values behind."

"Africans have been cleaning up white folks' mess for years, not just in the U.S. but in the Caribbean. We're not asking for handouts, just trying to collect what's owed us."

The large and crowded room was full of children, from infants to ten-year-olds. Surrounded by large and loving families who passed them from arm to arm, they were extraordinarily well behaved. The Freedom Singers, founded by SNCC, were white-haired, one unsteady on his feet, but they could still belt it out. "Music was the glue that held the movement together," said one before striking up "Oh, Freedom." Two teenage boys performed a hip-hop song they'd written called "Put the Guns Down," to a standing ovation.

The jubilee ended with a workshop called Truth and Reconciliation. Seven weeks after Donald Trump's inauguration, Bernard Lafayette played a hopeful note. "He's a blessing in disguise," said the preacher. "We celebrated for eight years, but we got work to do." Lafayette argued that we are living at the end of the second Reconstruction: every step blacks take forward leads to white backlash—which doesn't prevent us from moving forward again. Fania Davis, an activist lawyer who resembles her sister, Angela, had come from Oakland to the Selma she views as hallowed ground; the ancestors whose blood soaked this earth, she said, were very powerful. As a child, she lost two close friends in the Birmingham bombing, and she described her own journey from rage to reconciliation. "I get tired of people dissing 'Kumbaya.' It's the way our ancestors got through slavery and lynching. When you bad-mouth 'Kumbaya,' you're dissing my ancestors. In the end it's just saying we can't do it alone." Fania Davis saw progress in our current history: more truth being told.

Two women who lost family members to racist violence took the floor, one after the next. Gwen Carr, mother of Eric Garner, the black man choked to death for selling cigarettes on a New York City sidewalk, said that she must be his voice now. She described how he was demonized after he was killed: looking for traces of drugs at the autopsy, describing him as unemployed and uneducated. "Without that film they would have kept up the story that he had a heart attack. But there is a God."

Mary Liuzzo Lilleboe was seventeen years old when her mother, Viola Liuzzo, was murdered outside Selma. A white coal miner's daughter from Tennessee, Liuzzo was a housewife and mother of five living in Detroit when she answered the call to come to Alabama after Bloody Sunday. Driving some marchers from Montgomery back to Selma, she was shot by four Klansmen enraged by the sight of a white woman and a black man in the front seat of a car. Her passenger survived by lying in her blood, pretending to be dead. Mary spoke of the hate mail her family received after the murder, the cross burned in their Detroit yard, the stones thrown at her six-year-old sister. Still, she told us, she wouldn't change a thing; though she still feels the pain of absence, she is proud of her mother's sacrifice. Mary regularly comes to Selma, where she feels closer to her mother than anywhere else. The people there "would part the waters for me if they could." When Obama was elected, her family thought that "every drop of blood was worth it, because *that* happened in our lifetime." Still, she was worried about the violence Black Lives Matter had brought to the nation's attention—as well as the fact that the media still paid more attention to murders of whites than blacks. In that respect, little has changed in fifty years: like Goodman and Schwerner, Viola Liuzzo was all over the national media, while Jimmie Lee Jackson's murder went largely unknown.

As I listened to Liuzzo's daughter and Garner's mother, I tried to imagine how I'd feel if German cops were routinely shooting Jews today. My imagination failed again. The one time I needed my local police, when an alcoholic neighbor was regularly keeping the house awake by shouting racist slogans, they were more helpful and sympathetic than I'd ever known cops to be.

Driving back to Oxford, I stopped at a fast-food joint in Tuscaloosa, knowing there would be nothing better to eat on the long two-lane road that followed. The paunchy white customers barked at the black woman who served them. "Can you hurry that order, 'cause I got to get my mother-in-law's teeth back so she can go to choir practice. She won't go to church without 'em, and I borrowed hers 'cause mine are broken." No doubt he was a fierce opponent of Obamacare, like most in the region. The men at the other tables stared at me, their eyes spitting venom. I thought I looked respectable, still wearing the church dress I'd put on for the service that morning, yet somehow the dress revealed that I was an outsider. Or was it something about the way I walk? I returned to my car, put some Dylan on the stereo, and wondered whether Alabama was worse than Mississippi. There's a long-running contest between them.

✧

Aside from the legal claims that reparations for slavery have no precedent, arguments against reparations include a mixture of moral and practical claims. I want to reply to the most important.

1. *The Africans were slave traders too, often selling captured members of other tribes. Since they were just as complicit, Europeans should not be held responsible.*

This argument is sometimes dismissed by pointing to the differences between African slavery and the chattel slavery practiced in the Americas, but the history of neoslavery sketched above shows those differences to be irrelevant. Whatever the relative merits of African slavery may be, Africans did not develop Jim Crow, convict leasing, segregation, or redlining. The strongest case for reparations is based on the fact that subtler forms of subjugation were developed when slavery was abolished, creating conditions that continue to affect lives today.

2. *Reparations would enforce a narrative of victimhood that is unhealthy for its proposed beneficiaries.*

As I've argued elsewhere, a culture of victimhood is indeed unhealthy.[48] But objections to that culture can become reasons to support reparations, as long as that support is properly grounded. Proper grounding would come with an apology and a full description of the wrong that was done. Unlike welfare or affirmative action, reparations would be seen as a straightforward payment for an overdue debt. If our forebears failed to pay it, the responsibility to do so devolves on those of us who benefit from that failure, whether the benefits come directly from wealth or other privileges gained from belonging to the white majority of a powerful nation.

Interestingly enough, white conservatives in favor of reparations, like Charles Krauthammer and Ross Douthat, have argued that reparations are preferable to affirmative action programs because the latter convey the stigma of ongoing victimhood rather than the straightforward acknowledgment of a debt that is owed. I don't accept their proposals, largely because the amount of compensation they proposed is far too low, but affirmative action has indeed proved to be notoriously problematic. First, it's not clear that it helps those most in need of support. Giving preference in education or employment to members of disempowered groups *so long as it's arguable they are equally qualified* necessarily benefits the best qualified members of those groups, not those who need basic remedial education and other forms of support. Moreover, even when they have been faithfully applied, affirmative action programs can harm those they are designed to benefit. Don't tell me you never wondered: Did he get that prize for the quality of his work or for the accident of being born black? (This question can be asked by black as well as white folk, women as well as men. Even those who are oppressed may take the view of the oppressor: that's how ideologies work.) I cannot count how many Germans suspect I got my job for the dubious privilege of being Jewish and female; usually the suspicion is only insinuated. But that suspicion infects relationships between members of different groups, feeding resentment on one side and self-doubt on the other. Honest payment of a debt that both parties recognize avoids this. Sidestepping concepts like "trauma" and "victim," reparations are supported by simpler ideas of justice.

3. *Reparations look backward. It's more important and healthier to look to the future.*

This is an argument Jean Améry would accept—while insisting on the reasonableness and right of the victim to look back. Resentment, he wrote, nails the victim to the cross of his past. Still, Améry thought that anyone who was subject to slavery cannot help but look backward.

The sociologist John Torpey, writing on the rising demand for reparations during the 1990s, has an incisive take on this argument in his book *Making Whole What Has Been Smashed*:

> The phenomenon is a kind of transitional *substitute* for the progressive politics associated with the Enlightenment, cut out for an age of diminished expectations . . . In the absence of a horizon for which to aim, the excavation of memory and its mysteries compensates for those shortcomings of the present about which their opponents can do little, politically speaking.[49]

Not since the Romantics, he argues, has so much energy been spent digging through the past. Torpey believes this has everything to do with the enshrinement of the Holocaust as emblematic of our age. Though not opposed to reparations, he regrets the loss of the future-oriented politics characteristic of progressivism for the past two centuries.[50]

As do I. But the problem is not only the absence of a forward-looking vision that could command consensus, though this may be changing. More important, ignoring past wounds in favor of future hopes has not worked. Obama's politics were deliberately forward-looking. To the disappointment of some African Americans, he avoided discussions of race wherever possible. To the chagrin of others, he refused calls to examine the devastating war waged in Iraq by his predecessor. Those pragmatic decisions were understandable. As I shall argue in the following chapter, however, our refusal to face American crimes was central in fueling the emotions that led to the election of Donald Trump.

4. *My family had no slaves. They didn't even come to America until slavery was abolished.*

Most nonblack Americans are descended from people who came to the country in the waves of immigration that began after the Civil War. Nevertheless, in taking on the benefits of citizenship, they took on its responsibilities as well. It's usually only first-generation immigrants who consciously take on those responsibilities—if people fleeing poverty, or worse, reflect on such responsibilities at all. Most of us are citizens without active consent. We had no choice about the place where our mothers happened to give birth, and we could not possibly consent to it any more than we could consent to being born. Some of the most important things that determine our lives are entirely contingent, in ways that can be tragic or wonderful. We may begin by understanding our debts to the past by analogy with familial inheritances, but our responsibility to our nation's past is political. As Ashraf Rushdy has argued, to be a citizen is not merely to take responsibility for your country's history since the moment you, or your ancestors, claimed its citizenship. "When citizens accept responsibility for their nation's past, what they are doing is affirming that the past matters for the kind of encumbered, historically meaningful citizenship they desire."[51] Political identity cannot merely be a matter of acquiring the benefits that accrue to possessing one passport or another. Though the individuals responsible for slavery and all that followed are long gone, many of the corporate entities, public and private, that legalized and profited from slavery still exist. So do descendants of those who still suffer discrimination because they are part of a group that was brought to America in chains.

The philosopher Thomas McCarthy makes this argument forcefully:

> Our national inheritance was in considerable part unjustly acquired at the expense of African Americans; and as a result, it is now unfairly distributed in respect to them. The issue here is not whether individual citizens' ancestors owned slaves, or whether they have personally benefited from discrimination against blacks, but that they now share in and benefit from an unjustly acquired and unfairly distributed national inheritance. This is not a matter of collective guilt but of collective responsibility; and reparation is not a matter of collective punishment but of collective liability.[52]

McCarthy's argument is similar to that of Karl Jaspers. Although Jaspers was no Nazi and suffered considerable hardship during the Third Reich, he used the first-person plural throughout *The Question of German Guilt*. So long as they live in a society built on injustice, even those who have not incurred guilt are responsible for correcting it.

5. *Demands for reparations are divisive: the vast majority of white Americans, like the vast majority of white Britons, are against even an apology for slavery, much less reparations for it.*

So were the vast majority of Germans in the 1950s. Adenauer could muster the votes in favor of reparations only by going outside his own conservative Christian Democratic Union and appealing to the Social Democrats. Outside pressure from the United States played a central role in persuading Adenauer that significant reparations were necessary to gain readmission to what was called the family of civilized nations.

The United States is often remarkably indifferent to the "decent respect to the opinions of mankind" demanded in the Declaration of Independence, but there have been exceptions. Roosevelt's fear of enemy propaganda played a role in his decision to outlaw the peonage and convict labor system. Truman's worries about Soviet criticism were crucial in his decision to desegregate the army. During the anticolonial struggles of the early 1960s, Soviets condemned American segregation; it was the Cold War that helped pressure John F. Kennedy to get serious about civil rights. In the age of an American administration that demonstrates disrespect for the rest of the world on a daily basis, effective outside pressure is hard to imagine. Internal pressure would have more impact. It's easy to forget how long it took America to reach the consensus that civil rights are rights for all its citizens. The sanctification of Dr. King makes it hard to remember how deeply he was reviled, especially toward the end of his life. There's no reason why a serious and persistent public discussion of reparations couldn't shift public opinion, as discussion of civil rights has shifted common views of Martin Luther King. That would be progress even if it didn't result in material compensation. For white Americans,

> the massive gap between professional historiography and public memory
> might be narrowed somewhat . . . in which the dismal state of public aware-
> ness of the actual history of slavery and segregation in the United States, of
> the extent to which it has shaped our culture and institutions, and of the
> pervasive structural inequalities it has left behind could be improved.[53]

For African Americans, wrote Randall Robinson, "even the *making* of a well-reasoned case for restitution will do wonders for the spirit."[54] Both blacks and whites would benefit from acknowledging the debt that is owed. Few white Americans today do so; if they don't go so far as to think that blacks should be grateful for emancipation (or affirmative action), most feel no obligation of gratitude for what black people built. Nor are Britons likely to reflect on what the Industrial Revolution owed to slavery. As Robinson and others have argued, too many black Americans have internalized the idea that they should be grateful for whatever they might receive. Acknowledgment that reparations are due—even before they were paid—would be good for all of us.

6. *Achieving a social democratic system for all is far more important—and far more plausible—than pursuing reparations for a specific group.*
    This was Bernie Sanders's answer to a question about reparations in 2016, and it's been argued by black thinkers as different as Cornel West, Adolph Reed, and Glenn Loury. It's the objection that tempts me the most, and it calls for a brief digression to explain the difference between liberalism and social democracy.

❧

For liberals, all human beings have fundamental rights to say what they like, worship as they please, marry whom they love, vote as they choose, live or travel where they will. Liberals call this freedom. Socialists point out that those freedoms are worth little without conditions for realizing them. You needn't be a materialist to believe that our minds cannot work if our bodies are broken. Thus social democrats acknowledge liberal rights and add the right to fair working conditions, good education, health care, and housing. There's a long tradition of philosophical argument about the concept of rights itself; the utilitarian philosopher Jeremy Bentham called it nonsense on stilts. I will avoid those discussions and use the word *rights* as it is enshrined in the constitutions of democratic nations in order to highlight the crucial distinction between liberal and social democratic traditions. For liberals, health care, parental leave, and paid vacations are not *rights* but *benefits*, something you may be privileged to have, but not something you deserve simply by virtue of being human. How we conceive and call things has consequences for what we are able to demand—and what governments are prepared to grant.
    In arguing that it is humanly and fiscally possible to create a system

that regards health care, education, and fair working conditions not as benefits but as rights, both Bernie Sanders and Paul Krugman recently pointed to Denmark. I suspect that neither referred to Germany because the idea of Germany as a model for anything is still hard for other nations to swallow.[55] This was a mistake, because it's easy to reply that what works in tiny, homogenous Denmark would be impossible to achieve in large, diverse America. Had they referenced Germany, the world's fourth-largest economy, they could have pointed to a functioning system that, even under conservative governments, is far to the left of anything Sanders ever proposed.

Two examples must suffice here to illustrate the difference. The cost of comprehensive health care is deducted from every German employee's paycheck; the state pays the costs for those who are unemployed. Health care covers a wide range of services, including medication, testing, psychotherapy, and hospitalization. If you are hospitalized, you are charged 10 euros per day for the cost of your hospital meals. Should your hospitalization last longer than twenty-eight days in one calendar year, the state takes over the remaining cost of your food. The intuition behind this is one Americans find bewildering: if you have the misfortune to be hospitalized for so long, you shouldn't have to suffer financially as well. It's an intuition that rests on the Rawlsian assumption that a just society does what it can to protect its citizens from the slings and arrows of outrageous fortune. Few beneficiaries of that assumption have read John Rawls. Built into the structure of the health-care system, it has come to seem like common sense.

What happens to an employee's job if she falls ill? For the first three days, nothing at all, as long as she notifies her employer. If she's sick for longer, she must go to a doctor, who gives her a note that "writes her sick"—*krankschreiben*—for a certain period of time, which can be extended as long as necessary. Now, in addition to federal holidays, every German employee receives at least four weeks' paid vacation. Several years ago, a proposal to limit the vacation time of those whose chronic illnesses left them unable to work for long periods was indignantly rejected by Guido Westerwelle, then head of Germany's most business-friendly party. "Sick is sick, and vacation is vacation," he insisted. Westerwelle regarded the concepts as so fundamentally different that the idea of weighing one against the other seemed absurd. It was as if someone had suggested trading your freedom of travel for your freedom of expression because you'd used up your quota of blog posts. Despite all this, Germany enjoys a thriving economy with low unemployment. German businesses argue that generous vacation time improves employees' health and productivity.

When I try to explain such systematic conceptions of rights to Americans, they think I live in a utopia. Germans find the American system positively dystopian. They are baffled by the concept of a fixed number of sick days: "What if someone gets sick for longer?" In America, your bad luck is your problem. In Europe, if you suffer misfortune, you can usually expect the state to come to your aid. Now, even with a (partly) social democratic conception of rights, Europe remains resoundingly capitalist; there are large inequalities of wealth both within individual nations and throughout the Union as a whole. Left-wing parties rightly protest inequalities, but European citizens enjoy a system of rights that citizens of the United States, and most other nations, would envy—if they had the opportunity to learn of them.

That they rarely do is the result of a media that, even at its best, holds a neoliberal framework to be the only viable way to structure an economy and rarely reports on the success of alternatives. You can learn more than you want to know about celebrity baby bumps, but little about parental leave in other countries. Despite this, the last years have seen change. The word *socialism* no longer frightens a majority of Americans under thirty-five, and even *The New York Times* now prints articles suggesting that health care might be viewed as a right, not a benefit.

❧

A thoroughgoing revision of our economic system would be required to guarantee every American the right to good education, health care, housing, and, yes, even paid vacation. This possibility may seem as distant as the possibility of paying substantial reparations for slavery. Indeed, proponents argue, a wide-ranging social democratic program is far more likely to succeed, as it could appeal to the broadest coalition of citizens. Most supporters of reparations support not cash transfers, but programs that would provide education, health care, and housing to those African Americans denied these things by centuries of subjugation.[56] Why not renounce the demand for reparations in favor of programs that insist on those rights for all? As the political scientist Adolph Reed has argued, even if the injuries caused to African Americans were explicitly racialized, the remedy for those injuries need not take the same form. Reed insists that the problem with inequality is inequality, not the fact that inequality is distributed according to race.

[Race] politics is not an alternative to class politics; it is a class politics, the politics of the left wing of neoliberalism. It is the expression and active agency of a political order and moral economy in which capitalist market forces are treated as unassailable nature.[57]

The longer you live within one system of value, the more you come to regard it as self-evident. Having lived for twenty-five years in a system that regards economic and social rights as basic, I no longer see them as utopian but as normal. The shift in perspective takes place slowly but all the more surely for that. It's the difference between viewing a society that allows sick people to die for want of money as something unfortunate but ordinary, and viewing it with outrage. Today nothing seems more reasonable to me than a society that considers itself bound to provide the basic foundations for dignified living to all its citizens—though I'm well aware that few Americans, who have come to see another system as natural, will find this self-evident at all.

Martin Luther King's Bill of Economic and Social Rights, drafted shortly before his death in 1968, went further than any current proposal. His proposal included a right to a meaningful job at a living wage, as well as a secure income for those unable to work; a right to adequate education; a right to decent housing in a neighborhood of one's choice; and the full benefit of modern science in health care.[58] In one of his last speeches, he railed about the absence of reparations for slavery. Announcing the Poor People's Campaign, King concluded, "Now, when we come to Washington in this campaign, we are coming to get our check." King's struggle for civil rights was an attempt to ensure that African Americans could attain the basic liberal rights guaranteed within the existing American framework. The human rights he later championed would entail a revision of that framework itself, for it requires economic redistribution. It's therefore not surprising that despite King's iconic status, those rights have been largely ignored.

As one who has come to believe in the justice of social democracy, I strongly support King's economic and social bill of rights for all. If applied worldwide, it would require the world's richest nations to give up some of their wealth. The greater obstacle might be giving up the neoliberal ideology that economic growth is the key to human happiness—or at least that it's the real motive behind most of human action. This would entail so great a transformation in thought and practice that it seems impossible to achieve. Paradoxically, our greatest present danger could provide our greatest hope for such transformation: climate change could be the catalyst that forces us to abandon the view that economic growth is the key to human welfare.[59]

At the moment, the odds that government and industry will choose to change course and introduce international social democracy seem vanishingly small. Yet if we are reflecting on justice—not probability—we should perform a thought experiment. What if the United States instituted the kinds of social programs advocated by the thinkers previously mentioned? Whether, like Robinson, they regard them as reparations, or, like Reed, they reject the concept of reparations in favor of such programs, all agree that large-scale investment in good schooling from prekindergarten through college, full medical care, proper housing, and decent jobs would make a world of difference to African Americans in urgent need of them. Communities of color would rejoice. The thought experiment I'm proposing asks us to imagine that those services are guaranteed to all Americans as a matter of human rights. Would African Americans be owed something more?

Contrast this question with another. A Holocaust survivor who chose to remain in Germany after the war—and some did—would receive the same palette of social services as her ex-Nazi neighbors. Before Germany's Economic Miracle, those services were limited, but as the 1960s brought prosperity, their range expanded. Would we think justice served if the survivor were guaranteed the same economic and social rights as the rest of the nation, or would we think she deserved something more for the pain and terror most of the nation inflicted on her? No compensation could redeem the loss of her parents or children. Still, something more than regular social services—regarded as a right for everyone—seems owed to her. Something more than words of apology.

Now Améry's moral daydream entailed more than words. What he envisioned but dared not hope for was a broad program of public education that would bring about deep and genuine regret. This would require the kind of explicit and detailed truth-telling that is sure to cause pain. No story can put an observer in the place of a victim. But Améry's own writing, often broadcast on public radio, as well as that of other survivors, was so sharp and devastating that it helped force the guilty nation to wish time undone.[60] Indeed, Germans' wish to identify with the victims rather than their perpetrator parents produced a rash of people falsely claiming to be descendants of Jewish victims, or even victims themselves.[61] Those false testimonies were the perverse expression of a real desire to undo their nation's crimes. What has happened cannot be reversed, but it can be fully acknowledged, as it can be acknowledged that the irreversibility of the past is no excuse for looking to the future as if nothing had happened at all.

As the philosopher Thomas Brudholm has argued, the tensions so crucial to Améry's thought make the expression of resentment compatible with a striving for reconciliation and a mutual recognition of humanity.[62] Reconciliation would restore that basic trust in the world that the first blow of torture destroyed for Améry. Yet he also wrote that he had no resentment when he was freed from Bergen-Belsen, the last of the camps where he was prisoner. Being a surviving resistance fighter, a Jew, and a victim of a universally hated regime made him a hero in the first years after the war— "There was mutual understanding between me and the rest of the world."[63] Only after the political winds changed and German crimes were ignored as the price of integration into the Western camp of the Cold War, did Améry come to feel that the world had turned upside down.

I can imagine that an African American who fought for the Union might have gone through a similar process: celebrated—at least in some quarters— as a hero who suffered and struggled for a righteous cause, he would later be abused and disdained as the nation rejected Reconstruction and any form of regret. I can also imagine that a thoroughgoing working off of American slavery and all its consequences would restore African Americans' trust in the world that is lost, once again, every time they are followed in a department store. That working off must include complete reform of a justice system that grants little justice to black people. Might that be enough without the trouble of figuring out who owes what to whom? Isn't the commodification of everything, including suffering, part of what's wrong with the world?

I can also imagine voices saying: *Bull . . . shit. Those are just excuses to avoid paying up. Of course money can't make up for murder. But let them start by trying.*

Améry rejected financial reparations, and others might do so as well. I've come to believe they should nonetheless be offered, even were African Americans to share in a social democratic system that guaranteed economic rights for all. Financial compensation should be offered on the same grounds that it's awarded in cases of wrongful imprisonment. No amount of money can make up for years lost. Yet even most courts hold that to release a prisoner after new evidence proves his innocence and leave him with nothing but an apology would be simply shabby.

Nor does it matter whether the wrong was intentional. The historian Isaac Deutscher illustrated this with a parable: suppose a man jumped from a burning house in which many of his family had died, and hit a passing stranger, breaking her arms and legs in falling. If both people were reasonable, they would not become enemies. The jumper would try to console and compensate the innocent stranger, who would understand that she was a victim of accidental circumstance. If they were irrational, they will be caught in an endless cycle of resentment, fear, and revenge. Deutscher devised this parable to describe the justified claims of Israeli Jews and Palestinians in 1967, but it can be applied to many cases.[64] To this day, Israel has refused to recognize the justice of Palestinian claims that began when Jews fled a burning Europe, and those claims have only become more valid under the long occupation. All the more urgent are the claims of the victims of American racism, whose perpetrators can hardly be compared with someone escaping a burning home.

꩜

After his long career as a diplomat and a shorter one as Brandenburg's minister of justice, Hans Otto Bräutigam headed the Memory, Responsibility, and Future Foundation, which was established in 2000 to compensate those non-Jewish laborers enslaved by the Nazis. He knew that no sum could suffice, which is why he rejected the word *Wiedergutmachung*, but he believed that anything that made the survivors' old age more tolerable was worthwhile. He did not believe that material compensation, however generous, would be sufficient. "The consciousness of German past crimes had to become a basis—*Grundlage*—of our democratic system as a whole," he told me. To a large extent, that has taken place, but Bräutigam still believes that Germany hasn't accepted its responsibility to engage internationally to work for a better world.

I told him about the American debate over reparations for slavery and asked what he thought of it. Like any good German, he eschewed comparisons, insisting that the Holocaust was a singular, and singularly evil, event in human history. Still, he declared that from a moral standpoint, reparations for American slavery seem as justified as the reparations he sought for those the Nazis enslaved. "One must think carefully about the form," he said. "Above all, the descendants should be given the support their families were unable to give them." Given the research on redlining and wealth, this seems decisive. Even a small inheritance can spell the difference between making a down payment on a home and living your days at the mercy of landlords.

How far back do our obligations extend? Noting the British prime minister Tony Blair's apology for injustices committed against the Irish a century earlier, the author Robert Penn Warren asked if an apology should extend to Oliver Cromwell, who devastated Ireland in the seventeenth century. Penn Warren thought he was showing the absurdity of demands for historical justice, but the question is worth taking seriously. At the close of the twentieth century, the punk group the Pogues sang

> A curse upon you, Oliver Cromwell
> You who raped our Motherland

and hoped he was burning in hell as they sang it. As long as public memory is seething over unacknowledged injustice, the heirs of those who wreaked it should, at the least, acknowledge it. "Let My People Go" still rings in our ears.

The philosopher Janna Thompson has argued that obligations to right historical wrongs persist indefinitely, if not eternally. She believes that keeping transgenerational commitments, implicit or not, is the central moral and political good that gives nations the basis for trust. Philosophical theories of reparations depend on two different arguments: one emphasizing historical obligations, the other present needs. The case for American reparations for slavery can be made on both grounds—the historical obligation arising from the evil of slavery, as well as the present economic condition of most of its descendants. To those claims Thompson adds a third: "Maintaining a political society capable of acting justly in a world of nations depends essentially on a moral practice that requires each generation of citizens to take responsibility for keeping the commitments of its predecessors and repairing their injustice."[65] This way of grounding an obligation for reparations requires no appeal to guilt for the sins of long-dead ancestors, nor does it appeal to obligations automatically conferred by citizenship. It can be applied very widely, though determining the exact obligations must be decided case by case. Particular circumstances always matter.

If there's no algorithm that can calculate how far obligations may go back in time, there is also none that can determine how wide they may reach across space. The claim that the United States owes reparations for slavery has been followed by the argument that European nations owe reparations to the Caribbean community, where slavery was often even more brutal and devastating than it was in the American South. Given the importance of the slave trade, and the products of slavery, for building nineteenth-century Europe's wealth, no further argument might be needed. But the Caribbean community is right to focus on one fact that's particularly galling: after abolishing slavery in its colonies in 1833, Britain paid 20 million pounds to compensate former enslavers for the loss of what they considered their property. The amount, at the time, was 40 percent of annual government income and had to be financed by private loan. British taxpayers paid the interest on that debt until 2015.[66]

In demanding to receive at least the amount of reparations that slave owners received for the loss of property, Caribbeans demand elementary justice. They surely have every reason to demand an apology. Former prime minister David Cameron, whose distant cousin received compensation for the liberation of the people he had owned, refused to apologize during an official visit to Jamaica, saying rather, "I do hope that, as friends who have gone through so much together since those darkest times, we can move on from this painful legacy and continue to build for the future." Other nations guilty of profiting from slavery have been called to account, so far without result. Since 1993, the Organization of African Unity has called for reparations for the damage the continent suffered from slavery and colonialization. During a 2015 meeting with representatives of those countries, a European Union official dismissed their claims with the words, "We cannot correct history. What happened, happened." One wishes he'd read Améry: "What happened, happened. This sentence is just as true as it is hostile to morals."

Opponents of reparations will blanch: the case I've sketched does imply that there is no honest way to resist claims for reparations on a global scale. Lawyers may argue over legal precedent, but moral precedent was set when Germany first paid reparations for the Holocaust. There followed a small but significant number of reparations settlements: for U.S. treaties broken with Native Americans, for Japanese Americans interned during World War II, for black farmers denied loans. Britain even paid reparations to Kenyans tortured during the Mau Mau rebellion. By acknowledging that nations have an obligation to compensate for past crimes, Holocaust reparations opened uncounted doors.

Though the large reparations Germany made were prodded by political force, the principle is one of justice. The difficulty of figuring out how to allot what to whom is no excuse for refusing to try. It's probably impossible to calculate the amounts the United States owes to Native Americans, or European countries to their former colonies. Still, the U.S. could begin by restoring mineral rights on the reservations of the former, and Europeans by forgiving the debt of the latter.[67] This could initiate the sort of cleansing Karl Jaspers thought necessary and inescapable for Germany in 1946. After reparations to Israel began, other Germans spoke of retrieving lost honor.[68]

Some have suggested that an apology for colonialism is more important than material compensation. The Indian politician and author Shashi Tharoor said that a symbolic payment of one pound a year would suffice as reparations for two hundred years of British rule in India. Reparations, he argued in a 2015 speech at the Oxford Union, are "not a tool to empower anybody, they are a tool for you to atone . . . The ability to acknowledge your wrong, to simply say sorry, will go a far, far longer way than some percentage of the GDP in the form of aid."[69] This is a remarkable statement, given Tharoor's argument that Britain's industrial revolution was premised on the destruction of India's precolonial economy; as in many other colonies, what had been a self-sufficient system was turned into a source of raw material, often through barbaric means. An apology for those abuses would, at the least, acknowledge that foreign aid to developing countries—of which European countries contribute twice as much, relative to GDP, as the United States—is not a matter of generosity but of obligation. It might even restrain the development of the new forms of neocolonialism that many corporations practice today. But, for the reasons just sketched, I don't believe that acknowledgment is enough. Opponents of reparations counter that the cost of all that debt would be impossible to raise, which makes them reluctant to even acknowledge it.

Proposals to repair massive injustice are inevitably met with the claim that there isn't enough money in the world to do so. Several taxation policies that might finance reparations have been proposed, but if we are serious about seeking the means to restore justice, the real elephant in the room is the arms industry. Too many of us continue to ignore it. If no one ever produced or profited from another weapon again, we'd still have enough to defend (or kill) ourselves many times over. As in the fable of the emperor's new clothes, it takes a child to point out the obvious. When Malala Yousafzai's life was threatened for demanding girls' rights to education, the world took notice, and she became the youngest person ever to receive the Nobel Peace Prize. Very little attention was paid a few years later, when she used her education to argue that all children have a right to twelve years of free education—and that this could be paid for by cutting military spending for *just eight days every year.* That fact, confirmed for me by a Nobel laureate in economics, received little attention because we have no idea what to do with it. If there were an international referendum about priorities, a motion to replace military spending with education—at least for eight days—would surely win hands down. We do not even know what structures would frame such a decision process.

When I began writing this chapter, I was not entirely convinced of the arguments for reparations myself. Thinking through the questions made me certain that justice demands them, however challenging it would be to work out the details. Yet when I sent what I hoped would be the final draft to my editor in October 2018, I feared I was going out on a limb so long that readers who had followed me up to this point would refuse to go any further. I could not have guessed that a few short months later, what had been a minority position would play a role in the forthcoming presidential race, or that *The New York Times* would print an argument for reparations citing Lincoln's second inaugural address to support the claim that "sometimes the costs of repairing sin have to be born generations after the sin was first committed."[70] Polls show that the majority of white Americans still oppose them, as the majority of Germans opposed reparations for the Holocaust in the early years after the war. Yet the fact that what was so recently the province of a few intellectuals is now part of a national conversation is as good a sign of progress as any I know.

Only the ideal can make demands on reality. If we could acknowledge the justice of claims for reparations, we could begin to work out how to honor them. Acknowledgment would be enough for some, and a beginning for all. Britons might begin by recognizing that their colonial history is far less beneficent than they were taught. Americans could start by simply asking Congress to pass H.R.40, a resolution made and denied every year since 1987, which would create a commission to study appropriate remedies for slavery. It cannot be too much to expect the U.S. Congress to do in the twenty-first century what the German parliament did in 1952.

In Place of Conclusions

I began writing this book at a moment that seemed so much more promising than the present that remembering it can make me weep. And that was after a massacre.

Rarely have a few years made such a difference. Despite the slaughter in a Charleston church, it was an easier time to feel hopeful. For once, during that summer of 2015, America seemed to come together around President Obama's speech that followed a young white supremacist's murder of nine African Americans. It was a Republican governor who took down the Confederate flag in South Carolina; it was the Arkansas-based Walmart that stopped the sale of Confederate memorabilia. America seemed ready to face down its past, and I thought I could contribute by sharing what I know about the Germany I've studied for thirty-five years. My conviction that the country had learned most of the lessons it needed from its own racist past seemed confirmed a few months later, when Germans outdid themselves by welcoming a million brown-skinned refugees with open arms.

That moment of hope has receded. With the possible exception of protecting rich people's wealth, Donald Trump has no policy at all but to reverse every decision President Obama made, no matter the cost to the country or the world. He thereby exposed America's two faces: one that the world wanted to believe in, the other that it suspected and feared. Those faces reveal the American antinomy—a philosopher's word for two opposing claims that each look plausible, neither of which can ever be proved. It's an opposition over the soul of America. Obama personifies the American ideal: with intelligence and fortitude, we can move toward fulfilling the aspirations America wrote into its founding documents. Trump embodies sheer determinism: there *are* no ideals that can't be reduced to the naked struggle for wealth and power, the motor that moves us all. If Obama was the American dream—"Nowhere else on earth would my story be possible"—Trump is the American nightmare. After Charleston, we had a president who taught us grace. After Charlottesville, the voice from the White House praised "very fine people" who included unabashed Nazis.

It's impossible to say which vision represents America. No matter what happens in 2020, or before, we will have to come to terms with the fact that the Trump presidency was possible. Like much of the world, I didn't think it was. That's not only because—though I know all the arguments against Providence—I share Obama's belief in the power of reason and King's vision of a moral arc that bends toward justice. My certainty wasn't based only in faith, but in a 2016 statement signed by one hundred top brass in the U.S. military, who wrote that they'd take early retirement before they would serve under a Commander in Chief Trump. At the time, I found it ironic that the Pentagon would save us from disaster; now I am glad that military men of conscience have saved us from disaster by *not* resigning.

Americans aren't the only ones who remember where they were, and what they were doing, on that November night when Obama was first elected. The election was greeted with unmixed joy—not only in most American cities but in most of the world. Even in Israel, the first country where a majority later turned against him, a major popular newspaper celebrated the event with the headline HA-TIKVAH—the hope—which is all the more astounding when you know that it's the name of the Israeli national anthem, which has near-sacred status. Ireland proudly marked the birthplace of Obama's mother's great-grandfather as a national heritage site. The list could continue around the globe, but two events in 2009, when the rush of hope that accompanied the election was still fresh, now seem like premonitions.

The first was the public response to the arrest of Henry Louis Gates Jr. in July. As it happened, I read of that arrest just before boarding a plane from Berlin to Boston, and I was outraged. Harvard professor Gates is the world's foremost scholar of African American literature, whose achievements as a public intellectual made him widely known beyond the scholarly world; he is also a short older man who walks with a cane. Returning from a long journey after being feted in Beijing, he couldn't find his house key, and was arrested for forcing open the back door of his own home in Cambridge. Surely, it seemed, this would confirm that police forces routinely mistreat African Americans. By the time I landed in Boston, the reaction was the opposite of what I'd expected. Instead of outrage over the arrest of a distinguished black man, much of the country was angry at the president for calling the policeman stupid—an expression I thought far too mild. The matter was considered settled when Obama invited both Gates and the cop for a beer at the White House. Still, the public mood was ominous.

The next month brought another reason for misgivings. Shortly before Labor Day 2009, the president announced his intention to give a back-to-school speech that would be broadcast to schools throughout the nation. No one raised objections when Reagan and Bush Senior had done the same. Besides, anyone who'd read Obama's beautiful *Dreams from My Father* could predict what the speech would contain: he'd talk about how his mother woke him at four a.m. as a child in Indonesia to make sure he had more English lessons than were offered at the local school. *See, kids? Study hard and you too could become president.*

The burgeoning Tea Party staged protests against this innocuous message. Across the country, parents threatened to keep their children home from school that day so they wouldn't be "forced to listen to the president's socialist speech." The White House averted a crisis by releasing an advance copy of the speech that showed it was just as harmless, and just as American, as anyone with good sense had supposed. Still, the protests were the beginning of popular determination to oppose anything that came from a White House run by a black man. If he could hardly give a speech telling children to study, how was he supposed to close Guantanamo?

Since 2016, many have argued that it was white supremacist resistance that propelled the least qualified man ever to run for the presidency into the White House.[1] Donald Trump's ability to feed white anxiety and rage was demonstrated by everything from his entry into politics as a champion of the birther movement to his description of all Africa as "shithole countries." It's the same strategy Nixon and Reagan deployed to push the Republican Party toward the racist right. Trump's use of that strategy is so loud and clear that it hardly counts as a dog whistle. Anyone at all can hear it. But rather than repeat the many arguments that have shown how Trump's presidency is fueled and run through racism, let's turn to the closest thing the social sciences have to hard evidence: polling data.

The award-winning pollster Cornell Belcher devised a series of questions that connect what he calls "negative racial attitudes" with political decisions.[2] Belcher was careful to avoid skewing the data by avoiding questions that elicit only socially acceptable answers. Few people today will admit to being racist. Though some Republicans carried signs reading KEEP THE WHITE HOUSE WHITE before the 2012 election, most suggested that he was *not one of us* by focusing on his name. Obama sounded like Osama, who'd been responsible for the deaths of three thousand Americans, and Hussein could only be associated with the Iraqi dictator American troops had recently vanquished. After Obama's enthusiastic welcome during his 2008 trip to Europe, John McCain ran an ad suggesting that the European cheers implied that Obama wasn't a real American. (I reported on the crowd during Obama's Berlin speech; almost half of it actually consisted of expat Americans who'd come from all corners of Europe to express their weariness with George W. Bush.) The fact that Obama's absent father was a Muslim and that he'd spent several years in Indonesia were coded accusations for those who suspected that, in the twenty-first century, the N-word would fall flat.

Recognizing this, Belcher took polls that measured implicit negative sentiments toward black people, primarily in the political realm. Racial antagonism was measured by reactions to statements like "Reverse discrimination is a growing problem today" or "Too often minorities use racism as an excuse for their own failures." The statistics showed that in October 2008, racial aversion was similar among Democrats, Republicans, and Independents. Just after Obama entered the White House, the groups diverged in dramatically different directions, with a huge spike in negative sentiments toward blacks among Republicans and to a lesser degree among Independents. Racial attitudes were responsible for a thirty-seven-point difference in Obama's positive image. Belcher's team asked voters whether certain characteristics designed to measure racial stereotypes correlated with support for a presidential candidate in 2008. For example, Obama was viewed by a fifteen-point margin as "more likely to have benefited from unfair and undeserved advantage" than McCain. I leave the reader to wonder how Obama, who had barely finished paying off his student loans when he entered office, could be considered unfairly advantaged compared with McCain, who could not, on the campaign trail, remember how many homes he owned. (The answer turned out to be eight.)

Belcher's study went to print just before the 2016 election, but it included polls taken during the campaign that show that the racial aversion studies he correlated with antagonism toward Obama in 2008 and 2012 were just as useful predicting support for Trump in 2016.[3] "Let's stop pretending it's about something other than race," Belcher concluded. "The right has demonstrated time and time and time again that they'd rather sink the country and see its citizens suffer than do business with a black man."[4] Obama was not, as the right charged, responsible for worsening racial tension, but he was a catalyst for showing just how badly Americans need to face problems that have plagued the nation these four hundred years.

Obama preferred to face the future. In that, too, he was very American. He'd opposed the war in Iraq, but made clear he wouldn't consider investigating the previous administration for war crimes. His personal behavior in office was as forward-looking as it was flawless; indeed, his entire family was exemplary. "I can't imagine how awful it must be to be a teenager in the White House," said one of my daughters just out of her teens. "But the first African American teenagers in the White House? Talk about pressure! And they were awesome." As was their mother. After joking, "I hope the president will forgive me," Paul McCartney launched into "Michelle" during a concert at the White House, and the moment felt historic. When he sang it in the '60s, the only available images, at least for white people, were girls who looked like Carla Bruni. Now the strong, grown-up, black, and beautiful Michelle Obama was the emblem of desire. Hadn't the post-racial future arrived?

As Ta-Nehisi Coates observed, Barack Obama's unusual biography ensured that he grew up without distrust of white people. His international experiences only strengthened the universalism he learned in Hawaii. His personal behavior was so flawless because he had good reason to believe in the better angels of our nature. His inimitable combination of idealism, intelligence, and cool was not a mask.

Yet there was *something* he let slip at the fateful White House correspondents' dinner in April 2011. It was a time when right-wing politicians looking for another way to delegitimize America's first black president promoted the theory that Obama was secretly born in Kenya, hence ineligible for the presidency. Donald Trump became the face of the "birther movement," which claimed that Obama's Hawaii birth certificate was faked and insisted that the president release more evidence of his American birth. Coming onstage to the tune of "Real American," Obama proposed to lay any doubts to rest by releasing his birth video—and proceeded to show the beginning of *The Lion King*, playfully facing and trouncing the birthers' racism. The president continued his remarks by addressing Trump directly, with a few well-aimed jabs suggesting that the reality TV star had jumped on the birther bandwagon for lack of any serious work to do.

Later we would learn he'd delivered that brilliant performance while some part of his brain was occupied with weather reports from Abbottabad, and the not-yet-final decision to target Osama bin Laden the next day. Even without that knowledge, the evening was so stunningly funny that I have replayed the video of the dinner more than once. The man for whom I'd knocked on New Hampshire doors was finally pushing against the dim-witted racists who clogged our airwaves and minds. Let it rip, I thought, show them *The Lion King*.

Obama's speech was brilliant, but brilliance can be snarky. That speech was the only instance of public snark in his entire presidency. Donald Trump, the object of Obama's contempt, couldn't have deserved it more. The attack on his lies was just, but it proved to be dangerous because, more than any-thing else, snark is *uppity*. At the time, I loved it, for it reminded me why Barack Hussein Obama made me glad to be American. Trump's glowering face did not, at the time, seem portentous; a black man had just dismissed him as a fool.

Though I'm certain Obama has regretted the speech he gave that night, the evening was hardly the cause of Donald Trump's rise to power. But it did suggest that a black man must be not only perfect, but perfectly humble, to get a seat at the table. Although no one factor is enough to explain the results of the 2016 election, the white supremacists who gnashed their teeth over the presence of a black family in the White House played a crucial role. When Obama got uppity, they snapped.

Historians avoid counterfactual speculation, and philosophers should be wary of it too. Surely no single cause will explain the 2016 American elec-tion: Clinton's tone-deafness, Russian interference, and a mighty portion of sexism all played their parts. Yet it's hard to imagine that Donald Trump would have been elected had Americans done their historical homework. George Orwell distinguished patriotism, the simple devotion to a particular place, from blind and violent nationalism, which he believed to depend on historical lies. "Every nationalist is haunted by the belief that the past can be altered . . . Events which it is felt ought not to have happened are left unmen-tioned and ultimately denied."[5] The rise of the Tea Party following Obama's first election was the first hint of backlash revealing the extent of white supremacy. Its roots in America's psyche are too deep to be pulled up by the victory of one extraordinary black man. Those who hailed that victory as the dawn of a post-racial era were those who'd never fully faced American darkness.

ॐ·

All right, you may wonder, *America never did the hard work to face its past that Germany has done. But if German working off is so exemplary, what explains the rise of the AfD? Nazis rioting in the streets of Saxony?*

Just about a year after the Nazi demonstrations in Charlottesville, pictures of Nazi demonstrations went around the world again, this time from a small German city called Chemnitz. (Not all demonstrators in either place were Nazis, but it was chilling enough that the ones who weren't Nazis were willing to march with those who were.) Both demonstrations flaunted fury and fire, but there were important differences. First among them: Angela Merkel immediately condemned the violence. "Hate has no place in this country." A few days later, leading politicians from every party but the AfD came to Chemnitz to mourn the violence and to challenge the right. Counterdemonstrators carried homemade signs: I'M A JEW; I AM A FOREIGNER FROM CROATIA; I AM ROMA. The original right-wing demonstration was triggered by the killing of a local resident, allegedly by an Iraqi and a Syrian refugee. "If the police can't protect the people, it's natural for the people to take to the streets," commented the AfD party chief Alexander Gauland, but it's hardly natural they should take to the streets chasing brown people, as the mob had done. Chemnitz is located in Saxony, long considered the most right-wing state in Germany even before the Nazi era. Think Mississippi.

Although the riot of four thousand white nationalists was first-page news in much of the world, the concert that followed ten days later was not. Organized by seven bands that gave the free concert to protest right-wing violence, it drew sixty-five thousand people from all over Germany, with a hashtag that read #wearemore. The German historian Jan Plamper showed that even in 2018, far more Germans were actively engaged in supporting refugees than voted for right-wing parties.[6] But evil reliably attracts more attention than goodness. Six weeks later, the demonstration against right-wing racism that brought a quarter of a million people to the streets of Berlin— one of the largest demonstrations in postwar German history—attracted scant international notice.

To those who say that the mob in Chemnitz showed that German working off didn't get rid of German racism, and those who say that the election of a black president didn't get rid of American racism, I want to point to the half-full glass. It's unlikely that racism anywhere will ever be entirely uprooted; the urge to blame your troubles on strangers is too old and too deep. Yet in my own lifetime we've come some distance in reducing racism. On the other hand, I'd never urge complacence; to those who urge calm and take it all in stride . . . actually, there aren't very many. Much of the world is alarmed, and rightly so. Nonetheless, in an issue of *Die Zeit* devoted to the question, the historian Michael Wildt concluded, "No, we are not threatened with a new 1933. All the signs point rather to the country's determination to defend an open society of solidarity."[7]

The riots in Chemnitz made visible the fears that gripped Germany a year earlier, when the AfD won more than 12 percent of the vote and entered the national parliament, the first time a radical-right party had done so since the war. As of this writing, there's no indication that the AfD incited that riot directly, but they're the second-strongest party in Saxony, and they've been inciting racism for years.

The AfD shares a number of tendencies with Trump's most enthusiastic supporters. In a picturesque town overlooking the Rhine, its members celebrated Trump's victory the day after his election, together with leaders of right-wing parties from France, Holland, Austria, and Italy. The most extreme white supremacist supporters of those parties call themselves identitarians, decrying internationalism and insisting on the "right of peoples to determine their own identity." *If minorities can play identity politics, why the hell should we abstain?* They detest political correctness—*politische Korrektheit*—and prefer politicians who practice the kind of vulgar straight talk that exasperates the establishment. Those who speak moderately are suspected of being too close to traditional centers of power. They consider any reckoning with their country's crimes to be capitulation to a "guilt cult," and spend much of their time denouncing *Vergangenheitsaufarbeitung*, often to disguise the fact that much of their program comes dangerously close to the Nazis' own. They claim that immigrants are rapists, and sprinkle anti-refugee propaganda with repeated warnings of danger to *our women*. On a continent whose vast majority accepts the scientific consensus that human-caused climate change is a major global threat, the AfD denies it. Its economic program is vague but for a desire to eliminate inheritance taxes and promote other tax support for the wealthy. The party has fewer women than men, who are evidently moved by anxieties about manhood. "Germany has lost its masculinity," said one ranking party leader. They are systematically but not openly anti-Semitic. Some AfD politicians have cited the *Protocols of the Elders of Zion* and referred to "the Jewish truth of the Holocaust"; one member of parliament drives a car with a license plate that references Hitler. Most members know that anti-Semitism is taboo, so they raise their voices loudly for the State of Israel while seeking to court Jews with anti-Muslim positions. They come from a variety of economic and educational backgrounds. What unites them is not class, but mood: a sense of pessimism, nostalgia, and suspicion.

Those characterizations were taken not from the AfD's many center-left critics, but from the 2018 book *Inside AfD*, the first to be written by a former active party member.[8] Franziska Schreiber wrote that she joined the AfD before it was the nationalist, racist party its critics claimed it was from the beginning; only after 2017, she thought, did it move firmly to the right. Perhaps the critics noticed tendencies she initially overlooked; she was only twenty-three, after all, when she came to the party. What made Schreiber's book interesting was not the confirmation of the racist nationalism that most already suspected, but her description of the tactics she is now ashamed to have used.

"We need fearful people," said Frauke Petry, a former head of the party who was forced out for being too moderate. Schreiber described how the AfD manufactured fear without facts. The facts left little to fear: the German economy is growing, unemployment is declining, crime statistics are improving; after Germany took in one million refugees in 2015, even the flow of refugees sharply decreased. "Almost everything in the AfD began with a Facebook post," Schreiber wrote. "Facebook is the AfD's battleground." She described the competition between AfD members: who could write the most provocative claim that would put the party in the news; who could best twist establishment politicians' statements. When, for example, the interior minister said, "We will never be able to rule out the possibility of terrorism one hundred percent," she wrote the headline "INTERIOR MINISTER NO LONGER RULES OUT TERRORISM!" In fact, she revealed, the AfD had to restrain itself from loudly celebrating the terror they knew would strengthen their ranks. In addition to distorting statements and spreading outright lies, the AfD falsified Facebook accounts to make it appear that they supported one faction of the party while sowing dissention and chaos in all of them. As the moderates left the party, the number of conspiracy theorists grew.

Schreiber's claims about AfD's use of Facebook were validated by two researchers at the University of Warwick in 2018.[9] Karsten Müller and Carlo Schwarz confirmed that the AfD has by far the largest number of

Facebook users of any political party, and they scrutinized every anti-refugee attack from 2016 to 2018, analyzing the communities in which those attacks occurred for every relevant variable: demographics, wealth, political leanings, newspaper sales, number of refugees, and history of hate crimes. One factor stood out. Whether city or town, affluent or modest, liberal or right-leaning: wherever Facebook use was higher than average, so was the number of hate crimes. Wherever Facebook use rose to one standard deviation above average, attacks on refugees rose by 50 percent. That isn't to say that Facebook *causes* racism and violence. It's just a better tool for escalating them than any ever devised.

This will sound eerily familiar to observers of the U.S. and British politics that led to Trump and Brexit, but there are important contrasts. To assure its readers that having a radical-right party in parliament wasn't the first step to electing another Donald Trump, editors of Germany's distinguished weekly *Die Zeit* rushed to count seven structural differences between the United States and Germany. The AfD itself doesn't expect to win enough votes to lead the country. Its goal is to take enough votes from the center-right to be invited to join a government in Germany's complex coalition politics. So far, every party in the nation has vowed to refuse a coalition with them, and even the conservative tabloid *Bild*, Germany's most widely read paper, condemns the AfD. In the meantime, the AfD's goal is to push popular opinion toward the right. On the refugee question, they've had considerable success—which has forced one traditional party to adopt some of their positions.

Another important contrast between the AfD and American or British right-wing nationalism has to do with local history. Although most of the AfD leaders come from West Germany, where the party received the largest number of votes, a larger proportion of the population supports the party in East Germany, where Chemnitz is located. Those Westerners inclined to reflexive disdain for the former GDR have argued that those proportions are explained by the GDR's failure to work through the Nazi past. But we have seen that this claim is misleading, and there's a more likely explanation for the AfD's success in the East. The party plays on long-standing, often justified, East German resentment.

The old West German constitution mandated that a new constitution would be written when the country was unified. In the rush to reunification, that proviso was ignored. Easterners were never asked for their vision of the new state, but simply incorporated into the old one, leaving Easterners to feel less reunited than annexed. Jokes about Easterners are still regularly told in circles that wouldn't countenance anti-Semitic or anti-Turkish ones—only one of many reasons East Germans often feel scorned. The sociologist Naika Foroutan, director of the Humboldt University's Institute for Integration and Migration Studies, documents similar prejudice toward East Germans and migrants; both are still treated as second-class citizens. The discrepancy between East and West pensions, which are calculated on the basis of lifetime salaries, is a central source of resentment. With rent, food, transportation, and culture all heavily subsidized, GDR salaries were low, and its citizens had neither reason nor opportunity to save for retirement. Now pensioners in the East rage at refugees who receive state support. The AfD has succeeded in exploiting that rage and giving some East Germans that thin sense of self-respect that's so often built on the denigration of others.[10]

"The East was barely visible until it moved to the right," wrote Jana Hensel, an author who was born in East Germany in 1976. Her hometown, Leipzig, was splendidly renovated after the country was unified, but 94 percent of the restored old buildings belong to Westerners. Eastern hostility toward the Welcome Culture that embraced the refugees, she holds, stems from the fact that East Germans themselves feel unwelcome in the nation as a whole. "Inter-German resentments are one of the biggest taboos in our society." Hensel rejects the West German claim that right-wing tendencies in East Germany result from the GDR's supposed failure to work off the Nazi past. "That claim is a projection," she wrote. "West Germans cannot imagine the omnipresence of antifascism in the GDR, even in my generation, because they had nothing comparable." The era that needs working off, she argued, is the era just after reunification, when contempt for East Germans and disregard for their memories created resentment that has only grown since the 1990s. That contempt produced a picture of the East in the Western media that fuels a tendency to dismiss every traditional media report as *Lügenpresse*—fake news.[11]

The AfD's representatives present differently from the average Trump supporter. They appear mild, trim, well-dressed, and often well-spoken. When I met Andreas Kalbitz, head of Brandenburg's AfD, he insisted he was not an intellectual but a politician, yet he was smart, well-informed, and quoted Adorno. He also listened with interest to what I had to say. Ever since the AfD entered parliament, there's been a national debate about how to treat them. If they were democratically elected, should a democratic state ignore them? Or were they wolves in sheep's clothing who did not deserve the legitimization a conversation would confer? The Nazis, after all, came to power in the Weimar Republic's last democratic election. Initially, none of the parties was even willing to sit next to the AfD in the Reichstag. I was curious.

An accident of timing left me meeting eleven young women with foreign roots just before my appointment with Kalbitz. They were all studying German literature at a good university, training to be high school teachers or, with luck, professors. They were first- and second-generation immigrants, and some of them could pass for dark-haired ethnic Germans; the Afro-German and the Kurdish woman in a hijab could not. They wanted to talk about diversity and intersectionality, two words that have no real German equivalents. A woman whose parents were from Croatia was interested in African American history. "Doesn't the U.S. refuse to work off its history of slavery?" she asked. "I think we've worked off our history better." The Kurdish woman disagreed: industrial mass murder was worse than anything, anywhere, and it should never be compared. I smiled, for it was a very German discussion.

Two hours later, in the offices of the Brandenburg State Parliament, I mentioned the meeting to Kalbitz. Those young women had flawless command of the language; they loved German literature. Weren't they examples of the perfect integration the AfD thinks impossible? The state party leader looked disgruntled. "We have to be realistic and accept the foreigners who are already here," he told me, "as long as they don't become a majority."

❧

The AfD magnified German racism, and made its expression more acceptable, but it did not create it. Several people of color have told me that the German taboo on racism is confined to anti-Semitism and only extended to people who look white. Peggy Piesche, for example, has a Ph.D. in German literature, but she was the product of a tryst between a working-class white German and a Nigerian medical student. Though she believes the GDR was on the right side of history in its support for decolonizing countries and its antiapartheid stance, she experienced racism in East Germany, just as she does in Berlin today. Despite having taught German, gender studies, and Africana at both German and American colleges, when she tells people that she hails from Thuringia, she is regularly greeted with the question "Where are you *really* from?"

"It's better at American universities," she told me coolly, "but the universities there are so isolated. The distance from the university to public opinion is much shorter in Germany." Her experience was amply confirmed by a 2018 hashtag, #MeTwo, in which thousands of Germans of color described their experiences of ordinary racism. All had often encountered the ubiquitous question "Where are you *really* from?," which, Kwame Anthony Appiah wrote, actually means *"What* are you?" Many had experienced worse: elementary school teachers who tried to track them into vocational rather than higher education, Turkish men who used their German wives' names in order to obtain apartments or jobs. Worst of all: Germany had just concluded the trial of the only surviving member of the National Socialist Underground, which managed to kill nine people of color, most of them Turkish, before killing themselves in 2011. The surviving member showed no regret and was sentenced to life without parole, but those who helped her received milder sentences, and the country was shaken by what the trial revealed. The police had ignored the killings for a decade, imputing them to Turkish gangsters with foreign ways. There are indications that some policemen assigned to surveil the National Socialist Underground actually supported them.

Though some refugees posted tales of warm welcome under #MeTwo, ethnic Germans who never experienced discrimination were shocked by the outpouring. To their credit, the center- and left-leaning parties quickly issued statements declaring the need for more awareness of everyday racism. Unlike Britain or France, Germany had but a handful of colonies, so street scenes in Berlin are whiter than those of London or Paris. Unlike the United States or Canada, Germany never considered itself a land of immigration. Until the Social Democratic/Green government changed the law in 2000, German citizenship was based on German ethnicity. (Blood had been decisive, even when the soil on which ethnic Germans were born was as far away as the Volga.) Now that darker-skinned people have begun to appear as politicians, journalists, and media personalities, is it reasonable to expect that racism will decline?

Samuel Schidem doesn't think so. He's an Israeli Druze who came to Germany to study philosophy in 1999. He stayed in Berlin, where he married a German woman. Now his main job is educating new refugees about the Holocaust, which he does in the offices of the Topography of Terror, the museum devoted to the Gestapo torture chambers. Samuel dismissed the idea that Muslim anti-Semitism could be cured by a trip to concentration camps or bombed-out torture cells, as some politicians have urged. He believes it can be confronted only by the sort of personal, long-term education he practices in his seminars. "You need to relate the Holocaust to their own experiences," he told me. "These people have been close to death in ways few Europeans ever know. Every one of them is a hero." The Iranian in the class was severely tortured during nine years in prison. He walks with a limp and a cane, and he'll never be whole again. Several of the Syrians suffered in Assad's prisons; all lost homes and family members to his bombs. Over generations, even before the founding of the State of Israel, they'd been taught to fear Jews. It's not their fault they swallowed poison where there was nothing else to drink. Samuel encourages them to talk about their experiences under dictatorships and the everyday racism they meet in encounters with German bureaucracy. Then he relates it to what happened to Jews in Nazi Germany. "Every one of this group knows what it's like to be locked up without trial."

Samuel was willing to invite me to a seminar, provided I was willing to answer questions he'd ask his students to prepare. Though many were well-educated, most had never met a Jew. Did I believe in eternity? asked the sad-eyed, kind Iranian. Samuel emphasized similarities between Sharia law and traditional Jewish *halakhah*. A young Syrian threw what might have become a bombshell: "Aren't the Jews ashamed? Why don't they do something about the occupation of Palestine?" I exhaled slowly and said that many Jews, even in Israel, abhor Netanyahu's government. I talked about fear and the role of American Evangelicals, I hemmed and I hawed until Samuel interrupted. "Aren't the Arabs ashamed?" he countered. "Why don't they get rid of Assad? Al-Sisi? The Saudi monarchy?" As a Druze, a minority within a minority, he understands both sides, and he could say what I could not. Abashed, the students nodded, and the discussion turned to forms of effective political action. "Here's my hope for the future," Samuel concluded, pointing toward the Topography museum's exhibit on Nazi torture. "We'll all meet in Aleppo at the opening of an exhibit about Assad's war crimes."

Yet Samuel is not, in general, hopeful. Nor does he think German working off has succeeded. It has focused on the political forms of racism, not their day-to-day expression. Even worse, he thinks, educators have failed to universalize the Holocaust and have focused only on European history. As a result, they've missed the chance to teach general lessons about prejudice, persecution, and genocide. "The lesson most Germans learn from history is: be nice to Jews." I demurred; the 2015 welcome given to one million Muslims was a powerful counterexample, subsequent backlash not withstanding. But Samuel's experience, echoed by many other people of color, will not be denied. Nor is it easy to understand why his own work is so precariously funded. While the radical right is one source of the recent rise in anti-Semitism, the other is the increase of Muslim immigrants angry over Palestine. German media has repeatedly debated the question: How can we be fair to both Muslims and Jews? There are a couple of small community groups that bring Muslims and Jews together; the rabbi of the most liberal Berlin congregation went out of her way to show Jewish support for Syrian refugees. But there is, to my knowledge, nothing else like the sort of education Samuel practices. "They think it should come as a pill," he said. "One trip to a concentration camp, and you're cured of anti-Semitism."

I asked the journalist Mariam Lau whether she's experienced racism. Though she grew up in Germany, she was born in Tehran, and she takes after her Iranian father. "Never," she said. "Except perhaps the moment at the cash register when the cashier looks impatient because she doesn't know if I speak German. I don't look like I come from here, so they're confused." Both her skin tone and hair texture code: person of color. "But I never experienced real racism."

Mariam trained as a nurse and worked in a hospital for five years before deciding to go to university, where she majored in American studies. She wrote several books and worked as a journalist at different newspapers before landing a job as a political reporter at *Die Zeit*. For a time she was assigned to cover the Green party; since the AfD was elected in 2017, she's been responsible for covering it.

"It's fascinating," she said. "Normally I have no contact with people like that. I could write a long piece about them every week, but there's a consensus in the editorial board not to treat them like a normal party. Every time we write about them, we risk becoming part of their propaganda machine by putting their ideas in public. I ask myself before every interview how warmly I should treat them."

"How do they treat you?"

"I've asked directly what they think of my background," she replied. "There's no problem with you, Frau Lau," said party leader Gauland. She is fully integrated into German culture. Her family invites mine to Christmas dinner. "They know I'm Iranian and my father fled from the mullahs. What matters to them is that I'm not a Muslim." The AfD glorifies German culture, though they have no clear definition of it. "There are members who never heard of Hölderlin and those who quote Brecht and Goethe. Not *West-Eastern Divan*, of course," she said, and smiled. One of Goethe's late works was an enthusiastic dialogue with Islamic poetry. "They're full of contradiction."

Mariam believes things would have been different had Merkel taken full political responsibility for the refugees. "She should have said, *Look, people, we're a wealthy country, and the Syrians' homes are in flames. We'll get the UNHCR to check for terrorists, but we ought to take them in."* Had she gone on the offensive, Mariam thinks, a majority of the nation would have stood behind her. But Merkel's forte is waffling. The message she signaled was: things are happening that we don't want, but it's against the law to close the border. She waited and waffled and finally followed the majority mood, which in 2015 was welcoming—when she should have been leading it.[12]

Throughout Europe, the refugee question has become critical. Germany has been far more welcoming than any of its neighbors, but Mariam thinks the problems will continue until all European liberals find an answer to the question *Who are we?* But she knows that Europeans are anxious about patriotism, which is not the same thing as nationalism. "Germans have acknowledged our guilt, which is our great achievement," said Mariam. "No civilization before was able to face its own crimes and mature through that recognition. But in the long run it's not enough. People need to be able to show their flag." Now many Germans do, at least during soccer season. Gone are the days when liberal-left Germans rejected all of German culture because of those fatal twelve years.

"It's the AfD that keeps bringing them up," she added. They say that working off was imposed by Americans and Europeans who sought to weaken German citizens through guilt in order to exploit them economically. The AfD began as a tiny party opposed to the euro; many view the European Union as an "eternal Versailles," always emphasizing German guilt. "They don't understand that being able to say 'Yes, that was us' is a step toward adulthood," Mariam continued. "We not only did horrible things, we lost so very much. Think where Germany's film industry would be had we not eliminated so many Jews; think of science and literature. I suspect the AfD can't bear to admit that." Instead they argue that those Germans who do admit it suffer from pathological self-hatred.

Mariam granted that German history is easier for her to bear because of her own family background. Her German grandfather wasn't a resistance hero, but he wasn't a soldier either. As a member of the church founded by the theologian and anti-Nazi dissident Dietrich Bohnhoeffer, he engaged in small acts of sabotage at the factory where he worked. Still, she's astonished that few German soldiers ever owned up to their war crimes. Talking of Günther Grass, Mariam grew furious. "He could have done so much to help the country had he taken the lead. He should have said *I was in the Waffen-SS and here's why I did it and now I'm ashamed.*" Instead he spent forty years moralizing and pointing the finger at others, until the truth came out. "I was moved by John Kerry, who stood up and acknowledged that what he'd done in Vietnam was wrong," she concluded. "I would call that manly." Most AfD members she meets seem traumatized. They complain of a masculinity deficit, though what they mean is that traditional male roles have waned where feminism has made progress.

Mariam wishes that conservative politicians would stand up to the AfD by showing that their gloomy worldview is false. Unemployment has never been lower, exports have never been higher, and education has never been more attainable. By any objective measure, the idea that the country is headed for catastrophe is absurd. But conservatives fear losing votes to the AfD, and Merkel's sister party, the Christian Social Union, has been willing to create government crises just to fan anti-refugee flames. Mariam sees little hope that the AfD will abandon its radical-right stance. "They've tasted blood," she said, "and they've had success. Why should they ask themselves if they're doing anything wrong?"

"The older I become, the more I realize how much I owe to my parents." Gesine Schwan was born in 1943, but for the last twenty years, at least, she has looked timeless. Her blond hair is graying, but its curls are swept up in a playful style. Her energy is astonishing: she has been, among other things, a professor of political science, the author of many books, the president of two universities, and the Social Democrats' candidate for president. Through it all she finds time to mentor younger people seeking to echo her kind of pragmatic idealism. Her parents were socialists who admired Rosa Luxemburg, and kept a Jewish girl in hiding during the war years. Gesine and her brother were raised to honor one task: to work toward a world where what happened under the Nazis would never happen again. She has no truck with those who claim Germany's changes are merely superficial, and she insists the changes are not merely generational. "One can pass on racist, authoritarian attitudes from one generation to the next. They must be deliberately interrupted—and they were." Early on, she learned French and Polish, the languages of Germany's erstwhile enemy neighbors.

A devout Catholic, she remembers praying as a child that Adenauer would lose an election. His relationship to the Nazi past, she told me, was an example of the Christian Democrats' "tactical relationship to the truth." As head of the Social Democrats' Commission on Basic Values, she remains committed to finding alternatives to Christian Democratic policies— particularly in regard to the refugees. "Merkel never had a strategy beyond the catchphrase 'We'll manage,'" she said. "The problem began well before 2015." The German government refused to show solidarity with its neighbors, both in its dealings with Greece during the debt crises and in leaving the lion's share of refugees where they landed in Italy and Greece. "Why was the government surprised when other countries refused to show solidarity with us when we took in a million refugees?" A passionate defender of European ideals, Gesine believes the refugee question needs a European solution. "We have to begin by viewing this as an opportunity rather than a crisis. Given our demographics, the boat is far from full." Europe's population is aging, and its birthrate is falling. She finds current policies merely defensive, walking a halfhearted line that reduces neither nationalist anger nor the number of refugees who drown.

She has proposed a model that would bypass national antagonisms and work directly between the European Union and local communities. Small towns and rural communities have lost so many young people to the cities that their already meager infrastructures—one reason why young people leave in the first place—are on the verge of ruin. A central European fund could offer such communities a large carrot: figure out what you need in order to integrate the number of refugees you're willing to accept, and we'll not only pay for their integration, we'll give you an equal amount of funding for other projects you'd like to further. Improving schools, renovating housing, creating local culture. Theater, for example. "Don't groan," said Gesine, as she explained the proposal to an audience in Essen. "I was involved in theater groups when I was young. Putting yourself in different roles is an excellent way to create empathy for differences."

The key to the project is community self-determination. She envisions groups of citizen stakeholders—church groups, businesspeople, teachers, scientists—coming together to work out, in detail, exactly how they want their communities to grow. "Identity and integration require working together, not just receiving money from a distant government." Top-down solutions inevitably provoke resentment.

She doesn't believe enough consensus can be built at the national level, but she has faith in communities. Ninety percent of those who have taken in refugees say it has enriched them. Studies on anti-Semitism show that it's greatest in places where there are no Jews; the same is true of anti-immigrant sentiment. Gesine proposes a solution that would revitalize desolate communities, provide homes for refugees, and revive local democracy, all at once. "In English they call it killing two birds with one stone, but that sounds cruel." She smiled. "I prefer the German expression: two flies with one swat. You start with two, because people can be slow, but eventually we'll hit twenty-five." The European Parliament is enthusiastic about the proposal, the first that addresses both its current major crises at once: under-mining populist nationalism and providing refuge for those migrants who continue to wash up on Mediterranean shores. Gesine spends a considerable amount of time speaking to groups whose support will be needed, from labor unions to Brussels bureaucrats. She is hopeful that, with their help, she will convince the European Union to put its money behind the enthusi-asm. The cost, she says, should be seen as investment. Then again, Gesine is the kind of person who radiates hope on a daily basis. I asked how she maintains it; what keeps her activism so constant? "It's partly genetic," she acknowledged. "But staying active is the only way to ward off despair."

ᢙ

Even before the AfD came to power, many German intellectuals were un-easy with the way their country had worked off its past. In the '60s, the only doubting voices came from the right, which had its own reasons to discour-age talk of recent history; most of them had been on the wrong side of it. Now a different form of skepticism has risen on the left. Refusing to celebrate the success of *Vergangenheitsaufarbeitung* is in one sense natural, in another simply decent: taking pride in your own repentance would come close to a contradiction in terms.

Aleida Assmann explained other reasons for recent discontent with Ger-man memory culture. Formerly a professor of English literature, Aleida was awarded—together with her husband, the Egyptologist Jan Assmann—Germany's highest literary honor, the Peace Prize, for their work on histori-cal memory. In 2018, saluting their work at the Frankfurt Book Fair was a political act at a time when *Vergangenheitsaufarbeitung* is again under at-tack. The Assmanns responded by donating the prize money to three orga-nizations working to integrate different groups of refugees. "People *detest* the idea that Germans are memory world champions," she told me. "There are Europeans who say that Merkel is trying to do peacefully what Hitler did with war." Both, critics say, were determined to dominate Europe. Being self-critical about *Vergangenheitsaufarbeitung*, said Aleida, is a necessary part of the process itself.

Some of the criticism is generational. There is a (Western) tendency to view your parents' projects as failures, so the children of those who began the work are now counting the ways it went wrong. But even more troubling to some is its success. "We were the opposition," said Aleida. The movement developed in resistance to the dominant political culture; Willy Brandt was the great exception in postwar politics. Suddenly, in 1990, the project of working off was taken over by the state, beginning with Helmut Kohl, of all people, who had taken Reagan to the Bitburg cemetery to honor fallen members of the Waffen-SS just a few years earlier, and who claimed he did not need to think about Nazis thanks to "the mercy of a late birth." But re-unification, and the Western pressure that accompanied it, pushed Kohl's Christian Democratic Union toward *Vergangenheitsaufarbeitung*, at least in public. Anything taken over by a state is vulnerable to ritualization, leading to ceremonial pieties every politician is obliged to utter but no one is inclined to believe.

Now public rites of repentance are performed throughout the year: the liberation of Auschwitz is commemorated on January 27; the Warsaw ghetto uprising is remembered on whatever day in April coincides with the Jewish calendar's Nisan 27; May 8 marks the end of the war; November 9, Kristall-nacht. A standard ceremony includes two politicians, one Holocaust survivor, and a melancholy klezmer performance. The rites are predictable, formulaic, and boring. Much like American ceremonies marking Martin Luther King's birthday, they do not feel very deep. Critics complain of forced and inauthentic identification with the victims of Nazi terror.

Aleida argues, however, for the need to create that empathy with the victims that was missing in Germany for decades after the war. Here she thinks literature and film were more important than ritual. In 1979, millions of Germans watched the television series *Holocaust*. However kitschy the Hollywood show may have seemed, its emotional impact was enormous, for behind the abstract concept "six million," viewers finally glimpsed individual fates. "That series was for Germany what the Eichmann trial was for Israel," said Aleida. Both were catalysts for public discussion of the Holocaust that had been missing for decades. She also argues that those who complain about state-imposed ceremony overlook hundreds of smaller efforts in communities all over the country, which gain little media attention. Civic and church groups remember their history in grassroots initiatives that work to root out the last traces of Nazi symbols, to commemorate the victims who disappeared from their towns.

I have heard many views about what has gone wrong with German working off. Volkhard Knigge argued that it was emotional rather than analytic: instead of focusing on the horror of the Holocaust, we need critical thinking about how it came to pass. Samuel Schidem argued that it had been too European: rather than focusing on the murder of one tribe, we need to fight universal tendencies to racism. Mariam Lau argued that it hadn't been sufficiently personal: most people took refuge in abstract antifascist formulas rather than squarely facing up to their own crimes. My own view is that *Vergangenheitsaufarbeitung* has been too focused on victims in a world that is saturated with them. We're far more likely to be inspired by admiration for heroes than by pity for victims. As John Brown wrote in 1851:

> Nothing so charms the American people as personal bravery. Witness the case of Cinque, of everlasting memory, on board the "Amistad." The trial for life of one bold and to some extent successful man, for defending his rights in good earnest, would arouse more sympathy throughout the nation than the accumulated wrongs and sufferings of more than three million of our submissive colored population. We need not mention the Greeks struggling against the oppressive Turks, the Poles against Russia, nor the Hungarians against Austria and Russia combined, to prove this.[13]

I can imagine a television series that would appeal, among others, to teenagers. Why not tell a story of a fifteen-year-old who slowly comes to befriend a refugee, and in doing so must challenge not only her classmates but her authoritarian, right-wing teacher? (What fifteen-year-old doesn't want to defy a teacher?) If you'd like to produce it, you're welcome to the idea.

The problems with Germany's attempt to work off its past will probably only be resolved by responding to all the critiques and suggestions made above. Further thinking is also needed in view of the fact that 20 percent of its population now has an immigrant background. Currently, Germans are considering how to place the Holocaust in the center of its modern history for people whose grandparents had nothing to do with it. But despite some reasons for skepticism, the achievements are clear.

Nazi symbols, Holocaust denial, and hate speech, protected in America by the First Amendment, are illegal in Germany. The Washington Mall has a museum of the Holocaust, but no monument remembering American slavery and genocide. Would we object to Germans who acknowledged that the Holocaust was terrible—but built a monument commemorating American slavery in the center of Berlin? London's Imperial War Museum has an exhibit about the Holocaust, but doesn't bother to explore the violence committed in the name of Britain's empire. Berlin's new Humboldt Forum was meant to challenge Eurocentrism by showcasing non-European art and culture. There's dark irony in the fact that many objects in its collection were stolen from colonized peoples, but the museum has already returned sacred objects to the Chugach people of Alaska, and more returns are certain to come. In the meantime, exhibits will display the short, violent history of German colonialism, including the massacre of the Herero, the first instance of twentieth-century genocide. The historical museum in The Hague is full of scenes showing prospering burghers, but when you reach the twentieth century, you find an exhibit about Dutch suffering during the war. There's no reference to the fact that, thanks to Dutch collaboration with the Nazi occupation, a higher percentage of Jews were deported to concentration and death camps from Holland than from anywhere else in Europe.

I could multiply examples, but the point is surely clear: Germany's attempts to work off its past have stumbled many times, but compared with the efforts of other countries, they are steps in the right direction. I share Aleida Assmann's conviction that self-criticism is vital to the process of *Vergangenheitsaufarbeitung*. It's a process that's never likely to be finished or final, echoing Samuel Beckett's adage: "Try again. Fail again. Fail better."

⚬

But if failing better is the best we can hope for, what's the point of the attempt? If years of German working off have failed to uproot everyday racism or prevent the rise of the AfD, why bother with it at all? The past few decades have produced what's been called an international cult of memory, which itself failed to remember that the slogan "Never forget!" can be an injunction to anything. If the right use of memory can be healing, the wrong use can be toxic. "Remember the Alamo!" was a war cry; the memory of France's defeat by Germany in the Franco-Prussian War helped fuel World War I; Milosevic's insistence that Serbians remember the 1389 defeat at Kosovo only led to further battles. The best students of memory know this well. Tzvetan Todorov wrote, "The memory of the past will serve no purpose if it is used to build an impassable wall between evil and us, identifying exclusively with irreproachable heroes and innocent victims and driving the agents of evil outside the confines of humankind. This, though, is precisely what we usually do."[14]

Memory isn't magic. The philosopher George Santayana's famous warning—whoever fails to remember the past is condemned to repeat it—suggests that memory is an everlasting inoculation against past errors. We know this is false. Samantha Power's *A Problem from Hell* showed how many genocides took place after the world was reminded not to forget Auschwitz. The urge to remember can stoke grievance, encourage vengeance, power vendettas. The writer David Rieff recalled such examples in his book

In Praise of Forgetting. The best case for his argument is probably Northern Ireland. Rieff described how negotiations between Republicans and Unionists shattered whenever a member of the IRA began to sing the old Fenian classic "The Rising of the Moon." Hence Rieff quoted an Irishwoman who suggested that the next commemoration of Irish history should "raise a monument to Amnesia and forget where we put it."[15]

Rieff's argument turns on two important points. Memory is always partial, subjective, and political. This is true, but it needn't lead to the conclusion he drew: because memory of the past is always selected to serve the present, it's no better than propaganda. If history is an attempt to discover what actually happened, memory is an attempt to recover the experiences of it. At the very best they are complementary, but they should not be confused. We have no hard-and-fast criteria that determine when memory is a tool and when it is a weapon, when it is useful and when it's abused. Then again, we have no hard-and-fast criteria for most important judgments. But we don't need a concept of absolute truth in order to recognize lies. In the first decades after the war, Germans remembered nothing but their own suffering. Had they not been replaced by a combination of solid history and the memories of Germany's victims, Germans' memories of themselves as the war's worst victims would have been not only false but dangerous. Southern memories of a noble Lost Cause are false, and they're still dangerous today. Curiously, though Rieff's discussion surveyed an impressive range of countries, it treated the German case only in passing.

The second strand of Rieff's argument arises from political concerns about the ways in which justice can become the enemy of peace. Rieff rightly insisted that we attend to the world as it is; in a world that is not as it should be, many calls to remember have ended in tribal violence. Rieff allowed that if all were as wise as Avishai Margalit and Tzvetan Todorov, the dangers of manipulative memory would be slight, but, he concluded, "If history teaches us anything, it is that in politics as in war, human beings are not hard-wired for ambivalence."[16]

Indeed we are not. Nor are we hardwired for nuance. Babies have neither, and children grasp both slowly. Learning to live with ambivalence, and to recognize nuance, may be the hardest part of growing up. But the difficulty of learning them is hardly a reason for ceasing to try.

Margalit, an Israeli philosopher, acknowledged the dangers of memory but argued that we have an absolute moral obligation to remember. The need to be alert to radical evil requires us to construct a moral memory that can be universally shared. "The source of the obligation to remember," he wrote, "comes from the effort of radical evil forces to undermine morality itself by, among other means, rewriting the past and controlling collective memory."[17] Margalit's claim was echoed and expanded by Margaret Urban Walker, who insisted that memory—and the acknowledgment of others' memories—addresses not psychological but moral needs. Moral repair, she argued, is required to sustain moral relationships, which demand confidence in shared moral standards. When moral standards are violated, the community must reassert them, even if the wrongdoers themselves show no recognition of their crimes. To do otherwise is to leave the victim in what she called normative abandonment, and the rest of us prey to cynicism. Where some evils are acknowledged and others dismissed, it is easy to view justice as arbitrary—and ultimately merely a matter of power.

There may be as many ways to forget the past as there are to remember it. In the first decades after the war, the great majority of Germans followed Adenauer's informal taboo: forget and be silent. After the Civil War, once federal troops withdrew, white American Southerners took the opposite direction: they made a lot of noise. The Lost Cause myth was deliberately constructed; from statues of Johnny Reb to developments in the burgeoning film industry, there was a concerted attempt to create a narrative that made Confederates look at least as virtuous, and a great deal more attractive, than the Yankees. The success of that effort makes it imperative to create a counterweight that's just as deliberate. Although people should be punished for racist behavior, enforcing the law is not enough. We must change their attitudes, or at least their children's, with conscious education on the scale that Germany undertook. As the failure of denazification showed, it cannot be imposed from outside, but outsiders have something to teach us, if only through their mistakes. Forgetting past evils may be initially safer, but in the long run, the dangers of forgetting are greater than the dangers of remembering—provided, of course, that we use the failures of past attempts to learn how to do it better.

America's failure to face its past is evident not only in the vicious outbursts of white supremacy that Donald Trump encouraged, but in subtler ways as well. We saw that false memories of Reconstruction drive resistance to federal programs, such as Obamacare, that would serve everyone, not only in the South but in many parts of the country. By contrast, German efforts to confront its own crimes have made it a better country. Despite Germany's tendency to paint itself black, it is a far more open, free—and yes, joyful—place than it was when I arrived there in 1982. It is also far more trusted, even occasionally admired, by the rest of the world. As late as 1990, much of the world was frightened by the prospect of a reunited Germany. Now many other nations ask Germany to play a more powerful role in world affairs, a request that would have seemed incredible just thirty years earlier.

There are pragmatic as well as moral grounds for the United States to follow Germany's lead. American media may have largely ignored the reasons we decided to destroy Hiroshima or oust democratically elected governments in Iran or the Congo. Other nations' media has not. Few Americans are quite aware of how little credibility we retain in other parts of the world. Even Europeans, who are better served by their news media, can be surprised at the depth to which those outside the West suspect every appeal to Western values. They know just how often those values have been abused. Until we acknowledge the abuses, our moral authority will continue to recede, allowing critics to argue that any attempt to support universal values is just a smoke screen for violence and plunder. The Iraq War was only a recent example. The persistent weaknesses of the European Union rest in part on its inability to decide whether it stands for anything but the promotion of trade. Unfortunately, it's exactly those progressive Europeans who would be expected to support the ideas of liberty, equality, and solidarity, born in the European Enlightenment, who are most inhibited by their knowledge of Europe's colonial history. Britons who might have stopped Brexit with enthusiastic appeals to European values were unable to voice those values with anything like a whole heart. Conceptually, there's an easy way out of the problem, which is to grant that Europe and the United States cultivated values they also repeatedly violated. But the violations must be acknowledged before the values can be reclaimed, and the actual work of acknowledgment will not be easy.

In an Alabama jail cell, Martin Luther King penned an open letter to fellow clergymen who dismissed his work as extremist. Among the many reasons why "Letter from Birmingham Jail" became a seminal text, one is surely the bluntness of its truths. King explained that he stood between two factions: those African Americans whom the long terror of segregation had made resigned and complacent, and those who "have lost faith in America . . . and have concluded that the white man is an incorrigible 'devil' . . . whose bitterness . . . comes perilously close to advocating violence." The statement was tactical; King was a political man. Yet he was not issuing a threat, but stating a fact: if we do not stand up for justice for its own sake, Americans will face another civil war. If "our white brothers . . . refuse to support our nonviolent efforts," King continued, "millions of Negroes will, out of frustration and despair, seek solace and security in black nationalist ideologies, a development that would inevitably lead to a frightening racial nightmare."[18] At a time when Afro-pessimism has become a common watchword, King's warning rings truer than ever. At a time when demographics show that America will cease to have a white majority within decades, we have all the more reason to heed it.

❧

Understanding how the Germans are confronting their past cannot provide a recipe for confronting other historical evils, even were the German confrontation without flaw. Though I knew this in principle, I had to learn it in detail through writing this book. When I began, I meant to examine three countries. After Germany and the United States I chose Ireland, partly because it's a place I've come to love, and know a little; partly because the Irish are proud to be the first country to wage a successful anticolonial struggle in the twentieth century. I spent the summer of 2016 visiting museums and theaters and lectures in much of the Republic of Ireland, surveying commemorations of the centennial of the Easter Rising, the founding event of Irish independence. I gave up the project when I realized it would require at least another book. Any real understanding of working-off-the-past demands enormous particularity: to understand what memory means to a nation, you need to study not only the details of its history but its culture as it's lived today. That's the only way to get a sense of the omnipresence of memory: the way it penetrates kindergartens, affects preferences for tea and for colors of clothing, determines what's said out loud and what's left as allusion, what counts as an insult and what's taken as a compliment. And the omnipresence of memory is often complimented by the threat to put the past behind us, once and for all. Comparisons are interesting only when they convey the tone and texture of all these; otherwise they remain surface dives. Our experience is always tied to particular places and times. If we want to act morally, we cannot rest on general principle; we must attend to where we are. Even Kant, properly understood, knew that. This means there can never be one conceptual framework for dealing with every nation's past crimes. We can learn from one another, but we cannot transfer principle without paying attention to difference.

❧

If it is crucial to attend to empirical and historical differences in practice, it is possible to be universalist in principle. Few ideas today seem more suspect. On the left, universalism is regularly confused with its counterfeit. Critics point out that, from Enlightenment philosophers through the American Founding Fathers to the Kiplings of the nineteenth century, white men made claims to universality while ignoring the experience of most of the planet. It was the philosophers of the Enlightenment, however, who were the first to condemn Eurocentrism. Montesquieu wrote his critiques of European government from the (imagined) viewpoints of Persian observers; Christian Wolff lost his job, and very nearly his head, for arguing that the Chinese had perfectly good ethics though they had no Christianity; Diderot criticized European sexual mores from the perspective of Tahiti; Kant called colonialism evil, a word he used rarely; Rousseau complained that Europe knew nothing of the vast continent of Africa because its reports came from travelers "more interested in filling their pockets than their minds." All these men—and they were all men—wrote of other nations, and genders, with a brevity and ignorance we now find appalling, but they were on the right track. Those philosophers made statements we are right to regard as racist and sexist; for all they tried to rise above them, they shared prejudices of their day. They remain necessary thinkers because they nevertheless built the foundations to destroy these prejudices—not only with abstract commitments to universal justice, but with their nascent attempts to address Eurocentrism by looking at Europe through other (albeit male) eyes.

If universalism is often dismissed in today's academy, few outside are willing to defend it either. There are two historical reasons for this, and both revolve around the year 1989. After the collapse of state socialism, appeals to universal solidarity were associated with Stalinism. Ironically, in addition to his many other offenses, Stalin was deeply nationalist—the root of his battle with Trotsky, whom he erased from history with some success. Still, references to international solidarity were routinely invoked until the Soviet Union collapsed. Hardly anyone mourns the end of state socialism, but the idea of it served to expand our moral imagination. The now-common view that the rot that infected the Soviet Union dooms *any* attempt to create socialism has shrunk our imagination to a point where we can hardly envision more than mending the neoliberalism that replaced it.

The second reason follows from the first. Since the end of state socialism, the visible faces of universalism are the owners of Apple and Amazon and Facebook and other corporations hoping to imitate their success. The neoliberal, globalist ethos has nothing to do with universal values and everything to do with universal needs—however manipulatively they may be created. For neoliberals, universal human happiness is assured by the collection of stuff. The problem with neoliberalism is not only that its aversion to economic regulation has created a greater wealth gap than ever existed in modern times.[19] The deeper philosophical problem is its view of human nature, revealed in neoliberal assumptions that economic growth is the single key to human happiness, though that's rarely stated so baldly. Even those who may belong to the 1 percent know the meaning of life can't be found in stockpiles of gadgets and baubles. Neoliberalism makes passive consumption rather than active engagement the fundamental human stance toward the world. Though I admired much of Obama's presidency, his acceptance of neoliberalism proved a major flaw—not only because it resulted in bailing out Wall Street at the expense of Main Street but because it conflicted with his own philosophical ideals. Obama encouraged an active concept of human nature, urging his followers to civic engagement with slogans like "We are the change we've been waiting for." In most of us there *is* a flame that makes us want to live righteously, to give something back to the world for the gift of having lived in it. For those born in a place where hunger and war are the rule, not the exception, it can shrink to a faded spark. But unless they are thoroughly undone by despair, human beings have a need to act in the world, leaving it better than they found it in some way.[20] The worldview of neoliberalism, by contrast, treats us all, at bottom, as couch-centered, passive consumers.

This worldview has been supported in the last decades by the biological determinism encouraged by pseudoscientific versions of evolutionary psychology. To read an ordinary newspaper, you would think it's just common sense to explain all human behavior by reference to our earliest ancestors' attempts to reproduce themselves. Seldom is it asked what evidence we have for our ancestors' motivations, or how much of what drove hunters and gatherers to action is relevant today. Biological determinism is so widely accepted—*finally, a scientific explanation of human behavior!*—that its premises are rarely questioned.

Finally and fatally, both neoliberalism and biological determinism are reinforced by post-structuralist assumptions about power. Like the early Sophists with whom Plato argued, they have done us a service by showing how many claims to truth are actually attempts at domination. But like those early Sophists, they leave us with the sense that *every* claim to truth is a matter of perspective and power. Some post-structuralists have recently countered the charge that, by undermining the concept of truth, they bear some responsibility for climate change denial or the thoroughgoing mendacity of the Trump administration. They reply that post-structuralism seeks to describe reality, not to orient it. But post-structuralism often obscures the line between descriptive and normative statements, imbuing much description with a faintly normative air. It cannot be surprising that less subtle readers hear their statements as prescriptions and conclude that if there are any facts at all, they are facts about domination.

Most of us know from our own lives that all three worldviews are false. Even social psychologists have shown that as soon as we cross the poverty line, our happiness does not consist in consumption; we often act from love or faith in ways that have nothing to do with the reproduction of our tribes; and we make and defend statements because we have good reasons to believe them. Not always, of course, but we have enough ordinary counterexamples to those worldviews to call them into question. It is hard to think of anyone who consistently acts according to those views—with perhaps one exception. Despite his views on economic issues like trade, Donald Trump embodies all three ideologies: his claims to truth are nothing but assertions of power, his values are all material values, and he appears to care about nothing so much as reproducing as many copies of himself, or at least of his name, as possible. Fortunately, the theories that describe the behavior of this singular man cannot be extended to the rest of humankind. Most of us are differently constructed—though the omnipresence of the reigning ideologies makes many embarrassed to express other values out loud.

If these beliefs are the reigning faces of universalism, is it any wonder that tribal identities have resurged? The reduction of universalism to globalism has been key to the revival of identity politics, whether white, brown, or black nationalism. In questioning identity politics, I am not endorsing Mark Lilla's much discussed book, *The Once and Future Liberal*.[21] That book was flawed by its failure to recognize the centrality of white identity politics for the Republican Party ever since Nixon concocted the Southern Strategy; white identity politics also fuel resurgent European nationalism. But Lilla was right to argue that identity politics can only be overcome by a conception of the common good, something that left-liberal focus on tribal identity has neglected to sustain. His description of similarities between the individualism that has dominated American culture since the Reagan era and the self-absorption of many appeals to identity politics is insightful. And though Lilla ignored the depth to which successful efforts by women, people of color, and LGBT activists have reshaped political culture, with very real consequences, he is surely right to insist on the importance of ordinary political acts like voting.

Much of what's important in Lilla's critique was preceded by Todd Gitlin and Richard Rorty, who both warned of the dangers of the tribalism that was already emerging on the left in the 1990s.[22] It was Barack Obama's ability to transcend those dangers by appealing to a common good that got him elected. To this date, no Democratic politician has been so successful in making the appeal believable, but other thinkers have opened doors for balancing difference with solidarity. Cornel West's work exudes a love for black culture *within* a universalist framework that he views as a matter of humanity:

> Blacks and whites are in some important ways alike, that is, in their positive capacities for human sympathy, moral sacrifice, service to others, intelligence and beauty, or negatively, in their capacity for cruelty. Yet the common humanity they share is jettisoned when the claim is cast in an assimilationist manner that subordinates black particularity to a false universalism.[23]

And Kwame Anthony Appiah's powerful book *The Lies That Bind* argued that it is hopeless to explain why we are what we are by straightforward appeals to creed, country, color, class, and culture—collective identities that organize our lives. He concluded, "We live with seven billion fellow human beings on a small, warming planet. The cosmopolitan impulse that draws on our common humanity is no longer a luxury; it has become a necessity."[24]

~✧~

The citizenship ceremony I witnessed at the city hall of my neighborhood, Neukölln, worked hard to combine the cosmopolitan and the particular, beginning by acknowledging the power of national anthems. A violin-piano duet played a snippet of the anthem of each country from which the forty-eight new citizens came. Unlike her predecessor, the young district mayor Franziska Giffey deliberately encouraged diversity as she spoke of the twenty-two anthems the new citizens must have heard on the radio, in school, at a soccer game.

"Every time we do this I watch the faces to see if I can tell whose anthem is being played. Often I see people moved by memories of childhood, of loved ones."

Of scattered trees and worn-down stone and far-off skies.

"Some of you were probably nervous on your way to this ceremony," the mayor continued. "You may have even wondered about turning around and forgetting the whole thing." Since qualifying for permanent residency is the first step to qualify for citizenship, none in the room need to fear deportation. In applying for citizenship they had taken a further step. "I want you to know that no one will take away your music, your memories, your old identities. You're just receiving a new identity today."

Each new citizen was called to the dais, where they received a copy of the constitution in exchange for taking an oath to uphold it. "You don't have to memorize it," said Mayor Giffey. "But the world would be a better place if everyone learned its first three articles:

"One: The dignity of the human being is inviolable.

"Two: Everyone has the right to the free development of their person so long as they do not harm the rights of others.

"Three: Everyone is equal before the law. The state supports the real equality of men and women and works to eliminate existing prejudices."

After reading those passages, Mayor Giffey segued gracefully into one of the district's problems. "When men and women have equal rights, it means that no woman can be forced to marry against her will." The mayor concluded the ceremony with a call for civic engagement, before asking the assembled to sit still for the European anthem, and to rise for the German one. Staring at the backs of their programs, most of the new citizens made an effort to sing along before retreating to the foyer, where the mayor offered each one a piece of bread sprinkled with salt. Shortly after I watched her preside over the ceremony, Giffey's political talents won national acclaim; she became a federal cabinet minister in 2018. More politicians like her would provide the kind of leadership that Germany, and Europe, sorely need.

❧

"We have to remember that it's absolutely new: never before did perpetrators take over the perspective of their victims," Aleida Assmann reminded me. Since that shift of perspective is not only unprecedented but also at odds with our psychological need for approval, we can hardly expect it to go smoothly. Nietzsche wrote, "Memory says: I did that. Pride replies: I could not have done that. Eventually, memory yields."[25]

Put less cryptically: Shame hurts. Guilt hurts. They are not emotions we willingly feel. We seek admiration from the outside and peace from within, and we have powerful ways to deflect everything that threatens them. Rather than acknowledging our complicity in something shameful, we forget with remarkable ease. That's why memory is vital.

The burgeoning academic field called memory studies is mostly concerned with bad memories. It is crucial that the horror and shame we're so eager to repress not be forgotten, but no community can be built on them alone. That's the legitimate thought behind the demand to put the shameful past behind us that has accompanied German *Vergangenheitsaufarbeitung* since its inception—and keeps other nations from embarking on a similar path. When *memory* becomes interchangeable with *trauma*, no country can hope to heal any wounds. We need ground to stand on before we can stand up to our own shame. As the philosopher Richard Rorty wrote, "National pride is to countries what self-respect is to individuals: a necessary condition for self-improvement."[26] It's impossible to work for further improvement if you believe things have never improved. Without sources of light in our history we cannot penetrate its darkness.

"I bring you greetings from the other America." That's how Harry Belafonte opened a concert at the GDR's Palace of the Republic in 1983. Progressive Americans have always been able to appeal to an idea of another America, the home of those patriots who fought to force the country to be true to the ideals on which American pride was based. Frederick Douglass and Harriet Tubman, Henry David Thoreau and Walt Whitman, Susan B. Anthony and Elizabeth Cady Stanton, Ida B. Wells and Joe Hill, Eugene Debs and Mother Jones, Ella Baker and Martin Luther King, Paul Robeson and Woody Guthrie. All those names are known, if few have been memorialized as they deserve. Bryan Stevenson insists that we learn the names of the white Southerners who stood up to racism, even as he insists that Americans need to feel shame for our racist past before we can work to undo it.

German culture does not divide so neatly. Though it required a lot of editing, the Nazis did their best to incorporate cultural giants like Kant and Goethe into their pantheon. That can leave Germans seeking identities to fear that memory will lead to nothing but a boundless black hole. I have argued that Germany's ability to face its Nazi past can be a source of self-respect. But it's hard to be especially proud of cleaning up the unholy mess you made, even if the cleanup was a sign of the capacity for reflection that composed and sustained German culture.

The distinguished German writer Navid Kermani has urged that the strength and vitality of German identity be sought in its very brokenness.[27] Kermani, whose Iranian parents immigrated to Köln just before he was born there, wrote that he felt most German when he went to Auschwitz. He often quotes Rabbi Nachmann: "There is nothing more whole than a broken heart." It's a thought that was reflected in the speech given by the German president Frank-Walter Steinmeier on November 9, 2018—a date that was, among other things, the eightieth anniversary of Kristallnacht.

Among other things. November 9 has been called Germany's day of fate, for an uncanny number of entirely unconnected historical events took place on that date. In the rush of excitement when the Berlin Wall came down on November 9, 1989, many proposed to make it a national holiday—until someone pointed out that it could look as if Germans were celebrating Kristallnacht. For decades, the date has not been celebrated but mourned, for the pogrom that signaled the end of Jewish life in Germany.

In 2018, President Steinmeier took a bold new tack. Like dozens of politicians before him, Steinmeier began with a warning against forgetting November 9; unlike them, he reminded Germans to remember November 9, 1918—the end of imperial Germany and the beginning of republican democracy. His speech was a plea for "the ambivalence of memory," urging the nation to live with its own contradictions. "We can be proud of the traditions of freedom and democracy without repressing the sight of the Shoah. We can be aware of our historical responsibility for fracturing civilization without denying ourselves the joy in what we've done well. We can trust this land although—or because—it contains both. That's the core of enlightened patriotism." Steinmeier's speech was a masterful blend of pathos and nuance; how else could a politician urge his citizens to embrace ambivalence? Some critics predict the speech will prove as important as the epochal speech of his predecessor, Richard von Weiszäcker. If they are right, it will be one more thing that can be learned from the Germans.

For five years of my own life, I gave tribalism a try. Soon after the 1995 Oslo Accords, I moved to Israel, three children in tow. There were reasons enough to do so: Israeli friends in New Haven assured me I belonged in Tel Aviv, and the end of my first marriage made me hope to give my children the large extended family I thought the country would provide in place of the nuclear family I could no longer offer. There I discovered that tribalism becomes progressively narrower and narrower. (Just listen to Mizrachi and Ashkenazi Israelis talk about each other behind closed doors.) Tribal impulses go far beyond the mixture of resentment and contempt that Jews from Arab countries and Jews from Eastern Europe may express toward each other. When blood is the glue that holds people together, every single family becomes its own tribe.

Tribalism will always make your world smaller; universalism is the only way to expand it. My decision to leave Israel wasn't directly political; the situation there in early 2000 was better than it had been in years. The country was still reeling from Yitzhak Rabin's assassination, and a majority was committed to continuing the peace process for which he died. Benjamin Netanyahu was viewed as a fool in disgrace. Though I left Israel before the second intifada, I make no claim to political foresight; I'd just realized that my relation to the world is not tribal. I was raised on the universalism of the early civil rights movement and educated in theories of justice by Rawls, and I have led an adult life most would call cosmopolitan. But influences are one thing, convictions another. In becoming an Israeli citizen, I tried out voting for tribalism with my feet. There I learned I could not possibly feel more connected to an arms dealer who shares my ethnic background than to a friend from Chile or South Africa or Kazakhstan who shares my basic values. My ties are to agents, not genealogies. I choose friends, and loves, for reasons.

I understand the longing for the stability and succor of an idea about home; I shared it for many years myself. Even when you know that home was never idyllic, its pull is very strong. Yet the sense of home will grow more elusive with every passing decade. Many thirty-year-olds are now imprinted with a far more fluid vision of the globe than I have. Genetics have shown that ethnic purity is largely mythical; most of us are more biologically cosmopolitan than we know.[28] It isn't just a matter of morality: historical changes and scientific discoveries give us every reason to embrace genuine universalism.

This book itself is offered as an exercise in universalism, in the hope that understanding difference will help us find shared souls. (*Shared* is not *identical*, even for twins.) To do so, we must reject the fear of everything that could be adjacent to kitsch—a fear that now underlies educated culture, which is far more comfortable with irony. Above all, we must acknowledge our shared vulnerability to the silliest banalities of evil, the tendency to put fame or fortune above what we truly believe and desire. That acknowledgment makes it possible to critically examine our own histories without tribalism or trauma. If we fail to understand that we have more in common than all that divides us, we cannot pursue what Toni Morrison called the human project: "to remain human and to block the dehumanization and estrangement of others."[29]

Notes

Where not otherwise indicated, all direct quotations are taken from interviews I conducted between 2016 and 2018 in Germany and the United States. Where not otherwise indicated, all translations from the German are my own.

PROLOGUE

1. Jan Plamper, *Das neue Wir: Eine andere Geschichte der Deutschen* (Fischer Verlag, 2019).
2. Adam Nossiter, *Of Long Memory* (Da Capo Press, 2002), preface.
3. C. Vann Woodward, *The Burden of Southern History*, quoted in Curtis Wilkie, *Dixie* (Scribner, 2001), p. 142.
4. Tzvetan Todorov, *Hope and Memory: Lessons from the Twentieth Century* (Princeton University Press, 2003), p. 1.
5. See Susan Neiman, *Evil in Modern Thought: An Alternative History of Philosophy* (Princeton University Press, 2015 [revised edition]).

1: ON THE USE AND ABUSE OF HISTORICAL COMPARISON

1. James Q. Whitman, *Hitler's American Model* (Princeton University Press, 2017).
2. James Baldwin in discussion with Malcolm X, University of California, Berkeley, video, 1963.
3. Baldwin, National Press Club, video, 1986.
4. James Baldwin with Malcolm X, video, 1963.
5. British Foreign Office in Washington, D.C., January 12, 1943, quoted in Louise London, "British Government Policy and Jewish Refugees 1933–45," in *Patterns of Prejudice* (Routledge, 1989).

6. *Berliner Zeitung*, August 31, 2015.
7. Many argue that working-through-the-past cannot be translated. See Mischa Gabowitsch, ed., *Replicating Atonement* (Palgrave Macmillan, 2017).
8. See Carol Anderson, *White Rage* (Bloomsbury, 2016).
9. See Matthew Karp, *This Vast Southern Empire: Slaveholders at the Helm of American Foreign Policy* (Harvard University Press, 2017). See also the conversations with Charles Reagan and Diane McWhorter in the chapters that follow.

2: SINS OF THE FATHERS

1. See Wolfgang Schivelbusch, *The Culture of Defeat* (Picador, 2004).
2. Martin Heidegger, *Gesamtausgabe, Anmerkungen I–V (Schwarze Hefte, 1942–1948)*, vol. 97 (Vittorio Klostermann, 2015).
3. Quoted in Jürgen Habermas, *Die Normalität einer Berliner Republik* (Suhrkamp, 1995), p. 118.
4. Karl Jaspers, *The Question of German Guilt*, trans. E. B. Ashton (Fordham University Press, 2000), pp. 14–15. Translation modified.
5. Ibid., p. 41. Translation modified.
6. Winston Churchill, "Friendship and Germany," *Evening Standard*, September 17, 1937.
7. Jaspers, *The Question of German Guilt*, p. 90. Translation modified.
8. See Mark Clark, *Beyond Catastrophe: German Intellectuals and Cultural Renewal After World War II, 1945–1955* (Lexington Books, 2006).
9. Quoted in Ulrike Jureit and Christian Schneider, *Gefühlte Opfer* (Klett-Cotta, 2010), p. 117.
10. Theodor Adorno, "Schuld und Abwehr," in *Gesammelte Schriften* (Suhrkamp, 1997), vol. 9, p. 189.
11. Ibid., p. 192.
12. Ibid., p. 270.
13. Ibid., p. 227.
14. Ibid., p. 236.
15. Ibid., pp. 248–49.
16. Ibid., p. 235.
17. Ibid., p. 242.
18. Ibid., p. 298.
19. Ibid., p. 260.
20. Ibid., p. 298.
21. Ibid., p. 260.
22. Ibid., p. 258.
23. Ibid., p. 245.
24. Ibid., p. 321.
25. Ibid., pp. 205, 247.
26. See Susan Neiman, "Banality Reconsiderd," in *Politics in Dark Times: Encounters with Hannah Arendt*, ed. Seyla Benhabib (Cambridge University Press, 2010).
27. Bettina Stangneth, *Eichmann vor Jerusalem* (Arche Literatur Verlag, 2011), p. 298.
28. Ibid., p. 286.
29. Ibid., p. 454.
30. Bettina Stangneth, "Deutsche Kant, Jüdisches Kant," lecture given at the Einstein Forum, 2014.
31. Polina Aronson, "You're Better Than You Think," opendemocracy.net, January 2017.
32. Voltaire, *Candide*, trans. Roger Pearson, in *Candide and Other Stories* (Oxford University Press, 2006), p. 29.
33. Jan Plamper, *Das neue Wir: Eine andere Geschichte der Deutschen* (Fischer Verlag, 2019).
34. Alexandra Senfft, *Schweigen tut weh: Eine deutsche Familiengeschichte* (List, 2008), p. 104.

35. Omer Bartov, Cornelia Brink, Gerhard Hirschfeld, Friedrich P. Kahlenberg, Manfred Messerschmidt, Reinhard Rürup, Christian Streit, and Hans-Ulrich Thamer, *Bericht der Kommission zur Überprüfung der Ausstellung "Vernichtungskrieg. Verbrechen der Wehrmacht 1941 bis 1944,"* November 2000.
36. Jan Philipp Reemtsma, *Trust and Violence,* trans. Dominic Bonfiglio (Princeton University Press, 2012), p. 309.
37. Hannah Arendt, *Eichmann in Jerusalem: A Report on the Banality of Evil* (Penguin Books, 2006), pp. 521–22.

3: COLD WAR MEMORY

1. Daniela Dahn, *Westwärts und nicht vergessen* (Rowohlt, 1996), p. 36.
2. Michael Kimmelman, *New York Times,* December 20, 2016.
3. Günther Anders, *Wir Eichmannsöhne, offener Brief an Klaus Eichmann* (Munich, 1988), p. 89.
4. See James Zeigler, *Red Scare Racism and Cold War Black Radicalism* (University Press of Mississippi, 2015).
5. See Arkadi Zeltser, *Unwelcome Memory: Holocaust Memorials in the Soviet Union* (Yad Vashem, 2018).
6. "Aufruf der ZK der KPD vom 11. Juni 1945," in *Dokumente und Materialien zur Geschichte der deutschen Arbeiterbewegung,* Reihe III, Bd. 1 (Berlin, 1959), pp. 15ff.
7. Heinrich Himmler, *Geheimreden 1933 bis 1945 und andere Ansprachen,* eds. B. F. Smith and A. F. Peterson (Ullstein, 1974).
8. Arno Mayer, *Why Did the Heavens Not Darken?* (Pantheon, 1988), p. 446.
9. Ibid., p. 160.
10. Ibid., p. 90.
11. A. O. Lovejoy, "What Shall Be Done About Germany After the War?," EM10, 1944, American Historical Association Archives (www.historians.org./projects/GIRoundtable).
12. Timothy Snyder, "Tony Judt: An Intellectual Journey," *New York Review of Books,* August 31, 2010.
13. See Dahn, *Westwärts und nicht vergessen.*
14. Ingo Müller, "Die Verfolgung der Nazi-Verbrechen in Ost und West," talk at the 45th Bundesweites Gedenkstättenseminar (Halle, 2006).
15. Andreas Eichmüller, "Die Strafverfolgung von NS-Verbrechen durch westdeutsche Justizbehörden seit 1945" (Institut für Zeitgeschichte, 2008), and Malte Herwig, *Die Flakhelfer* (DVA, 2014).
16. Ingo Müller, "Die Verfolgung der Nazi-Verbrechen in Ost und West."
17. "Alt-Nazis beherrschten Justizministerium bis in die sechziger Jahre," *Der Spiegel,* April 4, 2013.
18. Christian Mentel, "Die Debatte um '*Das Amt und die Vergangenheit*'" (Bundeszentral für politische Bildung, 2012).
19. Institute für Zeitgeschichte München-Berlin and Zentrum für Zeithistorische Forschung Potsdam, "Die Nachkriegsgeschichte des Bundesministeriums des Innern (BMI) und des Ministeriums des Innern der DDR (MdI) hinsichtlich möglicher personeller und sachlicher Kontinuitäten zur Zeit des Nationalsozialismus," October 2015, p. 142. www.bmi.bund.de/SharedDocs/downloads/DE/veroeffentlichungen/2015/abschlussbericht-vorstudie-aufarbeitung-bmi-nachkriegsgeschichte.html (accessed October 20, 2018).
20. Ulrike Puvogel and Stefanie Endlich, *Gedenkstätten für die Opfer des Nationalsozialismus* (Bundeszentrale für politische Bildung, 2000).
21. Karl Hessdörfer, "Die finanzielle Dimension," in Constantin Goschler and Ludolf Herbst, eds., *Wiedergutmachung in der Bundesrepublik Deutschland* (De Gruyter Oldenbourg, 1988).
22. See Rainer Karlsch, *Allein bezahlt? Die Reparationsleistungen der SBZ/DDR 1945–53* (Christoph Links Verlag, 2013 [1993]); and Hans Günter Hockerts, Claudia Moisel,

and Tobias Winstel, eds., *Grenzen der Wiedergutmachung: Die Entschädigung für NS-Verfolgte in West-und Osteuropa 1945–2000* (Wallstein, 2006).
23. See Dahn, *Westwärts und nicht vergessen*.
24. Stanley Cavell, *Little Did I Know* (Stanford University Press, 2010).
25. I owe this insight to Dominic Bonfiglio.
26. Dahn, *Westwärts und nicht vergessen*, p. 58.
27. See Renate Kirchner, "Jüdisches in Publikationen aus DDR Verlagen 1945–90," in Detlef Joseph, ed., *Die DDR und die Juden: Eine kritische Untersuchung* (Berlin, 2010).
28. Mario Kessler, *Die SED und die Juden—zwischen Repression und Toleranz: Politische Entwicklungen bis 1967* (De Gruyter Akademie Forschung, 1996).
29. See, for example, Ottmar Ette, *Der Fall Jauss* (Kulturverlag Kadmos Berlin, 2016).

4: EVERYBODY KNOWS ABOUT MISSISSIPPI

1. See Eric Foner, *A Short History of Reconstruction* (Harper & Row, 1990).
2. James Meredith, with William Doyle, *A Mission from God* (Atria Books, 2012), pp. 43–44.
3. Carol V. R. George, *One Mississippi, Two Mississippi* (Oxford University Press, 2015), p. 208.
4. Susan Glisson, "Everything Old Is New Again: Storytelling and Dialogue as Tools for Community Change in Mississippi," *Oral History Forum d'histoire orale* 34 (2014), p. 3.
5. George, *One Mississippi, Two Mississippi*, p. 229.
6. Howard Zinn, *The Southern Mystique* (Knopf, 1964), p. 341.
7. Meredith, *A Mission from God*, p. 234.
8. Ibid., p. 239.
9. Ibid., p. 235.
10. Ibid., p. 236.
11. Timothy Ryback, "What Ole Miss Can Teach Universities About Grappling with Their Pasts," *The Atlantic*, September 19, 2017.
12. These statements were made by members of the audience at the meeting.
13. Jean Améry, "Aufklärung als Philosophia perennis," in *Werke*, vol. 6: *Aufsätze zur Philosophie*, ed. Gerhard Scheit (Klett-Cotta, 2004), p. 557.
14. Meredith, *A Mission from God*, p. 222.
15. Ibid., p. 27.
16. Ibid., p. 33.
17. Ibid., p. 44.
18. Ibid., p. 16.
19. Ibid., p. 41.
20. Ibid., p. 55.
21. Ibid., p. 89.

5: LOST CAUSES

1. See Grace Elizabeth Hale, *Making Whiteness: The Culture of Segregation in the South, 1890–1940* (Vintage, 1999).
2. Ibid., p. 65.
3. Ibid., p. 62.
4. Inscription at the Confederate Memorial Carving, Stone Mountain, Georgia.
5. Ibid.
6. "A Declaration of the Immediate Causes Which Induce and Justify the Secession of the State of Mississippi from the Federal Union," 1860.
7. See Wolfgang Schivelbusch, *The Culture of Defeat* (Picador, 2004).
8. Quoted in David W. Blight, *Race and Reunion: The Civil War in American Memory* (Belknap Press, 2001), p. 159.
9. Thomas Nelson Page, quoted in Hale, *Making Whiteness*, p. 43.

10. Anne Sarah Rubin, *Through the Heart of Dixie: Sherman's March and American Memory* (University of North Carolina Press, 2014), p. 180.
11. Quoted in Blight, *Race and Reunion*, p. 106.
12. Ibid., p. 92.
13. Ibid., p. 93.
14. Ibid., p. 106.
15. Andrew Young, *An Easy Burden: The Civil Rights Movement and the Transformation of America* (HarperCollins Publishers, 1996), p. 104.
16. John Cummings, *Why America Needs a Slavery Museum*, Atlantic Documentaries, August 25, 2015.
17. Ibid.
18. Ibid.
19. Bob Dylan, *Chronicles, Volume One* (Simon and Schuster, 2004), p. 86.
20. John F. Kennedy, *Profiles in Courage* (Harper and Brothers, 1955), p. 140.
21. A video of Myrlie Evers-Williams's speech can be viewed here at YouTube, www.youtube.com/watch?v=TzR6OTry0tk (accessed October 21, 2018).
22. Quoted in Arthur M. Schlesinger, *A Thousand Days: John F. Kennedy in the White House* (Houghton Mifflin, 1965), p. 966.

6: FACES OF EMMETT TILL
1. Mamie Till-Mobley and Christopher Benson, *Death of Innocence* (One World Books, 2003), p. 99.
2. Ibid.
3. Ibid., p. 14.
4. Ibid.
5. Ibid., p. 102.
6. Bob Dylan, "The Death of Emmett Till."
7. Till-Mobley and Benson, *Death of Innocence*, p. 310.
8. "The Shocking Story of Approved Killing in Mississippi," *Look*, January 24, 1956. The text has been amended to avoid the racist epithet *Milam* used for "those people."
9. See Edward E. Baptist, *The Half Has Never Been Told: Slavery and the Making of American Capitalism* (Basic Books, 2014).
10. "Mississippi Freedom Trail," State of Mississippi tourism website, www.mississippi.org/mississippi-stories/mississippi-freedom-trail/ (accessed October 20, 2018).
11. "The Apology," Emmett Till Interpretive Center, www.emmett-till.org (accessed October 20, 2018).
12. James Baldwin, *Blues for Mister Charlie* (Vintage International Edition, 1995), p. xiv.
13. Christopher Benson, "The Image of Emmett Till," *New York Times*, March 28, 2017.
14. See Jean Améry, "At the Mind's Limits," in *At the Mind's Limits: Contemplations by a Survivor on Auschwitz and Its Realities*, trans. Sidney Rosenfeld and Stella P. Rosenfeld (Indiana University Press, 1980).
15. Kwame Anthony Appiah, *The Lies That Bind: Rethinking Identity* (Liveright, 2018), p. 208.
16. Ibid., p. 327.
17. Ibid., p. 328.

7: MONUMENTAL RECOGNITION
1. See Susan Neiman, "Victims and Heroes," in *The Tanner Lectures on Human Values* (University of Utah Press, 2012).
2. William James, "Oration," *Essays in Religion and Morality* (Harvard University Press, 1982), pp. 65–66, italics added.
3. Ibid., p. 66.
4. Ibid., p. 67.
5. Ibid., p. 66.

6. Ibid., p. 73.
7. Birgit Schwelling, "Gedenken im Nachkrieg. Die 'Friedland-Gedächtnisstätte,'" in *Zeithistorische Forschungen/Studies in Contemporary History*, 2008.
8. See "Black and Unarmed," *Washington Post*, August 8, 2015.
9. See Susan Neiman, *Widerstand der Vernunft: Ein Manifest in postfaktischen Zeiten* (Benevento, 2017).
10. See Aaron Williams, "Hate Crimes Rose the Day After Trump Was Elected, FBI Data Shows," *Washington Post*, March 23, 2018, and *The Independent*, July 17, 2017.
11. See Mischa Gabowitsch, "Sites of Practice," talk at Einstein Forum conference *Imagine Solidarity!*, June 17, 2017.
12. Directive No. 30, Official Gazette of the Control Council for Germany, Nr. 7, May 31, 1946.
13. James Meredith, with William Doyle, *A Mission from God* (Atria Books, 2012), p. 6.
14. Jan Philipp Reemtsma, "Wozu Gedenkstätten?," *Politik und Zeitgeschichte*, June 21, 2010.
15. Ibid., p. 4.
16. Ibid., p. 5.
17. Ibid., p. 9.
18. See Susan Neiman, *Evil in Modern Thought: An Alternative History of Philosophy* (Princeton University Press, 2015 [revised edition]).
19. See Lorraine Daston, "When Science Went Modern—and Why," talk at Einstein Forum conference *Fetishizing Science*, June 11, 2016.
20. Friedrich Nietzsche, *On the Use and Abuse of History for Life*, trans. Adrian Collins (Digireads, 2009), p. 122.
21. G.W.F. Hegel, *Introduction to the Lectures on Philosophy of History*, trans. Hugh Barr Nisbet (Cambridge, 1975), p. 43.
22. *Buchenwald: Ausgrenzung und Gewalt* (Wallstein Verlag, 2016), p. 183.
23. Barack Obama, in *Crain's Chicago Business*, December 6, 2017.
24. See Seth Cagin and Philip Dray, *We Are Not Afraid: The Story of Goodman, Schwerner, and Chaney, and the Civil Rights Campaign for Mississippi* (PublicAffairs, 2006).
25. Howard Ball, *Justice in Mississippi: The Murder Trial of Edgar Ray Killen* (University Press of Kansas, 2006), p. 10.
26. See Sally Belfrage, *Freedom Summer* (University Press of Virginia, 1990).
27. Cagin and Dray, *We Are Not Afraid*, p. 279.
28. Ibid., p. 134.
29. Ibid., p. 362.
30. Ibid., p. 390.
31. Quoted in Carol V. R. George, *One Mississippi, Two Mississippi* (Oxford University Press, 2015), p. 29.
32. See ibid.
33. See ibid.
34. Ibid., p. 211.
35. Ball, *Justice in Mississippi*, p. 12.
36. Ibid., pp. 203–204.
37. Ibid., p. 27.
38. Ibid., p. 26.
39. Mitch Landrieu, *In the Shadow of Statues: A White Southerner Confronts History* (Viking, 2018), pp. 217–18.

8: RIGHTS AND REPARATIONS

1. Jean Améry, "Resentments," in *At the Mind's Limits: Contemplations by a Survivor on Auschwitz and Its Realities*, trans. Sidney Rosenfeld and Stella P. Rosenfeld (Indiana University Press, 1980), p. 81.
2. Ibid., p. 72.
3. Ibid., p. 77.

4. Hannah Arendt, "Auschwitz on Trial," *Responsibility and Judgment*, ed. Jerome Kohn (Schocken Books, 2003), pp. 228–29.

5. See Ta-Nehisi Coates, "The Case for Reparations," in *We Were Eight Years in Power* (One World, 2017).

6. See Coates, *We Were Eight Years in Power*; Randall Robinson, *The Debt: What America Owes to Blacks* (Dutton, 2000); Thomas McCarthy, "Coming to Terms with Our Past, Part II: On the Morality and Politics of Reparations for Slavery," *Political Theory*, no. 6 (2004): 750–72; and Charles J. Ogletree, "Tulsa Reparations: The Survivors' Story," *Boston College Third World Law Journal* 24 (2004): 13–30.

7. See Christopher Clark, *The Sleepwalkers: How Europe Went to War in 1914* (Penguin Books, 2012).

8. Hannah Arendt, *Ich will verstehen: Selbstauskünfte zu Leben und Werk* (Piper, 1996), p. 59.

9. See Tom Segev, *The Seventh Million: The Israelis and the Holocaust* (Henry Holt, 2000).

10. Ibid., p. 192.

11. Ibid., p. 204.

12. Paul Weymar, *Konrad Adenauer: His Authorized Biography*, trans. Peter de Mendelssohn (Dutton, 1957), p. 406.

13. Ibid., p. 445.

14. See Segev, *The Seventh Million*, pp. 230ff; and Constantin Goschler, *Schuld und Schulden: Die Politik der Wiedergutmachung für NS Verfolgte seit 1945* (Wallstein, 2005), p. 274.

15. Segev, *The Seventh Million*, p. 246ff.

16. John H. McWhorter, "The Privilege of Checking White Privilege," *Daily Beast*, March 15, 2015.

17. Jelani Cobb, "What We Talk About When We Talk About Reparations," *New Yorker*, May 29, 2014.

18. Ta-Nehisi Coates, *We Were Eight Years in Power*, p. 201.

19. See Susan Neiman, "Victims and Heroes," in *The Tanner Lectures on Human Values* (University of Utah Press, 2012).

20. See Edward E. Baptist, *The Half Has Never Been Told: Slavery and the Making of American Capitalism* (Basic Books, 2014); Sven Beckert, *Empire of Cotton: A Global History* (Knopf, 2014); and Walter Johnson, *River of Dark Dreams* (Belknap, 2013).

21. Baptist, *The Half Has Never Been Told*, p. xviii.

22. Ibid., p. 387.

23. Ibid., p. 317ff.

24. Ibid., p. 410.

25. Ibid., chapter 4.

26. See Special Field Order 15 in Roy L. Brooks, *When Sorry Isn't Enough: The Controversy over Apologies and Reparations for Human Injustice* (New York University Press, 1999), p. 366.

27. Baptist, *The Half Has Never Been Told*, p. 408.

28. Martin Luther King Jr., *The Radical King*, ed. Cornel West (Beacon Press, 2015), p. 243.

29. Douglas A. Blackmon, *Slavery by Another Name* (Anchor Books, 2008), p. 402.

30. Ibid., p. 73.

31. Ibid., p. 336.

32. Ibid., p. 380.

33. Ibid., p. 85.

34. See Michelle Alexander, *The New Jim Crow: Mass Incarceration in the Age of Colorblindness* (The New Press, 2012); and Bryan Stevenson, *Just Mercy: A Story of Justice and Redemption* (Spiegel & Grau, 2014).

35. For one summary of studies, see www.sentencingproject.org.

36. H. R. Haldeman, *Inside the White House* (G. P. Putnam, 1995), italics added.

37. Blackmon, *Slavery by Another Name*, p. 390.

38. Coates, *We Were Eight Years in Power*, p. 169.

39. See Dalton Conley, *Being Black, Living in the Red* (University of California Press, 2009).

40. See Elizabeth Anderson, *The Imperative of Integration* (Princeton University Press, 2010).
41. Coates, *We Were Eight Years in Power*, p. 177.
42. Ibid., p. 190.
43. José Brunner, Constantin Goschler, and Norbert Frei, *Die Globalisierung der Wiedergutmachung* (Wallstein Verlag, 2013), p. 296ff.
44. Blackmon, *Slavery by Another Name*, p. 394.
45. Coates, *We Were Eight Years in Power*, p. 207.
46. Thomas Chatterton Williams, "How Ta-Nehisi Coates Gives Whiteness Power," *New York Times*, October 6, 2017.
47. See Carol Anderson, *White Rage* (Bloomsbury, 2016), chapter 5.
48. See Neiman, "Victims and Heroes."
49. John Torpey, *Making Whole What Has Been Smashed: On Reparations Politics* (Harvard University Press, 2006), pp. 5, 23.
50. Ibid., 37.
51. Ashraf Rushdy, *A Guilted Age: Apologies for the Past* (Temple University Press, 2015), p. 171.
52. McCarthy, "Coming to Terms with Our Past, Part II," p. 12.
53. Ibid., 24.
54. Robinson, *The Debt*, p. 232.
55. Susan Neiman, "What Americans Abroad Know About Bernie Sanders and You Should Too," *Los Angeles Times*, June 3, 2016.
56. See Robinson, *The Debt*; and Ogletree, "Tulsa Reparations: The Survivor's Story."
57. Adolph Reed Jr., "From Jenner to Dolezal: One Trans Good, the Other Not So Much," *Common Dreams*, June 15, 2015, www.commondreams.org/views/2015/06/15/jenner-dolezal-one-trans-good-other-not-so-much (accessed October 21, 2018). See also Cornel West, "Ta-Nehisi Coates Is the Neoliberal Face of the Black Freedom Struggle," *Guardian*, December 17, 2017.
58. The original document is stored in the King Center Archives.
59. See Naomi Klein, *This Changes Everything: Capitalism vs. the Climate* (Simon & Schuster, 2014).
60. Works that were particularly influential in this regard include Primo Levi's *If This Is a Man*, Ruth Kluger's *Still Alive*, and Imre Kertész's *Fatelessness*.
61. See Binjamin Wilkomirski, *Fragments: Memories of a Wartime Childhood* (Knopf Doubleday, 1997).
62. See Thomas Brudholm, *Resentment's Virtue: Jean Améry and the Refusal to Forgive* (Temple University Press, 2008).
63. Améry, "Resentments," p. 64.
64. See Isaac Deutscher, *The Non-Jewish Jew and Other Essays* (Alyson Publications, 1968).
65. Janna Thompson, *Taking Responsibility for the Past* (Polity Press, 2002), p. 37.
66. Kris Manjapra, "When Will Britian Face Up to Its Crimes against Humanity?," *Guardian*, March 29, 2018.
67. See Wole Soyinka, *The Burden of Memory, the Muse of Forgiveness* (Oxford University Press, 1999).
68. Goschler, *Schuld und Schulden*, p. 226.
69. www.ibtimes.co.in, July 24, 2015.
70. David Brooks, "The Case for Reparations," *New York Times*, March 7, 2019.

9: IN PLACE OF CONCLUSIONS

1. Carol Anderson, Ta-Nehisi Coates, Tim Wise, and Cornel West are only the first names that come to mind.
2. Cornell Belcher, *A Black Man in the White House* (Walter Street Press, 2016), p. 128ff.

3. A similar poll conducted in August 2018 by *The Economist*/YouGov confirmed this again.

4. Belcher, *A Black Man in the White House*, p. 164.

5. George Orwell, "Notes on Nationalism," in *Polemik*, October 1945.

6. Jan Plamper, *Das neue Wir: Eine andere Geschichte der Deutschen* (Fischer Verlag, 2019).

7. Michael Wildt, "Droht Deutschland ein neues 1933?," *Die Zeit*, September 8, 2018. www .zeit.de/wissen/geschichte/2018-09/chemnitz-weimarer-republik-nazizeit-vergleich -rechtsextremismus/komplettansicht (accessed October 22, 2018).

8. See Franziska Schreiber, *Inside AfD* (Europea Verlag, 2018).

9. See Karsten Müller and Carlo Schwarz, "Fanning the Flames of Hate: Social Media and Hate Crime," May 21, 2018. Available at SSRN: https://ssrn.com/abstract=3082972.

10. See Schreiber, *Inside AfD*.

11. Wolfgang Engler and Jana Hensel, *Wer wir sind: die Erfahrung, Ostdeutsch zu sein* (Aufbau Verlag, 2018).

12. See also Robin Alexander, *Die Getriebenden: Merkel und die Flüchtlingspolitik* (Siedler, 2017).

13. Quoted in W.E.B. Du Bois, *John Brown*, ed. Henry Louis Gates Jr. (Oxford University Press, 2007), p. 45.

14. Tzvetan Todorov, *Memory as a Remedy for Evil* (Seagull Books, 2010), p. 80.

15. David Rieff, *In Praise of Forgetting* (Yale University Press, 2016), p. 28. Quote slightly modified.

16. Ibid., p. 141.

17. Avishai Margalit, *The Ethics of Memory* (Harvard University Press, 2002), p. 83.

18. Martin Luther King Jr., "Letter from a Birmingham Jail," in *A Testament of Hope: The Essential Writings and Speeches of Martin Luther King, Jr.*, ed. James M. Washington (HarperCollins, 1991), p. 297.

19. Branko Milanovic, "A Short History of Global Inequality: The Past Two Centuries," in *Explorations in Economic History*, vol. 48, no. 4 (Elsevier, 2011), pp. 494–506.

20. See Susan Neiman, *Why Grow Up?* (Farrar, Straus and Giroux, 2016).

21. Mark Lilla, *The Once and Future Liberal: After Identity Politics* (HarperCollins, 2017).

22. See Todd Gitlin, *The Twilight of Common Dreams: Why America Is Wracked by Culture Wars* (Henry Holt and Company, 1996); and Richard Rorty, *Achieving Our Country: Leftist Thought in Twentieth-Century America* (Harvard University Press, 1999).

23. Cornel West, "The New Cultural Politics of Difference," in *The Cornel West Reader* (Basic Civitas Books, 1999).

24. Kwame Anthony Appiah, *The Lies That Bind* (Liveright, 2018), p. 232.

25. Friedrich Nietzsche, *Beyond Good and Evil*, trans. Walter Kaufmann (Vintage Books, 1989), Part IV, Aphorism 68.

26. See Rorty, *Achieving Our Country*.

27. Navid Kermani, "Auschwitz Morgen," *Frankfurter Allgemeine Zeitung*, July 7, 2017.

28. See, for example, *Finding Your Roots with Henry Louis Gates Jr.*, PBS.org.

29. Toni Morrison, *The Origin of Others* (Harvard University Press, 2017), p. 37.

Bibliography

Alexander, Michelle. *The New Jim Crow*. New York: The New Press, 2011.

Améry, Jean. *At the Mind's Limits*. Bloomington: Indiana University Press, 1980.

Améry, Jean. *Weiterleben—aber wie?* Stuttgart: Klett-Cotta, 1982.

Anders, Günther. *Wir Eichmannsöhne*. München: C.H.Beck, 1964.

Anderson, Carol. *Eyes off the Prize: The United Nations and the African American Struggle for Human Rights, 1944–1955*. New York: Cambridge University Press, 2003.

Anderson, Carol. *White Rage: The Unspoken Truth of Our Racial Divide*. New York: Bloomsbury, 2017.

Anderson, Elizabeth. *The Imperative of Integration*. Princeton: Princeton University Press, 2010.

Andreas-Friedrich, Ruth. *Schauplatz Berlin*. Frankfurt: Suhrkamp Verlag, 1984.

Appiah, Kwame Anthony. *The Ethics of Identity*. Princeton: Princeton University Press, 2005.

Appiah, Kwame Anthony. *The Honor Code: How Moral Revolutions Happen*. New York: W. W. Norton and Company, 2011.

Appiah, Kwame Anthony. *In My Father's House: Africa in the Philosophy of Culture*. New York: Oxford University Press, 1992.

Appiah, Kwame Anthony. *The Lies That Bind*. New York: Liveright Publishing Corporation, 2018.

Arendt, Hannah. *Eichmann in Jerusalem*. New York: The Viking Press, 1963.

Assmann, Aleida. *Das neue Unbehagen an der Erinnerungskultur*. München: Verlag C.H.Beck, 2013.

Assmann, Aleida, and Ute Frevert. *Geschichtsvergessenheit, Geschichtsversessenheit: vom*

Umgang mit deutschen Vergangenheiten nach 1945. Stuttgart: Deutsche Verlags-Anstalt, 1999.

Baldwin, James. *Blues for Mr. Charlie.* New York: Vintage, 1964.

Baldwin, James. *The Fire Next Time.* New York: Vintage, 1963.

Baldwin, James. *Notes of a Native Son.* Boston: Beacon Press, 1955.

Baptist, Edward E. *The Half Has Never Been Told: Slavery and the Making of American Capitalism.* New York: Basic Books, 2014.

Belcher, Cornell. *A Black Man in the White House.* Healdsburg, CA: Water Street Press, 2016.

Blackmon, Douglas A. *Slavery by Another Name: The Re-Enslavement of Black Americans from the Civil War to World War II.* New York: Anchor Books, 2008.

Blight, David. *Race and Reunion.* Cambridge/Massachusetts/ London: The Belknap Press of Harvard University Press, 2001.

Bordin, Elisa, and Anna Scacchi, eds. *Transatlantic Memories of Slavery.* New York: Cambria Press, 2015.

Boxill, Bernard R. *Blacks & Social Justice.* Lanham: Rowman & Littlefield Publishers, 1992.

Boxill, Bernard R., ed. *Race and Racism.* Oxford: Oxford University Press, 2001.

Brenner, Michael. *Geschichte der Juden in Deutschland 1945 bis zur Gegenwart.* München: Verlag C.H.Beck, 2012.

Brooks, Roy L. *When Sorry Isn't Enough: The Controversy Over Apologies and Reparations for Human Injustice.* New York: New York University Press, 1999.

Campbell, Will D. *Brother to a Dragonfly.* New York: Continuum Publishing Corporation, 1986.

Coates, Ta-Nehisi. *Between the World and Me.* Melbourne: The Text Publishing Company, 2015.

Coates, Ta-Nehisi. *We Were Eight Years in Power: An American Tragedy.* New York: Random House, 2017.

Dahn, Daniella. *Westwärts und nicht vergessen.* Reinbek: Rowohlt, 1997.

Davis, David Brion. *Inhuman Bondage.* New York: Oxford University Press, 2006.

Davis, David Brion. *The Problem of Slavery in the Age of Emancipation.* New York: Alfred A. Knopf, 2014.

Delgado, Richard, and Jean Stefancic. *Critical Race Theory: An Introduction.* New York: New York University Press, 2017.

Didion, Joan. *South and West.* New York: Alfred A. Knopf, 2017.

Dittmer, John. *Local People: The Struggle for Civil Rights in Mississippi.* Urbana/Chicago: University of Illinois Press, 1995.

Duberman, Martin Bauml. *Paul Robeson.* New York: Alfred A. Knopf, 1988.

Dylan, Bob. *Chronicles Volume I.* New York: Simon and Schuster, 2004.

Dyson, Michael Eric. *Tears We Cannot Stop.* New York: St. Martin's Press, 2017.

Engler, Wolfgang and Hensel, Jana. *Wer wir sind: die Erfahrung, Ostdeutsch zu sein.* Berlin: Aufbau Verlag, 2018.

Ette, Ottmar. *Der Fall Jauss.* Berlin: Kulturverlag Kadmos, 2016.

Foner, Eric. *A Short History of Reconstruction, 1863–1877.* New York: HarperCollins, 2014.

Franklin, John Hope. *From Slavery to Freedom.* New York: McGraw-Hill Companies, 2011.

Frei, Norbert. *Vergangenheitspolitik: Die Anfänge der Bundesrepublik und die NS-Vergangenheit.* München: C.H.Beck, 1996.

Frölich, Margrit, and Ulrike Jureit. *Das Unbehagen an der Erinnerung—Wandlungsprozesse im Gedenken an den Holocaust.* Frankfurt/M.: Brandes & Apsel Verlag GmbH, 2012.

Fulbrook, Mary. *The People's State.* New Haven/London: Yale University Press, 2005.

Gabowitsch, Mischa, ed. *Replicating Atonement: Foreign Models in the Commemoration of Atrocities.* Palgrave Macmillan, 2017.

Gates, Henry Louis Jr. *Tradition and the Black Atlantic.* New York: Basic Books, 2010.

Gates, Henry Louis Jr., and Cornel West. *The African-American Century*. New York: Touchstone, 2000.

Gilman, Sander, and James M. Thomas. *Are Racists Crazy? How Prejudice, Racism, and Antisemitism Became Markers of Insanity*. New York: New York University Press, 2016.

Habermas, Jürgen. *Die Normalität einer Berliner Republik*. Frankfurt am Main: Suhrkamp Verlag, 1995.

Habermas, Jürgen. *Vergangenheit als Zukunft*. Zurich: Pendo Verlag, 1990.

Hale, Grace Elizabeth. *Making Whiteness*. New York: Vintage Books, 1998.

Hartmann, Christian, Johannes Hürter, and Ulrike Jureit. *Verbrechen der Wehrmacht: Bilanz einer Debatte*. München: C.H.Beck, 2005.

hooks, bell. *Killing Race. Ending Racism*. London: Penguin Books, 1995.

Jarausch, Konrad H. *After Hitler: Recivilizing Germans, 1945–1995*. New York: Oxford University Press, 2006.

Jaspers, Karl. *Der Schuldfrage: Von der politischen Haftung Deutschlands*. München: Piper Verlag, 1965.

Joseph, Detlef. *Die DDR und die Juden*. Berlin: Verlag Das Neue Berlin, 2010.

Jureit, Ulrike, and Christian Schneider. *Gefühlte Opfer*. Stuttgart: Klett-Cotta, 2010.

Kennedy, James Ronald, and Walter Donald Kennedy. *The South Was Right!* Gretna, LA: Pelican Publishing Company, 2014.

Klemperer, Victor. *So sitze ich den zwischen allen Stühlen: Tagebücher 1945–1949*. Berlin: Aufbau Verlag, 1999.

Knigge, Volkhard, and Norbert Frei. *Verbrechen erinnern. Die Auseinandersetzung mit Holocaust und Völkermord*. München: Verlag C.H.Beck, oHG, 2002.

Lilla, Mark. *The Once and Future Liberal*. New York: HarperCollins, 2017.

Mills, Charles W. *Black Rights/White Wrongs: The Critique of Racial Liberalism*. Oxford: Oxford University Press, 2017.

Moses, A. Dirk. *German Intellectuals and the Nazi Past*. Cambridge: Cambridge University Press, 2007.

Neitzel, Sönke, and Harald Welzer. *Soldaten-Protokolle vom Kämpfen, Töten und Sterben*. Frankfurt/M.: S. Fischer Verlag GmbH, 2011.

Novick, Peter. *The Holocaust in American Life*. New York: Houghton Mifflin, 1999.

Ó Dóchartaigh, Pol. *Germans and Jews Since the Holocaust*. London: Palgrave, 2016.

Parsons, Sarah Mitchell. *From Southern Wrongs to Civil Rights*. Tuscaloosa/London: University of Alabama Press, 2000.

Pilgrim, David. *Understanding Jim Crow*. Oakland, CA: Ferris State University and PM Press, 2015.

Piper, Adrian. "Recognition and Responsibility: Legacies of Xenophobia in Germany, Australia, and the United States." Unpublished Manuscript, 2002.

Reemtsma, Jan Philipp. *Vertrauen und Gewalt*. Hamburg: Hamburger Edition, 2008.

Rieff, David. *In Praise of Forgetting*. New Haven/London: Yale University Press, 2016.

Robinson, Randall. *The Debt: What America Owes to Blacks*. New York: Dutton, 2000.

Rorty, Richard. *Achieving Our Country*. Cambridge: Harvard University Press, 1998.

Rothberg, Michael. *Multidirectional Memory: Remembering the Holocaust in the Age of Decolonization*. Stanford, CA: Stanford University Press, 2009.

Rubin, Anne Sarah. *Through the Heart of Dixie*. Chapel Hill: University of North Carolina Press, 2014.

Rushdy, Ashraf H. A. *A Guilted Age: Apologies for the Past*. Philadelphia: Temple University Press, 2015.

Salomon, Ernst von. *Der Fragebogen*. Hamburg: Rowohlt, 1961.

Schivelbusch, Wolfgang. *The Culture of Defeat: On National Trauma, Mourning, and Recovery*. New York: Picador, 2001.

Schreiber, Franziska. *Inside AFD: Der Bericht einer Aussteigerin*. München: Europa Verlag, 2018.

Seck, Ibrahima. *Bouki fait gombo*. New Orleans: UNO Press, 2014.

Sereny, Gitta. *The Healing Wound*. New York: Norton, 2001.

Silver, James W. *Mississippi: The Closed Society*. Jackson: University Press of Mississippi, 1966.

Simpson, Christopher. *Blowback: The First Full Account of American's Recruitment of Nazis and Its Disastrous Effects on the Cold War, Our Domestic and Foreign Policy*. New York: Open Road Media, 2014.

Soyinka, Wole. *The Burden of Memory, the Muse of Forgiveness*. New York: Oxford University Press, 1999.

Stangneth, Bettina. *Eichmann vor Jerusalem*. Hamburg: Arche Literatur Verlag, 2011.

Stevenson, Bryan. *Just Mercy: A Story of Justice and Redemption*. New York: Penguin Random House, 2014.

Thomas, Laurence Mordekhai. *Vessels of Evil: American Slavery and the Holocaust*. Philadelphia: Temple University Press, 1993.

Thomason, Sally Palmer, with Jean Carter Fisher. *Delta Rainbow: The Irrepressible Betty Bobo Pearson*. Jackson: University Press of Mississippi, 2016.

Todorov, Tzvetan. *Hope and Memory: Lessons from the Twentieth Century*. Princeton: Princeton University Press, 2003.

Todorov, Tzvetan. *Memory as a Remedy for Evil*. Calcutta: Seagull Books, 2010.

Todorov, Tzvetan. *The Morals of History*. Minneapolis: University of Minnesota Press, 1995.

Torpey, John. *Making Whole What Has Been Smashed*. Cambridge: Harvard University Press, 2006.

Torpey, John. *Politics and the Past*. Lanham: Rowman & Littlefield, 2003.

Tyson, Timothy B. *Blood Done Sign My Name*. New York: Broadway Books, 2004.

Tyson, Timothy B. *The Blood of Emmett Till*. New York: Simon & Schuster, 2017.

Walker, Margaret Urban. *Moral Repair: Reconstructing Moral Relations After Wrongdoing*. Cambridge: Cambridge University Press, 2006.

Wallis, Jim. *America's Original Sin*. Grand Rapids, MI: Brazos Press, 2016.

Weiss, Peter. *Die Ermittlung*. Frankfurt/M.: Suhrkamp, 1991.

West, Cornel. *The Cornel West Reader*. New York: Basic Books, 1999.

West, Cornel, ed. *The Radical King*. Boston: Beacon Press, 2015.

Weymar, Paul, and Peter de Mendelssohn. *Adenauer: The Authorised Biography*. London: Andre Deutsch, 1957.

Whitman, James Q. *Hitler's American Model*. Princeton: Princeton University Press, 2017.

Williams, Robert F. *Negroes with Guns*. Mansfield Centre, CT: Martino Publishing, 2013.

Wolffsohn, Michael. *Die Deutschland-Akte*. Frankfurt: Bruckmann, 1995.

Woodward, C. Vann. *The Strange Career of Jim Crow*. New York: Oxford University Press, 2002.

Wyatt-Brown, Bertram. *Southern Honor*. New York: Oxford University Press, 1982.

Yancy, George, ed. *What White Looks Like: African American Philosophers on the Whiteness Question*. New York: Routledge, 2004.

Yancy, George, ed. *Reframing the Practice of Philosophy: Bodies of Color, Bodies of Knowledge*. Albany: State University of New York Press, 2012.

Acknowledgments

I have been thinking about German *Vergangenheitsaufarbeitung,* and what other nations can learn from it, since I first came to Berlin in October 1982. Initial attempts to understand these questions appeared in my first book, *Slow Fire: Jewish Notes from Berlin,* but both Berlin itself and my reflections about it have developed considerably since that book appeared in 1992. Along the way, my thinking has been furthered by more people than I can probably remember, but this is a place to thank as many as I do. Margherita von Brentano introduced me to the complexities of *Vergangenheitsaufarbeitung* and showed me that there were Germans who took it seriously from the very start. I am grateful to Jan Philipp Reemtsma for detailed comments on one chapter, and even more for years of friendship and dialogue that have played a crucial role in my conviction that German *Vergangenheitsaufarbeitung* can be serious and deep. In addition to furthering that conviction concerning Germany's past, Gesine Schwan has been a source of hope about its future. From Adrian Piper, who has written and spoken about these matters for many years, I have learned much. The same is true of Sander Gilman, who was also kind enough to read and comment on a controversial chapter. Conversations on the subject with Diane McWhorter have been as illuminating as they are delightful. A road trip with Diana Pinto, dashing from Jimmy Carter's Sunday school sermon in Plains, Georgia, to the Reconstruction sites in South Carolina, left me breathless, and grateful for her reflections and her company. My rabbi, James Ponet, taught me much of what I know about Judaism, and has been a source of dialogue and encouragement for the last three decades. Through him I met David Shulman, who has been an inspiration for thinking critically about Jewish values and history, and how to put them into practice. Jennifer Stollman was not only my main Mississippi mentor; she read and commented on several versions of the manuscript. Her criticism and knowledge challenged my thinking, and her encouragement kept me going when I was unsure about the point of doing so. Sadly, the William Winter Institute for Racial Reconciliation is no longer based at the University of Mississippi, but I am grateful to the original institute for providing inspiration, as well as a research base in 2017.

I am indebted to all those who graciously granted me their time and thoughts in the interviews that were crucial for this book—including those whose voices, for reasons of space, were not directly quoted. Had I incorporated all the things I learned from them, this book would be twice as long as it is now. They are: Polina Aronson, Aleida Assmann, Christopher Benson, Omri Boehm, Hans Otto Bräutigam, Chelius Carter, Maudie and Langdon Clay, Leroy Clemson, Daniela Dahn, Mischa Gabowitsch, Susan Glisson, April Grayson, Adam Flaherty, Bill Foster, Ainka Jackson, Hans-Christian Jasch, Volkhard Knigge, Björn Krondorf, Cilly Kugelmann, Mariam Lau, Michael Löffelsender, Robert Lee Long, Jackie Martin, Jimmie Jewel McDonald, Diane McWhorter, James and Judy Meredith, Markus Messling, Frank Mitchener, Buka Okoye, Wheeler Parker, David Person, Peggy Pietsche, Peter Pogany-Wendt, Jalda Rebling, Jan Philipp Reemtsma, Jens Reich, Chuck Ross, Stewart Rutledge, Benjamin Salisbury, Samuel Schidem, Friedrich Schorlemmer, Ingo Schulze, Alexandra Sennft, Herman Simon, Bettina Stangneth, Bryan Stevenson, Jennifer Stollman, Johnny B. Thomas, Charles Tucker, Mike Wagner, Mae Ruth Watson, Patrick Weems, John Whitten III, Curtis Wilkie, Willie Williams, and Charles Reagan Wilson.

The very first work that led to this book was presented as a Beamer-Schneider Lecture at Case Western Reserve University in 2014; I am grateful to Jeremy Bendik Keymer for the invitation and the engaging discussion that followed. Once again, I found reason to count my blessings in having Sarah Chalfant as my agent; her warm and wise support accompanied the project from proposal to finish. Eric Chinski, Julia Ringo, Helen Conford, and Karsten Kredel all made editorial suggestions that sharpened the arguments as well as the prose. Dominic Bonfiglio's expert research assistance was particularly helpful, not only because so many facts had to be checked but because his reflections on these matters were always incisive and thought-provoking. I am deeply indebted to you all.

Index

A Note About the Author

Susan Neiman is the director of the Einstein Forum. Her previous books, which have been translated into many languages, include *Why Grow Up? Subversive Thoughts for an Infantile Age*; *Moral Clarity: A Guide for Grown-Up Idealists*; *Evil in Modern Thought: An Alternative History of Philosophy*; *The Unity of Reason: Rereading Kant*; and *Slow Fire: Jewish Notes from Berlin*. She studied philosophy at Harvard and the Free University of Berlin and was a professor of philosophy at Yale and Tel Aviv Universities. She is the mother of three grown children and lives in Berlin.